I0540412

JUSTICE BY GUNBOAT

Warlords, Lawlords and the Making of
Modern China and Japan

Abridgment of the *Gunboat Justice* trilogy

Douglas Clark

EARNSHAW
B O O K S

Justice by Gunboat

By Douglas Clark

ISBN-13: 978-988-8422-74-6

© 2017 Douglas Clark

Cover design: Jason Wong

This book has been reset in 10pt Book Antiqua. Spellings and punctuations are left as in the original edition.

HISTORY / Asia / General

EB098

All rights reserved. No part of this book may be reproduced in material form, by any means, whether graphic, electronic, mechanical or other, including photocopying or information storage, in whole or in part. May not be used to prepare other publications without written permission from the publisher except in the case of brief quotations embodied in critical articles or reviews. For information contact info@earnshawbooks.com

Published by Earnshaw Books Ltd. (Hong Kong)

In memory of my maternal grandfather

The Honourable Mr Justice Russell Skerman

Supreme Court of Queensland

CONTENTS

Author's Note

Foreword

Introduction – Extraterritoriality: An Extraordinary System

This abridgement

In this abridgement I have reduced the original *Gunboat Justice* trilogy into one volume. The original trilogy told two stories: first, the history of the how extraterritoriality impacted and fundamentally changed the development of China and Japan and, second, the life and times of the judges and other individuals who played an important part of the British and American courts. This latter story, the small details of cases and cases or developments that are not directly relevant to the larger history of extraterritoriality have been removed or substantially edited. All footnotes have been removed. Those with an interest in sources and greater detail are recommended to the original trilogy.

Quotations

All quotations come from contemporaneous documents or reports.

Cartoon and illustrations

All cartoons and illustrations accompanying the text are contemporaneous drawings published at the time.

Romanisation and place names

I have used transliterations of Chinese personal and place names in accordance with the transliterations used during the period covered by this book. Where someone is now much better know by a Hanyu Pinyin transliteration, I have used this. For place names in China, for any reference prior to the Communist Revolution in 1949, I have generally used the contemporaneous English names, such as Canton and Amoy. For street names in Shanghai, I have used the pre-World War II street names. Where appropriate I give the current street name in parentheses.

For Japanese names, I have used modern romanisations, except in quotations or names of publications where the original spelling is kept.

FOREWORD

By Rt. Hon. Sir Robin Jacob
Former Lord Justice of Appeal

DOUGLAS CLARK ASKED ME to write this by an email. It ended with this: "If you are interested, I will send you through the page proofs so you can see if you would be happy to be associated with my work. Please do not feel any obligation at all to say yes." I am so glad I did. For this is a riveting work – almost novel-like with its rich content of quotations from the seemingly larger than life characters who set up and administered the outposts of law – mainly the English Common Law - in the Far East.

Yet this book is not a novel, and the characters were real. Living people. To today's eyes, the notion of the "Supreme Court of China and Japan" or, a little later in time, the "Supreme Court of China and Corea" seem surreal. But real they were, created and manned by men (had to be all men) of vision coupled with both energy and, largely a fierce sense of justice. Their jurisdiction was over the British men (and women) out in the Empire (and beyond). Although it was a jurisdiction taken from the countries concerned by the power of the gunboat it was frequently fair. Take for example this quotation from a direction of Sir Edmund Hornby to a jury hearing a case where an Englishman was accused of the manslaughter of a Chinese man: "A Chinaman's life is as precious as that of our own countrymen." The defendant had taken a pistol to confront a group of men who were protesting about the building of a lighthouse. In a scuffle the pistol had gone off, killing its victim." Sir Edmund clearly thought that taking a pistol to the confrontation was much more than was warranted. He directed the jury to convict, was deeply sorry when it refused, and said so. Or consider how the English Judge in Japan protected Chinese coolies from being transported as slaves from Macao (Portuguese) to South America.

Of course it was not perfect justice. Nor without its racism. Take an acquittal in 1898 Korea of a Briton accused of murder or manslaughter of a gardener in the British Legation. After the Judge described the death as follows:

"The defence was borne out in court by competent medical evidence that this was one of those interesting cases where an Oriental injured in his feelings will turn his face to the wall and die".

And the force of the all-powerful Royal Navy lay behind these courts – hence Douglas Clerk's vivid title. Yet another quote makes this come alive. This was when there were anti-missionary riots in the Yangtze Valley in 1891 (not perhaps all that surprising since the missionaries, like many zealots often rather aggressively ignored Chinese laws and customs). When the riots were threatened the telegram seeking help simply read:

"Riot Wuhu, catholic premises being destroyed; send gunboat immediately"

This book is full of such tales and of such gem quotes. The tales are not only told well but are full of these gems from the sources of the day, the newspapers in Shanghai and Japan, the reports of cases, letters from and to the participants, civil service records and so on. The original research has obviously been extensive, even though the style is easy and tends to disguise the erudition behind it. You are made to feel close to these people, almost as if you knew them.

The inquisitive might ask why Doug Clark asked me of

all people to write the foreword. The reason is my connection with the world of which he writes. My father was what was known in Shanghai as a Baghdad Jew. He was the third of ten children of Iraqi Sephardic Jewish parents who had come to Shanghai because of trade. My grandfather worked for Sir Victor Sassoon in Sassoon House (now the Bank of China) on the Bund, hard by the junction with the Nanking Road (now Nanjing Road West). From 1917 to 1923 Dad went to the Shanghai Public School for Boys, a sort of grammar school manned entirely by Oxbridge teachers – not as upmarket as the Cathedral School, a sort of public school. Little England in Shanghai! It was through his school that Dad learned about the law – he played the Attorney-General in a mock murder trial. And in Shanghai he first saw an English Court – the same one described in this book, with judge and counsel in the standard wig and gown. He said "I want to do that, but in London, home of Empire". That is what he did. And I followed.

My interest in the Shanghai court is therefore in part personal. I have tried to imagine how someone without such a connection might react. I think I can fairly judge – they will be riveted. This will particularly be so for those concerned today with the Far East. From these vivid stories and Douglas Clark's insight, they will have much to learn, not only about the past but how that past must inevitably influence the dealings between East and West today.

The Rt. Hon. Professor Sir Robin Jacob
University College London,
July 2014

PART ONE

White Man, White Law, White Gun
(1842 to 1900)

INTRODUCTION

Extraterritoriality – an Extraordinary System

IN 1874, SIR EDMUND HORNBY, Chief Judge of the British Supreme Court for China and Japan, entered a court room in the northern Chinese seaport of Chefoo in the full red robes of a British criminal judge. All those in court rose and bowed to him. As he took his seat, behind him was the British coat of arms bearing the words "Dieu et Mon Droit" ("God and my Right"). Before him in the dock was Thomas Fawcett, a British foreman accused of killing a Chinese man. After a trial in which Chinese witnesses were brought to court in chains to give evidence, Fawcett was acquitted by the British jury. For the next three days and two nights, the local Chinese population besieged Hornby's house demanding proper justice. He wrote later: "Of course, I never tried another British subject accused of killing a Chinaman at an outlying port, unless there was a gun-boat at hand."

What was a British judge, bewigged and fully robed in red, doing trying a criminal case against a British subject in northern China? Why was there a British jury? Why the gunboat? The simple answer is: extraterritoriality.

In China, for almost a century, Britain, America and other foreign countries ran their own civil and criminal justice systems. These legal systems were, as far as possible, entirely separate from the Chinese system. They had their own courts, judges, lawyers and, even, prisons. In Japan, almost identical foreign legal systems to those in China also existed for just over forty years.

These justice systems were created as part of the forced opening of China and Japan in the 1840s and 1850s. Until then, for more than 200 years, both China and Japan had been closed to Westerners and in both countries, only limited foreign trade had been allowed at a single port far away from the capital.

Britain and America changed this. In 1842, following the two-year Opium War, a British Navy flotilla led by Captain Henry Pottinger forced China to sign at the point of their gunboat barrels the Treaty of Nanking which opened five ports to Western trade. In 1854, an American naval squadron, led by Commodore Matthew Perry, forced Japan – also at the point of their gunboat barrels – to open to Western trade and sign a Treaty of Amity and Commerce. Other Western countries were quick to follow Britain and America's lead and signed similar treaties with both countries.

The Chinese and Japanese, not surprisingly, hated the "unequal treaties" that had brought foreigners to their shores. They, however, had no choice but to accept them. The treaties allowed the treaty powers to base army and naval forces in China and Japan, and on numerous occasions, British, American and other treaty powers' gunboats and armies were brought in to enforce "treaty rights." Peking was attacked and the Summer Palace burnt to the ground by the British and French in 1860. Kagoshima in southern Japan was shelled and all but destroyed by the British in 1863. Shimonoseki was held to ransom by the British, American, French and Dutch navies in 1864. China fought and lost numerous wars with foreign powers in the late 19th century. Right up to the 1940s, foreign navy boats, exercising treaty rights, patrolled the coast of China and the Yangtze River to protect foreign interests. Foreign troops were stationed in Peking and all along the railway line between Peking and Tientsin.

China and Japan's reaction to their forced opening to the

West continues to this day to have a strong impact on how they both view and treat each other and the rest of the world. Each country faced an almost identical challenge, but the results were diametrically opposite. Japan was the big winner from the unequal treaties while China was the big loser. Neither country has forgotten this – and neither country will. Ever.

This history explains the deep enmity that exists to this day between the two countries and why the 21st century tensions between the newly-strong China and still-strong Japan are so dangerous. If pushed, neither side will back down to the other.

For Japan, its forced opening is, now, a matter for celebration. All over Japan can be found memorials to the arrival of the foreigners and their contribution to the development of Japan. Museums commemorating the foreign settlements and the foreigners who helped build them can be found in all treaty ports. In a country where land is scarce, and despite having fought the British and Americans in World War II, foreign cemeteries from the 19th century have been preserved and are well maintained. On the 150th anniversary of the British and Japanese Treaty of Amity and Commerce, the Japanese Foreign Minster, at the Foreign Office in London, launched a "Japan-UK 150" celebration. In Yokohama, you can enjoy lunch at "Le Jardin de Perry" near where Matthew Perry landed.

For China, its forced opening and the 100 years that followed are now described as "the Century of Humiliation." Anti-foreign sentiment is taught in schools, fills China's history books and is on display in all its museums. Foreign cemeteries have all been destroyed. You could never imagine any Chinese Foreign Minister celebrating an anniversary of the Treaty of Nanking anywhere, let alone at the Foreign Office in London. There is no "Le Jardin de Pottinger" in modern-day Nanjing.

How can two countries which faced almost identical

challenges have travelled such different roads?

In Japan, the opening of the country led to a civil war between reformers and those who wanted to retain the old feudal government under the Shogunate. The reformers won. From the late 1860s, the basic policy of the Japanese government was "reform or die."

Japan launched headlong into a program of rapid and large scale Westernisation. The Shogunate and old feudal system was abolished; foreign laws were studied and adopted; and, democracy was steadily introduced. The results were amazing. Japan went through a period of massive industrialization and economic growth and year after year became, politically, economically and militarily stronger. In less than 40 years, by 1894, Japan was strong enough to be able to reach agreements with all foreign countries to abolish all the unequal treaties. The following year, it defeated China in war and imposed its own unequal treaty on China. It continued to go from strength to strength, defeating Russia, annexing Korea and, over time, taking over large parts of China. Ultimately, during World War II, Japan occupied almost half of Asia.

China, on the other hand, was at the time of its forced opening already ruled by foreigners, the Manchus from Manchuria in what is now northeast China. The basic policy of the Manchu-run Qing Dynasty can be summarized as "if we reform we will die." Any change in China's system of governance, they believed, would weaken Manchu rule. One large-scale revolt in the 1850s and 1860s, the Taiping Rebellion, did threaten the government (and the Foreign Settlement in Shanghai), but was put down. The Qing Dynasty futilely resisted reform, relying instead on "self-strengthening," modernization in certain limited areas. This response, which led to further wars with foreign powers which China almost invariably lost, allowed China's sovereignty to be chipped away by more and more unequal treaties.

The Republican Revolution in 1911 offered hope, but

collapsed into civil war. Germany's defeat in World War I and the Russian Revolution brought the end of extraterritorial rights for Germans and Russians, but saw Japan take over most of Germany's interests in China. The unification under the militarily powerful Nationalists in 1927 offered even more hope; the European powers and America were willing to give up some rights. But by this time Japan was too strong for China to resist alone. By the time World War II started, Japan occupied more than half of China.

To this day, anti-foreign and particularly anti-Japanese propaganda is a fundamental part of the Chinese Communist Party's hold on power. Regular anti-Japanese protests are encouraged (and then, when they get too big, discouraged) by the government. In the 2010s, Sino-Japanese tensions have been upped by the Chinese by the use of military threats to assert China's claims over the Diaoyutai/Senkaku Islands. In March 2014, almost seventy years after World War II finished, the Secretary General of the Chinese Communist Party and President of China Xi Jinping said on a visit to Europe that the "war of aggression committed by Japanese militarism alone inflicted 35 million Chinese military and civilian casualties. These atrocities are still fresh in our memory."

How Japan which until the mid-1840s had co-existed relatively peacefully with China has became China's sworn enemy is a story that for most Westerners has long been forgotten. But given modern-day tensions between the two countries, it is well worth remembering. The story is not just Chinese Communist Party propaganda: China was treated appallingly by foreign powers, including Britain and to a lesser extent, the United States, for over 100 years. Japan's treatment of China, after it threw off the unequal treaties that had been imposed on it, was even worse.

Extraterritoriality foreign justice in foreign lands was a fundamental part of this humiliation. Extraterritoriality underpinned the foreign presence in China. It served day

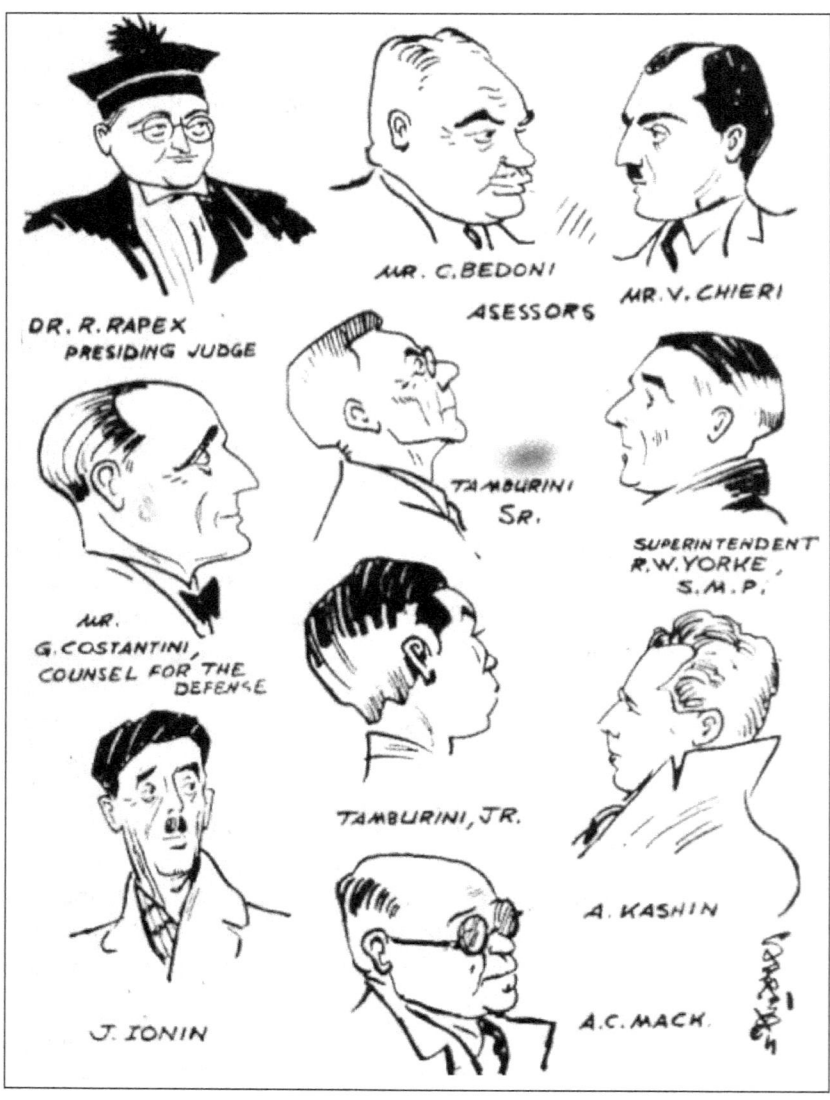

DR. R. RAPEX
PRESIDING JUDGE

MR. C. BEDONI

ASESSORS

MR. V. CHIERI

TAMBURINI
SR.

SUPERINTENDENT
R.W. YORKE,
S.M.P.

MR.
G. COSTANTINI,
COUNSEL FOR THE
DEFENSE

TAMBURINI, JR.

A. KASHIN

J. IONIN

A.C. MACK.

A scene from the Italian consular court in Shanghai in 1920s. Italian and British witness give evidence before an Italian judge and assessors.

to day to remind Chinese they were not sovereign in their own land and the assertion of "treaty rights" often resulted in military force being used against China.

Extraterritoriality meant that the governments of China and, while the treaties were in force there, Japan had almost no power to control foreigners enjoying treaty rights. Foreigners were allowed to freely enter the treaty ports, they were not subject to local laws and, could not be punished by local authorities. The most local officials could do was to arrest foreigners and hand them over to their own consular authorities for trial. They could not even deport them. Any threat by the Chinese or Japanese to breach these rights resulted in the dispatch of gunboats to enforce them.

Extraterritoriality created a remarkable system. Each treaty power established courts staffed by consular officers to try cases against their nationals. At its peak, in Shanghai, there were at least 23 different courts operating in the city: 19 foreign courts, three Chinese courts, and a Court of Consuls for bringing cases against the foreign-run Municipal Council. Close to twenty courts operated in the main Japanese treaty port, Yokohama. The consular courts were an alphabet soup of jurisdictions including German, Italian, Austro-Hungarian, Russian, Belgian, Danish, Dutch, French, Hungarian, Spanish, Mexican, Chilean, Norwegian, Swedish, Russian and Spanish courts.

While they hated the unequal treaties that allowed foreigners freely to enter and trade with their countries, Chinese and Japanese attitudes towards extraterritoriality, at least at the beginning, were equivocal. Despite later protestations and propaganda, neither China nor Japan were against extraterritoriality in the early years. Extraterritoriality had been demanded to protect treaty foreigners from the "barbaric" Chinese and Japanese legal systems which, to be fair to the foreign powers, did regularly torture parties before the courts. For both the Chinese and the Japanese, foreigners handling disputes between other foreigners seemed like a good idea.

Indeed, perhaps most telling of their early attitudes to extraterritoriality is that in the 1870s, China and Japan agreed to provide for mutual extraterritoriality for their citizens in each other's countries. In the 1880s, when foreign countries entered into unequal treaties with Korea, both China and Japan also imposed extraterritoriality on Korea.

The real problems with extraterritoriality came as more and more foreigners arrived in China and Japan and interacted with the locals. Particularly in China, foreigners in the form of missionaries, traders and officers of the foreign-run Imperial Maritime Customs spread across the country. Everywhere they went they mixed with local Chinese, creating friction that lead to disputes and, in the worst cases, to a number of killings. The Japanese managed, for the most part, to restrict foreigners to treaty ports but even in these ports, just as in China, disputes would arise with and crimes be committed against Japanese. Local Chinese and Japanese could only seek justice – in their own country by going to a foreign court using a foreign language and applying foreign law. They often felt that justice was not done when foreigner judged foreigner. This could lead to violence. The first British Chief Judge, Sir Edmund Hornby, quoted above, had had to call in the gunboat in Chefoo because a mob had besieged his bungalow for three days, angry at the acquittal of the British foreman.

The problems were exacerbated by the fact that most countries did not appoint trained lawyers to handle legal cases. Cases were instead handled by consuls, often with no legal training. For many countries, consuls were not even professional consular officers, but merely local merchants appointed to handle their country's interests. Cases could be, and often were, very poorly handled and decided.

In order to deal with some of the problems with consular

courts, the British, by far the largest Western power in East Asia, were the first to establish a formal court system in China and Japan staffed by professional judges. In 1865, the British Supreme Court for China and Japan was established in Shanghai. It was run from the British Foreign Office in London. The British Court for Japan, under the Shanghai Supreme Court, was established in Yokohama 14 years later. America, as its economic and political interests grew in China, established the United States Court for China in 1906 in Shanghai. This was for most of its life run by the Department of State from Washington DC.

These three courts tried in China, Japan, and, for a period, Korea (or Corea as it was then known), cases of every type imaginable: murder, sedition, rape, contract disputes, divorces, mass fights on board merchant ships, assault, battery, theft, fraud, ship collisions, and even, patent, copyright and trade mark infringement cases.

The courts were in almost all respects fully functioning British and American courts. They were staffed by professional judges. Qualified lawyers appeared before the courts. British or American law was applied and British and American rules of evidence and procedure were used. In the case of the British courts, juries were empaneled for all major civil and criminal cases. British judges and barristers all wore the traditional wigs and gowns, even in the oppressive heat of summer. Case reports were published and full records kept. Every quote from a judge, lawyer or witness in this book is from a contemporaneous report or record.

Needless to say being a judge or lawyer in an extraterritorial jurisdiction was challenging, requiring skills and knowledge beyond that of a judge or lawyer in their home jurisdiction.

Milton Helmick the last judge of the United States Court for China, who served right up to the commencement of the Pacific War, described the job of an extraterritorial judge:

"For ordinary every day judging he ought to
have known ... all about extraterritoriality, a little
international law, a smattering of the laws of other
countries, something of Chinese law, a great deal about
China, a lot about international politics, considerable
about diplomatic usages, a bit of anthropology and a
modicum about bomb dodging."

So, where did extraterritoriality come from?

CHAPTER 1

White Man, White Law, White Gun

CALEB CUSHING, A NOTED American diplomat, politician and lawyer, drafted the wording that would be the foundation of almost 100 years of extraterritoriality in China. Cushing, who had been sent by the US President to negotiate a treaty, said that he:

> "entered China with the formed general conviction that the United States ought not to concede to any foreign state, under any circumstances, jurisdiction over the life and liberty of a citizen of the United States, unless that foreign state be of our own family of nations, in a word, a Christian state."

Surprisingly, perhaps, given how long extraterritoriality lasted, it took only two short paragraphs to create the system. The paragraphs were Articles 21 and 25 of the Treaty of Wanghsia signed between the United States and China in 1844 to "establish firm, lasting, and sincere friendship between the two nations."

The articles provided that Chinese who committed crimes against Americans in China would be tried in Chinese courts but Americans who committed crimes in China against anyone would be tried by American consuls. All civil claims against Americans would be dealt with by American consuls.

Almost identical wording was used in every later treaty signed by China, Japan and Korea granting extraterritorial rights.

Article 21, as far as it dealt with criminal offences by Americans, the treaty provided that:

> "citizens of the United States who may commit any crime in China shall be subject to be tried and punished only by the Consul or other public functionary of the United States thereto authorised according to the laws of the United States."

Article 25, dealing with civil claims, read in part:

> "All questions in regard to rights, whether of property or person, arising between citizens of the United States in China shall be subject to the jurisdiction of and regulated by the authorities of their own Government."

Cushing had not needed to lead an American fleet or army

Caleb Cushing, American jurist who negotiated America's first treaty with China

to China to get the Chinese to sign the Treaty of Wanghsia. The British, two years previously, had already done that for him by convincingly defeating China in the first Opium War of 1839-1842.

China until the 1840s had been a hermit empire. Since the 17th Century, the country had been ruled by the Manchus from Manchuria in the northeast of today's China. The Manchus were foreign rulers of China. They spoke

Chinese boats blockade the Canton factories

and wrote their own language, wore their own clothes and garrisoned Manchu soldiers in the major cities of China in separate quarters. Chinese men were forced by the Manchus to wear their hair in a long braided ponytail, called a queue. The penalty for not doing so was death.

The Manchus had closed China off to foreign contact. They believed they had no particular need for foreign goods and, in particular, had no desire for the Chinese people to be infected by Western religions or thoughts. They did, however, allow for some limited trade in Canton (Guangzhou) in the far south of China. Foreign traders were restricted to the Canton factory so-called because factors, or agents, were based there. These were warehouses on the Pearl River in Canton. Foreign traders were permitted to deal with a select number of local merchants.

The trigger for Britain's attack on China was a war on drugs. China said "No." Britain had other ideas. Britain was running a huge trade deficit with China and started importing opium from India to even things up. The Chinese, not surprisingly, in 1836, banned its import. Two years later, in 1838, an Imperial Commissioner Lin Zexu started to aggressively suppress the domestic consumption of opium as well as the import of opium by foreigners. British merchants in Canton were blockaded in their factories until they agreed to hand over their opium stocks.

In March 1839, Captain Charles Elliot, the British Superintendent of China Trade, the most senior British official in China, agreed to the Chinese demands. He ordered the merchants to hand over more than 20,000 chests of opium. Elliot told the merchants that the British government would compensate them for their loss. Lin arranged for the opium to be destroyed by being released into ponds near the sea in the town of Humen in southern Guangdong province.

The reaction in Britain was one of outrage. The British government determined that the Chinese must be taught a lesson and dispatched an expeditionary force under the command of Captain Elliot. Elliot first headed north to Tientsin (Tianjin) where he was convinced to return to Macao for negotiations. When he realized the Chinese were prevaricating, he attacked Canton, taking it in May 1841.

Despite this success, when he returned to Macao from Canton, Elliot was dismissed for failing to prosecute the war with China properly. He was replaced by Henry Pottinger. China at the time had no major cities on the coast. Peking was located inland from Tientsin and was impossible to attack without land troops. Pottinger decided instead to attack Nanking, a major inland trading port on the Yangtze River, which controlled the supply of grain to northern China. After easily repelling Chinese counter attacks, they arrived at the walls of Nanking in August 1842 and threatened to bombard the city unless the Chinese agreed to their demands.

The Chinese Emperor in Peking finally realized the British forces were vastly superior to China's. He authorized his officials to negotiate whatever settlement they could. On August 29th 1842 a treaty was signed aboard HMS *Cornwallis* between Britain and China.

The treaty was the historic Treaty of Nanking.

The main terms of the Treaty of Nanking allowed for

Henry Pottiinger forcing opium on Lin Zexu

British merchants to trade with China. It opened five cities, Canton, Amoy, Foochow, Ningpo and Shanghai to foreign trade and allowed British merchants to live in these cities. The cities became known, along with all ports opened under later treaties, as "treaty ports." Hong Kong Island was also ceded to the United Kingdom in perpetuity to serve as a British base in China. China was also required to pay a total of $21 million, a massive sum at the time, as reparations for the war.

The Treaties of Nanking and Wanghsia only opened the

treaty ports to trade. They did not give free access to China for British or Americans. Foreigners could only travel short distances inland. Most importantly, foreigners were banned from the Chinese capital, Peking, and were not treated as equals by the Chinese government or officials. Not satisfied with the limitations in the Treaty of Nanking, the British over the years sought to reach a new agreement with China. China consistently rebuffed them.

In 1856, an opportunity came along to force the issue when the Chinese Governor of Canton seized what he believed to be a pirate ship, the *Arrow*. The British claimed that the Arrow was registered in Hong Kong and had been sailing under a British flag. In fact, its registration had expired. Nevertheless, Harry Parkes, the British Consul in Canton, was determined to teach the Chinese a lesson. Although Canton had been opened to foreign trade the local authorities refused access to the Chinese city. Using the seizure of the *Arrow* as an excuse, at Parkes' instigation, the British seized a Chinese warship and then attacked Canton. In December 1857, Canton was occupied by a joint British and French force. Early the next year, the fleet sailed to Tientsin where they negotiated and signed treaties with China. America also signed a treaty at the same time. All of these treaties were called the "Treaty of Tientsin" and had similar terms. They were much more detailed than the earlier treaties and gave foreigners far more rights in China.

The treaties loosened the restrictions on travel around treaty ports allowing residents to travel up to 100 li (about 50 kilometres) for a five-day period without restriction and to travel further in the interior with internal passports. The Yangtze River was opened to trade and five more ports were opened to trade. Christian missionaries were allowed to enter China to proselytize.

The Chinese government took responsibility for protecting foreign citizens and their property. Until 1860, no

Chinese official or ministry had been directly responsible for foreign affairs. The treaty required the Chinese to nominate a senior official to deal with diplomatic affairs. This resulted in the creation of China's first Ministry of Foreign Affairs the "Tsung Li Kekuo Shiwu Yamen" (Zongli Geguo Shiwu Yamen) or "General Office for Handling Affairs of Foreign Countries" usually shortened in English and Chinese as the "Tsungli Yamen." Foreign countries were given permission to establish legations (one rank below an embassy and headed by a minister) in Peking. China was required to treat foreign representatives on an equal footing. A specific provision stated that the term "barbarian" was not to be used to describe foreigners in official documents.

The signing of the treaties was not, however, to be the end of the matter. In 1859, the British and French returned to exchange ratifications of the treaties in Peking. They were repulsed leading to a war where Britain and France occupied Peking and in reprisal for the capture and killing of British representative travelling under a flag of truce, the British and French looted and burnt to the ground the Summer Palace, or Yuanmingyuan, a massive collection of palaces to the northwest of Peking.

For the next 50 years until the collapse of the Qing Dynasty, the Chinese continued to resist foreign encroachments. This led to wars that China almost always lost and to further unequal treaties.

Japan: The Black Ships

Just like China, Japan had been closed to foreigners since the 17th century. Dutch traders were allowed to trade in Nagasaki at the far western end of Japan in the small fan-shaped manmade island of Dejima.

The Americans took the lead to open up Japan. The negotiations were much easier, assisted in no small part by the clear military successes that the British and French had had

Commodore Perry of the US Navy arrives to force Japan open to trade

in China. The Japanese were, by the 1850s, well aware of the
China's defeat in the first Opium War and the overwhelming
firepower of foreign ships.

In 1853, Commodore Matthew Perry of the United States
Navy sailed into Tokyo Bay leading four ships. He demanded
the opening of Japan to foreign trade. Perry left a letter for
the Shogun and said he would return in a year's time for the
answer. In 1854 he returned with eight ships. The Japanese,
knowing they did not have the power to fight the Americans
and with the defeat of China in the Opium War in mind,
capitulated. The Shogunate, without obtaining the consent of
the Emperor, signed the Convention of Kanagawa with the
United States opening the ports of Hakodate, in Hokkaido,
and Shimoda, in Tokyo Bay, to foreign trade.

From 1856, the US Consul in Japan, Townsend Harris,
sought to sign an expanded treaty. In 1858, he was able to
get a treaty signed first by literally telling the Japanese "The
British are Coming" as the British and French sent a fleet to
Japan following the Second Opium War to negotiate treaty
rights in Japan. Harris told the Japanese they had better sign
up to the "favourable" terms he was offering (which included

a ban on importing opium) rather than have the British and French impose their own. The British and French were more than happy to sign treaties along the lines agreed with the United States without the need for war.

The treaties were signed with the Tokugawa Shogunate which had ruled Japan since the early 1600s. The Shogun as the head of the Shogunate was the senior military and political leader in Japan. Above the Shogun was the Emperor, but the Emperor held no true political power. Below the Shogunate, feudal lords, or Daimyo, ruled over their own domains. They were required to show allegiance to the Shogunate, but had substantial power in their own domains.

Not all Japanese or feudal Daimyos accepted the arrival of the foreigners and there was, initially, strong resistance to the treaties based in part on the fact that the Shogunate had signed the treaties without the approval of the Emperor. Two major battles, which the Japanese lost decisively, triggered rapid change in Japan. In 1863, a British citizen, Charles Richardson, was killed near Yokohama by a samurai who was a member of the Satsuma clan from Kagoshima in far Western Japan. When the Satsuma clan refused to punish the offender, seven British naval gunboats were sent to Kagoshima. When negotiations failed, the British ships bombarded the city, all but destroying it.

In 1864, the Choshu clan also from Western Japan, on orders of the Emperor who had directed the foreigners be expelled, closed the Straits of Shimonoseki by shelling any foreign ships seeking to sail through them. The narrow straits are the main routes for ships sailing from Japan through to China. The British, American, French and Dutch navies set out for Shimonoseki and after a short battle landed troops who destroyed the cannon. They then held Shimonoseki to ransom.

Following these defeats, the Choshu and Satsuma clans applied the maxim "if you can't beat them, join them." They sent a number of young men overseas to study, including

The British fleet bombards Kagoshima in retribution for the killing of Charles Richardson

Hirobumi Ito, who later became one of Japan's leading reformers and statesmen. The Choshu and Satsuma also pushed for a program of opening and westernization. This led to a civil war where the Choshu and Satsuma defeated the Shogunate. The Koumei Emperor who had ordered the expulsion of foreigners died in 1867. In February 1868, in what is now known as the Meiji Restoration, the very young and newly-installed Meiji Emperor issued a proclamation that the Shogun had been given permission to return the governing power to the Emperor. The Emperor then allowed the reformers to establish a new government.

The goal of the new Japanese government was to reform Japan's society, economy and legal system. The old feudal system and classes were abolished. The focus was on reform and the government adopted a hands-off attitude to the treaty ports. By 1875, reform was well under way. All foreign troops left Japan and gunboats were no longer needed to protect foreigners.

These treaties with China and Japan created the rules for extraterritoriality. How did the system work in practice?

Extraterritoriality in practice

In practice, extraterritoriality was a mess. At the beginning there were the teething problems one would expect in setting up a new system. Consuls had to be appointed and consulate buildings leased. That was the easy part.

Once appointed, the new consuls had none of the tools of state to run a legal system. They had no court rooms, no policemen and no prisons. The lack of court rooms could be easily solved. Any room will serve as a court if necessary. The lack of policemen and prisons was a far greater problem. The consuls often did not have police to arrest or prisons to hold criminals leading to weak enforcement of the law. Things improved as communities grew and police forces established in the major treaty ports.

Even after the initial teething periods, the exercise of consular jurisdiction remained fraught with difficulties. The early consuls, in particular, had to be chosen from a very small pool of people. Many countries, but not Britain, for many years appointed merchants living in the treaty ports as consuls. America appointed merchant consuls for the first 10 years but then shifted to political appointments. American consuls were expected to pay themselves from fees they collected. Most importantly, a "consul was never selected for his legal training."

It was not until the late 19th century that the United States sought to professionalize its consular service leading in 1906 to the passing of a consular reorganization law.

Britain from the outset avoided the worst of the merchant consul system by establishing a China Consular Service almost immediately with Henry Pottinger appointing many of the consuls. In the 1860s a system of examinations was introduced for appointing consuls in China, Japan, Korea and Thailand.

Consuls as Judges

Most consuls who tried cases were not lawyers and had no legal training. Because of this justice in the consular courts could be rough. The problem was exacerbated where a young consular officer could be called upon to act as a vice-consul.

British consular officer Ernest Satow, when he first acted as a vice-consul in the 1870s, wrote:

"Fancy me an acting Vice Consul. Such is the truth. It is quite absurd. I did not know how to register a birth till the constable showed me. Now I live in daily terror lest a case should be brought into my court and I am compelled to sit in judgement. Not having the faintest idea of how to preside. To say nothing of complete ignorance of the law."

Sir Edmund Hornby, the first Chief Judge of the British Supreme Court wrote to the then British Foreign Minister, Earl Clarendon, of the consular court system he found in Japan:

"[A]s the whole judicial business has to be done by Her Majesty's Consular Officers who have no legal education, and who are besides very young and inexperienced, the hearing of cases occupies a great deal of time, and the result is often most unsatisfactory. I do not think however, it would be fair to attribute any blame to the officers themselves, they conscientiously endeavor to do the work before them, but as they have neither the necessary education or experience the result is as unsatisfactory to themselves as to the public. Indeed, their position is very like mine would be if your Lordship insisted on appointing me to the post of Chief Surgeon to a London hospital."

Even before professionalization of the American consular service, some American consular officials were also lawyers. Thomas van Buren, the consul-general in Yokohama in the 1870s and 1880s was a former Civil War general and qualified lawyer. George Seward, the consul-general in Shanghai in the 1860s and later American Minister in Peking, was also a lawyer. This was a good thing because American consular courts in China and Japan had very broad powers, much

The Chaos of a Consular Court - A hearing in Kanagawa

broader than the British consular courts. They could and did
try serious cases including death penalty cases.

In the first 20 years of extraterritoriality, British consular
courts had much more limited powers than the American
consular courts. Hong Kong had, under the Treaty of Nanking,
become a British colony in 1842. The Supreme Court of Hong
Kong was established in 1844 (taking over the jurisdiction of
the Court for China that had been established in Canton). In
addition to having full jurisdiction in Hong Kong, the Hong
Kong Supreme Court was given extraterritorial jurisdiction
over China and, later, Japan. Death penalty and other
serious cases had to be tried in Hong Kong before a jury.
This created the serious problem that it was very difficult
to gather necessary evidence of a crime in China or Japan
that would satisfy a jury in Hong Kong that the accused was
guilty. Consuls would prefer to try British prisoners in the
consular courts even for serious offences rather than see them
acquitted in Hong Kong.

Appeals from decisions of British consular courts in China could also be brought to the Supreme Court of Hong Kong.

After the opening of Japan, the Hong Kong Supreme Court was also given appellate jurisdiction in Japan. This led to one case where Rutherford Alcock, then the British Minister in Japan, was sued in the Hong Kong Supreme Court for false imprisonment and lost because he had added a term of imprisonment to a fine imposed by a consular court.

Dissatisfaction with the Hong Kong Supreme Court continued for many years. *The Times* of London in July 1863 was scathing:

> "This Supreme Court of Hong Kong is the greatest nuisance in the East. Any Consul or Custom-House office who dares to take any measures against any of the 'scum of Europe' found running goods, or levying blackmail or shooting natives in China or Japan is immediately sued in the Supreme Court."

In early 1865, a question was asked in the British Parliament about whether it was proposed to take any steps to "remedy the evils arising from the Consular Courts in China being the only accessible Courts for the trial of Civil and Criminal as well as the ordinary Police cases; the Consuls not being lawyers by education, and the amount of business having become very large?"

The answer was "yes." To favourable comment from the *Times* and others, it was decided to relieve the Hong Kong Supreme Court of "most troublesome and burdensome work for which it never gained credit," and to establish in Shanghai Her Britannic Majesty's Supreme Court for China and Japan. To do so, the Foreign Office turned to a man who had already set up one extraterritorial legal system and had earned a reputation for getting things done: Sir Edmund Hornby.

CHAPTER 2

Establishing the British Supreme Court

SIR EDMUND HORNBY, the founder of the British Supreme Court for China and Japan, was one of those larger-than-life characters that populated the British Empire. He was by his own and others' accounts a "man's man," not only willing to face down a crowd of Chinese in a remote port angry at the acquittal of a British defendant with a shotgun in his hand, but as the *Times* said in a review of his autobiography to "berate a Secretary of State, rebuke an Ambassador, and bluff or bully for their own ultimate benefit any number of high foreign officials." He had his eccentricities. He kept as his "constant companion in all climes" for more than 40 years a parrot which a judge from the Gold Coast in Africa had given him in lieu of payment for helping him gain his appointment. He also wrote a long account of meeting a ghost in Shanghai, an account that to this day, given the position of the author, is still cited by many as clear proof of paranormal activity.

Despite his eccentricities and probably because of his strong personality, Sir Edmund, then Judge of the British Court at Constantinople was more than likely to have been the Foreign Office's first choice as the first Chief Judge in Shanghai. Hornby knew how to get things done and nothing and nobody scared him.

Hornby had originally been sent to Constantinople in 1855 as Commissioner of the Turkish Loan. Britain also had

*Sir Edmund Hornby, founder and Chief Judge of the
British Supreme Court for China and Japan*

extraterritorial rights in the Ottoman Empire. Hornby was asked by the Foreign Office to write a report on the exercise of judicial powers in Turkey by consuls who had no legal training or background. Hornby recommended setting up a court with dedicated staff to handle judicial work. This was accepted and on August 27, 1857, at the age of 32, Hornby was appointed Judge in Constantinople. He was knighted five years later in 1862 at the remarkably early age of 37.

Hornby was only 41 when he took up his post in Shanghai. One newspaper said on his death that he was a "man of extraordinary energy and varied experiences, and that as a raconteur he had few rivals." In particular, he had a sufficient sense of self-awareness that "he was never more amusing than when telling stories against himself." One story that the writer particularly remembered was when Hornby met with the British Attorney-General before heading out to Constantinople as the new Judge. The Attorney-General asked him how he intended to travel. Hornby told him he planned to go via Venice and take a steamer from Venice to Constantinople. The Attorney-General then said "Ah then, perhaps in the solitude of your cabin in the Adriatic you will employ your leisure in reading up a little – a very little criminal law."

It was true that as a judge, Hornby was not in the habit of writing long judgments or engaging in deep analysis of the law.

He also suffered from a particular virulent form of judgitis, "the smartest man in the room" syndrome. Every article on Hornby as a judge, and many of his judgments made it clear that Hornby was one of those judges whom lawyers hate to appear before. Hornby had no time for arguments by lawyers. In most cases, he would have already made up his mind before hearing counsel and would tell them so. Hornby was proud of the way he handled cases. Before a trip to Japan in 1870, he wrote:

"I can dispose of all pending cases – and the mere fact
of my being there will precipitate all those that are
hatching. There is always a lull in litigation after I have
been in place, because I talk people out of their absurd
grounds and settle those amicably which really have
any points in them without fighting – and in criminal
matters, I generally manage to inspire a wholesome
respect for the law, that the Rowdy chaps keep in order
for at least three months after I leave."

Another article published in Japan on his retirement saw
some silver linings in Hornby's attitude to judging:

"of course the faults in his judicial character were
severely commented on, for they were only too obvious
but really flowed from the most admirable quality of
his mind, his keen insight, and almost intuitive power
of discerning where the difficulty of a case lay. He
strove to strip every case of needless technicalities,
and to administer the Law according to the dictates of
common sense."

Perhaps not the sort of man you would look to become a
judge of an established court but, as the Foreign Office clearly
decided twice, the exact type of man you want to set up a court
in a remote foreign land where there are many opponents to
that court's authority.

Establishing the court
Having been appointed to set up the British Supreme Court
for China and Japan in Shanghai, Sir Edmund Hornby
travelled back to London from Constantinople in late 1864.
He recalled:

"I presented myself at the Foreign Office and set to

work with my old friend FS Reilly (afterwards Sir
Francis Savage Reilly, KCB) to draw an Order in
Council defining the jurisdiction of the new Court
to be established in China, and in hard work found
occupation."

An Order in Council is a regulation made theoretically by
the King or Queen, but in reality drafted by the government.
The Orders in Council governing the British Courts in China
and Japan were all made under the Foreign Jurisdiction Act,
which provided the legal foundation for extraterritoriality.

One of the goals of the British in setting up the British
Supreme Court in China and Japan as well as in Constantinople
was to set an example to the governments of all three places as
to how a legal system should function. In particular, Hornby
wanted to show the importance of judicial independence and
"how necessary it was to separate entirely the judicial from
executive and administrative authority." In order to do this,
the Chief Judge was given full authority over judicial matters
without reference to his nominal chief, the British Minister in
Peking.

Some years later, Prince Kung, the Emperor's uncle, asked
Hornby about his powers. Did he have to obey an order of the
Queen in relation to a particular case? Hornby said "certainly
not." Prince Kung then asked if he meant that if the Minister
gave him an order he would not have to obey it. Hornby said
that the Minister would never give him such an order and
that if he did he would not take any notice of it. Prince Kung
said this made Hornby all-powerful:

"Then you are, in your capacity of Judge, above not
only the Minister but also above the Sovereign."

Hornby replied with an explanation of the Rule of Law,
which even to this day would not be understood by most

Mainland Chinese leaders:

> "Not so, I am simply the mouth-piece of the law which, according to our system, rules alike Sovereigns and Ministers."

Prince Kung evidently did not appreciate this lesson. As we shall see, some years later, he would personally ask the British Minister to re-try a British defendant, who had already been acquitted of murder; and then, execute him.

Ordering the system

Hornby and Reilly's work in drafting an Order in Council ended with the issue of the China and Japan Order in Council, 1865 on March 9 of that year. The Order in Council provided that the Supreme Court for China and Japan be presided over by a Judge, who had to be a barrister with a minimum of seven years experience, as well as an Assistant Judge. The existing Consular Courts were renamed Provincial Courts and given very broad powers in relation to civil actions. They were also given a very broad criminal jurisdiction, except that the Supreme Court was given the sole authority to try death penalty cases. Capital cases were either to be tried in Shanghai or when the judges of the Supreme Court travelled around China and Japan on circuit.

In the Shanghai Consular District, the Shanghai Consular Court was abolished and the Supreme Court at Shanghai was given complete jurisdiction to handle all cases. Outside the Shanghai area, the Supreme Court was given concurrent jurisdiction with the Provincial Courts. Appeals could be brought to the Supreme Court in civil cases and by way of case stated in criminal cases. The Supreme Court and Provincial Courts were required to apply English Common Law, Rules of Equity and Statutes, as were from time to time in force in England.

The Deputy – Charles Goodwin

Hornby chose Charles Wycliffe Goodwin, a barrister practicing in London, as his assistant judge. Goodwin was much more famous (then and now) as an Egyptologist, but was also recognized as an expert on the Bible as well as being a music and art critic.

Goodwin had originally intended to become a priest, but had given up theological studies in the late 1830s. He first travelled in Europe and then studied for the Bar at Lincoln's Inn. According to his brother, he found the study of law uncongenial:

> "Oh, how he groaned under it. How often he demonstrated that the system of English jurisprudence was without philosophical foundation, and with what delight would he turn from law papers to hieratic papyri!"

Perhaps not surprisingly, after being called to the bar, Goodwin decided to give up the law and become a teacher. He became a fellow at St Catharine's Hall in 1840 and in 1843 returned to St Catharine's to teach. He, however, lost his fellowship four years later in very strange circumstances. The constitution of St Catharine's required that at least two fellows be priests and one a deacon. When Goodwin became a fellow in 1840, four fellows were priests. By 1847, following first a retirement and then a death, only two priests remained as fellows. St Catharine's therefore voted to forfeit Goodwin's

Charles Wycliffe Goodwin, Egyptologist, Bible scholar and genius – Hornby's Assistant Judge

fellowship. Goodwin appealed the decision to Queen Victoria who referred the matter to the Lord Chancellor. The Lord Chancellor upheld the decision of the Hall.

Having lost his fellowship, in 1847, Goodwin returned to London to practice as a barrister. His practice was principally in the probate courts although his work as a barrister did not keep him particularly busy. He did, however, keep himself occupied publishing three legal books on probate, succession duty and copyhold entitlement.

Egyptology remained his great love but he also dabbled in almost every other area of intellectual pursuit.

Goodwin had until the 1860s been able to live off income that his father had generated from a very successful solicitor's practice. But his father died in 1859 and his estate got caught up in a probate battle. Goodwin, desiring a more stable income, in 1861, made an application for a position as a judge through Sir Henry Layard, the Parliamentary Under Secretary to Earl Russell, then Foreign Secretary. Layard, when forwarding Goodwin's application, said he had only met Goodwin once but that he had struck him as "a hardheaded, able man." His letter made no reference to Goodwin's legal qualifications but supported the application on the basis of Goodwin's theological scholarship and especially of his study of hieratic papyri.

Earl Russell was a little more practical and wrote on the note from Layard that what was required was "legal and not theological orthodoxy." He asked that enquiries be made as to "Goodwin's standing and proficiency as a lawyer." These enquiries must have proved satisfactory because on 13 March 1865, four days after the Order in Council was issued, Goodwin received a letter from the Foreign Office on behalf of Earl Russell informing him he had been appointed Assistant Judge of Her Britannic Majesty's Supreme Court for China and Japan.

Two weeks after this, on 1 April 1865, Goodwin, at the age

of 47, married – or, as he put it in a letter to a friend "committed matrimony" to Augustine Anne Rutherford. Anne, as she preferred to be called, then aged 22, was the daughter of a long-term friend of Goodwin's, Edward Rudderforth, a London surgeon. This appears to have been Goodwin's first marriage. Despite this, Goodwin had a daughter, Agnes, who had been born in 1850 in an unknown place to an unknown mother. The Rudderforths must have been very good friends, because in 1861, Agnes was living with the Rudderforths as a boarder. Anne, Goodwin's new wife, who was eight years older, must have been like a big sister to Agnes. The marriage ceremony was conducted at St James' Church, Piccadilly by Goodwin's brother, the Reverend Harvey Goodwin.

Travelling to Shanghai
In June 1865, Hornby and John Fraser left England for Shanghai to set up the court. Fraser, whom Hornby had first met in a Vice-Consulate in Asia Minor, had been appointed Law Secretary. In this position, Fraser was responsible for administration of the court, trying as a magistrate minor criminal cases and prosecuting more serious cases before the court. Hornby and Fraser first stopped in Malta and then went on to Egypt. Goodwin and Anne, after a brief honeymoon, left a little earlier planning to meet up with Hornby and Fraser in Egypt. They went to France so Goodwin could meet another famous Egyptologist, Francois Chabas, in person in Marseilles. They then went on to Egypt because, as Hornby put it, Goodwin "longed to take a last fond look at some Papaqui and hieroglyphic slabs."

Goodwin had arranged to join Hornby and Fraser at Cairo to take the train to Suez. Hornby gave a delightful description of the scene that met him at Cairo station:

"I was surprised to find a guard of honour – several Pashas and Beys and the Corps Consulaire in full rig,

cocked hats, etc. A saloon carriage was attached to the
train, at the door of which stood an English guard. I
asked him what swell was going by the train, to which
he replied 'The English Judge'. Feeling certain that
I was not that distinguished individual, I patiently
waited until the guard saluted. All the cocked hats
were raised and an immense hand-shaking took place
--the object being my little fat friend Goodwin in a pith
helmet and green veil, his newly-married wife on his
arm. Of course I stood by whilst he was escorted to
the carriage, and when good-byes were said I humbly
asked if I might get in also."

After their train trip, Hornby, Goodwin and Fraser sailed
from Suez to Singapore and on to Hong Kong on board the
P&O Steamer, the *Carnatic*. They arrived in Shanghai on July
16, 1865. Hornby described landing in Shanghai:

"On landing I was agreeably disappointed to find,
instead of a second Wapping, as it had been described
to me in London, a handsome quay or bund, along the
length of which were visible a line of very handsome
buildings – indeed it would require but little stretch of
the imagination, and hardly then be an exaggeration, to
call some of them palaces."

Goodwin was not as enamoured of Shanghai as Hornby.
In a letter to his sister, he described Shanghai as "very like
England green and flat ... Everything here is in a state of
disorganization – People rob one another – and submit to be
robbed by their Chinese servants." In a later letter to a friend
he wrote: "Shanghai certainly is not the most interesting
place to come to – The City is a second or third rate one, & the
country around it is very dreary, flat and damp."

Shanghai as it was when Hornby and Goodwin arrived

Opening the Court: The First Cases

Her Britannic Majesty's Supreme Court for China and Japan was formally opened on September 4, 1865. The *North China Herald* reported:

> "On Monday, the Supreme Court of China and Japan was formally opened by Sir Edmund Hornby. The Royal Warrants appointing the Judge, Assistant Judge and Law Secretary were read, and Sir Edmund Hornby then proceeded to swear himself into office, after which the oath was administered to Messrs. Goodwin (Assistant Judge) and Fraser (Law Secretary). Messrs. Myburgh, Eames and Robinson signed the roll of practitioners in the Court, and the ceremony ended."

Goodwin was installed as Judge of Civil Cases and Fraser, the Law Secretary, as magistrate. Hornby reserved for himself all "heavy and appeal cases – civil and criminal."

The legal practitioners of the court were either barristers or solicitors admitted in England. Unlike most other English common law jurisdictions, from the start and for the lifetime of the court, there was no distinction drawn in the court between a solicitor and a barrister. Solicitors could appear as advocates in the court and barristers could practice in partnership with other barristers or solicitors and handle work traditionally within the realm of solicitors, such as conveyancing and drawing up wills. Many firms that would subsequently be set up in Shanghai would be partnerships between barristers or between barristers and solicitors. The legality of this was challenged unsuccesfully some 50 years later in the Privy Council.

The court almost immediately started work. At the end of September, and then six weeks later in November, the first three "heavy" cases came before Hornby. The first case challenged the right of the British to prosecute on behalf of the Chinese Emperor. The next challenged the entire foundation of the government of Shanghai and other treaty ports. The third was the first death penalty case to come before the court.

The right to prosecute

Messrs. Reynolds and Holt were the owners of a block of land on the Putong (Pudong) side of the river, opposite the International Settlement. They had extended the river bank to reclaim land and build a jetty. The Chinese Harbour Master of the Whangpoo River and the Conservator or the Yangtze River had complained about the works to the British Consulate because they were affecting the flow of, and navigation on, the river. The consulate issued a summons in the Supreme Court for Reynolds and Holt to show cause why they should not be punished for, and prohibited from, blocking the river. Reynolds and Holt had a number of defences, including that their lease entitled them to conduct the works. Of greater importance, they alleged that the British Consul had no power to bring a prosecution on behalf of the Chinese Emperor. Hornby made short work of this argument. He said that he was surprised the argument had been made because if it was allowed to succeed the result would be absurd. Either, the Government of China would have no remedy in cases in which British subjects were wrong-doers, or the "Emperor would be bound to appear as a suitor in a Foreign court on his own soil." Hornby ruled that by obtaining extraterritorial rights, Her Majesty had "implicitly undertaken that she will compel Her subjects to respect the laws of China, as well as the laws of their own country" and would not "subject the sovereign power the indignity of appearing on its own soil in the character of a suitor in a Foreign Court."

The Municipal Council's power to tax

In the next case, Hornby needed to decide if the Shanghai Municipal Council could impose and collect rates. Mr and Mrs Wills had died leaving an infant son. Rates were owed to the council on various pieces of land in what had been the British settlement as well as what had been the American Settlement, called Hongque, before the two settlements were merged. The council sued the Wills' estate for back rates.

This was a very important case that would confirm the legality of the management and financing of Shanghai International Settlement for its entire existence. The legal foundation of the International Settlement was the Land Regulations that had been agreed between the British Consul and Shanghai Taotai in 1853. Formally, the British Superintendent of Trade had issued them under power granted to him by an Order in Council. The Land Regulations provided the basic rules under which Shanghai was to be governed. They established a municipal council elected by ratepayers. The Shanghai Municipal Council could issue by-laws made under the Land Regulations.

The main question in the Wills case was whether the Land Regulations gave the Council the power to charge rates. The trustees argued that the Land Regulations were a private agreement between land renters in Shanghai and were thus not binding on those who chose not to participate.

The British Superintendent of Trade had been given

power to make regulations for the "peace, order and good government" of British subjects in Shanghai. This was the phrase used in all British colonies to give the colonial governments broad powers to pass laws. The trustees, however, argued that the making of land regulations that gave the power of government to private individuals, that is the Municipal Council, were not regulations for the "peace, order and good government" of the British subjects.

Hornby made short work of this argument saying that there was no reason why the Superintendent of Trade should not have as broad powers as a colonial government to control British subjects. Taking into account the special circumstances of extraterritoriality, the Superintendent had to have that authority:

> "Indeed I am inclined to go further and say it is incumbent on Her Majesty, by virtue of an obligation to be implied from the very privilege of exclusive jurisdiction granted to Her, to provide for the peace, good order and government of those of Her subjects who are within the Empire of China and removed by the consent of the Sovereign power of that country from the operation of its laws and the jurisdiction of its native Magistrates."

He found that the council could charge rates. The courts of almost all the other treaty powers in Shanghai at the time made similar decisions. The previous year the Prussian and Danish consular courts had upheld the Council's taxing power. The same year the French and American consular courts also issued similar decisions. The American Consul-General, George Seward, however, held that the power to charge rates came not from treaty rights but from a delegation of power from the Chinese government. He appreciated that he "was treading on delicate ground" because if this was the case, China could withdraw its consent at any time. But in a mixture of subtle diplomatese and legalese, he concluded by pointing out that the foreign military that was backing the treaties would make that difficult:

> "We are, moreover, so situated in virtue of the extraterritorializing provisions of the Treaties, that it would not be easy to enforce any regulations without our consent, and we are thus able to assert a certain pressure upon the authorities to uphold such Regulations as we deem right."

The first murder

Two days after hearing the Wills case, Hornby tried, with a jury, the first murder trial in the Supreme Court. Mohamed, a Malay seaman who lived in Bamboo Town in the northeastern corner of Hongque, had killed his Chinese wife, Leemah. Leemah was an opium addict who also worked as a prostitute when Mohamed was at sea. Mohamed and Leemah had adopted two Chinese girls aged nine and twelve. Mohamed doted on the girls.

Mohamed had heard rumours that Leemah was prostituting herself. Things came to a head when Leemah pawned his clothes and refused to allow him to see their daughters. After a quarrel, he stabbed Leemah seven times, twice in the kidney. She died quickly. Mr. York, the runner for the Ghaut Serang the senior supervisor of the Malay community had found Mohamed at his door. Mohamed told York that he had killed his wife. York did not find any knife. Mohamed said that he had thrown it away.

It appeared a very simple case. However, when Mr. York found him, there was no blood at all on Mohamed's clothes. Dr Johnston who gave medical evidence said that Leemah's clothing was very thin and there should have been some blood splatter.

Phillip Myburgh, a British barrister, prosecuted. Given that Mohamed was facing a death sentence, Mr Lawrance, a British lawyer volunteered to appear for the defence free of charge. All those present in the court were very aware that this was the first death penalty case to be tried by a British court in China. Myburgh and Lawrence both mentioned this in their arguments. After all the evidence was heard, Hornby summed up for the jury. He very properly cautioned the jury that they might feel sympathy for Mohamed who was facing the death penalty. However, referring to Leemah, he said there was "another being whom you have not seen for whom the same consideration is due."

Hornby said that the only possible defence Mohamed had was that of provocation. This could reduce his crime from murder to manslaughter. In order for provocation to be proved, it would be necessary for the jury to be convinced that Leemah's actions had been so bad as to cause Mohamed to kill her out of passion. Hornby made it clear that he did not consider this to be the case. He told the jury that "society should not be exposed to the consequences of a man losing his temper and surrendering himself to the dominion of his passions, until he is so overcome as to lose all power of regulating his actions."

The jury retired for 45 minutes. Upon returning, they convicted Mohamed of murder but with a strong recommendation for mercy. Before passing sentence Hornby asked if Mohamed had anything to say. He begged for mercy recounting Leemah's terrible behavior. Hornby put on the black cap and sentenced Mohamed to death. He said he would pass on the recommendation of mercy to the minister in Peking, saying it was "possible he might regard it favourably inasmuch as this was the first case of the kind brought before the Court."

Mohamed's sentence was commuted to 20 years in prison and he was sent to Hong Kong the next year to serve his sentence.

CHAPTER 3

The Younger Generation: Learning the Ropes

JUST BEFORE OR SOON after the opening of the British Supreme Court for China and Japan, almost all the men who would play important roles in the court in the 19th century, three young consular officers and two young barristers, commenced their careers in China and Japan.

One, Robert Mowat, very soon after the Supreme Court was established, took over as Acting Law Secretary when John Fraser fell ill in 1866. Fraser died in Marseille, France on 18 April 1867. Mowat had joined the China Consular Service in 1864. He had been born in 1843 in Edinburgh, Scotland making him 21 when he came to China. He was educated in Edinburgh before attending London University, which nominated him for the Foreign Office exam.

Mowat joined the consular service at almost exactly the same time as two other men who would be long standing colleagues and rivals for promotion: Hiram Shaw Wilkinson and George Jamieson. In 1864, all three of them took the Foreign Office examination for admission to the consular service made up of papers in Arithmetic, Compound Addition, Orthography, Handwriting, Intelligence, Geography, Precis, Latin, French and English. Mowat came second and Wilkinson third. Jamieson was placed either fourth or fifth.

Jamieson had graduated from Aberdeen University. Wilkinson had just completed a Bachelor of Arts at the

Queen's University Belfast. He was recommended by Lord Lugard and received a glowing reference from his professor, George Craick, who described him as a student of the "first rank." Unlike all other student intepreters he was married at the time, which was a surprise to British officials when he arrived in Japan. His wife Prudie died in Japan in 1870. They had two sons, Hiram Parkes (Harrie) and Thomas. Harrie later joined his father in practice in China.

Wilkinson chose to be based in Japan and Jamieson in China. After completing their language training in as student interpreters in Japanese and Chinese respectively, Wilkinson and Jamieson were both appointed consular officers. On January 1, 1868 Wilkinson was appointed to the rank of Third Assistant. In that position he acted as the accountant in the legation in Tokyo. In 1870, he was appointed a First Assistant, backdated to April 1, 1868. Jamieson was appointed a 2nd Class Assistant in 1867 and in 1868 appointed, despite his very junior rank at the time, Acting Consul in Tainan, Taiwan. Unlike Wilkinson and Jamieson, Mowat appears never to have entered full time consular service.

The trial of Robert George

Mowat was the Law Secretary when Robert George, an Indian foreman at Farnham and Co at Collier's dock, was tried for the murder of a Chinese co-worker, Wang Aran. The shooting had occurred some hours after a violent confrontation between them, which had started when Wang "broke wind" in front of George. Wang had also committed a "revolting act" over their food. George then insulted a carpenter and yelled "I'll have my revenge before 6 o'clock tonight." He returned later with a gun and shot and killed Wang and seriously injured another carpenter. After being arrested by a British co-worker, George told him, "I am not sorry for the Chinaman."

George was charged with the crime of willful murder. The Chinese authorities viewed the case very seriously and sent a Chee Seen or deputy magistrate to assist in the trial of the case. The bench in the old consular court was packed. Sir Edmund Hornby and Charles Goodwin were there in their scarlet robes and white wigs together with the Chee Seen, also dressed in his official robes. The British Consul in Shanghai, Walter Medhurst, also sat on the bench in his full dress consular uniform of dark blue with gold buttons.

The very tall Richard Rennie lights a cigar on a street lamp

Normally, Mowat, as the Law Secretary, would have prosecuted the case. However, probably given the seriousness of the charge and the Chinese authorities' interest in the case, a barrister, Richard Rennie was briefed for the prosecution. A young barrister, newly arrived in town, Nicholas Hannen, defended George. Rennie and Hannen were both destined to become judges and this case pitched them against each other for the first time in a major case.

Rennie, who had been born in 1839, was the fourth son of George Rennie who had been a well-known sculptor, Liberal Member of Parliament and Governor of the Falkland Islands. Rennie was called to the bar of the Inner Temple in 1860, having qualified by commencing a pupilage straight out of school. Rennie practiced before the Western Circuit for five years before moving to Hong Kong, where his brother, William Hepburn Rennie, had been serving as Auditor-General since 1858. As he put it himself, he had come to the Far East to "seek his fortune." He stayed in Hong Kong for two months before he moved to Shanghai in 1866, at the age of 27, and "fell in love with the place." Rennie was very tall. All cartoons from the time show him towering over everyone else.

Nicholas Hannen who had been born in 1842 was three years younger than Richard Rennie. He was the sixth son (and thirteenth child) of James Hannen, a wine merchant, of Kingswood, Dulwich. He attended University College London where he obtained a BA in 1862 with honours in logic and moral philosophy. He was called to the Bar at the Inner Temple in 1866. He arrived in Shanghai, via Hong Kong, in 1868, at the age of 26, and was admitted to the Supreme Court for China and Japan in that year. Like Rennie, he had a relative in China. His brother, Charles Hannen, was with the Imperial Maritime Customs. Another brother, James Hannen, was a judge in England and a good friend of Edmund Hornby. No doubt Hornby had told James Hannen that there were good opportunities as a barrister for his younger brother in China.

For George's trial, a jury of five Englishmen was empaneled. Rennie, for the prosecution, called three English and five Chinese witnesses to give evidence. The Chinese magistrate assisted with the examination of the Chinese witnesses. There was no doubt that George had killed the co-worker. The only question for the jury to decide was whether he was to be convicted of murder or manslaughter.

Hannen had a tough case. George had promised to get his revenge and had come back and done so. Hannen did the best he could. He objected to there being a jury of only five, arguing there should be 12 members, as in England. He also argued that the evidence of the Chinese witnesses as non-Christians could not be relied upon. Hornby overruled these objections.

In his closing speech, Hannen sought to convince the jury that the various attacks that had been made on George were sufficient for the jury to consider manslaughter the appropriate verdict. He said that it is "well known how easily people from his country can be roused to anger, and, how long it is before their blood cools." The jury should weigh all the provocations "with the known excitability of Indian men and take a favorable view of them."

In his summing up Hornby reminded the jury of their solemn duty to themselves and the public not to allow feelings or weakness to affect their verdict. The jury then retired. They returned twenty-five minutes later. Mowat, as Law Secretary, asked them for their verdict. "Guilty" said the foreman, but with a strong recommendation for mercy. English law at the time did not allow judges to show mercy for convicted murderers. There was only one sentence that could be passed. Hornby hated this aspect of being a judge. He put on the black cap and pressed a book between his left side and the bench to prevent his violently beating heart from bursting.

Doing all he could to control his voice, he said:

"You have been found guilty. The sentence is Death."

Hornby told George that he had no hope of mercy and earnestly exhorted him to:

"spend the rest of your short time on earth in making peace with your God."

The sentence was not yet the end of George. The case raised three important issues concerning the conduct of trials in extraterritorial China. First and probably most importantly for Hornby, he did not want ever again to sit with a Chinese judge. Soon after the trial was completed, Hornby wrote to the British Foreign Secretary, George Villiers, to "urgently entreat" Villiers to spare him "from being compelled to sit on the bench with a Chinese mandarin whose language I do not know, as he is ignorant of mine", but more importantly, "who cannot by any possible amount of interpretation be made to understand the principles of law and form of procedure which I am bound to follow." Hornby finished:

> "the presence of such an official on the bench of an
> English court must be an empty form and a farce,
> or – if it be supposed to give a guarantee for truth
> being vindicated or right being done – it is an insult to
> English justice."

Hannen also raised again his legal challenges. He argued that having a jury made up of only five jurors instead of 12 as was required in England, was unconstitutional. The Order in Council, as sub-legislation, could not take away a fundamental constitutional right such as trial by jury. Only Parliament could by enactment of a law amend the Constitution. Hannen also argued again that the evidence of the Chinese witnesses, as non-Christians, could not be relied upon. During the trial, the Chinese witnesses had been asked if they believed in a God who would punish them if they told a lie. The witnesses said that they believed in a God of Thunder who was able to punish them. They did not believe he would certainly punish them. Hannen argued that for pagans, the law should only accept their evidence if they believed they "would be assuredly punished." He concluded, "the God of Thunder is not an all seeing Being, and any rate, not that Being that the law of England requires in its oath."

Rennie tried to keep his argument in response simple, pointing out that the British Parliament had recently passed an act that allowed for unsworn testimony in certain cases. The Chinese witnesses had given sworn testimony even if to a non Christian god. This had to be better than unsworn evidence.

But with judges like Hornby and, in particular, Goodwin, a leading bible scholar, on the bench, it was never going to be kept simple. Hornby and Goodwin both pondered as to what were the motives that restrained a man from doing wrong. Hornby considered that "it is an innate consciousness that it is wrong." Goodwin asserted, "it was a conception of punishment in the background, inexpressible, but which was the deterring power."

Hornby gave a ruling four days later. He gave short shrift to the argument that a trial with five jurors was unconstitutional. He held that the Foreign Jurisdiction Act, which established the court and empowered the making of Orders in Council, gave more than sufficient authority for the Orders in Council to limit the size of a jury to five jurors. He gave more consideration to the question of whether a non-Christian witness could give evidence and ruled that "the object is to know whether the witness believed in the existence of any superhuman Being, who take cognizance of his action and to whom lying is offensive," and that the law of England "is ready to recognise any variety of this belief." He said that he and Goodwin were satisfied the Chinese witnesses had the appropriate fear of God and dismissed the applications.

Nothing now stood between George and the gallows. He was hanged at the British Consular Gaol, just southwest of the consulate, six weeks later at 5.30am on August 31, 1869. Robert Mowat, along with the British Consul, Mr Medhurst, the British Chaplain, the Chee Seen and the Chinese Magistrate of the Mixed Court, had the unpleasant duty of witnessing the execution. The machinery of death, even in those days, was expensive. Consul Medhurst charged to the consulate's accounts the cost of erecting and dismantling the gallows, a coffin, extra food and beer for 44 days for George and a cash bonus and new suit for the executioner.

CHAPTER 4

Order Out of Legal Chaos

SIR EDMUND HORNBY was clearly a bundle of energy. He had been chosen for the position of Chief Judge because in the Ottoman Empire he had "showed his special fitness for dealing with an imperfectly developed legal system, and for eliciting order out of legal chaos." There was no greater legal chaos in the British legal world than the consular courts in China and Japan and: "once more he set to work drilling junior members of the Consular service into police magistrates, establishing precedents and 'organising' in the fullest sense of the word a system of legal and judicial coherency out of a confused and random entanglement."

Hornby had been instructed by the Foreign Office to visit each port in China and Japan in turn "so as to form some idea of the mode in which judicial and magisterial work was done and how it might be improved."

In Peking, Hornby recalled, "the only European who did not condescend to call on me … was Mr Robert Hart (now Sir Robert Hart) the Chief Inspector of Chinese Customs." The Chinese Maritime Customs Administration had been established in 1842 with the opening to foreign trade. From 1855, the service began to employ foreigners to assist with collecting customs duties from foreigners. In 1865, Robert Hart had just been appointed the Inspector General of the Customs Service. He remained in that position until 1910. Throughout China, the Customs Service employed numerous foreigners, and used English as its official language. The Service was structured like the British Customs service and included below the Inspector General, a Commissioner in each port. Other positions included watchers, whose job it was to watch for smugglers, a tide-waiter who would board ships as they entered harbour to ensure they tied up at a controlled dock and a tide-surveyor whose job it was to supervise tide-waiters. Until 1912, the Customs service did not directly collect duties. They were paid directly to the Chinese government based on assessments made by Customs.

Hornby either with great prescience or 20/20 hindsight set out the reason why Hart did not want to meet him:

"His object was to ignore the fact that he himself and the other English officials --Commissioners, Clerks, Revenue Officers, Tidewaiters etc, etc, -in the employment of the Foreign Customs Department were under the jurisdiction of the Supreme Court."

Hornby said that if they were not subject to the authority of the Supreme Court they could become corrupt, or as Hornby put it: "revenue officers and men have opportunities for doing things not only hurtful to their own countrymen but to natives." On the other hand, if they were subject to local Chinese jurisdiction, they could be unfairly punished as foreign scapegoats.

Some years later, Hart did in fact seek to avoid liability in the British court regarding statements that he had made about Baron von Gumpach to the Tsungli Yamen. Hart had employed von Gumpach on behalf of the Tsungli Yamen as a professor of mathematics and astronomy at a new college they had set up to teach Western languages and science.

Von Gumpach sued Hart personally in the Supreme Court. The case was heard by Hornby and Goodwin with Richard Rennie appearing for von Gumpach and Nicholas Hannen for Hart. Hart in his defence pleaded that as an employee of the Chinese government, he could not be held liable in the British courts for making defamatory statements. Von Gumpach applied to strike this part of the defence out. The effect of striking out parts of a defence is that the court is deciding that the defence will not succeed as a matter of law. Hornby and Goodwin agreed with von Gumpach and struck out the paragraphs. In giving judgment, Hornby stated:

> "The Order in Council expressly gives jurisdiction to this court in all cases between British subjects (and these parties are British subjects). To say that this plea is a good answer in law would be to say that anything Mr Hart might do or say against another British subject who happened to be in service of the Chinese government, however false or malicious, he might do with impunity. For all acts done, within the sphere of duty, persons in Mr Hart's position are protected, but they are not protected from the consequence of false statements or misrepresentations, because it can never be an act of duty to make false statements or misrepresent facts."

The case was tried some time later by Goodwin with a jury. The jury found in von Gumpach's favour on two out of three claims. Hannen made an application to set aside the jury verdict on the grounds it was not supported by the evidence. Hornby refused to do so. Hart appealed to the Privy Council in 1873. The Privy Council dodged the question of whether the Supreme Court had jurisdiction over Hart by holding that Hart had not properly raised the point. The Privy Council then found in Hart's favour on the ground that Hart should have been allowed to plead that his communications with the Chinese government were privileged and sent the case back to the Supreme Court for a new trial. The Privy Council said it did not expect there would be a new trial. There was not.

As we shall see, in a later murder case Hart employed two of the top British lawyers in China to argue that employees of the Customs service were not subject to the jurisdiction of the Supreme Court.

Bricks and Mortar: A Home for the Court

When the Supreme Court for China and Japan was established in 1865, it took over the small and unsatisfactory consular court in the British consulate on the northern end of Shanghai's Bund. Hornby lost no time in trying to get a permanent building for the court erected. There was considerable correspondence between Hornby and the Foreign Office about the need to have a proper court building and whether the court and the consulate should be in the same building. After various proposals, a decision was made that a new court building would be built next to the Consulate, but the judges' offices and Magistrate's Court would remain in the Consulate. The building that was build was a simple two-storey structure with offices for servants and messengers on the ground floor and one large court above it.

The new Supreme Court building was opened on June 1, 1871 on Yuenmingyuen Road. Hornby was on leave at home at the time. The *North China Herald* described the building in glowing prose:

> "The design, free Ionic, is carefully carried out in Soochow granite, and for grace, elegance of design and careful workmanship is surpassed by few buildings of its kind at Home and certainly by none in the East with which we are acquainted.
> "The Courtroom is lighted by ten large windows, five on each side; and the walls are panneled in oak, finely polished. The domed and deeply coffered ceiling with its cornices is also of the same material, and the dais and canopy above is a beautiful specimen of workmanship."

A cartoon showing the inside of the Supreme Court in 1908. The case related to the quality of sherry. No alcohol was imbibed during the actual hearing.

And indeed it was. The only surviving photo of the original court that I have found shows a beautiful, if somewhat small building that is a fine specimen of workmanship. The courthouse ran parallel with Yuenmingyuen Road. The court room was about 50 feet (16 metres) long by 30 feet (10 metres) wide. It had a spacious verandah on the front side. Access to the court was provided from the front by two large flights of stone steps immediately inside the entrance door leading up to a front verandah. One set of windows opened out onto the verandah. The other set of windows faced onto what was planned to be a courtyard between the court building and Consulate office building. The windows were essential in providing good lighting in those pre-electric days. For the most part, the court relied on natural lighting. When trials went on after nightfall, the judges and counsel had to rely upon paraffin lamps and candles for light. Immediately below the courtroom was a large room the same size as the courtroom for the servants and messengers of the court.

New consulate building and Supreme Court offices
The new Supreme Court building was complete, but not everything had gone according to plan. There was no Consulate building for it to be connected to. Two days before Christmas 1870, on a freezing cold night, the original consulate building burnt down.

Fortunately for the Supreme Court, the majority of its property and papers, including, the most important documents, the Judges' notebooks, judgments, and originals of pleadings were saved. Some books from the Law Library were burnt but most were recovered. Current bankruptcy accounts were saved. However, the bankruptcy accounts and private papers of deceased people where the court was waiting for instructions as to how to dispose of them were destroyed. The Supreme Court supply of stationery was also burnt.

Unfortunately for Goodwin, almost everything in his room, which was next to the room in which the fire broke out, was destroyed. This included his dispatch box, "which was once rescued almost at the risk of his life by Mr Stripling, and handed to a member of the Consulate, who handed it to a constable, who appears to have put it down again in a passage and left it to be burned." Goodwin also lost his wig, although his gown "turned up safe, though not altogether sound." "Several specimens of natural history" which were standing in Goodwin's office were also lost. An unnamed member of the bar also lost his official toga and perruque. Hornby's wig and gown were burnt and Hornby later claimed six guineas and nine guineas to replace them.

The consulate building that stands to this day on the Bund was built to replace the old consulate. The building was specifically designed, in addition to housing consular staff, to house the judges, court staff and a police court.

At the time of planning for the re-building, Mr Medhurst, the Consul, advocated that the offices of the court and the consulate be in separate buildings because of the inconvenience of having two sets of offices under the same roof. One suspects that Medhurst was also sick of having two other officials, and particularly Hornby, in his consulate who outranked him. Hornby and Goodwin, on the other hand advocated strongly that both sets of offices should be in the same building because of the convenience of being able to call upon consular officers and staff when handling cases. Hornby said in a letter to the Foreign Secretary, Earl Granville:

"Not a day passes but that in the ordinary transaction of business, continual communication is necessary between the Judge and the Consul. I can answer for myself that I am constantly and continuously obliged to refer, not only to the Chief Consular Officer, but to his Subordinate Officers, and in the same way these officers are always coming to me with questions to answer, or for advice."

Hornby described the inconvenience of communication if the offices were apart and the "immense value" he found of the assistance of consular officers. He "did not hesitate therefore to commend that the new Consulate should be rebuilt on the same site and pretty much on the same plan." He also asked that all rooms be shaded and have a verandah to deal with the heat.

The final decision was to re-build the consulate on the foundations of the old building, but with the consular offices on the north side and the Court offices to the south. As the new consulate was being completed, the *North China Herald* reported on a foundation stone laying ceremony. The plan was that the new consulate would be built with the outline of the original building being maintained with an architectural style to harmonise with the new Supreme Court. The main court and registry would be located in the new building with the judges office upstairs in the consulate and the police court downstairs in the counsulate.

In 1912, just after the Chinese republican revolution, it was decided to expand the court by building two new courtrooms. The courts had seen a substantial increase in cases, and it had often been necessary for one of the Judge's Chambers, to be used for hearings "to the inconvenience of everybody." A new law library and extra rooms for the Consular shipping office were included in the plan.

The two new court rooms were built on to the south side of the main court. To balance these extensions out, new rooms of the same size were built on the north side for the Consular shipping offices. The Police Court was built on the ground floor and a second court for the Supreme Court on the first floor. The Police Court had a door opening directly into the gardens of the Consulate for the public to enter. Both courts measured about 35 feet (10 metres) by 20 feet (6.5 metres). The second court had a raised dais and teak panelling with a seat for one judge. There was a section fenced off from the main public area in the front for counsel and witnesses. Electric lighting and fans were installed in the court from the beginning and were presumably added to the main courtroom at the same time.

CHAPTER 5

Reform in Japan

HAVING SORTED OUT THE major issues with the British Justice system in China, Edmund Hornby's next task as Chief Judge was to get the British court system in Japan working properly.

In 1869, Hornby visited Yokohama to investigate the workings of the consular courts in Japan. He was not impressed commenting that the young consular officers were particularly unsuited for handing legal cases. After returning from Yokohama, Hornby wrote to the Foreign Secretary, Earl Clarendon, that the consular staff in Yokohama were for a number of reasons "unable to cope" with judicial work due to the complexity of cases as well as their youth and inexperience. Hornby, acknowledging that there may not be a budget for an extra judge in China and Japan, proposed that the Assistant Judge, Charles Goodwin, be transferred to Yokohama.

The plan may not have just been about improving the quality of judicial decision making in Japan. Hornby may have also decided that distance was the best way to maintain a good relationship with Goodwin. Goodwin as a judge was the complete opposite of Hornby.

After Goodwin's death, all obituaries, which were absolutely glowing in all other respects, were remarkably silent on his judicial abilities. The *North China Herald*, in a heartfelt obituary, merely mentioned that "a more congenial field than a Judgeship in Shanghai" may have been "more adapted to his taste and adapted to his powers." The *London and China Telegraph* was faint with its praise: "Mr. Goodwin was universally respected as a thoroughly upright and conscientious judge, who would spare no pains to arrive at the true merits of the cases before him."

As a genius, Goodwin was, like Hornby, the smartest man in the room. Compared to Hornby, this produced a completely different type of judge. Goodwin was so smart that he knew there were things he did not know (or as it has been put, that there are "unknown unknowns.") Goodwin, who it should be recalled had spent his life deciphering hieroglyphics, wanted to investigate everything and get everything right. This meant he took a long time to deal with his cases. A one-hour hearing could turn into a one-day hearing. A short trial could become a marathon. Hornby on the other hand, dealt only with known knowns. He just decided the cases on the facts presented to him. A long trial became a short sprint.

Before Hornby's plan to have one judge in China and one in Japan could be put into effect, Hornby then Goodwin were scheduled to take 18 months long leave each; Hornby from late 1870 to 1872, and Goodwin from 1872 to 1873. Someone would need to be appointed to Japan in the interim.

Hornby considered that Robert Mowat was too young and inexperienced to be sent to Japan. He proposed instead "a barrister practicing at Shanghae who appears well fitted for such a post, a Mr Hannen, brother to Mr Justice Hannen of the Queen's Bench. He is well educated in his profession, firm and well calculated to maintain his position in a mixed community like that of Yokohama."

Hornby's proposal was accepted and Hannen was appointed as Acting Assistant Judge of the Supreme Court for China and Japan to be based in Yokohama. The *Japan Herald* reported this decision had been taken "when the judicial business at Yokohama attained large dimensions while that of Shanghai decreased, it was (with good reason) thought desirable to transfer the Assistant Judge to Yokokama and thus give the chief court of Japan the advantage of a Court presided over by a professional judge."

In a letter to Hannen dated January 10, 1871, Goodwin, as Acting Chief Judge, confirmed the appointment. Hannen was to reside in Yokohama while Goodwin was Acting Chief Judge in Shanghai. As to Hannen's powers, Goodwin wrote:

"Under Order 38 of the China and Japan Order in Council you are empowered to … hear and determine any cases civil and criminal arising in the district of Yokohama, but this authorization does not include the trial of capital crimes."

Order 38 of the Order in Council provided that the Judges of the Supreme Court could visit any Provincial Court and hear any civil or criminal cases pending in the district at the time.

The Court in Kanagawa styled itself as the Supreme Court and from early 1871 to mid-1872 judgments and case reports

Nicholas Hannen arrives as Acting Assistant Judge in Japan

were headed "In HBM's Supreme Court for China and Japan." Hannen requested that he be provided with a seal for the Supreme Court for China and Japan for use in Yokohama rather than the seal of the Kanagawa Consulate. Goodwin replied that "in the present state of things, it does not matter one fig what the Yokohama seal is." As we shall see later in this chapter, Hannen decided many years hence that, in fact, it did matter what the Yokohama seal was.

The first reported case to be tried by Hannen in Japan dealt directly with one of the major problems of extraterritoriality, the appointment of merchants without legal training as honourary consuls. The issue was exacerbated if someone had a claim against a consul. The consul would either be the one to try the case or there would be no judge to hear the case. Mr Strauss the Belgian Consul, was one such person. In February 1871, the *Japan Weekly Herald* published an article headed "The Belgium Consulate." The article strongly criticized the fact that Strauss was allowed to engage in trading activities through his company, Comptoir Belge, in addition to his consular duties. The *Herald* claimed that he abused his position as consul to be hard on Japanese traders and that he "has disgraced the civil service of his nation and prostituted the uniform which he wears." Harsh words. Not surprisingly, Mr Strauss brought a libel case against the publisher of the *Herald*, Mr Howell. English defamation law is very proplaintiff. Howell was going to have a hard time proving his case, even if what he had written was true. Hannen had no trouble finding that the article was clearly defamatory and awarded damages, inclusive of costs, of $600. Hannen added: "so long as a newspaper proprietor confines himself to attacking a system he will be protected; when he descends to specific and personal charges, he must run the risk and bear the penalty of being unable to fully substantiate the accusations which he brings."

A withered branch

One year after its establishment, in July 1872, in the case of *Findlay Richardson & Co v Pitman & Co*, the nature of the court in Japan was questioned. The unsuccessful defendant, Pitman, made an application to appeal to the Supreme Court in Shanghai, rather than to the Privy Council. Pitman's counsel argued that the Court in Japan was not a branch of the Supreme Court for China and Japan but remained the Provincial Court at Kanagawa. The point was important because appeals could be made from provincial courts to the Supreme Court, whereas if the court was a branch of the Supreme Court, the only appeal lay to the Privy Council in London.

Hannen gave an oral judgment that he was sitting as a judge of the Supreme Court "visiting" Japan under Order 38 and that accordingly there could be no appeal from his decisions to the Supreme Court, but only to the Privy Council. But, he said the parties could apply directly to the Chief Judge for a rehearing and "he hoped the Chief Judge would take such a view as would enable the rehearing to be, in reality, an appeal from his (the speaker's) decision – a view which would be manifestly for everybody's benefit, and also a personal relief to himself." He went on that he fully appreciated the absurdity of appeals only being allowed to the Privy Council. But, he added, it was not appropriate to seek to patch up the jurisdiction of the court by "twisting the words of the Order in Council to the present circumstances."

Accordingly, he had to dismiss the motion for leave to appeal.

The *Japan Weekly Mail* in an editorial, agreed that Hannen's judgment was correct, but deplored the loss of the right to appeal, saying that an:

> "inalienable right has been alienated from us. We have been thrown into a pit and sold into bondage. We are

lesser Englishmen than our brethren over the world; shorter by a whole right; weaker by a whole invaluable privilege."

The Mail congratulated Hannen for boldly facing the defect in the rules so the "legislature may deal with it." Pitman then applied to Hornby for a re-hearing. Hornby gave an extremely practical, but perhaps not legally correct, judgment. He held that because the parties had brought the case to the Supreme Court for China and Japan, they could not now say this was not the court they had sued in. The judgment should be treated as a judgment of the Supreme Court and the only appeal was to the Privy Council. Then doing a complete about-face, he also found that the Court should in fact be a Provincial Court and ordered that henceforth the court would be treated a Provincial Court under the presidency of Her Majesty's Assistant Judge. Hornby added, for good measure, that from reading the court documents and Hannen's judgment, he agreed with Hannen's original finding.

Hornby's judgment was a fudge. The parties had no choice but to bring the case to the Supreme Court for China and Japan. This was the only court available. If the plaintiff had tried to file his case in the Provincial Court of Kanagawa it would have been rejected because such a court did not, in the eyes of the officials administering it at the time, exist. Hornby, however, realizing that the argument that the Orders in Council did not allow for a branch of the Supreme Court for China and Japan was correct, used a judicial sleight of hand to cover up his own mistake.

From then on, Hannen was treated as a judge of a Provincial Court when trying cases. Despite losing its status as a branch of the Supreme Court, the court at Kanagawa remained the key British Court in Japan and from 1873 jury trials were extended to the court.

Nine years later, in 1881, when Hannen was acting as

Chief Justice in Shanghai, he was able to have the last word on the nature of his appointment in 1871. The case of *Langfeldt & Mayer v Green* came on appeal to the Supreme Court in Shanghai before Hannen and Robert Mowat (who by then had been promoted to Assistant Judge). The Defendant challenged again the legality of the establishment of the branch of the Supreme Court in Kanagawa in 1871. The case involved the enforcement of a judgment given by Hannen, himself, when he was Acting Assistant Judge in Japan in 1871. Hannen had ordered that Green pay the plaintiff $300. The parties had agreed, however, that the judgment should not be enforced for some time. Eight years later, in 1879 the plaintiff applied to the British Court for Japan for enforcement. The defendant opposed the application on the basis that while purporting to be a judgment of the Supreme Court for China and Japan, it was sealed with the seal of the Consulate for Kanagawa – the very issue which Goodwin had told Hannen "did not matter one fig." In the British Court for Japan, the court declined to enforce the judgment because there was nothing to establish which court had given the judgment.

Langfeldt & Mayer appealed to the Supreme Court in Shanghai. Nowhere in the appeal judgment does Hannen mention that he was the original trial judge, but it is clear from reading the judgment that he had a strong personal interest in the case. Hannen and Mowat dismissed an argument by the Defendant that the court that had made the decree was not the Supreme Court for China and Japan by applying the same logic that Hornby had used nine years before. That is, that the Supreme Court for China and Japan was the court in which the parties filed the case. If they had an objection they should have raised it when filing the case. Hannen and Mowat added that, in any event, they would be bound by Hornby's decision in the *Pitman* case.

As to whether the judgment had been properly sealed by using the seal of the Kanagawa consulate seal, Hannen and

Mowat agreed with the defendant. They ruled that it had not been properly sealed and therefore could not be enforced. As to why the wrong seal had been used, Hannen, obviously still smarting from Goodwin's refusal of his request for a proper seal, said:

> "The seal affixed to the decree is not the seal of the Court in which in our opinion the decree is pronounced. That it was the only seal ever used in the Court – that there was no other seal available – that it was used, moreover, as the archives of this court show, in deference only to the instructions from his official chief (the then Acting Judge, the late Mr Goodwin) to the Acting Assistant Judge [that is, Hannen] who had requested to be furnished with a seal of the Supreme Court for use at Kanagawa – none of this can avail against the respondent who relies upon the irregularity, purely technical though it is."

This was not the end of the matter. On the basis that this decision would cause a "grave miscarriage of justice", they gave the Langfeldt & Mayer leave to amend their complaint to plead the court the judgment was given in was the Supreme Court and apply for the judgment to be re-sealed with the seal of the Supreme Court. Once correctly sealed they could then enforce it.

Wilkinson returns to Japan

1872 also saw the return to Japan of H.S. Wiliknson from Home leave. Wilkinson had completed his LLB and qualified as a barrister becoming the first consular officer in Japan to be legally qualified. He was appointed a Vice-Consul in Kobe. This gave him responsibility as one of the British judges in Kobe and Osaka and marked the beginning of his career in law in the British Courts in China and Japan.

Wilkinson as a newly qualified barrister was able to bring some judicial majesty to the Kobe Consular Court. John Carey Hall, who had arrived as a student interpreter in Kobe in 1868, recalled being called upon to carry out the "unpleasant duty" of prosecuting in Kobe two British for assault and battery on the complaint of some Chinese. The British together with an American had seen the Chinese gambling late at night, had broken into their residence and sought to disperse them. One of the Chinese lost his queue during the scuffle. Hall recalled:

"The case was tried by the Vice-Consul, Mr (now Sir) H.S. Wilkinson, afterwards Chief Justice of the British Court at Shanghai. The court-room was crowded and the scene was very impressive. The judge wore his barrister's wig and gown and looked the very impersonation of judicial dignity."

Wilkinson imposed a heavy fine with the alternative of imprisonment. The American ringleader was tried in the American Consular Court and got off with a light fine. Hall recalled that the penalty imposed by Wilkinson greatly enhanced the respect of the Chinese in Kobe for British Justice.

Goodwin replaces Hannen
Charles Goodwin returned from long leave in late 1873. He was now ready to take up the role of British judge in Japan replacing Nicholas Hannen who would return to private practice in Shanghai. After spending two months in Shanghai, Goodwin, his wife, and his now large family of four young children, plus his older daughter Agnes, headed south for Hong Kong before then travelling to Yokohama. They arrived in Yokohama in early April 1874 aboard the *Volga*.

On Wednesday April 8, 1874, Goodwin took his seat on the bench at a special ceremony to welcome him. Mr JF Davidson of the Public Works Department spoke on behalf of

Charles Goodwin returns to Yokohama to the joy of local lawyers

the bar to welcome Goodwin to Japan. He then expressed in "highly lengthy and highly eulogistic terms, the great respect and regard in which Mr Hannen was held by the members of the legal profession in the community and the regret at his approaching departure from among them." Goodwin thanked the bar for their welcome and said, perhaps with a hint of jealousy, he hoped that when his turn came to vacate the bench, "the same feelings might exist which had just been expressed for Mr Hannen."

Goodwin was not as universally liked in Yokohama as Hannen had been. Soon after Goodwin transferred to Japan, the *Japan Punch* published a cartoon headed "the prodigal's return" showing Goodwin returning to Yokohama from a trip with all the lawyers in the city spinning cartwheels of joy. The *Japan Punch* clearly took the view that Goodwin wasted time and worked to make lawyers rich and happy.

Building the New Japanese Legal System
The British-Japan treaty of 1858 provided that revisions could be made after 14 years, namely July 1, 1872. Accordingly in 1871, Count Terashima, Minister of Foreign Affairs, wrote to Sir Harry Parkes, the British Minister, a private memorandum

requesting reciprocity in the treaties.

Nevertheless, the Japanese knew that in order to bring an end to extraterritoriality, they had to reform their own legal system. To achieve this, in December 1871, a mission of 50 of some of Japan's ablest politicians and lawyers, led by Tomomi Iwakura, went on a study tour of the US, Britain and Continental Europe to study their legal systems and at the same time seek an end to extraterritoriality. In a letter to the President of the United States, presented on arrival in the US, they stated:

"We expect and intend to reform and improve the Treaties so as to stand upon a similar footing with the most enlightened nations and to attain the full development of public right and interest. The civilization and institutions of Japan are so different from those of other countries that we cannot expect to reach the desired end at once. It is our purpose to select, from the various institutions prevailing among enlightened nations, such as are best suited to our present condition, and adapt them, in gradual reforms and amendments of our policy and customs so as to be an equality with them."

Cooling the coolie trade

Six months after the Iwakura Mission left Japan, a major test of the developing Japanese legal system sailed into Yokohama Harbour. The case resulted in a rare display of diplomatic amity between Japan and China, and even rarer praise from China for the work of foreign consular officers.

In July 1872, a Peruvian Ship, the *Maria Luz*, heading from Macao to Peru lost her topmasts in a storm and limped into Yokohama port for repairs. Macao at that time played a key role in China's human slave trade. Although it was illegal to do so, Chinese coolies would be sold into bondage under

China Punch shows the "Embarking of 'Free and Independent' Emigrants at Macao"

alleged contracts of employment.

When the *Maria Luz* arrived in Yokohama, one of the Chinese coolies on board escaped over the rails and was picked up by the British Man-Of-War, the *Iron Duke*. The coolie, Mo Hing, was handed over to the British consular authorities, who then handed him to the Japanese authorities. After receiving assurances that Mo would not be mistreated, he was returned to Captain Hereira of the *Maria Luz*. The captain of the *Iron Duke* reported to the acting British Consul in Yokohama, R.G. Watson, that they could hear moans and cries coming from the *Maria Luz*. Watson then decided to intervene and inspected the ship.

The China and London Telegraph carried a report later of the conditions aboard ship, quoting an unidentified source, possibly Watson:

"We found them (the coolies) sitting or lying closely together in their numbered berths, reeking and sweltering in an atmosphere which would extinguish

the life of an American or European in half a day.
Though not confined, except in a few instances, they
were not allowed to stir from their cramped quarters.
An imaginary ventilation was afforded by a few small
holes in the side of the ship, which from their position
could only be opened in a quiet sea. To attempt to
depict the agony of despair in which the countenances
of most of these unhappy creatures were fixed would
be a hopeless task …. When we were about to return
to the deck, as if by common impulse, they all sprang
from their ranks and, clustering about us as closely
as they could, fell upon their knees, lifted their
clasped hands, and with piteous cries implored our
intercession."

Watson, wrote a strongly worded plea to the Japanese
foreign minister Soejima to intervene saying:

"The coolie trade between Macao and the western ports
of South America, particularly the Peruvian, has been
characterized by such barbarity and such disregard to
the rights of the Chinese government, that it has most
justly excited the strongest feeling in Europe and all
civilized countries … Hitherto the shores of Japan have
been free from the scandal of this abominable traffic …
but in the present case there is grave reason to believe
that more than one person on board has been treated in
a manner, which no law could sanction."

Watson was stretching the truth when he said that feeling
had been excited in all civilized countries. Many of the other
foreign consuls in Yokohama opposed any action by the
Japanese as an undue interference in international commerce.
The American position was mixed. America was at the time
the representative of Peru in Japan. When the matter first blew

Magistrate Chen of Shanghai chases Capt. Hereira

up, Captain Hereira contacted the American Consul, C.O. Shephard, who was also at the time Charge d'Affaires of the US Mission. Shephard, who supported the Japanese taking action to help the coolies, declined to assist Hereira. But soon after this, the US Minister, Charles De Long returned from leave and tried to help Hereira. This resulted in him being strongly rebuked by the US Secretary of State, Hamilton Fish.

The Japanese Foreign Minister, Soejima, ordered an investigation. Japan had abolished slavery during Tokugawa Shogunate, ironically, partly to stop the export of Japanese as slaves to Europe. The Japanese removed the coolies from the *Maria Luz* and formed a court of inquiry into what had occurred. This was presided over by the Governor of Kanagawa, Oe Taku, a young man of only 25 years of age. Oe was advised by an American legal adviser, G.S. Hill. Nicholas Hannen also sat on the bench with Oe. Consuls of other nations and Magistrate Chen of the Shanghai Mixed Court, who had been invited to Japan by the Japanese government, observed the trial.

Hereira was represented by a British barrister, Frederick

Dickins. The Court of Inquiry, even though it was not a criminal court, as Dickins had pointed out in a formal protest, found that Hereira was guilty of abusing his passengers and said that under Japanese law he should be sentenced to 100 lashes or 100 days house imprisonment. But because the court had decided to "judge him leniently," it had been decided that the Captain should in this case "be pardoned his offence and permitted to depart with his vessel."

This was not to be the end of the matter. Hereira wanted his valuable cargo, the coolies, back and he brought a civil claim for their return. Hannen again sat on the bench with Oe who refused to return them. After their release, the coolies were returned to Shanghai by the Japanese Government accompanied by Magistrate Chen. China in return, at its own expense, repatriated 45 Japanese sailors who had been shipwrecked near Chefoo.

The Chinese were very pleased with the result of the case. The Chinese Minister of Foreign Affairs wrote an effusive note to the American Minister in Peking thanking them for Mr Shephard's assistance in the case:

> "This action on the part of American officials is
> satisfactory in the extreme; it is a new and complete
> manifestation of the sincere friendship and goodwill
> now happily existing between the two nations and
> is quite in accord with your express desire to rescue
> and save our people from harm. To acknowledge our
> obligation and express our thanks is the object of this
> note."

Peru made a formal claim for damages against Japan, which was referred to arbitration by the Czar of Russia, Alexander. Czar Alexander found in favour of Japan finding in perfect diplomatese:

"The Government of Japan is not responsible for the consequences brought about by the stay of the Peruvian vessel *Maria Luz* in the port of Kanagawa."

Reform in Japan

While the *Maria Luz* case had made its way through the Japanese courts, the Iwakura Mission had continued its overseas study trip. While not successful in getting the foreign powers to end extraterritoriality, the mission was extremely successful in its main goal of studying foreign legal systems and beginning the process of reforming the Japanese legal system. Upon their return to Japan, the mission made recommendations for changes that were in part influenced by a "burning desire to secure the abolition of extraterritoriality."

In 1873 Japan revised its Penal Code, abolishing the use of torture to extract confessions, reducing the number of crimes where the death penalty would be imposed and almost abolishing corporal punishment. At the end of 1873, with assistance of French experts, work was begun on a comprehensive criminal code. In 1875, drafting commenced on a Civil Code to be based on the French Civil Code. By 1876 the Japanese had developed full procedures for handling first instance and appeal cases in their courts.

H.S. Wilkinson had by then become the key British legal adviser in Japan. Wilkinson was therefore entrusted with drafting and agreeing with the Japanese authorities procedures for British subjects to bring complaints and appeals to the Japanese courts. The procedures drafted by Wilkinson provided that British subjects could either file their cases or appeals through the consul or could handle them directly if they preferred. Appeals by Japanese against decisions favourable to British subjects would be transmitted to the consul for onward transmission to the British party.

The situation in China was starkly different to Japan. In China there were no Chinese lawyers, no independent

Chinese courts and no system for appeals. The handling of mixed cases, in particular, remained a serious issue of dispute between the foreign powers and Japan.

CHAPTER 6

Mixed Justice in China

IN CHINA, UNLIKE IN JAPAN, the question of how to handle mixed cases involving Chinese and foreigners remained a vexed issue. Three cases in the mid 1870s brought the issue to the fore. In two of the cases Chinese had been killed by Britons. In the third, Sir Edmund Hornby made himself very unpopular with all the foreign powers when he confirmed the right of the Chinese government to be involved in mixed trials a right soon taken away by another treaty signed at the point of gunboat barrels.

The Shantung lighthouse

In the first case, in 1874, Hornby sailed to Chefoo for the trial of Thomas Fawcett for manslaughter. Fawcett was the supervisor of the construction of a lighthouse by Chinese Customs in Shantung (Shandong). Fawcett was acquitted, resulting in the British Minister, Thomas Wade, questioning why Hornby had allowed Fawcett to go free. Wade's reproof greatly angered Hornby. In his autobiography, he described it as "still an open wound", adding that the case "might have ended badly for me as well as have become an awkward precedent for his successors."

The British-run Imperial Maritime Customs had decided to build a lighthouse on the Shantung Promontory, a dangerous headland on which many Chinese and foreign vessels had been wrecked. According to Hornby, the local people did not like the idea of the loss of income they would suffer from ships no longer being wrecked off the coast whether by accident of by the use of false beacons to lure ships to destruction. Regardless of the reason, it is clear that there was significant local opposition to the building of the lighthouse. The local people regularly attacked workers on the site, seeking to stop the work.

Though outsiders were forbidden from coming within a mile of the site, fights continued with the locals attacking the site at night and trying to destroy the work that had been done. Fawcett patrolled the site at night and one evening around sunset, according to Hornby, "seeing some men approaching from several points within the limits, he went to meet them – the two nearest him had the usual heavy pronged hoe used to break up the ground. He ordered them back, drawing his revolver; they refused and one of them raised his hoe. On this, the Englishman, seizing his revolver by the barrel, jumped on one side and struck the man over the arm and caused him to drop his hoe; but the blow caused the revolver to go off." The bullet killed another man standing nearby and Fawcett was detained by the local Chinese magistrate. Hornby, upon hearing of the case, requested Fawcett be handed over to the British authorities for trial. The Mandarin in charge of the district refused. Hornby sent a couple of officers to collect Fawcett and he was handed over. While he was in detention by the Chinese, a confession was obtained from Fawcett that he intended to kill one of the men, but mistakenly killed the other. At his committal hearing in the British Provincial Court, Fawcett asked the Magistrate who had detained him, Keng Tien-ken:

> "Was I not put in irons in your city, and my life threatened, if I would not say that there was a man shot and that I had shot him?"

Keng replied:

"I was afraid you would run away, and I ordered you
to be handcuffed because you expressed a dislike to
being chained by your neck. I did not threaten you;
you made your confession yourself that it was your
intention to shoot Wang-chih but that by mistake you
shot the other man."

Fawcett was ordered to stand trial before the Supreme
Court. The case was tried by Hornby with a jury of five at
Chefoo with two Mandarins in attendance. Mr W.M. Cooper of
the Yantai consulate prosecuted. Nicholas Hannen, now back
in private practice in China, came from Shanghai to defend
Fawcett. The Chinese prosecution witnesses were brought to
court in chains. When Hornby asked why, the answer was
given that they refused to give evidence otherwise. Hornby
ordered the chains be removed and they were examined by
the Chinese officials. The two Chinese who had met with
Fawcett gave evidence. They denied trying to hit him and
claimed that Fawcett had turned around and deliberately
shot the victim.

It was clear that not all the Chinese witnesses were
there voluntarily. One witness, after being pressured by the
Mandarins, finally exclaimed: "How can you expect I can
recollect all you have told me to say, you half starved me, and
look here [showing his wrists] see how I have been treated,
locked up in a beastly hole, taken away from my family and
work for the last moon. I have forgot all, I wasn't there, and
I know nothing about the affair, nor do any of them except
the two," referring to the men who had met Fawcett. Another
Chinese witness said that he had received 150 blows at the
Yamen before giving evidence.

An American doctor said that from the drawing of the
wounds it appeared that the victim was shot from behind
because the wound at the front was larger. A number of the

Ningpo workmen also gave evidence that supported Fawcett. Hornby summed up and made it clear that he thought Fawcett should be convicted. He said that illegal use of a weapon that causes death is manslaughter. A weapon should only be used when absolutely necessary. There was no evidence the use of the revolver had been necessary. Hornby completed his summing up all but directing the jury to convict:

> "And then you can, under my direction, have no
> difficulty in finding the prisoner guilty of the offence
> with which he is charged … I tell you distinctly that in
> my judgment the use of a loaded pistol was unlawful
> and unnecessary. I trust you will view the case as if it
> happened between two Englishmen. A Chinaman's life
> is as precious as that of one of our own countrymen,
> and you are called upon to do justice."

Hannen objected to the way the law had been explained. Hornby gave leave to argue this later if necessary. The jury then retired, returning in a few minutes, with a verdict of Not Guilty. Hornby then said:

> "Gentlemen, I must record your verdict, but I regret it;
> you have not taken the Law as I laid it down to you,
> which you ought to have done; it is a most mischievous
> verdict."

Hannen also protested against this, to which Hornby said:

> "I consider it my duty to do so, and most emphatically
> I say in this case that the jury have ignored the Law as
> I laid it down to them, and which they were bound to
> take from me, and they have come to a conclusion not
> warranted by the evidence. I greatly regret the course
> they have pursued, and although I have no right to,

and do not, interfere in any way with their verdict, which is final and conclusive; but I do claim the right, and shall always exercise it, when I think necessary, to express my disapproval and regret."

The acquittal caused much indignation to the local Chinese, perhaps more than normal given Hornby's comments about the verdict. The next evening, Hornby's bungalow on the beachfront in Chefoo was surrounded by a mob of villagers headed by the supposed widow, demanding that Hornby hand Fawcett over. Fawcett had in fact already, and wisely it seems, left Chefoo. Hornby's house was besieged for three days and two nights. Hornby sought assistance from the Chinese authorities who sent an officer who told Hornby to give the crowd a dollar or two each and 50 dollars for the widow, which Hornby refused. Instead:

"I closed all my windows, loaded a couple of doublebarreled guns and a couple of revolvers, and walked up and down my verandah."

Eventually, his Chinese servant, or "boy" as Hornby called him, learned that there was a British gunboat down the coast and the boy and a boatman went to find it. The next morning, to Hornby's "intense delight," the gunboat HMS *Hornet* steamed into port and landed a party of Marines and Jacks. Having controlled the crowd by the presence of the British military, Hornby went to see the Mandarin, who said he "was very sorry, but he really had no control over the villagers," but offered a guard. Hornby declined; he now had his own. Hornby remained in Chefoo for a further three weeks, to try other cases, with a guard of six Jacks. Complaints were made to the Chinese authorities in Peking, but according to Hornby, he never received "the slightest expression of regret."

Having now had a practical lesson as to where the power

supporting extraterritorial jurisdiction really came from, Hornby wrote:

> "Of course I never tried another British subject accused of killing a Chinaman at an outlying port, unless there was a gun-boat at hand."

Railroaded

The Fawcett case arose due to problems resulting from the Maritime Customs' desire to build lighthouses, a very welcome modernization. A case in Shanghai two years later involving the death of a Chinese, on the other hand, showed just how strong official and local objections to most forms of modernization were.

The case involved an accident on the Woosung Railway between Shanghai and the port of Woosung, 30 kilometres to the north, where the Huangpu River meets the Yangtze. Planning for construction of the line had commenced in 1865 and a company was formed to build it. But the plan met strong opposition from the Chinese authorities. Eventually, the British promoters received permission to build a road rather than a railway, which they did. They later announced the intention to build a tramway along the road. When the rails were landed, it was clear that they were for a railway. The Taotai objected and requested the promoters stop construction until he could refer the matter to Peking. Construction nevertheless went ahead and the line as far as Kiangwan (Jiangwan), halfway between the International Settlement and Woosung, was completed and opened on June 30, 1876. The train consisted of a small steam engine, like that now seen in amusement parks, and two carriages.

Less than five weeks after the line was opened, on August 3, 1876, a Chinese man walking along the tracks was hit by the train and killed under circumstances, which one contemporary English commentator "suggested either

The opening of the Woosong Railway. After a Chinese was killed by the train, the tracks were ripped up and dumped on a beach in Taiwan.

extremely dense stupidity or a malicious intent to commit suicide, and thereby create a prejudice against railways."

Following the accident, the Chinese population became so hostile to the railway that the British Minister, Sir Thomas Wade, who was in Shanghai at the time, ordered the trains stop running temporarily.

The Chinese carried out an inquest into the man's death, at which the driver of the train, Edward Banks, was called as a witness. The Chinese demanded that a mixed court be convened to try Banks for the killing. The British Consulate refused, but instituted a prosecution for manslaughter against Banks in the Supreme Court. At the preliminary hearing before Robert Mowat, sitting as Police Magistrate, Richard Rennie appeared for the Crown and Nicholas Hannen appeared for Banks. Rennie started by asking Mowat to immediately transfer the case to the Supreme Court for trial. He said the Chinese authorities were "deeply interested" in the case but that the Consulate had been unable to convince them that the Supreme Court had authority to try the case, rather than there being a mixed trial. Because of this, no Chinese official was present in the court and that as a matter of "political expediency" a Chinese official should be present at a Supreme Court hearing. Hannen objected saying that the "question of political expediency had nothing whatever to do with the Police Court." Mowat agreed, adding that the court was an open court and that anyone could attend. Mowat ordered that the case should continue.

Mr Cooper, Acting Vice-Consul who had attended the Chinese enquiry and acted as an interpreter, the fireman of the train and an employee of Jardine Matheson who was a passenger on the train all gave evidence. Criminal defendants at the time could not give evidence in their own defence. But Cooper repeated the evidence that Banks had given at the Chinese inquest. This was that he had seen a man on the rails about 100 yards away and had sounded his whistle. The man had got off the tracks. When the train was about 15 yards away, the man had then walked back on the tracks and the train hit him. The fireman, who was Chinese, corroborated this story saying:

"When I first saw the deceased, he was in danger, but after he crossed the rails he was in a place of safety. If he had remained there he would have been safe. He made no signs that he intended to re-cross the rails; he merely stood looking on."

Mowat found that there clearly was no evidence of culpable negligence to support a charge of manslaughter.

Following the case, during 1876 and 1877, the Chinese authorities negotiated to purchase the railway line from the promoters. A deal was done and the local authorities bought it for 285,000 taels, the actual costs incurred by the promoters. Then, in an act of what can only be described as official Ludditism, they had the rails ripped up. The track and rolling stock were dumped on a beach in Taiwan. A railway line was not seen again in Shanghai for another 20 years.

Joint trials or sole trials

The Woosong Railway case came before the British and Chinese courts in Shanghai in the same month that Britain and China were finalizing a new treaty that would settle for many years to come how mixed trials were to be handled.

The right of Chinese officials to be involved in trials of foreigners under the Treaty of Tientsin, had been brought to a head by a decision of Hornby the year before in 1875. The British steamship, the *Kwangtung*, registered in Hong Kong, had collided with a Chinese junk, *Kui-tsai-fay*. The junk and her cargo were lost but the crew was saved by the steamer. The owner of the junk brought a complaint to the British Consul General at Foochow, Charles Sinclair, who along with the local Taotai, Mr Pao, established a Mixed Court to try the case. The court found in favour of the junk owners ordering the Kwangtung to pay damages. The owners of the *Kwangtung* made an application to the Supreme Court in Shanghai for the judgment of the Mixed Court to be set aside. Surprisingly, perhaps, given Hornby's clear disapproval of the Chinese legal system, Hornby found that the creation of a mixed court by the British Consul-General in Foochow sitting with the local Taotai was fully compliant with the Treaty of Tientsin. Hornby also held that no right of appeal lay to the Supreme Court from such cases. The Treaty of Tientsin did not make clear provision for Chinese to make claims against British subjects. Article 17 provided that if a Chinese had a complaint against a British subject, they should seek the assistance of the Consul. If this could not resolve the matter then the Consul "shall request the assistance of the Chinese authorities, that they may together examine into the merits of the case, and decide it equitably."

Hornby said:

"I must refuse this rule. I do not entertain, and never
have entertained, the slightest doubt on the subject
of the right of Chinese litigants to invoke 17th clause
of the Treaty of Tientsin, and insist on any matters of
difference between them and British subjects being
decided in accordance with such clause."

He explained that the treaty was clear and even if
the Orders in Councils may be interpreted otherwise, no
legislation could override treaty rights. He went on to state
that if he was to consider the British defendant's protest
"or attach any weight to it, the result would be to send the
Chinaman whose junk had been run down, as he reports, in
the China Seas, to a British Colony, [that is, Hong Kong] to a
place, the law of which he is ignorant of, and of the language
of which he is also ignorant." With regard to the role of the
Supreme Court in Shanghai, he said that "it was true that
Chinese were willing to sue in the Supreme Court," but that
he had "often seen them and explained to them that they
can go and lay their case before the Consul, who will call on
the Tautai to decide it under the Treaty. Chinese parties had,
however, often refused, and expressed themselves contented
to abide by the decision of the Supreme Court."

The *London and China Telegraph* published a long editorial
denouncing Hornby's decision as "a sudden and unexpected
reversal of the established order of procedure" which had
"the effect of entirely overthrowing the order of things." The
Telegraph beseeched the Crown Law Officers in London to
look at the case and put things right.

Hornby's decision caused great consternation amongst
all the treaty powers. The Americans were particularly
dismayed by the decision coming from the British Supreme
Court. George Seward, who had been promoted from

Shanghai Consul-General to American Minister in Peking, as part of a joint statement issued by the treaty powers regarding the *Kwangtung* decision stated categorically, "the treaties concluded between the United States and China give, in effect, full jurisdiction in civil matters to the court of the defendant in all cases between Americans and Chinese arising within the territory of China." He added that "this principle has been rigidly adhered to since the date of the first Treaty." Interestingly, the representatives of Russia, Germany, France and Spain all considered that their treaties provided for mixed tribunals although they admitted that, in practice, "the state of affairs is different."

The joint statement was highly critical of the Chinese legal system saying "no codes of procedure worthy to be called such exist. The magistrates, secretaries and constables are often corrupt," adding that it was often difficult to find a court with jurisdiction and no appellate court existed. The statement finished with a the strong comment on the weakness of the Chinese legal system:

> "for the latter reasons, questions which should be
> decided by appeal can only be treated by political
> recourse through Diplomatic agents, and become the
> subject of long and annoying negotiations."

Gunboats resolve the issue: The Chefoo Convention

From a distance of more than a century and a half, it is clear that Hornby's decision was right. Hornby was not the type to worry about the "established order" of things. If the established order was wrong, he would make a decision to that effect. The only way to return to the "established order" was to reach a new agreement with the Chinese. This is exactly what Sir Thomas Wade, the British Minister, did the following year when he forced a treaty upon China that reversed Hornby's decision and established the principle that would apply for the remainder of the life of extraterritorial courts in China. The treaty, the Chefoo Convention, was a "catch-all" treaty that was intended to clarify issues that had remained open from the Sino-British treaties before it.

The treaty had been negotiated by Thomas Wade with Li Hongzhang, to resolve a number of issues that had arisen including the murder of a British interpreter in Yunnan. The Chefoo Convention was one of many unequal treaties Li negotiated, making him a very unpopular figure in Chinese history.

With regard to the handling of legal cases, the Convention set out that in order to fulfill its Treaty obligations, "the British Government has established a Supreme Court at Shanghai, with a special code of rules." Further, "the Chinese Government has established at Shanghai a Mixed Court." The Convention added, however, that "the officer presiding over it, either from lack of power, or dread of unpopularity, constantly fails to enforce his judgments." It was agreed that the Tsungli Yamen would consult with the legations on ways to improve the Mixed Court.

The Convention then dealt with how Mixed Cases were to be heard by providing that the each side would try their own nationals with the other side attending to observe proceedings. Article 2(3) provided:

"It is farther understood that so long as the laws of the two countries differ from each other, there can be but one principle to guide judicial proceedings in mixed cases in China, namely, that the case is tried by the official of the defendant's nationality, the official of the plaintiff's nationality merely attending to watch the proceedings in the interests of justice. If the officer so attending were dissatisfied with the proceedings, it will be in his power to protest against them in detail. The law administered will be the law of the nationality of the officer trying the case."

In the Shanghai International Settlement, this principle was extended by a consular assessor sitting with a Chinese magistrate to hear all cases in the International Mixed Court. A similar court was established in the French Concession.

The Chinese soon ratified the Chefoo Convention, but in Britain there was much opposition to its terms relating to trade. It was not until 1885, after much lobbying by Wade, that the Chefoo Convention was finally ratified by Britain.

The United States also signed a short treaty on Commercial Relations and Judicial Procedure in 1880 to implement directly between the United States and China some of the provisions that had been agreed in the Chefoo Convention. With regards to judicial procedure, the treaty provided that cases would be tried by the officials of the defendant's country under that country's laws. An official of the plaintiff's nationality was permitted to attend the trial and was to be "granted all proper facilities for watching the trial," and the right to "examine and cross-examine witnesses."

The Chefoo Convention and the US-China treaty of 1880 completed negotiation of treaties underpinning the British and American extraterritorial legal systems in China and formed the bedrock of the exercise of extraterritorial jurisdiction for the next 60 years. From then on, cases against British and Americans were tried in British and American courts and cases against Chinese were tried in Chinese courts. The Shanghai Mixed Court also continued to function and, up until 1911, the Chinese judge was, for the most part, in charge.

The Chefoo Convention was signed just as the British courts in China were about to see great changes.

CHAPTER 7

Change and Reorganisation

The End of an Era

A little more than a decade after its establishment, the British Supreme Court suddenly lost its two founding judges. Sir Edmund Hornby retired on a generous pension in 1876 and Charles Goodwin died at a relatively young age in early 1878. Hornby's decision to retire appears to have been quite sudden. There were no rumours of his retirement published in the *North China Herald* or *London and China Telegraph*, both of which kept a close ear to the ground on judicial movements. Rather, Hornby appears to have been preparing to sit on the bench in Shanghai for years to come. He had just re-married to a much younger (20 years old) Ms Roberts and perhaps decided to enjoy retirement. It is also possible his "lack of judicial temperament" had caught up with him.

On Hornby's retirement, Charles Goodwin was appointed Acting Judge from May 22, 1876. He sat in at least one case in Shanghai as "Acting Chief Judge" soon after Hornby left. However, shortly thereafter, he returned to Yokohama, leaving Robert Mowat to act as "Deputy Chief Judge" in Shanghai. Goodwin stayed in Japan for six more months sitting as the Acting Chief Judge. He returned to Shanghai with his family in early 1877.

Before leaving Japan, Goodwin appointed H.S. Wilkinson as Acting Law Secretary of the Supreme Court with "power to dispatch all summary criminal offences, to appoint prosecutors and even exercise the Supreme Court's authority to dispense with a jury where it would ordinarily be required." Wilkinson had just returned from an attachment to the court in Shanghai where he had acted as Law Secretary from October 1876.

During 1877, the local newspapers in China and Japan carried reports that Goodwin would be promoted to Chief Judge. But by late 1877, the decision had been made that a new Chief Judge would be brought in from outside and Goodwin would be appointed to a new position as Judge for Japan. The *Japan Weekly Mail* welcomed this news, if true, saying "we trust the community may soon have the pleasure of welcoming back a gentleman whose rare attainments and social qualities won him universal regard, and whose temporary absence has been a great loss to his friends."

The news was true and Goodwin was offered the appointment in Japan. It is not clear if he accepted it, in late 1877 Goodwin was struck down by a "prolonged and serious illness" and he applied for a year's sick leave.

Goodwin's illness, which he bore with "perfect patience and fortitude," took a turn for the worse in early 1878 and he died on January 17. He was buried following a grand funeral in a vaulted grave in Shanghai Cemetery.

Goodwin was an extraordinary man, with extraordinary gifts. This was reflected in the emotional outpouring that occurred on Goodwin's death. Flags were flown at half-mast and the British Consulate closed for two days. The American Consulate also closed for a day. There were many fond remembrances of Goodwin published in numerous obituaries in China, Japan and England. The *North China Herald* published a long obituary that after reciting his many achievements said:

"But those who enjoyed the great privilege of Mr
Goodwin's acquaintance remember him with that
affectionate regard which is secured by qualities
not always associated with profound antiquarian

scholarship; He was one of the most charming companions that it was possible to meet. His conversation was studded with recondite allusions, with 'happy expressions', and with all the evidences of learning alike accurate and profound; but it was lighted up with the most playful fancy, and enhanced by the modesty which Chaucer describes as inseparable from the true scholar.

'And gladly wolde he lerne, and gladly teche.'"

The *North China Herald* concluded its obituary:

"We may sometimes regret, in the interests of science, that a more congenial field than a Judgeship in Shanghai was not found for a man so peculiarly and richly endowed with gifts; and whose bias certainly pointed out other spheres as far more congenial to his taste and adapted to his powers; but at the same time we were fortunate for many years in having amongst us a man of rare learning, who was at the same time, an embodiment of some of the most loveable qualities, and a model of honour, simplicity, and purity of aim. Those who knew him intimately learned something fresh from every conversation they had with him, and feel that the loss made by his death is in many senses irreparable. But far deeper is the bereavement sustained by his family, with whom we can only express our sincere sympathy — "

This was followed by two lines from a sonnet by the Italian poet Petrarch:

"Non Omnia Terra
Obruta: vivit amor, vivit dolor."

CHANGE AND REORGANISATION   95

Or, in English:

"Not everything is buried
in the earth. Love lives, grief lives on! "

The next two lines of the poem were not published, but well-educated readers of the *Herald*, would have known they translated into English as:

We are denied the sight of those sweet features; but it is left for us to weep and to remember.

Reorganising the Courts

The retirement of Sir Edmund Hornby and death of Charles Goodwin, the two founders of the British Courts in China and Japan, not surprisingly, led to major changes in the structure and staffing of the British courts in both countries. Even before Hornby had announced his retirement, changes to the Orders in Council were under consideration. With Hornby's retirement these moved ahead.

First, a new Chief Judge had to be appointed. Mr Philip Currie of the Foreign Office proposed, in order to save costs and also to follow the practice that had been introduced in Constantinople after Hornby had moved to Shanghai, that the positions of Chief Judge and Consul in Shanghai be amalgamated.

The matter fell to be decided by Sir Julian Pauncefote, the

Sir Julian Pauncefote, now at the Foreign Office in London – architect of the new British legal structure in China and Japan

Legal Assistant Undersecretary for Foreign Affairs who had served as Attorney General in Hong Kong. Pauncefote in a memorandum dated September 1877 rejected Currie's proposal on the basis that executive and judicial positions should be kept separate. There would be particular problems if the Judge was called on to decide on the legality of actions of consular officers. Clearly reflecting his own personal experience in Hong Kong, he said:

> "Those who have not had experience of British
> Colonies and Settlements in that part of the world
> can hardly form an idea of jealousy with which
> the relations between the Executive and Judicial
> Authorities are watched. In Hong Kong and Singapore,
> the slightest appearance of interference with the
> Chief Justice in the way of pressure in the discharge
> of his functions is the signal for violent attacks by
> the public press, indignation meetings, petitions and
> demonstrations of every kind. The community look to
> the Chief Justice as their protector against any attempt
> by the Governor 'to trample on their liberties.'"

The idea of amalgamation did not, however, die. Currie himself moved up in the Foreign Office and later resurrected the idea of amalgamating the office of Chief Justice and Consul-General. As we shall see, Pauncefote must have been using a crystal ball with 20/20 vision when he wrote his memo. All he said would come to pass, did come to pass.

New judges

George French, the former Chief Justice of Sierra Leone, was appointed Chief Judge. French was born in Tortola in the West Indies in 1817, making him 60 at the time of his appointment. He had been called to the Bar at Lincoln's Inn in 1844. As a barrister, French "did not have a large business in court," but he was well known in the courts as a law reporter for the *Times* and the *Law Journal* in the court of the Vice Chancellor.

At the same time, Robert Mowat after nine years as Law Secretary at the age of 34 was promoted to Assistant Judge.

Mowat's old position of Law Secretary as a dual administrator and prosecutor of cases was peculiar and did not exist in any other British court in the world. In the same memorandum that rejected the amalgamation proposal, Pauncefote directed that the

Robert Mowat promoted to Assistant Judge

position of Law Secretary be abolished and that positions for a Registrar, to handle administrative matters and act as a magistrate, and Judge's Clerk, to assist the judges, be created in the new Order in Council then being drafted. Mowat was made Registrar of the Court.

The Crown Advocate

Pauncefote also decided to change the way in which prosecutions were handled. This was done by the creation of a new role, that of Crown Advocate, to conduct prosecutions on behalf of the Crown as well as to advise the British legations on legal issues. The role was similar to that of a colonial Attorney General (which Pauncefote had himself been in Hong Kong). The Crown Advocate was a practising barrister and was allowed to also handle cases for private clients so long as they did not conflict with their duties advising the Crown. He was paid a relatively low stipend of GBP500 per year (compared to the annual salary of GBP1,200 for an assistant judge).

Nicholas Hannen was appointed to be the first Crown Advocate in October 1878, a position that became a stepping stone for four out of six Crown Advocates to judicial appointments. For the remainder of the existence of the court, the office of Crown Advocate continued to be a part time position with the Crown Advocate also working for private clients as far as his position allowed him to. Remuneration also remained a live issue.

Challenged in Japan

The situation in the British Courts in Japan still needed to fixed by the establishment of a proper court system. Throughout 1877 H.S. Wilkinson had continued in his role as Acting Law Secretary as the principal British judge in Japan. He had taken up the task with relish. A number of cases came before him which, as he put it himself in a letter home, "were of considerable international importance, involving questions of civil and criminal jurisdiction of Her Majesty's Court in those countries." He, as he was to do for the rest of his life, wrote long decisions dealing with the issues. Wilkinson was justifiably proud of these early decisions and kept printed copies of them for the remainder of his life. Wilkinson noted in the same letter home in early January 1878 that "no appeal has been prosecuted from any of my decisions."

This was not to last long. Very soon after sending his letter, a case came before Wilkinson which shook the foundations of British justice in Japan. In late 1877, a British pharmacist in Edo, John Hartley, had tried to import opium into Japan, allegedly for medical purposes. The Trade Regulations under the British-Japan Treaty of 1858 specifically prohibited the import of opium and provided that if any British ship came to Japan for trade carrying more than 3 catties (about 2.5 kilograms) of opium, the surplus quantity could be destroyed by the Japanese customs authorities. A fine of $15 per catty could also be imposed on anyone smuggling or attempting to smuggle opium.

Despite the ban in the treaties, until 1872, Japan had not sought to restrict the import of opium intended for medical purposes. In 1872, they seized a shipment of opium and, after protests, in 1873 brought in regulations seeking to restrict the import of medicinal opium by charging double the tariff. Between 1872 to 1875 the import of powered opium as medicine had generally been allowed by the Japanese authorities. Some shipments were stopped by customs, but the majority of them were allowed to go through. From 1875 to July 1877 the Japanese then allowed foreigners to import opium freely, before again banning it.

In December 1877, Japanese Customs found 20 pounds (10 kilograms) of opium in a shipment destined for Hartley and brought a prosecution against him in the British Court. Even before this case was heard, Hartley was caught trying to smuggle another 14 catties (about 10 kilograms) of opium in early 1878. Japanese Customs brought another prosecution against Hartley.

Both cases were heard in Yokohama in early 1878, by Wilkinson. John Lowder, a former consular official (who had arrived in Japan as a student interpreter in 1862) now practicing as a British barrister in Japan, appeared for the prosecution on behalf of the Japanese Government. Hartley represented himself. In the first case, Hartley claimed that the opium was for medicinal use and was therefore not prohibited.

The trial lasted six days. Hartley called evidence was that the Japanese government also considered medicinal opium to be a medical necessity and that in fact to meet demand in Japan the Japanese government had allowed it to be imported. Lowder, the prosecutor, himself told the court that the Minister of Foreign Affairs was drawing up rules to allow for the import of medicinal opium.

Wilkinson wrote a very long judgment agreeing with

H.S. Wilkinson delivers judgment in the Hartley case
John Hartley is on the left, John Lowder is to the right

Hartley. He held that the distinction between smoking opium and medicinal opium had been clearly established.

"The only point, therefore, to be decided is, whether the regulation which speaks of opium without any express qualification was intended to apply to medicinal opium."

He looked at the evidence that showed medicinal opium had a much higher quantity of morphia and was unsuitable for smoking. He went on:

> "It was assumed throughout that opium smoking is
> a great evil, which having happily no hold over the
> people of Japan, it is desirable to avert from them,
> even if stringent measures should be necessary for
> that purpose; and it is admitted that the object of the
> regulation is to avert that evil. As to medicinal opium,
> on the other hand, the evidence shows it to be an
> inestimable blessing to suffering humanity."

Wilkinson, relying on various rules of international law

a bitter pill to swallow.

Harry Parkes forcing Opium on the Japanese. H.S. Wilkinson looks on.

and statutory interpretation, held that the tins of opium Hartley had tried to import "are not prohibited to be imported; and the person importing them, even though he smuggled them, is not liable to punishment either of fine or confiscation under that particular provision of the regulation." In the second case, the opium was of a lower grade and could not be used for medicinal purposes. Wilkinson convicted Hartley and imposed a fine of $165 dollars being $15 for each catty in excess of the limit in the treaty. He ordered that the remaining three catties should be re-exported.

The first decision upset Japanese officials and the public very much. They considered the treaty to clearly prohibit any import of opium. This was a fair contention. The relevant regulation in the treaty stated: "the importation of opium being prohibited..." before setting out the three catty rule and fine. The *Hioron*, a Japanese newspaper, commented on the decision, questioning "will the public believe the judgment to be impartial and just? Will our government be satisfied with that judgment or try to have it reversed? Or does it intend to appeal?" The *Hioron* said that it could not agree with the decision: "the misery brought upon China by the opium trade is so notorious." This is why the Japanese government decided to prohibit it. The fact that Wilkinson had made this decision made things worse. *Hioron* was "greatly surprised by the British judge whose impartiality and uprightness are so well known, having acquitted the accused." There was no difference between "medicinal" and "smoking" opium. If opium smoking became a habit in Japan it would be "a great calamity."

Finally, addressing the way in which the Japanese government was handling extraterritorial cases, *Hioron* commented unfavourably on the practice of the Japanese government using foreign barristers to argue cases on its behalf in the consular courts. The reason given for this was that "Japanese are not sufficiently learned in foreign jurisprudence and not accustomed to plead in foreign courts." However, foreign barristers are "countrymen and have many feelings in common, however much each of them may want to serve his client, he may occasionally labour under impediments." Japan now had hundreds of judges, one of whom could surely act for the Japanese government, and the fact they did not, "is it not a great shame for a great Empire like Japan?"

The Japanese government was not taking the matter lying down and instructed the Japanese Minister to Great Britain,

Kagenori Ueno, to file an appeal to the Privy Council. They also made a formal protest to the Foreign Office, first to Sir Julian Pauncefote and then directly to the Foreign Secretary Marquis of Salisbury. They protested that the decision breached the "absolute prohibition of opium" and that the decision opened the possibility of Japan being "flooded" with opium.

Wilkinson's position was at the forefront of the attack on the decisions. First the Japanese said that the servant of one treaty party (that is, Wilkinson) could not make a decision as the interpretation of a treaty between the parties. Second, they questioned Wilkinson's right to hear the case given he was, officially, the Vice-Consul in Niigata and not assigned to Kanagawa. Third, they questioned the legality of his appointment as Acting Law Secretary of the Supreme Court for China and Japan.

This latter argument caused great concern to Pauncefote and the Foreign Secretary Lord Derby. They asked the government Law Officers for an opinion on the legality of the appointment of Wilkinson as Acting Law Secretary and whether he had been acting within his powers when he decided the Hartley case. The answer was, not surprisingly, a resounding "No." They stated that the only power the Judge or Acting Judge had under the Order in Council was to appoint an Assistant Judge or the Law Secretary to hear a specific case, not cases in general.

The Japanese government's appeal to the Privy Council was a very real threat to the Foreign Office and to the legality of almost all judgments handed down in Japan by Hannen, Goodwin and Wilkinson in the last eight years.

The Law Officers' opinion put great urgency into the need to reform the set up of the British courts in Japan. In May 1878, a decision was made to establish a British Court for Japan as part of the planned amendments to the Order in Council. The Japanese government was informed of this in August.

In order to deal with the threat of an appeal, in February 1879 the Marquis of Salisbury officially told the Japanese that the British Law Officers had advised that Wilkinson's decision could not be upheld. In public, however, the British authorities maintained that the decision was a judicial decision that they could not interfere with. Pauncefote, in an answer to a question in the British parliament, said that the Foreign Office had no power to confirm or reverse the judgment. The Japanese appeared to be satisfied with the communication that the decision could not be upheld. They did not go forward with an appeal, partly so as not to cause the Foreign Office to lose face and further strain relations between the two countries.

The British Court for Japan
The new Order in Council establishing the British Court for Japan removed the Supreme Court's concurrent jurisdiction to hear cases from Japan. Instead, the Court for Japan became the sole British first instance court for the Kanagawa consular area and the appellate court for appeals from all Provincial Courts in Japan. First instance cases from other consular districts could also be brought directly to the Court for Japan. Appeals were to be heard by the Chief Justice (the new title for the Chief Judge) and Judge (formerly the Assistant Judge) in Shanghai with a final appeal to the Privy Council.

The Order in Council provided for the appointment of a full time judge in Japan, the Judge for Japan, and that the British Consul in Kanagawa would ex officio be the Assistant Judge of the Court.

To the surprise of many, Richard Rennie, the barrister from Shanghai, was appointed as the first Judge of the Court for Japan. The *Japan Weekly Mail* reported that this was a surprise to Yokohama residents, "simply because it was always expected that Mr Hannen would have been nominated."

The British Court for Japan formally opened on January

1, 1879. The Provincial Court for Kanagawa was abolished and all pending cases transferred to the Court for Japan.

The first reported case for the Court for Japan was in *H. Ahrens & Co v Ellies*, master of the British ship *Zingra* on January 4, 1879 where an application was made to Rennie for increased security for costs. The application was refused as being premature. This case came on for trial at lightning speed, six days later, on January 10. The Plaintiff alleged that the Defendant had failed to deliver gunpowder shipped aboard the ship *Zingra*. The defence was that due to an emergency, certain parts of the cargo had had to be thrown overboard. Under English maritime law, when this occurs, under the principle of "general average" all those who have shipped products on board are expected to share in the loss. Rennie found that a general average had occurred and found in favour of the Defendant.

HER BRITANNIC MAJESTY'S COURT FOR JAPAN.

THE China and Japan Order in Council, 1878, having commenced and having full effect from and after this date, Her Britannic Majesty's Court for Japan has this day been opened by the undersigned, who has been appointed Judge of the said Court by Her Majesty, by warrant under Her Royal Sign Manual, bearing date the 30th day of October, 1878.

Mr. HIRAM SHAW WILKINSON has, under instructions from Her Majesty's Principal Secretary of State for Foreign Affairs, been appointed by Her Majesty's Minister in Japan to be Acting Assistant Judge of the said Court in the absence of Mr Consul ROBERTSON. Under section 6, sub-section 1, of the said Order in Council, Her Majesty's Consul for the district of the Consulate of Kanagawa has ceased to hold and form a Provincial Court, and by section 12 of the said Order in Council, all suits and proceedings, civil or criminal, instituted or taken in the district of the Consulate of Kanagawa before and pending at this date, are transferred to the jurisdiction of the said Court for Japan, and the same may be carried on and shall be tried, heard, and determined in and by the Court for Japan as nearly as may be as if the same had been instituted or taken in the district of the Consulate of Kanagawa after the commencement of the said Order.

RICHARD TEMPLE RENNIE,
Judge.

Kanagawa, 2nd January, 1879.   3in

When the appointment of Rennie had first been announced, the *Japan Punch* published a cartoon showing Rennie arriving in Japan and Wilkinson been packed off to Niigata carrying a big bag of judgments. Japanese were shown presenting him with a box of "Genuine Medicinal Opium." The clear suggestion was that his decision in the Hartley case had taken him out of the good books of the Foreign Office.

Contrary to the suggestion of the Japan Punch, Wilkinson

Rennie arrives in Japan with Wilkinson packed off to Niigata

remained in the Foreign Office's good books and his strong claims to being appointed to the bench were not overlooked. At the time the Court for Japan was established, the Consul in Yokohama, Russell Robertson, who was by virtue of his position, the Assistant Judge, was on leave. Wilkinson was immediately appointed Acting Consul and Acting Assistant Judge during Robertson's absence.

When Russell Robertson was due to return from leave in April 1879 an even better opportunity arose. Around the same time Robert Mowat was due to depart Shanghai on long leave. At Chief Justice George French's request, Wilkinson was offered the position of acting Assistant Judge of the Supreme Court in Shanghai during Mowat's absence.

The British courts in Japan did not, however, deal with a major case involving a British citizen. Rather the Americans insisted they had the jurisdiction to do so.

CHAPTER 8

The Bullion Dollar Question: The Ross Case

IN WHAT WAS TO become a major diplomatic incident, very soon after the establishment of the Court for Japan, a British subject, John Ross, killed a fellow sailor on board a United States merchant ship, the Bullion.

The United States consular authorities prosecuted Ross in the US Consular Court for murder causing much diplomatic correspondence to pass between the Britain and the United States. The US President, Chester Arthur, even devoted three paragraphs of his State of the Union address in 1881 to explaining the United States' position. The case eventually found its way to the US Supreme Court, challenging both the jurisdiction of a US consular court to try a British subject and the constitutionality of trial without jury in the American consular courts in the Far East. The decision became the leading decision on the constitutionality of trials before US consular courts.

The facts of the case were relatively simple and fairly brutal. Ross, 30, who had been born in Canada, making him a British subject, had signed on to the United States Merchant Marine, joining the Bullion. While the Bullion was anchored in Yokohama Harbour, Ross had gone ashore drinking with the second mate of the ship, Robert Kelly, and the cook. Kelly and Ross had a heated argument and then returned drunk to the ship around 4.00am on May 9, 1880. The cook was making

US Consul General Thomas van Buren in front of the US Consulate

Kelly a cup of coffee in the galley when Ross came in with a long knife and asked Kelly if he was "as good a man on board as he pretended to be on shore." Kelly told Ross to lie down and came part way out of the galley. Ross stabbed Kelly in the neck, arm and face. Kelly died almost instantly. Ross was immediately arrested by the crew and the US deputy marshal was called to the Bullion.

John Read, the captain of the Bullion, filed a formal complaint against Ross with the US Consul, first describing him as "supposed to be a citizen of the United States." This was later amended to read that he was an "American seaman, duly and lawfully enrolled and shipped and doing service as such seaman on board the American ship Bullion."

At his trial before the US Consul, Thomas van Buren (the famous Civil War general), Ross challenged the authority of the US Consular Court to try him by presenting an affidavit that he was a native of Prince Edward Island, and thus a British

Subject. This was rejected on the basis that, as a seaman on a United States ship, he was subject to American jurisdiction. The British Acting Consul-General at the time then formally demanded that Ross, as a British subject, be released, but this request was rejected. Ross also challenged the fact that he was not being tried by a jury, as guaranteed by the United States Constitution. Van Buren rejected this argument on the basis that the statutes creating consular jurisdiction did not provide for a trial by jury.

When Ross was asked to plead he replied that he "remembered nothing about it as he was in liquor when he went on board." A plea of Not Guilty was recorded. Given the evidence, it is not surprising that van Buren and the assessors found Ross guilty of murder saying, "a more deliberate, foul and malicious murder it would be difficult to conceive." They added: "You were not drunk but had swallowed just enough of the vile compounds sold in the dens of Yokohama to fit you for the deed you contemplated." Ross was sentenced "to suffer death in such manner and at such time and place as the United States Minister in Japan may direct according to law, and may God have mercy on your soul."

Ross replied, "I do not remember the first thing about it, your Honour. If I did it I would not be ashamed to own it."

The sentence was confirmed by the American Minister, but with a recommendation that the sentence of death be converted to one of life without parole. The US President, Rutherford Hayes, pardoned Ross on the condition he agreed to be detained at Albany penitentiary in New York State for the term of his natural life.

Ross' trial and conviction created a huge diplomatic incident between Britain and America. Interestingly, given that it was usually the Americans who were legalistic and the British who took a practical view of extraterritoriality; in Ross' case it was the Americans who were practical and the British legalistic. The British position was that the treaties with Japan (and China) did not allow one treaty power to try nationals of another country. Extraterritorial jurisdiction was personal and the treaties only allowed the British to try British subjects and the Americans to try American subjects. The British Secretary of State wrote to the United States Secretary of State stating that because "Ross was a British Subject, his offence was justiceable only in the British Consular Courts and that the arrest, trial and conviction by the Consular Court of the United States were unlawful."

The United States' formal position was set out in a very long letter of June 3, 1881, from the new US Secretary of State, James G. Blaine, to the British Minister in Washington, Sir Edward Thornton. Blaine had been appointed Secretary of State on the election of James Garfield as president. The first point Blaine made was that "if the fact of nationality is to be the test of jurisdiction, who is to decide it?" Blaine said that if the Captain of a US ship denied a seaman's nationality this would need to be decided on a preliminary basis by the US Consul who would otherwise only make an arrest on the basis of comity. Second, prisoners would seek to play a nationality game – claiming to be a different nationality as it suited them to avoid arrest and punishment. Third, if the British Court assumed jurisdiction it would need the assistance of the US Court to compel witnesses and detain the ship pending trial. Blaine conceded that in "heinous" cases, cooperation would no doubt be forthcoming but in lesser cases there may be "differences of opinion" that would render assistance impossible. Fourth, in the case of smuggling by crew members, the ship's owners or officers would, in fact, be very happy to see jurisdiction transferred to make it easier to avoid liability themselves.

Turning to the treaties, Blaine conceded that the wording of the treaties made it clear British subjects were to be tried by British courts and Americans by American courts. But, there was an exception that applied to seamen of the mercantile marine. Article 9 of the US-Japan treaty of 1858 provided that the Japanese would assist in arresting any deserters from American ships. The US had enacted legislation to enforce this and the "position of the United States Government was that a foreign seaman duly enrolled on an American merchant vessel, is subject to the laws and entitled to the protection of the United States to precisely the same extent that a native born seaman would be during the period of his service." This principle Blaine said was also maintained by the British Government in the Merchant and Shipping Act of 1854 which declares that "all offences against property or person, committed ... afloat ... by a seaman" shall be dealt with by British Courts in the same manner as if the seaman was British. Blaine then cited a number of British cases where British jurisdiction had been asserted against foreign seaman and said that US practice was in "entire conformity" with British practice.

Richard Rennie holds the scales of justice while British and American officials look on

Finally, Blaine pointed out that in a number of cases, the British had not assisted where America had asked for assistance in Japan. In one case, a witness subpoena had been refused. In another case a British subject had helped to facilitate an escape from an American jail. The British consul had told the Americans that the alleged offender could not be punished because the jail was not British – it was only an offence for a British subject to help an escape from a British jail. Blaine concluded his letter by stating that going forward, the US would exercise jurisdiction over all foreign sailors on their merchant ships and hoped that the British Government would "recognise the advantages of the approach." As we shall see, the British did, but with a classic British bet each way.

Ten years later, in 1890, Ross made a habeas corpus application against the superintendent of Albany Penitentiary, Mr McIntyre. The case found its way to the US Supreme Court under the name *Ross v McIntyre*. Ross alleged that McIntyre was illegally detaining him because his original conviction was unlawful on the basis that as a British subject, the United States Consular Court in Kanagawa had no jurisdiction to try him and because he was constitutionally entitled to a jury. The first objection was rejected on the basis that, having voluntarily enrolled on an American ship, he was subject to American jurisdiction. The Supreme Court reviewed the State Department correspondence, which cited numerous British cases to show that the British had also asserted jurisdiction over foreign seamen aboard British ships. The court agreed with these decisions and finished by stating that the views were "in harmony" with the long standing position that England could not claim seamen from United States ships. In a nationalistic flourish, the Supreme Court added that "its enforcement was deemed a great indignity upon this country, and a violation of our right of sovereignty; our vessels being considered as parts of our territory. It led to the war of 1812, and, although that war closed without obtaining a relinquishment of the claim, its further assertion was not attempted."

With regard to the constitutionality of trial by assessors, the court took a purposive approach by saying that by the time the Constitution was enacted, consular jurisdiction already existed and thus "the framers of the constitution, who were fully aware of the necessity of having judicial authority exercised by our Consuls in non-Christian countries." When trading with these countries, the founding fathers "never could have supposed that all the guaranties in the administration of the law upon criminals at home were to be transferred to such Consular establishments." Such a requirement would destroy the whole purpose of having consular jurisdiction in the first place. While Americans subject to consular jurisdiction may lose some rights, on the other hand, they gained rights by being "withdrawn from the procedure of their tribunals, often arbitrary and oppressive, and some times accompanied with extreme cruelty and torture."

For the remaining half century of American extraterritorial jurisdiction in East Asia, the Supreme Court decision that there was no right to trial by jury in an American extraterritorial court stood despite a number of challenges. The decision was so important that it simply became known as the "Ross case."

CHAPTER 9

The Chinese Challenge

GEORGE FRENCH, the new British Chief Justice, had a tough time in his few years on the bench in China. For most of the time he was physically ill. His condition cannot have been helped by the two very tricky cases that came before him involving the rights of British missionaries to lease land and to what extent British employees of the Imperial Maritime Customs were subject to the jurisdiction of the court.

The position of missionaries

Foreign missionaries in China created numerous frictions and problems. Most foreigners were happy to live in treaty ports and have as little to do as possible with local Chinese. Even for trade with Chinese they relied on compradores, or Chinese middlemen, to handle the buying and selling of products. The majority of cases involving Chinese in the British and American courts were therefore criminal cases where a foreigner had killed or injured a Chinese.

Missionaries on the other hand were on a mission to convert Chinese to Christianity. They wanted to live amongst the Chinese, they learnt the language and tried to talk to Chinese and deal with them on a daily basis. The local Chinese were suspicious of these foreigners and what they were doing in China. Numerous rumours were spread, including that the missionaries ate babies they took into their orphanages. Riots broke out frequently against missionaries all over China and throughout the Qing dynasty. One of the major duties of foreign gunboats was quelling anti-missionary riots.

These disturbances could be very serious. Frederick Bourne, who later became a judge of the British Supreme Court, early in his career when he was the British Consul in Chungking (Chongqing) deep inland on the Yangtze River almost lost his life when he was attacked by a Chinese mob protesting against the activities of foreign missionaries. The riots had started due to the activities of American missionaries at the China Inland Mission. Bourne had gone to the local magistrate's Yamen to ask for assistance. For his return journey he was provided with 40 armed men to protect him, but they were no match for the mob and his chair was destroyed. His arm was badly hurt and a stick hit him on the temple. For at least half an hour he thought that he might be killed at any minute. The magistrate arrived with more armed men just in time to save his life and take him to safety.

Even after being saved by the mob, Bourne thought he would be killed and wrote a dispatch which ended: "The affair looks now as bad as it can be and I am very doubtful whether I shall write another letter." He then spent the next seven months living in various yamens, wearing Chinese clothes and eating Chinese food until the Chinese authorities thought it safe for him to publicly resume duties. Bourne blamed the affair on American missionary imprudence in building a new building that offended Chinese sensibilities.

A few years before in Foochow (Fuzhou) on the coast of Fukien (Fujian) Province, riots had broken out, triggered by the construction by British missionaries of a large foreign building that by its shape and height was offensive to Chinese sensibilities.

The Church Missionary Society (CMS) had first arrived in Foochow in 1850 even before missionaries were allowed by treaty into China. Originally, the missionaries were not permitted to live inside the walls of the city but they soon signed a lease for a piece of land owned by Taou Shan Kwan

* In the engraving, the hill in the left foreground is Black-Stone Hill. About the left centre of the picture, on this hill, will be observed a white wall; behind it a house with a slightly gabled roof looking as if it were on the highest point of the hill; and behind that, the top of a small pagoda. This wall surrounds the C.M.S. Mission compound; and the house is the old mission-house, now burnt down, but replaced by a new one built by the late Rev. J. E. Mahood. To the right, but lower down, and almost exactly in the centre of the picture, is another English-looking house, which is now used as a girls' school, and as the residence of the Native Pastor, the Rev. Wong Kiu-taik. Between the two houses, and a little behind, is the temple of the "Pearly Emperor Supreme Ruler," the great idol whose title (Shangti) is the term used by most of our missionaries to express "God." Another hill, crowded with buildings, will be seen in the background, with a famous pagoda half-way up it. Just beneath this pagoda, between the two hills, a building stands up from the mass of houses: this is the city gate, the lower ground to the right being the suburbs.

A view of Wushishan and the CMS compound

(Daoguanshan) Temple on Wu Hsih Shan (Wushishan). The Mission was located in a beautiful position with a wonderful view over Fuzhou.

The CMS had a very difficult relationship with the local Chinese. The local gentry did not want them in the city at all. Complaints were made about their encroaching on land not leased to them or building buildings larger than those allowed for in the lease. In 1869, the mission chapel was attacked, allegedly by Chinese soldiers, and its furniture destroyed. Serious damage was also inflicted on the building.

In 1878, the Society leased more land from the Temple and started to build a new theological college. They planned to build a three-storey building that would lie against the side of the hill. Because of this, the second storey was larger than the first and the third larger than the second. The building was planned to have 48 small rooms for study and a large dining room and lecture room. The local Chinese gentry complained to the local Chinese authorities about the construction of such a large building of "foreign design" and the officials passed on the complaint to the British Consul. The Chinese officials offered to relocate the mission to an old telegraph building, but the Society refused and continued the construction work.

In the heat of summer, in late August 1878, a Chinese mob took matters into their own hands and, while local Chinese officials and British consular officials looked on, burnt the new building down. The riot appears to have been, as far as riots can be, a relatively civilized affair. Nobody's life appears to have been threatened and none were lost. The local Chinese gentry were reported to have looked on while smoking their water-pipes.

There were rumours that two weeks later, the "mob, elated by their previous success, have determined to burn down the whole of the buildings belonging to the Church Missionary Society on September 11, 1878." Two days before this planned attack, the HMS *Swinger* arrived in port and over the next 10 days another three British and one American men-of-war arrived to deliver the clear message that destruction of the mission would lead to the destruction of Foochow.

Under pressure from the Tsungli Yamen and the British, the local authorities punished some locals for their role in the riots. The local authorities, however, wanted to get the mission out. Having no other option, they decided to take action in the British courts. They instructed a senior lawyer from Hong Kong, Thomas Hayllar QC, to act for them. In October 1878, the Foochow Office of Foreign Trade sent an eviction notice drafted by Hayllar to the Society. Later in early March 1879 they formally filed a petition in the British Consular Court in Fuzhou seeking eviction of the Society.

Sir Thomas Wade, the British Minister in Peking took a personal interest in the case. He arrived in Hong Kong on March 10, 1879 on his way back to Peking from long leave and decided to first go to Foochow to try to reach a settlement. He negotiated directly with the new Chinese Governor General of Fukien, Ting Jih Chang, and Reverend John Wolfe, the head of the mission, but failed. Despite generous offers from the Chinese and British authorities to provide new premises in the old telegraph office that had been offered before, Wolfe refused to leave.

The only way to solve the problem was for the case to continue in British courts. However, given the issues at stake, the case was transferred to the Supreme Court. Chief Justice George French came from Shanghai in early April 1879 for the trial in a specially leased house large enough to accommodate all who wanted to attend. This included the British Minister, Sir Thomas Wade and the local Governor General Ting who both sat near the bench. A number of other senior Chinese officials including the local magistrate and the President of the Foreign Trade Board and the Judicial Commissioner also attended.

Hayllar represented the temple at trial. The mission also called in a big gun, getting Nicholas Hannen, who at the time was the Crown Advocate in Shanghai to represent them.

The case itself, as almost all landlord and tenant cases are, was as dull as watching paint dry. The temple alleged that the lease agreements with the Church Mission Society were void or that the Society was in breach of the agreements. The trial lasted eight days from April 30, 1879 to May 9, 1879. Numerous witnesses were called on behalf of the temple to show the breaches of agreement. Two Chinese officials also testified on the requirements of Chinese tenancy law. Reverend Wolfe, the actual Defendant in the case, also gave evidence regarding the signing of the tenancy agreements. He was adamant that the Society had not breached the agreements.

At the end of the hearing, Chief Justice French said that given the importance of the case he would reserve his judgment and arrange for it to be read later in Foochow.

Two months later the judgment was read out in courtroom of the consulate in Foochow. French had spent his time writing a masterful judgment that gave something to everyone and could allow both sides to claim to be winners.

The first issue French had to decide was whether to apply English or Chinese law to the contract. Hannen had insisted during the trial that English law should be applied in particular because there was no pleading of Chinese law. French dealt with this quickly. He simply stated that the general principle of English law was that the "law of the place where the land, the subject of the contract, is situate, governs its construction," and accordingly, "the law of China applicable to the contract in question must govern its construction."

French then found that the evidence did not show any breach of contract by the Church Missionary Society in rebuilding its buildings. French added, however, that he could not, sitting in a British court in China, decide the boundaries of the land, as this would affect other neighbours not before the court. He then came to his formal decision. Before doing so, he sounded a warning to all involved that they should not be hoping for too much from a court judgment:

"I may here observe that the case is an anomalous one, and not likely to be of value as a precedent. Nor is the value of the interests involved in it of much moment. But other circumstances have drawn to it a factitious degree of attention which neither the value of the interests involved nor the importance of the points raised justify."

He dismissed the temple's claims – a victory for the missionaries. But, and this was a big but, he found that the lease agreement could be terminated by the temple on three months notice if they genuinely needed the land for use of the temple. This was a very big victory for the Chinese.

French also ordered that each side bear their own costs. The decision was very diplomatic. It effectively gave the Chinese an easy way to terminate the tenancy if they wanted to but also the Society the face of not having been found in breach of the agreement. By not ordering either party to pay the others costs, he also did not establish who the real winner or loser was. And perhaps in this case, the real winner was justice. The decision was a fair one that defused a difficult situation. Following the decision, the temple immediately terminated the tenancy on the basis that it needed the land. The Chinese authorities showed great flexibility and, after some further negotiations, offered the Society the telegraph office that the Society had previously turned down as a site for their new mission. The Society initially said that they would appeal to the Privy Council, but cooler heads prevailed and they agreed to move. All that remains of their mission in Wushishan today is a stone marker in Chinese recording the site as the "Former Location of the Wushishan Church Case."

Servants of the Chinese Empire

A year and a half later, in March 1881, French had to deal with an even trickier case over the rights and duties of foreigners employed by the Chinese Emperor. The case was particularly difficult because it involved the Imperial Maritime Customs, a Chinese government body run by foreigners. As a foreigner, the Scottish Inspector General of the Customs, Robert Hart, was much more willing to challenge the powers of the foreign courts in China. He did everything in his power to obtain a decision that would find that foreign officers employed by

Customs were not subject to the jurisdiction of the foreign courts for acts done in their position as employees of the Chinese Emperor.

Edward Page, a watcher in the Maritime Chinese Customs, was charged with the murder of two Chinese smugglers, Li Amai and one unknown person. He had killed the two in the course of trying to catch them smuggling opium.

The case caused Hart "much worry." When he first heard of the case, he contacted the British Minister, Thomas Wade, to ask him to intervene. However, Wade told him that he could not interfere if the consul in Canton "was proceeding judicially," and thus the case had gone ahead.

Hart fully supported Page in defending the charges. He engaged two of the leading British lawyers in Hong Kong, Thomas Hayllar QC, and the Attorney General of Hong Kong, Mr (later Sir) Edward O'Malley, as defence counsel. The case therefore pitted the Queen's most senior lawyer in China, the Crown Advocate, against her most senior legal representative in Hong Kong, the Attorney General. Nicholas Hannen did not himself appear for the Crown. He was on leave at the time of the trial. John Francis, a senior barrister from Hong Kong, who later became a Queen's Counsel, acted as Crown Advocate in Hannen's place.

In addition to defending Page, Hart went on the attack. He instructed Hayllar and O'Malley to bring a civil claim for false imprisonment against the British Consul in Canton, A.R. Hewlett, for arresting Page. This was scheduled

Sir Robert Hart, British Inspector-General of Chinese Customs who was willing to challenge the authority of the British courts (The Chinese characters are reversed in the original)

to be heard after the prosecution of Page.

Before Page's criminal trial started, Hayllar and O'Malley filed a demurrer, or objection, to the charge. They argued that because Page was employed by the Emperor of China with the consent of the British Government, the British courts in China could not have jurisdiction over him for acts done in the course of that employment. Two cases where British employees of the government of Chile and Portugal were found not to be subject to British jurisdiction were cited to support this argument. French dismissed the demurrer on the basis that under the terms of the Treaty of Tientsin, the Emperor of China did not have jurisdiction to try British subjects. If the argument of the Defendant were correct, no one would have jurisdiction to try them. The Chilean and Portuguese cases could be distinguished because in those cases the governments of those countries had not given up their rights to try British subjects.

Page was asked to plea to the charges. He pleaded not guilty and was put on trial before a five man jury. The Acting Crown Advocate, Francis, commenced by telling the jury that the jurisdiction the court had over Page was purely personal. Some of the witnesses in the court would not be British subjects and the court had no coercive power over these witnesses to force them to give evidence.

Francis then set out the case for the prosecution. One of Page's colleagues, a Mr Davis, had received information that smugglers would be attempting to bring opium into China aboard the steamer *Tung Ting*. Davis was too unwell to try to catch the smugglers so he passed the information on to Page. If Customs officers were successful in interdicting opium they were paid a considerable percentage of its value as a reward. Page sought permission to try to catch the smugglers. Customs' rules prohibited the use of firearms without the specific consent of a superior. Customs' rules also provided that firearms should only be used in self-defence. Page, however, took a rifle given to him by Davis on his expedition.

Rather than directly trying to stop the Tung Ting in a Customs boat, which most likely would have resulted in the opium being thrown overboard, Page boarded an ordinary Chinese boat dressed in Chinese clothing. The Chinese boat fired across the bow of the Tung Ting to try to force it to stop. Captain Homes of the Tung Ting testified that he then saw a sampan being rowed from his ship towards the shore of the river. He said he also saw a man dressed in Chinese clothing in the bow of the Chinese boat standing and shooting at the sampan and that one of the men in the sampan fell. The Chinese boat then went alongside the sampan. Captain Holmes said that that was all he could see.

Page returned to Canton and told Davis what had happened. Davis then took him to the Customs Office where he reported to Mr Eldridge, the principal tide-surveyor and Mr Parkhill, chief tide-surveyor. Subsequently, he also reported to Mr McKean the Commissioner of Customs in Canton. The dead man in the sampan was brought to Customs jetty where Dr Carrow examined him and determined that he had been killed instantly by a bullet that went through his heart and lungs.

Parkhill, McKean, Eldridge and Dr Carrow were all called as witnesses to testify as to what Page had told them or, in the case of Dr Carrow, what he had found in his examination of the victim. Robert Hart officially ordered them all not to give evidence. In court, they all refused to testify on the basis that the information was the property of the Chinese government. They wished to serve the Chinese government honourably and it would be a dishonor to disclose the information. Dr Carrow and Eldridge were both American citizens. The court had no power to make them give evidence and Francis was not able to get any statements from them.

Parkhill and McKean, however, were both British subjects. Parkhill was the first to be questioned. He was asked what

Page had told him when he spoke to him after the incident. Hayllar objected to the question on the basis the answer given by Page was in obeyance to an order and not voluntarily and under English rules of evidence, therefore, not admissible. He also argued that any answer given was the property of, and a secret of, the Chinese government. Hayllar said that if the incident had occurred in England, it would be for Page's superiors to decide whether to prosecute and in this case they clearly did not want to. The argument raised some tough issues. French said he would need some time to consider the matter and would resume the trial the next day.

In the morning, French overruled the first objection on the grounds that it appeared the answers had been given voluntarily. Turning to whether the information was a secret of the Chinese government, he said that a government document could be ordered to be made public when it was in the public interest do so. French said that this was clearly the case here. Parkhill then returned to the witness box. He continued to refuse to answer any questions regarding what Page had said to him on the basis that it would be dishonesty to the Chinese government. In what must have been a very tense exchange, French ordered Parkhill to answer:

French: I have held you must do it. Now, the powers of this Court are very considerable, and if you, being a British subject and in a British Court of Law, although in China, refuse to answer the question which the court thinks you ought to answer, I need not tell you that you are subject to punishment at the hands of the Court, with a view to consider whether you expose yourself to that punishment or answer the question.

Parkhill: I consider it a very dishonest thing. French: I don't care about that at all. You have to answer it. It is not a question for you to consider.

Parkhill: With all respect, I decline.

Francis then asked that Parkhill be found in contempt

of court and punished for refusing to obey French's order. French said that he would deal with that at the end of the day and said Parkhill could leave the witness box.

McKean was then called. His evidence lasted longer, but he also refused to answer any questions as to what Page had said to him and refused to disclose the statement that he had been taken down on the basis that he had been ordered by Robert Hart not to answer the question or disclose the document. McKean explained why he was refusing:

> "It involves a question of immense principle, I may be summoned every day of my life to this Consulate in consequence of the credulity of some Consular assistant to answer for my acts. …. My acts are of the Chinese Government only."

McKean refused to produce the statement. The prosecution then sought an adjournment to allow the British Consulate to serve a notice on the Chinese Superintendent of Customs (called the Hoppo), who had last had the document asking him to produce the document. This was done. But the next day, no one attended to produce the document.

Francis then sought to get evidence from Mr McKean as to what the document said. This was objected to as secondary evidence as to the contents of a document that has been refused to be produced as the property of another state. French upheld the objection and ruled that McKean could not be asked further questions on this topic. McKean was then allowed to leave the witness box.

Without the evidence of what Page had told his colleagues, Francis did not have much of a case. He, however, did the best he could relying on the undenied evidence that two people were dead and Captain Homes' testimony. French summed up for the jury and directed them that it would be murder if they were satisfied the firing was deliberate and intentional.

Despite the lack of evidence, the jury took a long time to consider its verdict. They returned at one time to clarify the direction given by the judge regarding the shooting. French had told them they should acquit if they "should be satisfied the prisoner did not fire the fatal shot." They asked if they could alter this to "should not be satisfied the prisoner did fire the fatal shot." French allowed this and the jury acquitted Page. While an apparently small change, the jury was effectively saying they accepted someone had fired the shot and it was likely to be Page, but could not be satisfied it was him. When Page was acquitted applause broke out in the court.

French quickly suppressed it. Francis then sought an order that Parkhill be punished for refusing to answer questions. French, whose attitude had clearly softened during the trial, said that given Parkhill had been ordered by his superiors to refuse to answer, he would not punish him. Francis argued strongly against this. He said if witnesses could refuse to answer based on a superior order it would be impossible to obtain evidence for prosecutions in the future. French, however, was not in the mood to punish anyone. He said it was a "peculiar case" and that he did not suppose a similar case would need to be dealt with again soon, and hopefully not at all. He told Mr Parkhill that he was free to go.

With the decision, Robert Hart ordered that the false imprisonment proceedings against the Consul, Hewlett, be withdrawn, recording in a letter to a colleague, "they are wroth with McKean for refusing to give evidence and will be wroth with me if I go on with the prosecution of the Consul." He went on in a long-winded stream of consciousness that reflected the difficult position he was in as a foreigner heading a Chinese government agency:

"Under the circumstances – after a full review of
the situation, comprising a Yamen too weak to back

me up, a possible defeat with an 'I told you so' to
swallow afterwards, a possible victory in one court
but renewed opposition elsewhere and intensified ill
feeling everywhere, and an indisposition to sacrifice
a mountain because tripped by a mole-hill – I have
decided to take my own course, which is a) to stop
Hewlett, b) to send home the report of the trial etc., for
legal opinions at home, c) to give instructions to Canton
specially and the Service generally (vide forthcoming
circular) of a kind to 'save face' and d) by changing my
tack, and remembering we are under sail and without
steam, bend to the storm and save the ship. – But it is a
bitter pill to swallow, all the same!"

The circular he issued to "save face" read:

"If any foreign employee of the Chinese customs kills
or wounds any person, he shall at once resign his
place and report to the Consul of his nationality within
whose jurisdiction he resides; if the Consul tries and
convicts him, his resignation is to be permanent; if the
Consul acquits him, or decides that there is no cause for
trial, he may resume his official position with full pay
during the time since his resignation."

Two years later in Shanghai, in what Hart remarked
was an odd coincidence, another man named Page was the
Defendant in a case in Shanghai that again raised the question
as Hart put it "are China official employees if foreigners
obliged to answer judicial questions concerning their official
knowledge?"

In April 1883, Hart had issued instructions to the Customs
Commissioners in each port concerning when and when not
Customs employees should give evidence in consular courts.
The rules were that if a Commissioner instructed any customs

employee to attend any foreign court of law the employee should do so. The Commissioner was required to obtain from the Superintendent, Hart, a memorandum of what actions the employee was to take and what evidence he was permitted to give. If an employee was summonsed to court, he must go but he would be treated as being on leave without pay. Except where they had permission from the Commissioner, they were "forbidden to answer questions on subjects of which he had knowledge only by reason of, or through his position as an employee of the Chinese Government."

In late August 1883, William Page, the Quartermaster on the P&O Steamer *the Ancona*, stole 163 balls of opium. They had been found during a search by Customs. Page offered John Roberts, an assistant examiner and diver with Customs, a bribe of one sovereign if he would let him throw the opium away. Page was prosecuted in the Police Court at Shanghai before Robert Mowat sitting as the police magistrate. Roberts was called to give evidence against Page. Roberts first refused to appear in court unless he was subpoenaed. After he was subpoenaed he appeared the next day. He refused, however, to answer any questions concerning what happened on board the *Ancona*. He recited almost word for word Hart's instructions:

> "I cannot answer that question, as I am strictly
> forbidden to answer any questions on subjects of which
> I have a knowledge only by reason of my position as a
> servant of the Chinese Government."

He then said he had been ordered by the Commissioner of Customs in Shanghai, Mr Glover, not to answer any questions. Mowat told Roberts that the law did not allow him to refuse to answer, unless the answer would incriminate him, and said:

"If you do not answer, I shall have, unwillingly, to commit you to prison. Will you answer?"

"No, Sir."

Mowat explained the law again and told Roberts that if he did not answer he would send him to prison for seven days unless he answered in the meantime and added: "I hope you will be enabled to answer. I very much regret the course I have to take."

Roberts simply asked: "Will you allow me one favour – to get my room locked up?"

"Oh, yes," replied Mowat.

Mr Wainewright who was in court to watch the case for the Customs service then tried to argue with Mowat that the prosecution could get the evidence it needed if they applied to the Superintendent of Customs "and it is for him to say whether he will allow them to give the evidence required."

Mowat was having none of that and said with finality: "It is for the Court to say whether he must answer."

Robert Hart was very upset by the case, not because Roberts had been locked up but because Roberts should have answered the question and Glover should not have ordered him not to. He wrote furiously: "the case is such a bad one for us – Glover having shut his mouth to keep in what should have come out in the public interest." Glover later told Hart that he had ordered Roberts not to answer because he thought Hart had wanted a test case and "the stronger the reasons for a man's speaking out, the more necessary for us [Customs] to get Government to say he may be silent!"

Six days later, the case took a surprising turn when Page, who was presumably in the same consular gaol as Roberts, confessed to having been given the opium after it was stolen. Mowat convicted him of possession of stolen property and sentenced him to two months in prison. Then, because

Roberts was no longer required to give evidence, Mowat ordered that he be released from prison. To add to the pain for Roberts, Hart said that he expected his pay to be docked for being absent without leave, even though he had been sent to jail for complying with a superior's order.

Hart considered taking action against Mowat for damages for false imprisonment and appealing against the Mowat's decision to the Privy Council. He received advice from "eminent London lawyers" that the foreign courts had no jurisdiction over any "matters immediately connected with a foreigner's employment in the Customs service," and that an appeal would most likely succeed.

In the end, he determined discretion was the better part of valour. No doubt he would also have been concerned that an unfavourable decision from the Privy Council would make Customs' position even weaker.

Hart did modify his instructions concerning giving evidence in foreign courts so that he required the Commissioners to take the initiative to seek his instructions as to what evidence should be given.

CHAPTER 10

Justice Demanded

Some Corner of a Foreign Field

The trial of Edward Page at Canton was to be George French's swansong. Soon after the trial, French went on sick leave. He had been unwell almost from when he first arrived in China, and became gravely ill during early 1881. In early July, French was placed on reduced salary and Robert Mowat formally took over as Acting Chief Justice. When French first went to Kobe, Nicholas Hannen was still on leave in England. When it became apparent that French would most likely either not recover or retire, Hannen was called back to act as Chief Justice. He arrived in Shanghai in October 1881 and immediately took up the role.

Around the same time that Hannen got back to Shanghai, it was reported that French was feeling slightly better. But it was not to be. He died two weeks later on November 13, 1881 and was buried in Onohama Cemetery in the foreign settlement in Kobe. His grave – which was along with others in Onohama moved after WWI - can still be found today in a beautiful corner of Futatabi Cemetery high up in the hills of Kobe.

Jockeying for Promotion

George French's illness and death led to jockeying for the positions that would become vacant when French retired or died. Richard Rennie, as Judge for Japan, and as an experienced barrister was the clear choice for the position of

Nicholas Hannen arrives in Japan

Chief Justice. The prize on offer was, then, the position as Judge of the Court for Japan. Nicholas Hannen, Robert Mowat and H.S. Wilkinson all had good claims for the job. Hannen and Wilkinson had both acted as a judge in Japan. Wilkinson spoke Japanese. Mowat had been Law Secretary and Assistant Judge in Shanghai for over 12 years. In the end, Rennie was appointed Chief Justice in Shanghai and Hannen was appointed Judge for Japan. H.S. Wilkinson was appointed Crown Advocate in Shanghai to replace Hannen.

Big Trouble in Little Canton

Soon after his appointment as Crown Advocate in 1882, another killing by a Customs Officer in Canton handed Wilkinson his first big case. First, he had to travel to Canton to prosecute the officer, James Logan, for murder. Then, the next year, he returned as a British Commissioner to clean up the aftermath of the killing, which had led to large-scale riots in the city. During the riots, the rioters took over the foreign settlement on Shameen Island and destroyed many foreign warehouses and properties.

Logan and a group of four or five other Customs officers had been put aboard a ship, the *Kiangping* off Macao on August 11, 1883. They had remained on board almost all day as the ship sailed upriver to Canton and searched the ship until midnight. They had not eaten all day and, after completing their search, went to Hing-Kee Tea House, in Honam where they were based. Honam was a local area well away from the Shameen settlement. They had food and beer and went back to their house where they played cards and drank until 6 o'clock in the morning. About 18 foreign Customs officers lived in the area and one of them had, on a number of occasions, insulted a Chinese woman living in the tea house. This had led to bad relations between the Customs Officers and the locals. Logan himself had also complained to the District Magistrate about the performance of a watchman. This had resulted in the watchman being flogged. Logan's son had been told by some Chinese a few day previously that they were going to take Logan and his son's heads soon.

As Logan and the party of drinkers passed the tea house, a large crowd formed. Logan was fearful that they were going to be mobbed. The party went back to Logan's house where they got two revolvers. Logan said that he intended to use the revolvers to scare the mob. When the customs officers returned, up to 1,000 people were on the street and they started throwing stones. One officer was hit in the ankle and another on his body.

Logan fired his revolver. He hit a young boy as well as a woman and an old man. The crowd dispersed and the officers quickly returned to their homes. Three of them were subsequently arrested and locked up in the British consular gaol. One was Norwegian and he was taken before his Consul. The other was a Russian Finn, and having no Consul in Canton appeared before the British Consul. After further investigation, the Norwegian and Russian suspects were released.

The young boy died and so, allegedly, did the woman. To settle the matter, the District Magistrate gave the uncle of the boy $100, and the woman (who was in fact still alive) and the man $30 each. This did not satisfy the shopkeepers who put up posters demanding Logan's head.

The rioting in Canton. 1. Chinese looting the Foreign Settlement. 2. A house in the foreign settlement being burnt. 3. Viceroy's soldiers defending Shameen.

On September 10, 1883 matters came to a head when a Portuguese watchman on board a Portuguese ship, the *Hankow*, killed a Chinese by kicking him and then throwing him in the water. A mob first burnt down the wharf where the Hankow was docked. The *Hankow* withdrew to the safety of the river. The mob of up to 1,000 Chinese then attacked the foreign settlement in Shameen Island at 8 o'clock in the morning looting all that could be carried away and burning down foreigners' offices and houses. The telegraph cables to Hong Kong had been cut so no gunboats could be called. Women and children were evacuated to two merchant boats the *Ningpo* and the *Hankow* that were moored off Shameen. The foreign men armed themselves to fight off the mob. A small force of Chinese troops arrived at 11 o'clock in the morning but was too small to restore order. At about 1 o'clock in the afternoon a battalion of Chinese troops arrived "with the ling ki or warrant flag, which, after being held up in presence of the mob, authorizes the military to fire upon any rioters who refuse to disperse." According to the *North China Herald*'s correspondent, the blowing of the mandarin's horn

The docks in Shameen in 1883

acted like magic, and they fled in all directions helter skelter." After the mob left, a "sad scene was presented at Shameen" with 13 houses burned down and four others looted. The newlybuilt icehouse and the Concordia Club were also destroyed. The US consul estimated that total losses were in the order of $200,000 of which only $10,000 was the property of US citizens. The main losses were to British properties.

After this, foreigners would be molested on the streets and whenever a foreigner passed the words "Fan-Kwei" ("barbaric ghost") would be shouted at them. The Viceroy issued a reward of $50 for the apprehension of anyone inciting violence against foreigners. The British Minister, Sir Harry Parkes, sent the Viceroy a telegram stating that the lives and properties of British subjects were in the Viceroy's hands and that "if any more riotous attacks take place, the consequences will be most disastrous for China." This prompted the Viceroy to arrest upwards of one hundred rioters who were dealt with in a "summary way." He subsequently issued a proclamation that anyone who so much as assaulted a foreigner would be decapitated. Gunboats were stationed in the river and a code of signals was arranged between the British Consulate and the gunboats in case of attack with landing parties at the ready to land within five minutes of the first alarm.

A month later, Logan was put on trial for murder of the boy he had shot. Originally Logan had not instructed a lawyer to defend him. It appeared that he thought the customs service would provide him with counsel, but as the killing had nothing to do with Logan's official duties, Customs had not done so. After a two week adjournment, Logan had instructed Mr A.G. Wise, a barrister from Hong Kong who later became a judge of the Hong Kong Supreme Court, to represent him.

J.J. Francis (who had prosecuted the Edward Page case) from Hong Kong was instructed to watch the case on behalf of the Viceroy. Taotai Pang, representing the Viceroy, sat on the bench to the left of Rennie.

Wilkinson called numerous Chinese and foreign witnesses to the events that had occurred to show essentially that the boy had died; that Logan had fired a gun; and that no one else had fired a gun. Wise, in defence, emphasized that all the events that had occurred after the shooting should be put out of the jury's mind. They should only consider the evidence before the court. He said that the jury had to be certain that Logan fired the shot to convict him.

Logan was acquitted by the jury of murder but convicted of manslaughter. Rennie though it was murder: in sentencing commented that Logan "might congratulate himself he had not been convicted of the higher crime of murder." Given that there appeared to be no self-defence involved, Rennie sentenced him to a relatively long term of seven years imprisonment. Because there was no long-term accommodation for prisoners in Canton, Logan was sent to Hong Kong, where he had previously been a policeman, for imprisonment. The fact that he was found guilty satisfied the locals briefly, until they discovered that the penalty was not death but imprisonment. The Viceroy formally protested the verdict and requested a new trial. He also intimated that he could not be responsible for any outbreak that occurred due to the result of the case. He, however, did issue a proclamation asking for calm because he had protested the verdict and asked for a new trial.

The British took the Chinese complaints seriously. Julian Pauncefote, the former Attorney General of Hong Kong and now Permanent Under-Secretary of the Foreign Office reviewed the file personally. He thought the sentence was far too lenient and that Logan should have been sentenced to at least 20 years in prison, a view that the Law Officers in London concurred with.

Long discussions subsequently went on between the foreign powers and Tsungli Yamen as to how to settle the claims for damages from the riot. Originally, it was proposed that the issue be resolved by a panel of arbitrators. Discussions went quite a way forward with John Russell Young the American Minister leading the discussions on behalf of the British, Americans, French and Germans. But the Chinese side through Prince Kung then insisted:

"it having originated in murder, an investigation into the circumstances of the riot should be the objective point. These circumstances being correct, the guilty parties could be punished according to their desserts."

Prince Kung, with whom it may be recalled Hornby had discussed due process and the separation of powers, was effectively demanding that Logan be re-tried and then executed. It seems that, perhaps, the prince had not been listening as attentively to Hornby as Hornby imagined.

Young told the Chinese that the Logan case could not be reopened. Logan "had been tried by an English judge, before an English jury, according to English law, and there was no power, not even the power of the Queen which could put him in peril of his life a second time." Young said that the same law applied in the United States and "other civilized nations" and it was not appropriate to mix up the question of the losses suffered by foreigners and whether Logan had received his "just desserts." The Chinese would not budge. In a meeting with Young they said that because a British subject, Logan, had caused the riot by killing an innocent Chinese, it was the British who were responsible and they should pay the damages claimed by the foreigners, pointing out that China had paid an indemnity when British interpreter Augustus Margary had been killed in Yunnan.

Ultimately, the British and Chinese agreed to establish a joint Commission to decide on British claims arising out of the riots to sit in Canton. Crown Advocate H.S. Wilkinson was appointed to sit as the British Commissioner and Mr Kung Fan-tai was appointed to sit as the Chinese Commissioner. The Commission commenced hearings in August 1884. This was a time of great tension in Canton because the French and the Chinese were coming very close to war over rights in Tonkin, Vietnam. The Chinese claimed suzerainty over Vietnam; the French rejected this. One correspondent for the *North China Herald* reported on the situation in early August 1884 saying that the town had been "placarded all over with inflammatory appeals to the Chinese to rise and kill all the 'foreign devils.'" Gatling guns had been brought on shore to defend the British and French settlements and all foreign Customs employees were ordered to leave Honam.

Into this cauldron of hatred and fear sailed Wilkinson to sit with Mr Kung to decide the claims from the previous year. The British Consul and Vice-Consul in Canton, Dr H.F. Hance and Robert Mansfield as well as Sit Min Kook the former magistrate of the Namhoi District also sat on the bench. The Chinese government instructed Victor Deacon, as solicitor from Hong Kong, to represent them. The firm of Deacons in Hong Kong, which still exists to this day, is named after Victor and his nephew. Some of the claimants represented themselves whilst others were represented by counsel. From the reports of the cases, it appears that the claims work went relatively smoothly. The procedure was semi-judicial and semi-"market bargaining." The British claimants would make the claims detailing items lost and their value. Deacon then cross-examined the claimants as to their value. An offer of compensation would then be made by the commissioners. The claimants were free to reject this and to make a counter-offer. In one case, involving a Dr Wales who had lost his entire house and contents, including his 200-volume medical library, his total claim came to approximately $15,000. After cross-examination, Deacon put the value of the claim at about $10,000. Following an adjournment, Dr Wales' counsel said that he had been instructed to accept $12,000 but may be able to meet the commissioners half way. This resulted in a "somewhat lengthy private discussion between the commissioners and other occupants of the bench" which resulted in the offer being raised to $11,000, which was accepted. Other claims proceeded in a like manner.

One claim for damages to the ship the Ningpo, by its owners was rejected. Wilkinson told the owner's counsel, Mr Schroeder, that if the Ningpo had left immediately it would have left with no cargo. It would not have been able to claim compensation for leaving without cargo. As it was, after calm had been restored it had taken on cargo and, therefore, the claim ought not to be met. The other claim the Ningpo had was for $120 for provisions they had used to feed the people of Shameen. Wilkinson said "he was sure that neither the owners of the ship nor any persons concerned would wish him to ask the Chinese Government to pay $120 for feeding the Shameen community." In fact, Mr Schroeder did want to ask for this but Wilkinson cut him off when he started speaking.

This brought the claims process to a close after only two days of hearings mainly, it seems, due to the close cooperation between the Chinese and British commissioners. One suspects that Wilkinson had a strong desire to be cooperative so that he could get in and out of Canton as quickly as possible without his work triggering further riots.

The French and Chinese did go to war soon after this, with the French attacking Foochow and Zhenhai Bay, occupying Keelung in Taiwan and blockading Taiwan. The Chinese agreed in April 1885, in another unequal treaty, to abandon their claim to suzerainty over Vietnam and withdraw troops they had sent there.

Enlarging jurisdiction

In 1884 a new Order in Council expanded the jurisdiction of British courts in Asia in three important ways. First, the Order in Council was extended to Korea after Korea had signed treaties allowing for extraterritoriality there. Second, the definition of British subject was extended to include "a British protected person" and third, jurisdiction in admiralty was extended to any act committed on board a British ship anywhere in the world, and not just within 100 miles of the coast of China, Japan or Korea.

The second change was, as we shall see later, to have far-reaching effects on the rights of individuals from British protectorates or foreigners enrolled in the British army. More immediately, however, it provided a solution to the question of who had jurisdiction over British sailors on American ships and American sailors on British ships that had arisen in the *Ross* case. The issue was resolved in a case that Wilkinson prosecuted before Rennie. relating to an affray that had occurred on the *Lennie Burrill*, a British ship based out of Yarmouth, Nova Scotia.

One of the seamen charged, George Lee, was an American. Lee pleaded not guilty so that he could challenge the jurisdiction of the court to try him. Chief Justice Rennie disposed of the argument quickly. He said that while before the new order had been enacted there was an argument as to the jurisdiction of the British Courts in China and Japan over seaman on British ships, "he was clearly of opinion that under the new Order, the prisoner came within the jurisdiction of the Court." He noted that a representative of the United States Consul-General was in court and that correspondence had been sent to the American Consulate about the case. The American Consul-General had responded, stating, "they could not interfere in the case, in which the Court had proper jurisdiction." Rennie concluded that he was certain the British Supreme Court had jurisdiction. Lee then changed his plea to one of guilty to unlawful wounding and was sentenced by Rennie to 12 months hard labour.

The Captain did not go down with his ship

In Japan, another shipping case in 1886 became the *cause celebre* for the end of extraterritoriality. The case is still mentioned to this day in Japanese writings on extraterritoriality as one of the prime example of the evils of the system. On October 23, 1886, the *Normanton*, a British ship, set sail from Yokohama bound for Kobe. She had on board a British crew of 47 and 23 Japanese passengers. Somewhere off Ooshima the boat struck a pinnacle rock and started to take in water. The crew tried to convince the Japanese passengers to abandon ship but they refused. The captain and the crew took to the life rafts leaving a boatswain with the Japanese passengers to try to convince them to get into the remaining life rafts. They continued to refuse and the boatswain jumped off the ship just as it sank. All 23 Japanese passengers together with one British sailor and 12 British firemen died in the disaster.

A Naval Board of Enquiry to investigate into the causes of the disaster headed by the British Consul in Kobe and two mariners was formed. In what the *North China Herald*, normally a supporter of the British courts, was to later term a "farce", a "miscarriage of justice" and a "complete whitewash" the captain, John William Drake, was cleared of all responsibility. This was met with shocked disbelief by the Japanese public and the Japanese government and there were many public protests against the decision.

The Japanese government determined to seek to make Drake criminally liable for the deaths. John Lowder, a former consular officer now practicing as a barrister in Japan, was instructed by the Japanese government to bring a criminal prosecution against Captain Drake for manslaughter in the British Court for Japan.

The criminal trial commenced on December 7, 1886 before Hannen and a jury of five and lasted for five days. Various witnesses gave evidence as to what occurred including the Chief Officer and boatswain. Hannen in his instructions to the jury first dealt with a suggestion by Drake's defence counsel that the Captain could not be found to be negligent if the Japanese passengers had been contributorily negligent in failing to get into the lifeboats. He said clearly this was not the law of England. The captain had the authority to and should have forced the Japanese into the lifeboats if necessary. Drake had also failed to arrange boat stations and drills and had given contradictory orders. The jury was left to answer the question as to whether this was negligent so that the death of the passengers could be considered manslaughter.

The jury retired for an hour and a half and returned with a verdict of guilty. The foreman, however, added:

"But the Jury desire to record their sense of

French artist Bigot shows Capt Drake demanding money from Japanese passengers

the difficulties of the position in which the captain was
placed, aggravated by the fact of the engineers having
left the ship in the port life-boat, thereby diminishing
the means of saving life at his command, and also by
the unwillingness, if not actual resistance, offered by
the Japanese passengers to the efforts made to get them
out of the alley-way towards the boats."

Following the verdict Hannen turned to Drake to sentence
him saying: "that it can not but be a matter of deep regret, not
only to us all, but also no doubt, to you now, that you did not
take such steps as would have been more effectual towards
the saving of life." He added in a true British dressing down:

"We have been accustomed to expect from the
merchant service of England heroism and devotion to
the interests of the crew and passengers that I am afraid
in this case were wanting."

He then passed sentence saying it was his "painful duty"
to order Drake to serve three months imprisonment.

The relatives of the dead had also brought a civil case
against Drake, which they withdrew after the conviction on
the basis he had suffered enough. Drake in a letter from his
counsel expressed his deep sympathy for the loss of life.

The case nevertheless continued to be used by Japanese
to agitate for an end to extraterritoriality, a goal that was
achieved in the 1890s.

CHAPTER 11

The Amalgamation

THE 1890s SAW the continued rise of Japan with agreements reached with all the powers for the end of extraterritoriality there. Japan also defeated China in a war weakening the Chinese government even more and increasing further the rights of foreigners.

Nicholas Hannen continued his own personal rise. Richard Rennie had retired as Chief Justice in Shanghai in April 1891. Hannen returned from Yokohama to Shanghai as Chief Justice of the Supreme Court. Robert Mowat replaced him as Judge for Japan in Yokohama.

Hannen was made an offer he could not refuse. In addition to making him Chief Justice, he was appointed Consul-General in Shanghai. Any man would find it hard to turn down the second and third most important Foreign Office appointments in China, behind only the Minister in Peking. Hannen, despite misgivings he later expressed, accepted. George Jamieson, who by now had close to three years experience as an acting judge, was appointed to the amalgamated position of Judge and Consul in Shanghai. Hannen could not speak Chinese, so it was essential to have a Chinese speaker who could deal with local Chinese officials as his consular deputy.

The appointments of Hannen as Chief Justice and Jamieson as Judge were welcomed. On the other hand, the amalgamation of their judicial and consular positions was bitterly opposed. The amalgamation was put into place by Sir

Nicholas Hannen, the new Chief Justice and Consul-General
George Jamieson, the new Judge and Consul

Philip Currie, the new Under-Secretary for Foreign Affairs, who had replaced Sir Julian Pauncefote. Currie had originally proposed that the position of Chief Justice and Consul be combined in 1877. As we have seen, Pauncefote soundly rejected this in a long memorandum. But with Pauncefote gone, Currie was able to push through the amalgamation of the positions as a cost saving measure. Currie was very happy with the result and regretted that money had been wasted for many years by paying salaries for two positions. He had short shrift for the idea of the British Courts in China and Japan being an example to the Chinese and Japanese of the Rule of Law. What was needed, he said, was "to promote British trade and administer consular jurisdiction, not set up caricatures of British courts of law."

The amalgamation of the consular and judicial posts faced fierce criticism from the local British community. It was argued that the two posts were too important to be held by one person. The Chief Justice was required to travel on circuit to try important cases. If the position was held by one person the Consul-General would be absent for long periods. In addition, a judge should not play an active role in the community whereas the Consul-General should be encouraged to. Further, the Consul-General needed to deal with Chinese authorities on diplomatic issues and served as a referee for the Municipal Council when grievances were brought to him. It would be difficult to have the same person serving as Chief Justice and be seen as delivering impartial justice.

On March 10, 1891 a "largely attended and influential meeting of British residents" was held at the Shanghai Club to protest the changes. A petition to the Foreign Office was circulated and agreed to at the meeting that made the above points, but also emphasized the difficulties merchants faced dealing with conflicting jurisdictions:

> "Our position here is an exceptional one. We have
> a local Municipal Government constituted under
> the Land Regulations for the Foreign Settlements
> … while we live and have our warehouses on land
> held under the Chinese Government and our ships
> and merchandise in transit are subject to Customs
> regulations made by the Chinese Government, and
> which it claims to be enforceable by its Officials, while
> we are governed by British Law."

The petition stated further that in these circumstances, British subjects would have to frequently resort to Chinese courts and would often need the intervention of an independent Consul-General with long experience dealing with Chinese officials. The Chief Justice and Judge were required to have long experience as practising lawyers meaning they would not have this experience.

Nevertheless, the amalgamation proposal was a fait accompli having already been approved. The *North China Herald* laid the blame for this directly on the Sir John Walsham, the British Minister to China. Currie had sent the amalgamation proposal to Sir John. He did not respond for one month, so the Foreign Office took it that the proposal was acceptable.

How the two positions of Consul-General, protecting British interests, and Chief Justice, administering impartial justice could be reconciled boggles the mind. Julian Pauncefote's memo in 1877 had made clear the many reasons why it was not appropriate. Perhaps more importantly, the Consul General could be actively involved in the use of British force to maintain the British presence in China. Mowat, before leaving for Japan, acted as Chief Justice and Consul-General from April to October 1891. During this time he had to deal with anti-missionary riots that broke out in the Yangtze Valley. On 13 May 1891 Mowat received a telegram, which he passed on to the Vice Admiral of the Navy:

"Riot Wuhu, catholic premises being destroyed; send gun-boat immediately"

Back in Shanghai, during the riots, the Municipal Council, after consultation with the Consular Body, of which Mowat, as Acting British Consul-General, was one of the most important members, issued a notice in Chinese and English to the effect that if riots broke out, a warning bell would be rung, the volunteers would disperse the riot by force.

The warning had the desired effect and no riots broke out in Shanghai. However, if riots had broken out and the legality of the warning had to be considered by the court, Mowat would have been severely compromised. Indeed, one missionary, George Cockburn, whose Church of Scotland Mission in Ichang had been destroyed, wrote in a letter to The Glasgow Herald that he had seen "Judge Mowat in Shanghai who is also acting for the Consul-General," to discuss his claim for compensation. Mowat told him to make a claim in full. This is not the sort of position a judge should be in, particularly if he later has to decide on the claim.

Changing the subject, Cockburn finished his letter with the teaser: "Great revelations are expected on Monday at the Mason trial. Mason is the Customs' clerk caught smuggling arms and dynamite."

Mason – A terrorist in service of Chinese Customs?

There were indeed great revelations. Charles Mason, a midlevel employee of the Chinese Customs in Chinkiang (Zhenjiang) on the Yangtze River, was accused of six counts of possessing dynamite. The Chinese government believed that Mason was a member of a secret triad society, the Kolao Hwei (the Society of Brothers and Elders), which was engaged in active rebellion to overthrow the Qing Dynasty. The rebellion had many thought triggered the 1891 anti-missionary riots. Mason had arranged to smuggle dynamite and other weapons from Hong Kong. The Chinese Government pushed the British Government very hard to prosecute him.

The case, which illustrated the difficult position the holder of the amalgamated position of Chief Justice and Consul-General could face, commenced in the Supreme Court in September 1891. In the lead-up to the case, the British Minister in Peking telegrammed Mowat, as Acting Consul-General, directing the institution of proceedings "through the Crown Advocate against Mason, and recommending the charge should be laid under the Explosives Act if Mr Mowat thought that act applicable, and otherwise under Article 81" of the then current Order in Council.

Mowat, as Acting Consul-General, was deeply involved in bringing the case to trial before the Supreme Court. However, at this time Mowat was also Acting Chief Justice. The effect of this was that the Chief Justice of the Court was being instructed to bring a case to trial and to decide under which legal provisions he should do so. This was clearly inappropriate and would have been even more so if Mowat had tried the case. The court would certainly have been a "caricature" of a British court, to use Philip Currie's words. Luckily, Hannen had by the time the trial commenced arrived in Shanghai from Japan.

Mason's trial was Hannen's very first hearing as Chief Justice. The Judge (and Consul), George Jamieson, accompanied him on the bench. Before the proceedings began, H.S. Wilkinson, the Crown Advocate, offered a welcome to his old friend saying he had the "very pleasant duty to bid your Lordship in the name of the Bar a most cordial welcome to Shanghai." Making a reference to Hannen's previous time on the bench and the amalgamation, Wilkinson added "Since that time changes have taken place, the expediency of which this is neither the time nor the place to discuss; but we as members of the Bar are satisfied that we shall see in you a Chief Justice of whom we may feel that the noble traditions of the Bar are safe in your hands."

The Taotai and Liu Ta-Jen the Director of the Kiangnan Arsenal were observing the case from the bench, while Mr Yu, a deputy of the Viceroy, sat at a table below the bench. What they made of this Wilkinson's coded pleasantry, one will never know. What they will have seen was that the British Consul-General was sitting as the British Chief Justice and they cannot but have wondered about British representations as to the importance of the separation of powers.

A jury was empanelled and Mason was asked to plea. He pleaded guilty. After doing so, Mason read a statement giving an almost unbelievable explanation that the conspiracy was an invention of his and that he ultimately intended to report to both the Customs service and the British Government. Wilkinson was asked to comment on what sort of sentence should be imposed. Wilkinson said he would be very happy to leave the matter in Hannen's hands.

Hannen, noting "that confinement here in China is a much more serious punishment than it would be at home," and that this matter meant the "loss of your position and the entire ruin of your career here in China," then sentenced Mason to nine months imprisonment and to deportation upon release unless he could obtain two sureties.

This light sentence drew a vehement protest from Minister Sieh Tajien of the Chinese Legation in London directly to the British Foreign Minister, the Marquis of Salisbury. Sieh expressed the "surprise and disappointment" at the light sentence and entered a "formal and emphatic protest ... on the grounds of it being incommensurate with to the gravity of the offence." Sieh went on to make the specific point that the British extraterritorial courts were administering justice in China against British subjects on behalf of the Chinese government:

"It is the opinion of my Government, neither the Judge nor the Crown Advocate seemed to realize either the importance of the case, or to feel the responsibility imposed on them by the vicarious function devolving on the Crown, in virtue of British subjects being the objects of extra-territorial jurisdiction."

Sieh said that the evidence showed that Mason was an avowed member of the Kolao Hwei and that he recruited another 19 Europeans with plans to import weapons and dynamite to fight the Chinese government. Sieh complained that the Crown Advocate had been wrong to frame a charge as only one of possessing dynamite and that Hannen had been wrong in passing such a lenient sentence, stating in particular that "there was nothing in [the case] which called for a mitigation of the punishment: a traitor to the trust reposed in him." Sieh called the case a miscarriage of justice and requested that after Mason had finished his sentence in Shanghai he be sent to Hong Kong for trial on a more serious charge.

Wilkinson was asked to prepare a report on the case. He wrote a long 18-page document setting out the full background to the case explaining why, given the lack of evidence, he had only preferred charges under the Explosives Act. He said that the Taotai had been very satisfied with the case and had wanted to give Wilkinson some Chinese scrolls in recognition of his good work.

Before the Marquis of Salisbury could reply to Minister Sieh based on Wilkinson's report, on May 14, 1892, Sieh wrote back a long letter in reply to the Marquis' first letter. This made a number of substantive comments on English law and was most likely drafted by, or on instructions of, a British employee of the Chinese Customs Service. The letter criticized the lightness of the sentence against Mason by comparing it to a sentence given to Chinese in England and pointing out that on that very date the letter was being sent, a "Chinaman will be liberated from Wandsworth Prison after having undergone an imprisonment of three months, with hard labor, for smuggling – an offence which was only one, and that the lightest, of the various offences of which it was held Mason was guilty."

The Foreign Secretary, the Marquis of Salisbury, replied to Sieh on July 2, 1892, setting out Wilkinson's report in detail. Then with regard to Hannen's position as Chief Justice, hypocritically, given Mowat's earlier role in the case, he wrote:

"As regards the sentence inflicted by the Chief Justice, I may observe that it is not in accordance with Constitutional practice in this country that a judicial officer should be called upon to render an account to the Executive Government of his action in his judicial capacity it being the essence of his office that it should be discharged with complete freedom from administrative interference."

Sieh responded on August 2, 1892 in another long letter challenging Salisbury's interpretations of the law. At the end, he made a clear demand for reciprocity of treatment:

"I much regret the theory that Mason's actions were the 'outcome of a crazy imagination' should have been allowed to figure so largely in the case. It was started immediately after his arrest before the trial, and seems afterwards to have been accepted without sufficient examination. I regret it, because 'crazy imaginations' are so common, or can be so easily feigned that at some future time Mason may have his imitators; a thing that would greatly add to the difficulties of the Imperial Government. For I am afraid that, should at any time hereafter, it be sought to extenuate the burning down of a Mission station, or the perpetration of any other outrages such as those which took place in China last year, the plea that they were the outcome of a 'crazy imagination' would have little chance of being accepted, and if advances, would be little calculated to promote the harmony of our international relations."

Sieh put the matter to a close by saying even though Wilkinson had "positive proof" to do so in his hands it appeared Mason could not be tried for other offences. He concluded by expressing the "hope of the Imperial Government that it may be long before the good feeling which happily exists between the two Governments shall be troubled with such an unsatisfactory case again."

Gunboat *Redpole* to the rescue

Not long after the Mason case, the trial of another customs officer meant that HS Wilkinson's son, Harrie Wilkinson, and George Jamieson required the services of a British gunboat to protect them from threatened mob retribution if the officer was not convicted of murder. Compared to Hornby's problems in Chefoo, better communications made it much easier to get a gunboat to port, warning the mob off before it formed.

A customs tide-waiter, Robert Jackson, had gone out shooting early in the morning and had, as Harrie Wilkinson, described it "a difference of opinion with a Chinese ferryman." Jackson's gun was loaded and "it went off, and the Chinaman was killed."18 Evidence from two doctors, including a Dr Lyall, was that ferryman had been shot in the back. Jackson also told Dr Lyall that, "his foot slipped as he was entering or leaving the boat, he fell forward and his gun went off, the charge hitting the deceased."

Jamieson went on circuit to try the case with a jury. Harrie Wilkinson, who had come out to China in 1890 to practice was assisting his father in his work as Crown Advocate, went with Jamieson as the prosecutor. An important Chinese official attended the trial on behalf of the Viceroy and during the first day's hearing asked to speak to the judge. He was told that it was better that he spoke to the prosecutor, Wilkinson and the Consul at Swatow, William Henry Wilkinson (no relation). The Chinese official told the Wilkinsons that as a Chinese had been killed, if the Defendant was not found guilty, the official "could not restrain the populace from wiping out the British Officials concerned." W.H. Wilkinson told the Mandarin that Jackson's guilt or innocence was a matter for the jury to decide, and refused to pass the message on to Jamieson.

W.H. Wilkinson, did, however, immediately cable Hong Kong for a gunboat to be sent. He also told the Mandarin that if what he said would come to pass did, in fact, come to pass, it would be "very inconvenient" for the Mandarin as a gunboat was expected. Harrie Wilkinson recalled much later that the accused was "found not guilty of murder, the gunboat arrived and the incident blew over."

Jackson was, in fact, found guilty of manslaughter and sentenced to six months imprisonment, a sentence that according to the *Hong Kong Daily News* was "considered light" and "caused great dissatisfaction among the natives" and "as a precautionary measure against a possible outbreak of feeling against foreigners HMS *Redpole*, in response to a request by Mr Wilkinson, Consul at Swatow, for a gunboat to held in readiness, was despatched yesterday morning." The *Daily News* felt sure that "upon the arrival of the Redpole, the popular feeling, if it has not quite abated by this time, will doubtless subside."

The sinking of the *Chishima*

In Japan, popular feeling has also been excited by a major case before the British Courts. However, unlike China, no gunboats were needed to quell the anger. Instead Japan focused on seeking abolition of extraterritoriality.

On 30 November 1892, the *Chishima Kan*, a Japanese war ship, and P&O steamship the *Ravenna* collided in the Inland Sea of Japan in the Gogoshima straits between the islands of Musuki and Gogo, less than three miles offshore from the island of Shikoku. The Japanese Government in the name of the Emperor or Japan sued P&O for damages. P&O sought to counterclaim against the Japanese Government in the British Court for Japan for damages to the *Ravenna*. Mowat said the issue to be resolved was whether the point of the collision was in Japanese waters or in international waters. If the ship was in Japanese waters, the Court for Japan, as an extraterritorial court, did not have jurisdiction to allow a counterclaim unless the Emperor consented. If the collision was in international waters, the Court for Japan was sitting as a British Admiralty Court and had jurisdiction to allow a counterclaim. Mowat held that the collision was in Japanese waters as it occurred within three miles of the Japanese shore. Therefore, the counterclaim was not allowed.

P&O appealed to Shanghai. Hannen and Jamieson agreed with Mowat that the issue to be decided was whether the ship was in international waters but disagreed with Mowat as to whether it had been. They held that locations within three miles of shore could be international waters when they were used for international shipping. Hannen went further and held that the waters were part of the "highway of nations." Both Hannen and Jamieson held that the court, sitting in admiralty, had jurisdiction to allow a counterclaim to be made against the Japanese Government.

The Japanese government could not accept this and sought leave to appeal to the Privy Council, which was granted. Reflecting the importance of the case, the appeal was heard by seven law lords; two Queen's Counsel appeared for each side and both the Attorney-General and Solicitor-General held watching briefs. The Privy Council stated in the first paragraph of their decision that the appeal "raised a question of considerable importance in regard to jurisdiction possessed by British Consular Courts in China and Japan." The Privy Council reversed the judgment of Hannen and Jamieson and restored Mowat's decision, ruling that on a proper reading of the treaties that granted extraterritorial rights, the Court for Japan (and the Supreme Court for China and Japan) did not have jurisdiction to allow counterclaims in any actions, including admiralty actions.

They rejected an argument that had been made that by choosing to sue in a British court, Japanese nationals had to take the consequences of that election on the simple ground that there was really no election. The treaty required a Japanese national to sue British subjects in the British Court for Japan. He "has no choice," but to do so. It was therefore a violation of the treaty and an excess of jurisdiction to allow a counterclaim. Perhaps more importantly, the Privy Council added that if British courts allowed a counterclaim against Japanese or Chinese subjects in British courts, the Japanese or Chinese courts would be able to allow a counterclaim when a British subject sued in those courts, destroying the whole foundation of extraterritoriality.

Following the Privy Council decision, the Japanese Government's claim against P&O was re-listed for hearing in the Court for Japan in October 1895 more than two years after it had been filed. The Eastern World noted sardonically, "when it is ended the lawyers in the case will probably own the Japanese navy and the P&O Company." Perhaps for this reason, P&O decided soon after to settle the case by paying the Japanese government GBP10,000.

Movements and changes

Soon after the Supreme Court decision in the *Chishima* case, Mowat went on long leave. Wilkinson, who had previously discussed the possibility with Mowat, was appointed acting Judge in Japan. W. Venn Drummond, the senior member of the bar in Shanghai, was appointed Acting Crown Advocate in

W. Venn Drummond, pro-Chinese lawyer who was briefly appointed Acting Crown Advocate

Wilkinson's absence. Drummond regularly represented the Chinese government and other Chinese bodies in the court and on other matters including acting for the Chinese government in a dispute with Japan over Chinese extraterritorial rights in Nagasaki. He was perceived in the British community, for this reason, as being pro-Chinese. Drummond's appointment was, therefore, strongly opposed by the China Association – a newly formed merchants' association representing the interests of British businesses in China and Japan - on the basis that his appointment would "prejudice the interests of British subjects in China." Hannen, as Consul-General, was asked to pass on a telegram to the British Minister opposing the appointment. Hannen did so. In a clear slight to

Drummond, Hannen's letter to the Minister was published in the *North China Herald*. Nevertheless, Drummond was appointed Acting Crown Advocate in February 1894. Due to continued opposition, he resigned eight months later. HP Wilkinson's son, Harrie Wilkinson at the tender age of 28 was appointed Acting Crown Advocate for the rest of his father's absence.

OUR LEADING LAWYERS
No. I.—Mr. H. P. Wilkinson, Crown Advocate

Harrie Wilkinson succeeds his father as Crown Advocate

HS Wilkinson returned to Shanghai as Crown Advocate in 1895. At the beginning of 1897 he was back in Japan to prosecute, before Mowat and a jury, the beautiful Edith Carew for the murder of her philandering husband in Yokohama. The case had been extremely high profile and was reported in newspapers around the world. After a long trial, Carew was convicted. The exhaustion of the trial broke Mowat who retired due to ill health soon after this. HS Wilkinson was appointed to replace him in Japan and Harrie Wilkinson replaced his father as Crown Advocate in Shanghai.

A little later to very little fanfare, the amalgamation of the consular and judicial positions was ended with Nicholas remaining as Chief Justice and George Jamieson becoming Consul-General. Jamieson retired the following year but remained in China acting for a number of commercial interests.

The Extraterritorial boot on the other foot
In his last major involvement as Consul-General Hannen had to handle one case which almost certainly he would have been very happy to pass on to a consular official. This was a

claim made by a British company Bennertz & Co against the Kiangnan Pay and Defence Department (PDD) in relation to four ships that it had hired from the PDD. Bennertz claimed that the PDD had agreed to pay for repairs on the ships that Bennertz had carried out. The PDD alleged that Bennertz had become insolvent and had not paid its charterparty fees. The PDD arranged for the ships to be stopped by Chinese Customs officials and in the case of one ship applied to the Hong Kong Supreme Court for it to be arrested. This led to additional claims by both parties. Bennertz claimed for lost profits because the ships had been seized. The PDD claimed for losses because it could not use the ships and had to hire other ships.

The case was the subject of intense diplomatic negotiations. At one point the Chinese side offered to have the case arbitrated by two foreign arbitrators. Bennertz rejected this proposal, stating that he would only accept it if the Chinese first admitted they had breached the contracts and that the arbitrators should only decide how much damages should be paid.

The Chinese did not agree to this. In the end a special *ad hoc* court was established to hear the case. Tsai Chun, the President of the Bureau of Foreign Affairs at Nanking was appointed as judge by Imperial High Commissioner Liu of the Nanyang Administration and Viceroy of the Liang Kiang provinces. Pursuant to the Chefoo Convention Nicholas Hannen attended "merely ... to watch the proceedings in the interests of justice." Hannen, who by this time had sat as a judge for almost 20 years, clearly chafed at being a mere observer. At the trial, Mr Tsai sat on a raised dais with his interpreter, Mr Fung Yee, to the left. Hannen also sat on the dais to Mr Tsai's right with his interpreter, Mr James Scott, the British Assessor at the Mixed Court, on his right.

Harrie Wilkinson, together with Mr E. Nelson of the law firm Johnson Stokes and Master, appeared for Bennertz. Venn

Drummond appeared for the Defendants.

The first day of the hearings was in early summer starting on 30 June 1897. The Court was held in an improvised court in a building known as the Ambassadors' Hall adjoining the Temple of Heaven in Shanghai. All of the arguments and submissions were made in English with the proceedings being interpreted into Chinese by the interpreters. The proceedings effectively took place in the open air, as most of the court was open to the sky. This was described as "a most satisfactory arrangement under the circumstances of the weather." Towards the latter part of the proceedings, tea and cigarettes were passed around.

On the first day of the hearing, Wilkinson was not able to attend, so Nelson opened the case for Bennertz. The PDD had filed a counterclaim against Bennertz. Nelson immediately raised an objection to the counterclaim on the basis that a claim against a British subject should be brought in the British Court. Drummond responded that while under the decision in the *Chishima* case this may be correct in a British court, "that decision had no binding effect upon a Chinese Court, as that now sitting was. He thought it was within the power of the Court to take all such circumstances into consideration on both sides and give judgment."

Tsai retired to consider the matter and then without making a ruling told Nelson to proceed with his case. Nelson then read out the Plaintiff's claim and the Defendant's defence and counterclaim.

While the proceedings may have started in beautiful weather, they were to go on for six weeks, dragging into midsummer. At some point they were moved to the Canton Guild Hall. Drummond was well-known for taking his time on cases. He was ably assisted by the fact that as an ad hoc court there were no rules of procedure and by the fact that Tsai was more than willing to allow the case to run on and on. Numerous witnesses were called on each side, with

Drummond, in particular, taking his time over questioning them.

This lead to fireworks in the first week of August, the peak of Shanghai's unpleasantly hot summer. Drummond was cross-examining a Mr Pollack concerning the accounts of Bennertz and Co. Pollack said that he "could not speak accurately upon the accounts as he was not familiar with the details."

Hannen asked Drummond if it was not a waste of time to ask questions about the accounts if the witness did not know about them. Hannen made clear what he thought, saying that if it were his court he would consider it a waste of time.

Drummond responded that he was entitled to ask any question he liked.

Hannen had had enough and the following testy exchange occurred:

Hannen: I say it is a waste of time, and I think that the length to which this enquiry has gone is a scandal. However, if the Court chooses not to take any notice of it I cannot do any more, but I would point out that in my own Court I should regard this as a waste of time. If this Court chooses to go on hearing questions which the witness cannot answer, then all I can say is I have done my best.

Drummond: I should like to know what particular matter you refer to when you speak of this being a scandal. Hannen: This case has been going on from the 30th of June; and I say the mere length of it is a scandal.

Drummond: That is a very strong statement and a very general one to make. I should like to know whose fault it is.

Hannen: I did not direct it at anybody.

Drummond was not willing to back down and after some further discussion lay the blame for much of the delay on Hannen, saying: "All the difficulty in this I think has arisen from your own action in the matter. A good deal of time has been wasted on discussion arising out of points raised by you." Drummond then added that the case raised very intricate issues, to which Hannen responded that those issues had not even been broached.

Things then got even hotter than the weather when Drummond accused Hannen of bias:

Drummond: Well, that is your opinion, but my opinion is they have been broached to a very great extent. I am quite aware that your opinion is entirely different. I have known that from the beginning; and before the case began.

Hannen: That has nothing whatever to do with it; if you have it in any of my dispatches you have a right to say so.

Mr. Drummond: I have it from your dispatches and your own language.

Hannen: Anything that can be discovered from my own dispatches you have a right to mention. I am not aware I have ever expressed an opinion.

Drummond: I am distinctly of the opinion that you have so committed yourself to the support of Mr. Bennertz' case long ago that it would be impossible to take this case into the English Court. That is a simple question.

Hannen then sought to dampen down the flames by bringing the question back to whether the witness should be questioned further on the accounts.

The case ran for another three weeks, eventually finishing on August 29. Tsai said that his decision would be announced in open court after notice was given to the parties.

Two weeks later, on September 11, 1897, Tsai issued his decision to the newspapers without a hearing. He repeated in the decision the various arguments that had been made and then found for the Chinese Defendants, dismissing Bennertz's claim in its entirety. He said that the evidence was that Bennertz and Co were in financial difficulties and the PDD had been right to have the ships seized. He added a, perhaps justified, flourish of nationalism:

"The power of detaining the said steamers, according
to my opinion, rested solely on the fact that they
were flying the Chinese flag, hence the steamers were
amenable to the Chinese law. Moreover, China is an
independent country and the Chinese authorities had
a perfect right to detain their own ships. Hence, the
claims of the plaintiffs are ordered by me to be refused.
I find that the plaintiffs are wholly in the wrong, and
that they unreasonably detained the said vessels for a
whole twelve months."

He said that the Plaintiffs should compensate the
Defendants but "as the latter have not given any evidence of
the amount they have lost, nor have they pressed the Court to
make an award, there is no necessity for dealing further on the
point," adding finally that the Plaintiff should return the ships.

The true reason for not ordering the Plaintiff to compensate
the Defendant was probably more political than legal. While
the Chinese may have liked to assert a right to try British
companies and subjects, this would have been certain to
provoke a strong reaction as being a breach of the treaties
granting extraterritorial rights.

The judgment as it stood produced a strong enough
reaction. First, British gunboats were ordered to prevent
Chinese officials from moving the ships from their
moorings. Second, Hannen issued a blistering protest. He
complained first that Tsai had ordered there be no personal
communication between himself and Hannen concerning the
case. Hannen said this was without precedent, noting that
in the Mixed Court, the Magistrates and Assessors would
regularly confer privately. He then complained about the
length of the proceedings and that the proceedings were "as it
seemed to me, controlled entirely by the defendants' counsel
whose suggestions on important or unimportant points
were adopted in every instance, sometimes without hearing

the plaintiffs' counsel's objections." He made some other criticisms of the procedure and then addressing Drummond's behaviour said:

> "During the course of the case, the defendants' counsel made remarks and addressed me in a manner which everybody acquainted with the ordinary rules of courtesy in courts must have felt to be unseemly; and this was done without one word of remonstrance from the presiding judge. Had such remarks been made to a Chinese magistrate sitting at the bench with me, I should have insisted on an apology and I should have known how to enforce it."

Hannen did not, however, want to be personally critical of Mr Tsai and added:

> "I desire to add that so far as Mr. Tsai himself is concerned I have experienced the greatest courtesy and consideration I make every allowance for the position in which he was placed, in conducting an important case in a novel and unfamiliar manner, and I quite see that his position was a very difficult one."

He then said that it was unfortunate that Mr Tsai would not consult with him because their views of the case had proceeded on "different planes."

Pausing for a moment, it is worth considering how Chinese officials felt in the British Courts. No doubt they were treated with the greatest courtesy and consideration. However, they were not allowed to speak to the jury nor to even address it. They must have felt very much like Hannen felt: frozen out.

Hannen in his protest then addressed the substance of the decision shortly saying that if the Defendants had a claim against the Plaintiffs under the treaty they should have made a claim to the British Consul or the British court. He finished by saying that if Tsai's comment that the steamers should be returned was an order, Tsai had no jurisdiction to make it.

The British did not let the matter end there and continued negotiations with the Chinese. Bennertz went bankrupt, perhaps due to the losses and costs of dealing with the case. The British Official Receiver took over the claim and it was subsequently reported that the case was resolved with the Chinese paying 72,000 taels of the total claim by Bennertz of 170,000 taels and the ships being returned.

The Bennertz bankruptcy was handled by Hannen in the Supreme Court. One can imagine that he must have felt a tinge of guilt at not having been able to help Bennertz more in the case.

Harrie Wilkinson as acting judge

Soon after the Bennertz case, Hannen went to Bangkok to sit as an arbitrator in a dispute between Siam and America over the seizure of the business of an American business. Harrie Wilkinson continued his meteoric rise and, despite having only been formally appointed Crown Advocate on December 10, 1897, was just one month later in mid January 1898 appointed Acting Chief Justice for two months – for that period he technically outranked his father, the Judge for Japan.

Later that year, in July 1898, Harrie Wilkinson was again appointed Acting Assistant Judge of the Supreme Court to conduct the first-ever trial of the British Supreme Court sitting in Korea. Wilkinson travelled to Seoul to try a case where the Legation constable, Mr O'Neil had, as Wilkinson put it, "physically reproved" the Legation head gardener who subsequently died. The case was tried before Wilkinson and a jury of five whch acquitted O'Neil.

Harrie Wilkinson later described the case in what to modern ears, appears very strange terms:

"The defence was borne out in court by competent medical evidence that this was one of those interesting cases where an Oriental injured in his feelings will turn his face to the wall and die."

One wonders what the competent medical evidence could be to show that a man had just decided to die.

Bourne to be a Judge

With the reversal of the amalgamation decision and George Jamieson being returned to full-time consular duties, the Foreign Office needed to appoint a new Judge of the Supreme Court. Frederick Samuel Augustus Bourne, a long time consular officer in China was appointed to the position. He had at the time of appointment been in consular service for over 20 years. Bourne had been called to the Bar of Lincoln's Inn in 1890 during long leave at home in England. Bourne had served all over China, including Chungking, Pagoda Island, Wuhu and Tamsui (near Taipei). He was almost killed by a Chinese mob early in his career and spent nine months living and dressed as a Chinese.

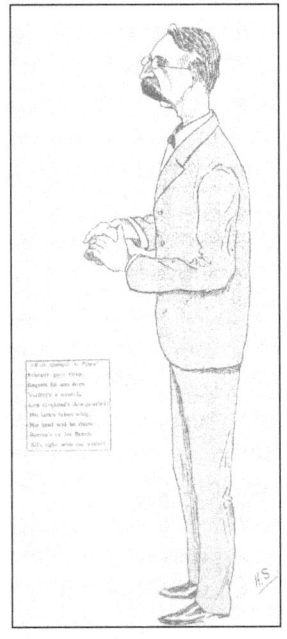

Bourne as a judge of the British Supreme Court for China and Japan was the last British judge with appellate jurisdiction over Japan. The role was soon to come to an end.

Frederick Bourne
Hannen's new Assistant Judge

CHAPTER 12

Japan Asserts Itself

Negotiations to end extraterritoriality

In the mid-1890s, the British and Japanese governments were able through negotiations in London to reach an agreement to terminate extraterritoriality in Japan by the end of the 19th century. Ironically, at the same time in 1895 under the Treaty of Shimonoseki, Japan was to extract from China greater extraterritorial rights than any power had to date.

Throughout the 1880s the Japanese had worked hard to bring an end to extraterritoriality by reforming their legal system. In 1882 the new Penal Code came into effect and a Commercial Code was also being drafted. Japan continued its program of political and economic reform and by the end of the 1880s had elections for parliament, with limited suffrage, and its first Western Constitution.

In the mid 1880s, serious negotiations had begun between Japan and the treaty powers to bring an end to extraterritoriality. Japan proposed that as soon as the Japanese Civil Code was enacted, consular jurisdiction should be abolished outside the treaty ports. Inside the treaty ports, consular courts could continue to operate for three years but should apply Japanese law. As a concession to foreign concerns, mixed courts would be established with Japanese and foreign judges on the bench. Also, as the biggest carrot, Japan was to be opened completely to foreign trade and residence with foreigners being able to own property. The British and Germans proposed that the mixed courts follow the model in Egypt where there was a majority of foreign judges and that all cases involving foreign parties would be heard by these courts.

Once these proposals leaked in the Japanese press, the Japanese public violently opposed them, particularly, with the *Normanton* case fresh in their memories. With no chance of reaching a settlement, Japan adjourned the negotiations in 1887. They proceeded fitfully under a number of different Japanese foreign ministers.

In order to satisfy the British that Japanese courts would be up to standard, Japan originally offered in a draft diplomatic note attached to a draft treaty to have foreign judges on their courts for at least 12 years. This had already been agreed with United States, Russia and Germany in unratified treaties. But the disclosure of the terms of these unratified treaties, particularly the idea of having foreign judges sitting on Japanese courts again aroused violent public opposition.

The British eventually accepted that foreign judges not sit on Japanese courts but requested that while the treaty be signed as soon as possible, its coming into force be delayed five years so the operation of the new legal system could be observed. The Japanese said they could negotiate on these

Foreigners fear being subject to Japanese law

terms but in 1890 the member of their negotiating team retired.

Two years later a new committee was formed. The Japanese, however, postponed the enactment of their new legal codes, resulting in a delay in when negotiations could re-commence. The Japanese Foreign Minister gave a speech in the Japanese Upper House on May 26, 1892 saying that while "Japanese public opinion was unanimously in favour of immediate revision of the treaties," the only method to achieve this was to enact a "Code of Laws fit to be accepted by the civilized nations of the world."

He added that one should not look back and criticize those who signed the original treaties:

> "The Treaty Powers could not have been induced
> to subject their precious lives and property of their
> subjects to the laws of Japan, and that for the very
> good reason that there were at the time no laws fit to
> enforced in a civilized society, to whose protection their
> lives and property could have been committed."

Japan was at this time, planning to negotiate treaties with other countries that would provide for extraterritoriality for Japanese subjects. The Foreign Minister therefore needed to be able to justify why Japan would ask for extraterritoriality from other countries while at the same time they were seeking to rid Japan of extraterritoriality.

By late 1893, the question of treaty revision had become a political hot potato. The democratic representatives in the Japanese parliament, the Diet, opposed any treaty that gave foreigners any residual rights. Others were opposed to the idea of allowing foreigners freedom to travel anywhere in Japan. Hirobumi Ito was now Prime Minister of Japan again and determined that strong measures needed to be taken to get the treaties signed. In order to silence criticism, he recommended to the Emperor that the Diet be dissolved. The government also prohibited several political societies and certain newspapers.

Negotiations went forward relatively quickly and an agreement reached in mid-1894. On July 16, 1894, Earl Kimberly and Viscount Aoki on behalf of Great Britain and Japan signed a Treaty of Commerce and Navigation in London. The treaty completely ended the treaty port system in Japan. The foreign settlements were to be returned to Japan and foreigners were allowed to freely travel and reside anywhere in Japan. The British treaty provided that Japanese could also travel and reside anywhere in Britain, even though this was a right that they already had.

With regards to extraterritoriality and the Court for Japan, Article 20 of the treaty provided that from the date the treaty came into force that all previous treaties shall cease to be binding and the British Courts in Japan would cease to have jurisdiction.

It was agreed that the treaty would not come into effect for at least five years after its signature. The Japanese government was required to give one year's notice that it wished to activate the treaty. The earliest date the treaties could come into force, therefore, was July 17, 1899.

The United States quickly agreed to sign a treaty on very similar terms to the British with a treaty being concluded on November 22, 1894. This needed to be ratified by the Senate. War had already broken out between China and Japan that year and just before the Senate vote, there were news reports that the Japanese had massacred Chinese soldiers at Port Arthur, leading the Senate to amend the treaty in a way unacceptable to Japan. After further negotiations, and assurances from Japan that there had been no massacre, the Senate agreed to a form of wording acceptable to all and the treaty was ratified in February 1895. Under the treaty, US extraterritorial rights were set to expire at the same time as British rights.

Over the next year, Japan continued to negotiate with the other treaty powers, obtaining agreements from all for the end of extraterritoriality on July 17, 1899. The only exception was France where it was agreed extraterritoriality would come to an end on August 4, 1899.

Sino–Japanese War

Just as Japan agreed to abolish extraterritoriality, the Sino-Japanese war of 1894-1895 ended with Japan imposing an "unequal treaty" on the Chinese. The war had broken out over control of Korea over which China had for centuries claimed rights of suzerainty. The newly-strong Japan did not wish China to occupy too strong a position in the country, so, they invaded Korea and subsequently China, occupying large parts of Manchuria and Shantung Province.

Li Hongzhang had been put in charge of defending China but his supposedly modern army and navy proved far too weak many say because funds had been syphoned off by corrupt officials leading to a series of quick Japanese victories. In order to end the war, Li led a Chinese delegation to Shimonoseki, in Western Japan, to negotiate peace.

The Japanese delegation was led by Hirobumi Ito, the Prime Minister. The Japanese had purposefully chosen Shimonoseki as the place for the negotiations. The site overlooked the Kanmon Straits between Kyushu and Honshu, which was heavily trafficked by Japanese warships making their way to China or Korea, thus sending a clear message every day during the negotiations as to Japan's military strength.

The Japanese clearly had the upper hand. The only trouble to arise in the negotiations for the Japanese was that a Japanese nationalist tried to assassinate Li during the course of the negotiations. Li was shot and wounded. The loss of face to the Japanese of having a peace envoy injured while in their care caused them to agree to a ceasefire while negotiations were ongoing.

The key terms of the treaty were that China and Japan agreed that Korea was an independent nation and China would no longer seek tribute; the Liaotung (Liaodong) Peninsular in Manchuria, Formosa (Taiwan) and the Pescadores Islands were ceded to Japan; Japan was accorded Most Favoured Nation status with other territorial powers; China agreed that Japanese (and hence under Most Favoured Nation clauses, all foreigners) could manufacture in China and import manufacturing equipment; and, a number of other cities were opened to foreign trade. China agreed to pay an indemnity of 200 million taels and Japan was also allowed to keep troops in Weihaiwei, Shantung Province, until the indemnity had been paid in full. The treaty gave Japanese citizens full extraterritorial rights in China and took away Chinese citizens' extraterritorial rights in Japan.

The granting of manufacturing rights was to change the face of China. Such rights had long been sought by foreign companies and had been opposed by China. In negotiating with the Japanese, Li had strenuously opposed the granting of manufacturing rights on the basis that the Diplomatic Corps in Peking had agreed it not be sought. Li emphasized that if foreigners could manufacture in China it would "tend to destroy the livelihood of Chinese and work a serious injury to native industry."

The colonial land grab
The Russians, who had their own territorial ambitions in China were strongly opposed to the cessation of Liaotung Peninsula to Japan. Together with the Germans and French, the Russians staged a "tri-partite intervention" where they warned the Japanese that taking the Liaotung Peninsular was not acceptable. Under pressure from all three countries, Japan agreed to retrocede the peninsula and asked for an increase in the indemnity to be paid from 200 million taels to 250 million taels. The Russians negotiated the additional payment down to

30 million taels and offered a loan to China to pay the amount.

The Japanese considered this intervention by Russia to be humiliating, particularly as Russia was expanding its own interests in Manchuria. The Japanese set about building their own army and navy so as to be in stronger position in future. In 1896, Ernest Satow who, after serving in postings in Uruguay, Morocco and Siam, had been appointed British Minister in Tokyo the previous year, sent a note to the Marquis of Salisbury reporting on a conversation with the Japanese Minister of Foreign Affairs. Japan was building a large army and navy that would be seen as a threat to her neighbours. The Japanese Foreign Minister, Count Okuma, was unapologetic about this, telling Satow:

"as every nation these days was arming to the teeth, it behoved Japan to follow suit. If she had no such neighbours as China and Corea these extensive armaments would not be required; but in case of serious complications such as a civil war in either country, the Japanese people would be unable to look on unmoved, and it was necessary to have an army large enough to admit of troops being dispatched to the mainland. Besides, the downfall of China could not long be delayed, and Japan must be prepared to play her part in the events that would follow."

And, indeed, the late 1890s did see an unseemly scramble for concessions in China. In 1897 the Germans took a lease on Kiaochow Bay (Jiaozhou Bay) around the Tsingtao (Qingdao) area; the Russians took a lease on Port Arthur and obtained concessions to build railways in Manchuria. The French took a lease over Kwangchow Bay (now called Zhanjiang) in Guangdong Province. The British as a foil to the Russians, in 1898, took a lease over Weihaiwei after the Japanese armed forced evacuated it and extracted a promise that no rights would be granted to other powers in the Yangtze River Valley. They also obtained a 99-year lease over the New Territories in Hong Kong.

A time for rejoicing not for revenge

On 17, 1899, the British and American treaties ending extraterritoriality in Japan were due to come into effect. The end of the treaties was very much welcomed in Japan. A local Japanese newspaper, the *Mainichi Shimbun* called July 17, 1899 "a day of festival unprecedented in the twenty five centuries of Japan's national existence." Japan was the first Oriental State to obtain admission to the comity of Occidental Powers. The *Mainichi Shimbun*'s explanation was that Japan had, unlike other Asian countries, not hesitated to adopt the best of Occidental civilization. Another Japanese newspaper, the *Chuo Shimbun*, equally rejoiced but emphasized that the end of extraterritoriality was only the beginning of the task of achieving equality. Numerous celebrations were held throughout Japan, including in all the treaty ports.

A ball was held at the Imperial Hotel in Tokyo in August organized by the Economical Society, and attended by Prince Kanin and other Japanese notables as well as members of the diplomatic corps. Baron Osaki, the President of the Society was effervescent:

"As subjects of His Imperial Majesty, we can not
but rejoice over the revision of the treaties, which
has become an accomplished fact, as an epoch
making event in the history of this country's foreign
intercourse. From the moment the revised treaties come
into operation, we enter into new relations with all
the countries of the world, nay, are admitted into the
comity of civilized nations."

Osaki commented on the position of foreigners under the

old treaties:

> "Heretofore foreign residents in Japan were like
> drops of oil in a glass of water. There may have been
> a mechanical intermixture, but there was no chemical
> combination. Heretofore though our foreign friends
> lived in the same land as us they were standing, as it
> were, outside the walls of our residence."

Then in a spirit of goodwill and welcoming he said:

> "But now we throw open our gates, and invite them to
> come in to the inner most part of our residence and feel
> themselves at home. Come friends, come!"

Viscount Aoki, the Minister for Foreign Affairs, speaking in English, added that Japan had now entered a new era in which it was opened fully to foreign intercourse and that all foreigners could live safely in Japan.

The Japanese Government wanted the Japanese people to understand that the end of extraterritoriality was a time for rejoicing, not for revenge. On July 1, 1899 just before the treaties came into force, an Imperial Rescript which was countersigned by all members of cabinet together with a separate Cabinet Instruction concerning the operation of the new treaties were issued. The Imperial Rescript recited the "joy and glory" of the Imperial heart brought about by the end of the treaties. The Emperor then directed:

> "We wish Our loyal and public spirited subjects, acting
> under strict observance of Our desire, to behave in
> strict conformity with the national policy of opening
> the Empire, and with one accord to let their intercourse
> with aliens be on the best of terms, maintaining the
> high character of the nation, and making it their utmost

endeavor to manifest the glory of the Empire."

Both the Imperial Rescript and the Cabinet Instruction emphasized that it was the responsibility of all Japanese officials to ensure subordinates and the people did not cause harm to foreigners who were now able to freely travel and live anywhere in the country.

Murder at the Rising Sun
The Japanese judiciary did not have to wait long to show how

Foreigners' worst fear of the end of extraterritoriality

they would enforce their new powers over foreigners. One American was in a great hurry to test out the new Japanese legal system. Within hours of the US-Japan treaty coming into effect, before the sun had even risen on July 17, 1899, Robert Miller, an American sailor, killed two Japanese women and an American man, Nelson Ward, in a Yokohama saloon called, ironically, the Rising Sun.

Miller used a claw hammer and a straight razor to kill his victims. The case was tried in the Yokohama District Court before four judges on August 20, 1899. Four Japanese lawyers and a British barrister appearing by special permission represented Miller. Miller was convicted and was sentenced to death. The judges in passing verdict noted their reluctance to do so by saying:

> "It is the benevolent desire of His Imperial Majesty the Emperor that all strangers within our Empire should be treated with magnanimity . . . . It is most distressing to the judicial officials to be placed under the painful necessity of sentencing a citizen of one of the Treaty Powers to death."

Miller appealed to the Tokyo Appeal Court but his appeal was rejected. The sentence was carried out on January 17, 1900 with Miller being taken to the gallows in Ichigaya Prison in Tokyo. He was allowed a last cigarette from which he took a few contented puffs. After that, a mask was put on his head and the trap sprung. He was buried in an unmarked grave.

Winding down of the Court for Japan

Despite the celebrations of the Japanese, the British Court for Japan did not cease to exist on July 17, 1899. The 1894 treaty did not make it clear what was to happen for cases that were pending or for crimes or civil disputes that were committed or which arose before July 17, 1899. Viscount

Aoki, Japan's Minister for Foreign Affairs, and Ernest Satow, the British Minister for Japan, signed a protocol on May 3, 1899 providing that any cases before the court at the date that extraterritoriality ended were still to be handled by the Court for Japan.

By November 1899 there was only one case pending trial in any extraterritorial court in Japan. This was a case brought against a Mr Reynell, which had been filed on July 30, 1899 in the British Court for Japan. The Japanese Foreign Minister, Viscount Aoki, was very keen that this case not be heard as he wanted to have all remnants of foreign jurisdiction "wiped out of existence." Reynell had applied for the case to be transferred to Japanese courts and Aoki asked Satow to communicate to Wilkinson that he should not oppose this. The response was, of course, that Satow could not tell Wilkinson, as a judge, what to do. The matter was resolved by Wilkinson hearing the case as an arbitrator, rather than as a judge.

Wilkinson was able to finalise all pending cases by January 31, 1900. On that date, he sat to deliver the final judgment of the British Court for Japan. The case related to a gift that James Joseph Enslie, the British Consul in Kobe, had made to his housekeeper, Kozawa Tori, out of "love and affection." He had also left Miss Kozawa an annuity in his will. The question was which had precedence, the gift or the annuity.

For the final hearing of the Court for Japan, Wilkinson delivered a lengthy judgment directing the way in which the annuity was to be paid. Wilkinson was accompanied in court by the Vice-Consul and Assistant Judge, Henry Bonar. Wilkinson's son and successor as Crown Advocate in Shanghai, Harrie Wilkinson came from Shanghai to attend the hearing. The principal members of the British bar in Japan, Henry Lichtfield, Crown Prosecutor, John Lowder, Ambrose Walford from Yokohama and H.C. Brushfield and Charles Crosse, from Kobe, appeared in court in their wigs and gowns. George Scidmore of the US Consulate also attended. Mr Idaura, a Japanese barrister who had been watching the Enslie case on behalf of Miss Kozawa, was granted a seat at the barristers' table out of courtesy.

Lichtfield gave a farewell speech saying this was probably the last time Wilkinson would preside over the court, which had been in existence since 1879. The old order had changed in the course of evolution and change in Japan. Naturally, many who had worked with the court could not but feel regret at the change. Turning to Wilkinson as a judge, Lichtfield said that Wilkinson had given strict attention to business but that also they could feel they had a friend in him. He then hinted as to Wilkinson's next position: "if rumour was right, some of the members of the bar present would shortly practice before His Honour in another court."

Wilkinson gave a short reply in thanks. With regard to the new order:

"he wished with others that the difficulties connected
– and inseparably connected – with the change would
be successfully overcome, and that over time the
excellence of the court in dispensing justice may be
attained under the new regime."

He then thanked the bar for their valuable assistance and wished them "all success and a hearty farewell."

C.D. Moss, the Clerk of the Court, then stood and brought an end to 42 years of British extraterritoriality in Japan by announcing:

"Know all men, this court stands adjourned. God Save
the Queen."

The death of Nicholas Hannen

Very soon after this, Nicholas Hannen died of Pneumonia in Shanghai just two and half weeks before he planned to retire. Hannen was given a funeral service with full honours, and perhaps the most international recognition ever given to an English judge. Hannen's coffin was paraded through the streets of Shanghai from his house to Trinity Cathedral. The parade was led by the Shanghai Volunteers, which consisted of companies A and B of the Light Horse Artillery, as well as the German Companies and French Volunteers. The gunboat HMS *Hermione*, which was in port, landed a company of 125 blue jackets and 18 marines to accompany the procession. The procession from Hannen's house travelled to Kiukiang Road (Jiujiang Road) and then to the Bund where a line of mourners was waiting. Once the party reached the Trinity Cathedral, the strains of Chopin's "Marche Funebre " ushered in the coffin and its attendants.

At a special hearing in the British Supreme Court before Acting Chief Justice Frederick Bourne, Crown Advocate Harrie Wilkinson gave a fitting eulogy:

"We have lost a chief; we have lost a friend; and this Court, and all Her Britannic Majesty's subjects and indeed all those who have any business with Her Majesty's subjects have lost a wise, good, and just judge, a lawyer of sound learning, a man with a legal mind, one with a gift which amounted to intuition as to what were the rights and wrongs of a case when it was laid before him, and one whose special gift was his knowledge of the law of evidence."

Bourne expressed the feeling of all over Sir Nicholas' death lamenting the loss of "a high-minded English Gentleman our national type of all-round human excellence". He finished his speech:

"Gentlemen, speaking for myself, for the officers of
the Court and for you, it is with the keenest sense of
personal loss of a wise and considerate chief, of a kind
friend passed out of our lives, that we remember we
can see and hear Sir Nicholas Hannen on this bench no
more."

Hannen was cremated and his wife, Jessie, took his ashes
back with her to their home at Lake Lodge in Wargrave,
England. She died 7 years later and both their ashes were
interned in the recently completed Hannen Columbarium.
The Columbarium had been designed by the famous English
architect, Sir Edwin Lutyens, and stands to this day in
Wargrave. On a beautifully sunny, but slightly chilly, autumn
day in October, I visited the churchyard in Wargrave. The
Columbarium, which is a very private affair, is tucked away
in the left hand corner of the churchyard where a number of
members of Hannen family are also buried. In keeping with
Hannen's own personality, the Columbarium serves as an
understated reminder of Sir Nicholas' long and meritorious
service in East Asia.

St Mary's Churchyard, Wargrave, where Sir Nicholas Hannen's ashes were interred

HS Wilkinson appointed Chief Justice

Following Hannen's death, HS Wilkinson achieved his greatest ambition, being formally appointed as Chief Justice of the Supreme Court for China and Corea in May 1900. At the time, Wilkinson had not yet returned to Shanghai. He had left Japan in February, travelling Home via America. The end of

Wilkinson CJ

extraterritoriality was a big story in the United States and "he was pounced upon by reporters" in Chicago. His view of the new system was mixed. He told the reporters:

> "It is an open question whether or not the new Court system in Japan was not inaugurated too soon. The law of Japan is derived largely from the French and German codes, which are not as adaptable to the Japanese uses, and especially with reference to English and American subjects, as would have been English common law."

He had originally intended to return to Yokohama in May to meet Hannen on his homeward voyage – this, of course, could not happen. He did, however, go back to Yokohama where he took final steps to close the Court for Japan transferring remaining moneys either to the Treasury or Consulate and passing the archives of the court to the Yokohama Consulate. On 1 June 1900 he issued a final Circular to all Consuls informing them of the formal closure of the British Court for Japan.

H.S. Wilkinson first sat as Chief Justice in Shanghai in June 1900.

At the time, China was facing an existential crisis.

PART TWO

Destruction, Disorder and Defiance
(1900 to 1927)

CHAPTER 13

China Boxed In

THE 20TH CENTURY STARTED very badly for China and the Qing Dynasty. Things got so bad that British Judge Frederick Bourne thought that there may be full out war in China between the foreign powers which if won by one of Britain's rivals could result in the "Chinese being exported as industrial slaves."

Starting in the late 1890s, a rebellion begun by the Boxers, a religious group that claimed to be immune to foreign bullets and weapons, swept Northern China. The Boxers were particularly ferocious in Shantung and Manchuria, driving most foreigners out from remote areas or killing them. The Chinese government supported attacks on foreigners. In June 1900, the Boxers descended on Peking with the slogan "Support the Qing, exterminate the foreigners." The battles resulted in June 1900 in the killing of senior German and Japanese officials.

China declared war on all eight major foreign powers: Great Britain, France, Germany, the United States, Russia, Austria-Hungary, Italy and Japan. From June 1900, Chinese troops laid siege to the foreign legations in Peking where most foreigners had retreated. Given that five years before China had not been able to defend themselves against the Japanese alone, this was foolishness of the greatest degree. The dowager Empress, Cixi, in one of the war councils justified the support of the Boxers on the need to retain the support of the people. She said:

"China has been extremely weak; the only thing we can
rely upon is the hearts of the people. If we lose them,

Kang-I, another high-ranking official, emphasized the
anti-foreign feeling by saying:

"When the legations are taken, the barbarians will have
no more roots. The country will then have peace."

Needless to say, many other high Chinese officials did
not support attacks on foreigners. Provincial governors,
including Li Hongzhang in Canton and Yuan Shikai in
Shandong as well as the governors in Nanking and Wuhan,
all refused to recognise the declaration of war. They reached
agreements with the foreign powers that there would be no
fighting between their troops and foreigners in areas they
controlled. More importantly, Rong Lu the commander in
chief of the Beiyang forces in Peking and in charge of the siege
of the legations, only attacked half-heartedly. He ordered that
blanks be fired and refused to bring up larger caliber cannon.

During the siege, London newspapers, particularly the *Daily
Mail* and *Daily Express* published lurid accounts of a massacre
of the foreigners in the legations. The *Daily Mail* published
a "Massacre Telegram" from its Shanghai correspondents
recounting a heroic last stand of the foreigners seeking refuge
in wrecked buildings and then running out of ammunition:

"A rush was determined upon. Thus standing
together, as the Sun rose fully, the little remaining
band, all Europeans, met death stubbornly. There was
a desperate hand-to-hand encounter. The Chinese
lost heavily, but as one man fell others advanced, and
finally, overcome by overwhelming odds, every one
of the Europeans remaining was put to the sword in a
most atrocious manner."

The Daily Express reports on the "Peking Massacre"
Robert Hart, Inspector-General of Chinese Customs was one of those reported killed.

The *Daily Express* followed with an even more lurid account of a massacre sourced from its correspondent, Henry O'Shea, who was also publisher and editor of the *China Gazette* in Shanghai.

"The end has come, and the worst horrors have been but too terribly accomplished. Every European in Peking has been massacred by the savage, bloodthirsty miscreants who now represent the supreme authority in China ... A last desperate sortie was made by the doomed victims. It is a picture that will live for all time. The horror square led by soldiers and civilians, the hapless women and children in the centre, the last murderous attack by the infuriated Boxers. 'Then the foreigners went mad,' said the courier who brought the story to Sheng. 'They killed the women and children, shooting them with their revolvers instead of using them on the Boxers.' Upon this awful climax, the true inwardness of which we realise with a shudder of fiercest indignation, the curtain went down on a worse tragedy than Cawnpore."

In Cawnpore, India in 1857, the British had been under siege and brutally massacred by Indian troops. As it would turn out, this was no Cawnpore and no tragedy, at least, not for the foreigners. Both stories were complete tissues of lies. Thanks mainly to Rong Lu's lackluster attacks, the legations were able to hold out until they were relieved.

While not a tragedy for foreigners, it was a tragedy for the people of Peking and the people of China.

Peking's position inland meant that gunboats could not come to the rescue of the legations. But on August 4, 1900, a foreign army of over 18,000 men, made up of 8,000 Japanese, 4,800 Russian, 3,000 British, 2,100 American, 800 French, 58 Austrian, and 53 Italian troops set out from Tientsin and made their way very quickly to Peking in 10 days. They arrived on August 14, 1900 to relieve the legations. German troops were also sent to join the attack but did not arrive in time.

After taking Peking, the troops looted the city and massacred the Chinese population. The looting went on for many months, leaving behind a devastated city. Ernest Satow, previously British Minister in Japan who had just been appointed British Minister in China, described his arrival in Peking in October 1900:

"So through the Hatamen and along legation street, which showed terrible marks of devastation. A feeling of profound melancholy took possession of me, such as I have never experienced. It was like entering a city of the dead where the tombs had been thrown down and enveloped in dust."

During the war, the Emperor, Empress Dowager and all other officials fled Peking. Li Hongzhang was called upon to negotiate with the foreigners. While the capture of Peking could have led to the end of the Qing Dynasty, this did not suit the foreign powers who were more content to continue to carve up China while leaving a weak government in power.

The negotiations for a peace settlement resulted in yet more onerous terms being imposed on China. This included a massive indemnity of 450 million taels (GBP67.5 million pounds at the time) to be paid over 39 years. The "Boxer Indemnity" was divided up between the foreign powers with Russia and Germany receiving 49% between them. Japan, despite having contributed the largest number of troops and also having seen one of its officials killed, only received 7.7%. Russia, which had occupied Manchuria during the fighting, stayed there despite promises to leave. The result of these negotiations were seen as a great failure in Japan and were one of the principal drivers of Japan's attack on Russia three years later. Payment of the Boxer Indemnity crippled China economically for years to come.

Liar, Liar, the legations were not on fire!

On January 18, 1902, the *Shanghai Times* published an article reporting on an expose by the Chinese Times in Tientsin of how the famous "Massacre Telegram" came about. The report said that the two temporary correspondents for the *Daily Mail* had made the story up and sent it to the *Daily Mail*. "The *Daily Express* determined to do as well as the Mail or better wired to its Shanghai Correspondent H. D. O'Shea to get a move on or words to that effect."

Then, coming to the crux, the *Shanghai Times* said:

"So O'Shea then wired as much blood and thunder as his conscience permitted and the *Express* came out next day with a bigger pack of lies than the Mail."

The *Shanghai Times* added the caveat that the *Daily Mail* had published the original telegram it received to show it had been misled. The *Express* did not do so, so therefore "part or all of lies therefore may be not O'Shea's." The next paragraph all but destroyed this caveat by adding:

"But he is a man who can lie when he tries and he certainly had in this case a chance to 'tell the truth and shame the devil' by wiring a flat contradiction of the massacre or some reassuring message discounting the story instead of which he or his London accomplices told a lie big enough to put the devil in the amateur class."

This was clearly intended to attract a defamation suit. The article ended:

"Now watch for the Shanghai libel case."

O'Shea took the bait. He sued the editor of the *Shanghai Times*, Mr T.C. Cowen, for defamation claiming 15,000 taels in damages.

The trial was heard by Frederick Bourne as Acting Chief Justice and a jury of five. Cowen's defence was that what had been said about O'Shea was true. There was no doubt that the massacre stories were false. The foreigners had not been massacred. The question to be answered was: had O'Shea sent telegrams to the *Daily Express* knowing them to be false?

In court, O'Shea said that the *Daily Express* had used his and other correspondents' materials to prepare their reports and what he had sent, he believed to be true based on information that he had received. He added that "he considered it was the duty of a correspondent to send home what rumours he heard; but at the same time it was his duty to warn his papers at home that these rumours were not to be accepted as news."

He suggested that the defendant had published the article about him out of spite because, at the time Cowen had also been a correspondent for the *Daily Express* and O'Shea had rejected some of his articles.

O'Shea recovered from the archives of the Chinese Telegraph Office 86 telegrams that he had sent. A key problem was that none of these were a telegram detailing the massacre as reported in the *Daily Express* on July 16. O'Shea swore that these were all of the telegrams he sent. He added, in cross-examination, that on July 16, he had been informed that the Japanese Consulate in Tientsin had received a telegraph from Baron Onishi that the legation was safe. He had sent a telegram to London to that effect.

In another report, O'Shea reported that the British Consul General, Sir Pelham Warren, had officially told him he believed that all in the Peking legations had been killed. In a separate deposition, Sir Pelham denied he had ever made such a statement officially, although there had been times when he felt the legations had fallen. He added, interestingly, that he had been in direct telegraphic contact with Yuan Shikai who had been providing him and other Consuls with information about the siege. Yuan had never told him the legation had fallen.

Cowen gave evidence and denied that he had written the article out of ill will to the defendant, but rather that "because I thought it a matter of duty for anyone able to go into it, that this massacre telegram should be sifted and exposed if possible. I thought it would be for the public good."

Bourne summed up for the jury. He told them they needed to be satisfied that what Cowen had written was not true. If so, they could consider how much Cowen should pay in damages. The jury went out "for some considerable time." Upon their return they said they considered the words were untrue, but that the damages should only be a very small amount of 100 taels or, less than 6% of the 15,000 taels O'Shea had claimed. O'Shea was thus partially vindicated by the verdict, but the small award of damages suggests strongly that the jury were not impressed by him.

Beginning of Legal Reform in China

The Boxer Rebellion and its aftermath acted as a catalyst for reform in China. The Chinese now appreciated that Japan had been able to abolish extraterritoriality because it had made significant improvements in its legal system.

In a Commercial Treaty made between China and Britain in September 1902, the abolition of extraterritoriality was explicitly tied to improvements in the Chinese legal system. Article XII of the Treaty provided:

> "China having expressed a strong desire to reform her judicial system and to bring it into accord with that of Western nations Great Britain agrees to give every assistance to such reform and she will also be prepared to relinquish her extraterritorial rights when she is satisfied that the state of the Chinese laws, the arrangement of their administration and other considerations warrant her so doing."

The United States and Japan made similar promises in treaties signed at the same time.

A commission was formed to draft civil, criminal, commercial and procedural codes. The commission, logically given Japan had just completed the process of adapting European laws to Asian circumstances, appointed a number of Japanese experts and borrowed from the Japanese codes. The Chairman of the Chinese Civil Codification Commission, Foo Ping-Sheung, writing much later, explained the reason for relying on the Japanese experience:

> "Japan had just emerged from her old feudalism into

a modern state. Her signal success in the process of modernization China was anxious to follow. It was quite natural for China to try to profit by her neighbour's experience... Japan at the time had completed her civil and commercial codification, which she had modeled after the German Codes. She had created a technical legal Japanese vocabulary, translated a number of the leading juridical textbooks of Europe, and produced a large Japanese legal literature. The Chinese could then find in Japan an adaptation to the Far Eastern mind, in a language closely relate to their own, of what represented at the time the most advanced stage of western scientific juridical science."

By 1907, regulations providing for modern courts and a modern Criminal Code were promulgated. Sweeping reforms were introduced, including the abolition of torture and the use of the cangue. The overthrow of the Qing dynasty in 1911 and World War I intervened, thereby putting legal reform and the abolition of extraterritoriality on the backburner. It was not until the 1920s that serious discussions on the end of extraterritoriality resumed.

Japan's victory over Russia

China was not the only country to suffer defeat in the early 1900s. Following the trip-partite intervention after the signing of the Treaty of Shimonoseki and Russia's occupation of Port Arthur and Dalian in 1898, Japan was concerned about Russia encroaching on its own territorial gains. In particular, following the Boxer Rebellion, Russia had not withdrawn its troops from Manchuria as they had promised to. Japan felt that its own interests in Korea were under threat.

As a first step to being in a position to challenge Russia, in 1902 Japan signed a treaty with the British that obliged the other party to enter a war if a third country did not remain neutral. In 1903 Japan then commenced negotiations with Russia seeking to reach an agreement that Korea was in Japan's sphere of influence while acknowledging Russia's interests in Manchuria.

Japan at the time had a much smaller navy than Russia and most people thought that it would be impossible for Japan, an upstart Asian country, to defeat a European power. The Russian Tsar certainly thought so and negotiated at a very slow pace. In early 1904, the Japanese navy attacked Port Arthur and landed land troops in Korea to enter Manchuria across the Yalu River. After a number of naval and land battles, the Russian Fleet was blockaded in Port Arthur. The Japanese, at the cost of great life, captured the hills around Port Arthur and destroyed the remainder of the Russian Pacific Fleet with artillery firing from the hill tops. They then captured Port Arthur.

The only hope for the Russians was their Baltic Fleet, which had been renamed the 2nd Pacific Squadron, which was heading to Asia around Africa and via the Suez Canal. By April 1905, the fleet had arrived in Manila and then set sail for Vladivostok. In order to get there, they would either have to sail around the North of Japan or through the Straits of Tsushima between Korea and Japan. They chose the Straits of Tsushima. Based on intelligence supplied by the British, the Japanese were able to attack the fleet as they sailed through the straits on the evening of May 14, 1905. The Russians, exhausted from months of sailing and outgunned and outmaneuvered, were convincingly defeated with the Japanese sinking all eight Russian battleships with limited loss to the Japanese side.

After this defeat, the Russians sued for peace. United States President Theodore Roosevelt acted as a mediator and a treaty of peace was signed in Portsmouth, Maine, in 1905. Under the treaty, Port Arthur and Dalian were ceded to Japan along with the Southern half of Sakhalin Island. No indemnity was to be paid. The lack of any payment outraged Japanese public opinion, which considered that Japan had been treated badly in the negotiations. Japan did, however, now have its first full colonies and naval ports in China from which it was able to further extend its influence in China.

Many British were ecstatic at the Japanese victory. At the China Association dinner in November 1905, the President, Mr Gundry, hailed the victory "as of good augury for peace and successful commerce for many years."

Mixed Court Riot

Shanghai saw its own battles. In late 1905, rioting broke out in Shanghai originating from a fight over who had the right to detain prisoners on trial at the Mixed Court.

The Municipal Council had long been concerned about corruption in the Mixed Court as well as the filthy conditions of the cells of the womens' jail attached to the court. The Municipal Council arranged that Municipal Police should be stationed at the Mixed Court to keep prisoners in custody as well as to keep a record of the cases. The first policeman to be sent was a Sikh. The Chinese Magistrate objected to any policemen being there as an infringement of Chinese sovereignty writing to the British Consul-General, "as I have sole charge of the Court from the front door inwards, the Police have no right to interfere therewith, and I should be entitled to expel the Indian at once." Eventually, a compromise was reached where a European policeman was stationed in the court.

Matters came to a head on December 18, 1905 when a Madame Li from Sichuan province was brought before the court on a charge of kidnapping girls for unlawful purposes. The case was adjourned to be heard on another day. Magistrate Kuan ordered that Madam Li and the girls be detained in the cells of the Mixed Court and instructed the Chinese runners accordingly. The British assessor, Mr Twyman, ordered that

Mr B. Twyman, the British Assessor who sparked the Mixed Court riots.

the Municipal Police keep Madam Li and the girls in custody. This led to an all-in brawl between the police and the runners. The police won. They then put Madam Li and the girls in a police van. The Magistrate ordered the doors to the court to be locked and said that the police would have to kill him if they wished to leave. The police broke the door down and left.

The incident inflamed Chinese sentiment against foreigners. Chinese merchant associations encouraged a boycott of foreign businesses and products. Riots broke out around the city. Louza Police Station, which was located at the western end of Nanking Road at the corner with Kweichow Road (Guizhou Road), was attacked. The police, who had orders not to use weapons, were overpowered and the building burnt down. The Town Hall, a few hundred metres back towards the Bund on Nanking Road was also attacked. At the Town Hall, the police did use their weapons. They fired into the crowd and killed two rioters and three bystanders. The riots were finally put down after landing parties from gunboats in the harbour were called upon to help restore order.

As a result of the riots, it was agreed with the Viceroy that Chinese prisoners would be kept in the Mixed Court cells, but that their conditions would be improved. It was also agreed that Municipal Police could be stationed in the court. However, as a result of the riots the Chinese magistrates were able to

The Eastern Sketch's view of the Mixed Court Riots.

recover some of the power they had been losing to assessors. Foreign assessors were instructed to comply with the original agreements whereby the assessor was there to observe, but not try, cases.

The Chinese authorities also agreed to pay compensation for British losses caused by the riots. Crown Advocate Harrie Wilkinson was appointed sole commissioner to determine the claims. He commenced sitting almost exactly two years after the riots and he dealt with the claims with dispatch, completing the work in two days.

Harrie Wilkinson had only returned to his role as Crown Advocate just before the Mixed Court riots. He had been required to step down while his father was Chief Justice and had sat as Acting Assistant Judge in the British Court for Siam. His father had sat as Chief Justice until 1905. No major cases had come before HS Wilkinson – he had been on leave when Bourne tried the O'Shea case. He retired to much deserved accolades after 40 years of service in the Far East.

Havilland de Sausmarez, a career judge of the Foreign Office was appointed to replace HS Wilkinson as Judge, the new title for Chief Justice. De Sausmarez had served in Africa and most recently had been the British Judge at Constantinople. De Sausmarez was a true servant of empire. He had been born into an aristocratic family in Guernsey on May 30, 1861 to the Reverend Havilland de Sausmarez and Anne Priaulx Walters, and had been brought up in the de Sausmarez manor in Guernsey.

In early life, he studied at Westminster and then went up to Cambridge. He graduated from Trinity College in 1883 with a Bachelor of Arts. He was admitted as a barrister of the Inner Temple in 1881 and called to the Bar in November 1884. He practiced on the Southern Eastern Circuit in England and then moved to Africa, where he practiced in Lagos, Nigeria from 1891. In June 1892, he joined the Foreign Office Judicial Service. From 1893 to 1897 he was Assistant Judge of the Consular Court in Zanzibar. In 1897, he transferred to Constantinople where he was Assistant Judge until 1903 when he was promoted to Judge. He was knighted at the end of 1905 after his arrival in Shanghai.

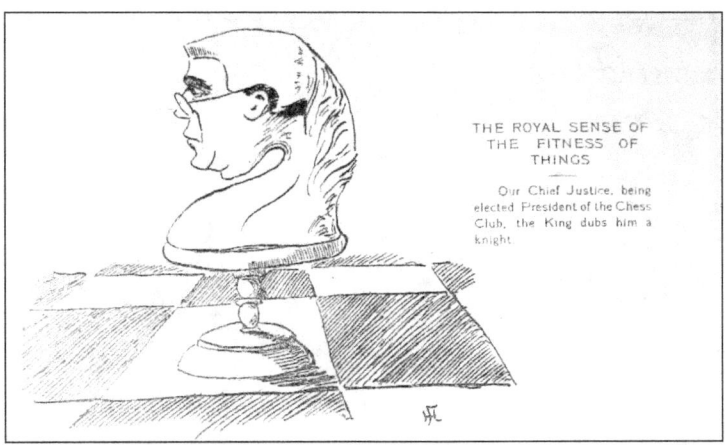

THE ROYAL SENSE OF THE FITNESS OF THINGS

Our Chief Justice, being elected President of the Chess Club, the King dubs him a knight

The Eastern Sketch on de Sausmarez's investiture as a knight

The rise of Yuan Shikai

1905 also saw the continued rise of a man who was soon to become the first President of China. That year, the Mixed Court riots had helped the Chinese magistrates to recover some lost rights in Shanghai. Provincial Governor Yuan Shikai, could see that only a far more organized force stood any chance of making China strong. In 1905, British consuls were invited to watch military exercises by Yuan's new army. The reports impressed the British Minister, Ernest Satow, immensely. He wrote back to the British Foreign Secretary, Lord Landsdowne, that Yuan and Tieh-liang, a Manchu general, instead of being carried around in a sedan chair had been "on horseback in European military costume and wearing swords. Such a thing was never before seen in China." The troops had been trained by Japanese "professors" and organized on the Japanese model and were intended to be nucleus of a modern army. One of the consuls estimated that a foreign force fighting this army would need at least half its strength "with plenty of guns."

Satow thought the days of foreigners being able to intimidate Chinese into ceding portions of territory were over. He commented that:

Foreign observers watch Yuan Shikai and his new army

"if the present numbers are only doubled and if the Yangtze is held by troops disciplined like Yuan's, with an uniform armament, it will be difficult for any European Power to invade either North China or the Yangtze valley. Our only means of coercion then will be attacks on coast ports, and on the occupation of islands."

He added two caveats:

"One difficulty is that of finance, and the second the jealousy naturally felt of the commander in chief of such a national army, who would be all-powerful."

He was right about finances and jealousy. He was also right about the days of European power being almost over. Only the Japanese were much later able to invade North China and the Yangtze valley.

As Satow's note suggested, change was coming to China, but not quite yet. For Americans in China, however, a new court was about to be established and, while no riots broke out, the court and its judge would go through a baptism of fire.

CHAPTER 14

The United States Court for China: Taming the Wild East

SHANGHAI AND THE OTHER treaty ports in China were the Wild East. In a report to President Roosevelt, Elihu Root, Secretary of State, called the behaviour of Americans in China a "disgraceful condition of affairs" that was "discreditable to the United States and humiliating to American self-respect." The problem was, Root explained, that under extraterritoriality there was not one court with power over all the residents of Shanghai.

> "As a result of this peculiar arrangement the vice which seems to thrive in the atmosphere of the Orient has long tended to seek shelter under the flag of the country whose administration is the most lax and ineffective. American administration in Shanghai had long been notoriously lax and ineffective, and the gamblers and prostitutes of Shanghai generally flourished under the claim of American citizenship and the protection of American indifference. To such an extent had this gone that prostitutes generally in Shanghai, and, to a considerable extent in the other cities, whether American or not, were called American girls and the two expressions were practically synonymous."

The problems were attributed to the weakness of the American consular courts, and indeed, they were not very effective. An American writer in 1904 gave this colourful description of consular court hearing held at the US Consulate on Whangpoo Road (Huangpu road) just north of the Bund:

> "The US Consular Court at Shanghai 'happens' in a back room of a brick building in the Whangpoo Road. The furniture is Quakerishly simple. Item, a plain table and with two rows of wooden chairs. In one corner a metal stove. Across one end of the table is a dais, and upon that a narrower table, with three chairs beside.

> Opposite the stove, a new looking 'stand' for witnesses, with a chair in which they sit upon the 'stand'."

After describing how witnesses were sworn almost inaudibly and how an official had noisily stoked the stove during the course of the hearing, the writer recounted the rough and-tumble behavior of the lawyers:

> "Both advocates are in ordinary Shanghai attire. While one is speaking, the other tilts back his chair upon its hind legs, and winks at the official aforesaid. Official spits in the stove. First advocate puts a leading question. Crash! The tilted chair finds its level, and the other forensic champion is on his feet. 'No! no! I object! I object! My boy, only seventeen knows better'n that. You can't do it.' Then follows a dispute in which 'the Court' is temporarily ignored. During the resumed pleading, advocate Number Two saunters over to the stove and warms his hands. Occasionally he wrangles with the Plaintiff while his learned friend continues to address the Bench. When his turn comes to speak, and an interruption is made, he advances to the Judge, places the palm of his hand on the judicial blotting pad,

and truculently demands to know if the Court is going
to allow him to be 'cheeked' in this manner within
these 'holy precincts.' A witness is peremptorily bidden
to 'shut up' and the irate advocate further warns his
learned brother that he (the speaker) has 'been too long
at this game to learn anything from him.' Beyond a
mild suggestion that the Court's time is being wasted,
the President of the Court takes no step to vindicate the
dignity of the Law."

An increasingly strong and proud United States of
America could not let this situation continue. In the 1880s, the
State Department had tried to get a bill passed to establish a
United States Court for China and Japan, but the proposal
died in committee. In 1906 Root revived the idea and found
a strong backer in Congress, Edwin Denby, whose father had
been American Minister in Peking. Denby had himself lived
in Peking from 1894 to 1895. Denby went to a lot of effort to
get the bill through Congress, pushing for the bill to be passed
by the Senate in the last hour of the last session of June 1906.

The new law established the United States Court for China
at Shanghai and provided that it would also sit at Tientsin,
Hankow and Canton and elsewhere in China as necessary.
Given the rush, a number of defects were left in the bill to
be sorted out later. The new law established the United
States Court for China with one judge, a clerk and a district
attorney. The court was to act as the peak court for American
consular courts in China. The law provided that the court
would apply United States Law and Common Law in China.
There was no provision for jury trials or other constitutional
protections; nor was there provision for the appointment of
acting judges. If the sole judge was not available for whatever
reason, the court could not sit. Over the years, many defects
in the court structure would be fixed by legislation but this
was a labourious process. To get legislation through the

US Congress requires a sponsor, but
no member of Congress represented
overseas Americans, meaning that bills
would often fall by the wayside.

The bill did provide one substantial
improvement over the old system.
A proper appellate procedure was
provided for, with appeals going from
the United States Court for China to the
Ninth Circuit Court of Appeals in San
Francisco.

Lebbeus Wilfley

The US Court for China was itself given appellate
jurisdiction over decisions of the US consular courts in China
and Korea. This included the Consular Court in Shanghai
which continued to exist. The US Court for China took over
all serious criminal cases, where the penalty exceeded 60
days in jail or a fine of $100 and civil cases where the amount
claimed was more than $500. US consular courts in China,
including the Shanghai Consular Court, continued to hear
smaller cases.

Sherriff Wilfley rides into town

With the court established, President Theodore Roosevelt
needed to appoint a judge of the court. After the bill was
passed, Denby met with Roosevelt to tell him what he hoped
for in the court and "begged him to make certain that the first
judge should be a man of calibre and character and vision
sufficient to attempt to realize the dream." Denby was asked
for a recommendation; he had none. Roosevelt said that he
had received a recommendation from Mr William Taft, then
Secretary of War, who had previously been Governor-General
of the Philippines that Lebbeus Wilfley, the Attorney-General
of the Philippines, be appointed. Roosevelt, a Republican,
made the point that he would be appointing a Democrat,
"thinking to accomplish the best results thereby."

Wilfley was a native of St Louis having been born in Mexico, Missouri in 1866 and a graduate of Yale Law School. He had been admitted to the bar 13 years before in 1893. In 1901, just after the United States had colonized the Philippines, he was appointed as a judge of the Philippines Court of First Instance, but very soon after, at the very young age of 35, was promoted to become the Attorney-General of the Philippines. He was 40 when he was appointed as Judge of the US Court for China and was clearly a young man in a hurry.

Wilfley was formally appointed in July 1906 and travelled immediately to Shanghai from Manila. Finding that the statute creating the court had not yet arrived in Shanghai, he went to Washington DC to meet with the State Department. He returned to Shanghai in December. At a dinner held by the American Association just before the court was formally opened, Wilfley told the American Association that the Court had been created for them. He said:

> "This Court was their Court. It had been established
> at their behest and in their behalf. It would be largely
> what they made it. The success of this Court was
> largely in their hands; the standard of this Court would
> not permanently rise much higher nor sink much lower
> that the standard of good Americans in Shanghai."

Wilfley then set out his intended philosophy for presiding over the court, saying that Americans were in China "at the sufferance of the Chinese Empire and this made it more incumbent that they should be more orderly governed, conduct themselves in a most orderly way." For Wilfley, just as it had been for Sir Edmund Hornby, this was particularly important. He wanted to set an example to the Chinese and show them what "the reign of law" meant. He added that "it was more incumbent upon Americans here than at home to be always law abiding under all circumstances and conditions."

Wilfley said that court would operate in a very similar way to a court in the United States, except there would be no jury trial. Then, perhaps with a nod to the Assistant Judge of the British Supreme Court for China and Corea, Frederick Bourne, who was in attendance, he added, "it came naturally to members of the Anglo-Saxon race that they should have purity of administration, secondly fearlessness, and thirdly common sense." Saying that these characteristics were common to Anglo-Saxon courts everywhere, he continued, to applause from the audience: "Wherever the English flag or the American flag floated they found the symbol not only of power but of justice."

Wilfley then turned to his first major task: improving the local bar. He said, again to applause, that it was his "purpose to raise the standard of professional ethics in the Court of the United States for China so that they would be such as America would be proud." To a further round of applause, he continued that "it was highly important that the lawyers should be well grounded in the law, but of the two he laid more stress on character." In conclusion, he said that his hope was that the US Court would achieve the "high standard of repute" of the British Supreme Court for China and Corea.

The Court officially opens

The United States Court for China held its first hearing at 10.30

am on December 17, 1906 sitting in the court room of the Consular Court at the American Consulate. Wilfley declared the court officially open and then requested the new District Attorney, Clerk of Court and Marshal to all present their commissions. The Hon Arthur Bassett, Dr Frank E. Hinckley and Mr O.R. Leonard all did so. Hinckley took charge of the

Arthur Bassett

The New Broom - Wilfley forces US lawyers to take an examination
Thomas Jernignan and Stirling Fessenden, the only two to pass,
are standing at the back of the courtroom.

commissions. Bassett who was only 28 had been Assistant Attorney-General in the Philippines under Wilfley while Dr Hinckley had just published a book on extraterritoriality in China. He had been appointed Clerk of the Court on the strength of this.

Wilfley, having thrown down the gauntlet at the American Association dinner a few nights before, then turned to the expected qualification of lawyers to appear before the court. He announced that American attorneys who wished to be admitted to the bar of the United States Court for China would be required to produce a certificate of good moral character as well as taking an examination in eight legal topics, namely,

Equity, Evidence, Contract, Torts, Conflicts of Laws, Criminal Law, the law creating the US Court for China and Wills and Probate. Certificates of moral character were to be filed within five days, before December 22, 1906, and the first examination would be on December 24, 1906.

Wilfley was effectively locking out American lawyers from appearing before the court unless they passed an exam on seven days notice. What must have been most galling to the American attorneys was that Wilfley ordered that foreign practitioners would be allowed to practice before the United States Court as a matter of courtesy.

First day at work
On January 2, 1907, the first formal session of the United States Court for China was called to order. On his very first day sitting as a judge, Wilfley notched up the first strike that would lead to his downfall as a judge. He also had, as the very first case before him, a case that would lead very soon to the second strike.

The first strike came with the announcement that of eight practitioners who had taken the examination, only two had passed. These were Mr Thomas Jernigan, a former US Consul-General, and Mr Stirling Fessenden. Fessenden, as we shall see, went on to become a pillar of the Shanghai community when he became the Chairman of the Shanghai Municipal Council. Wilfley described the testimonials he had received for Jernigan and Fessenden as having come from leading citizens of both Shanghai and their home jurisdictions and of being of the highest order. Wilfley also admitted Mr Noel Home, a British barrister, and Mr Musso of the Italian court. Bassett, as the District Attorney, was also allowed to practice without taking the exam. Those who had failed included, Lorrin Andrews, who had formerly being the Attorney-General of Hawaii. In the end, after other rounds of exams sixteen American lawyers in Shanghai took the exam and six failed.

Wilfley's rush to disbar those lawyers he considered unsuitable was overzealous and unnecessary. He created enemies who would, as we shall see, strike back.

Criminal and civil cases within the jurisdiction of the

US Court were then called for directions. The very first case was to become, a few days later, Wilfley's second strike. Wilfley, himself, admitted later that he made a "grave error in judgment." This was the case of the *United States v R.J. McCord*. McCord was charged with obtaining $301.50 by false pretences. Stirling Fessenden appeared on behalf of McCord and the case was adjourned until the following Tuesday.

Wilfley then gave directions in a number of other criminal cases involving an assault that had occurred on an American boat; assault with a deadly weapon; and, theft. One defendant had to find a new lawyer because his lawyer, Lorrin Andrews, had not passed the examination.

Civil cases were then called. As with the British Crown Advocate, the District Attorney was allowed to handle civil cases that did not conflict with his duties as District Attorney. Mr Bassett appeared in some of the cases. In a number of cases, the defendants said they needed to find new lawyers because their lawyers had failed Wilfley's examination.

McCord sows discord

The McCord case was a very simple case that was to take on extraordinary importance in the short career of Judge Wilfley. McCord, who had previously lived in the Philippines, worked on commission for an American company, Mustard & Co. he had pocketed some money he had been paid rather than passing in on to his employers. District Attorney Bassett prosecuted and Fessenden defended McCord.

First, Wilfley had to deal with the question of what the "common law of the United States" was. McCord had been charged with the common law offence of obtaining money by false pretences. At the outset of the trial, Fessenden on behalf of McCord applied for the indictment to be quashed on the basis that it charged an offence that was not indictable under common law because the common law had been amended by an English statute before the common law had been received in the United States. Fessenden argued that the common law, as received in the United States, could only be judge-made law. Bassett, on the other hand, argued that all English statutes that amended the common law prior to independence of the United States were received in the United States as common law, even if that statute had subsequently been repealed in England. Wilfley ruled that the common law as amended by the English statute was the common law of the United States and that the trial should proceed.

There followed a short trial where witnesses from the Alhambra Gardens and Mustard & Co were called. McCord admitted that he owed money to a third party and had taken the money due to Mustard & Co to pay that third party in order "to avoid any trouble."

Wilfley found the offence was proved beyond any reasonable doubt and convicted McCord. He said he would sentence McCord the next day at 9.00am. He then, in a decision he later described as "a mistake," continued McCord's bail allowing him to be free until sentencing. Not surprisingly, McCord did not appear the next morning. He had taken a ship out of Shanghai the night before. Wilfley ordered that his bail be forfeited.

What is not mentioned in the record of the court is that the last person in court that day to see McCord was Judge Wilfley. After the hearing, McCord had come to the Astor House Hotel the night before to see Wilfley. Wilfley met him in the lobby and told McCord: "If you are here in the morning I will give you a heavy sentence."

Heavy sentences

While Wilfley was not able to impose a heavy sentence on McCord, he did impose them on others. He also stopped the practice of granting bail even to those who were appealing against a conviction.

The first case where a defendant was to suffer the wrath

of Judge Wilfley was *United States v Biddle*. Biddle, who was the manager of the Metropole Hotel, had rented out a house in Mohawk Road (now Huangpi North Road) next to the racecourse for 3,000 taels to some Chinese on the basis that the municipal government would allow gambling at the house during the autumn races. Gambling was illegal in Shanghai and there was no chance that such approval would be given. The Chinese in a civil case had sued Biddle. At the conclusion of the civil case, Wilfley said Biddle should be charged with a criminal offence. District Attorney Bassett then charged Biddle with the criminal offence of obtaining money by false pretences under the common law.

At his trial, like McCord, Biddle argued that there was no common law offence of obtaining money by false pretences. It was not a federal crime and should be dealt with by state law. Wilfley disagreed and found Biddle guilty, but gave him the opportunity to refund the money. Biddle appealed the decision to the Ninth Circuit in San Francisco which nine months later allowed the appeal on a technical ground that at common law, the crime of obtaining money by false pretences was not made out where the promise made related to some future fact. The statement that the council would allow gambling in the future was not sufficient to make out the offence of obtaining money by false pretences.

Most importantly, the decision of the Court of Appeal was groundbreaking because it redefined the entire basis of United States extraterritorial jurisdiction in China in two significant ways. First, the court found that there was a "common law of the United States." This common law was, as Wilfley had found, the common law in force when the United States "separated from the mother country," England. Second, and far more importantly, the court ruled that the "laws of the United States" included the laws of the District of Columbia and Alaska, both federal territories at the time. The United States Court for China, could therefore, as necessary, apply the statutes that Congress had passed for Alaska and the District of Columbia. This principle became the bedrock for the future jurisprudence of the US Court.

The next case to bring problems for Wilfley was the prosecution of S.R. Price for assault with a dangerous weapon. Price had been tried, and acquitted, in the Shanghai Consular Court before the Consul-General on related charges. He had then been brought before Wilfley and pleaded "double jeopardy"; that is, that he had already been acquitted and could not be tried again for the same offence. Wilfley rejected this on the basis that the Consul-General did not have jurisdiction to try a charge of assault with a dangerous weapon. Price also argued that because the gun was unloaded the offence of assault with a dangerous weapon was not made out. Wilfley rejected this too and convicted Price, sentencing him to six months imprisonment. Price appealed to the Ninth Circuit in San Francisco. His lawyer, Lorrin Andrews who had by now passed Wilfley's examination, applied for bail pending

Wilfley presiding in the US Court for China

appeal. Wilfley refused bail, partly because of his experience of McCord jumping bail. Later, the Ninth Circuit found that Wilfley was right in rejecting Price's double jeopardy plea but wrong in holding that pointing an unloaded gun at a person was assault with a deadly weapon. They remitted the case back to Shanghai for a new trial.

Wilfley's strict enforcement of the law and in one case, at least, convicting US citizens where the British Court acquitted British citizens on the same facts was welcomed by some and not by others. Secretary of State Root, in a letter to President Roosevelt, said that "the lawyers whose most liberal clients have been the gamblers and prostitutes of Shanghai never complained of the old order of things, but they are now full of bitterness against the Judge, who has driven their clients out of business, but the decent and virtuous Americans in Shanghai were indignant and humiliated over the former conditions, and are now grateful and approving."

Secretary for War William Taft, who had recommended Wilfley for the position, in a public speech during a visit to Shanghai added support for Wilfley saying the US government had been "fortunate in the selection as the first judge of that court" of Wilfley who had intimate knowledge of Asia. Taft fully supported Wilfley's policy of "raising high the standard of admission to the bar and in promoting vigorous prosecutions of American violators of law" as to cause the "elimination from this community of undesirable characters who have brought disgrace upon the name of Americans in the cities of China."

He then praised Wilfley further, saying:

"it involves no small amount of courage and a great
deal of common sense to deal with evils of this
character and to rid the community of them. Interests
which have fattened on abuses cannot be readily
disturbed without making a fight for their lives,

and one who undertakes the work of cleansing and purifying must expect to meet resistance in libel and slander and the stirring up of official opposition based on misinformation and evil report."

A Tibetan tragedy

Wilfley did not convict everyone who came before his court. In late 1907, he tried a very difficult case where Henry De Menil, a medical doctor from a wealthy family in St Louis, Missouri (Wilfley's home town), while travelling in Tibet had shot and killed a Tibetan Lama. The lama, Pu Keng-lung, had been walking on a hill nearby. De Menil whose behavior had become erratic due to altitude sickness had become angry with one of his guards, Li Yu-shan, and had fired two shots in his direction to warn him. One of the bullets had hit the Lama. De Menil was brought back from Tibet to Shanghai for the trial. One of the Chinese guards who had been travelling with him was also brought to Shanghai to give evidence. This was the first time a case involving a killing of a Chinese by an American to come before the US Court for China. The Shanghai Taotai asked Magistrate Li to watch the case. Magistrate Li was given a place on the bench next to Wilfley. District Attorney Bassett prosecuted the case and William Fleming defended.

Magistrate Li must have found the whole proceeding bizarre. Fleming objected to almost every witness and piece of evidence. On a number of occasions Wilfley had to admonish Fleming for going too far and in one case said he had transcended "the bounds of professional ethics" for accusing Bassett of improper conduct and violating his oath of office. On another occasion, an "animated discussion" between Wilfley, Bassett and two witnesses could be heard from the backroom of the court during the lunch break.

The witnesses were not much better. De Menil had given an interview to the *Shanghai Mercury* on his arrival in Shanghai.

Bassett wanted to rely on what De Menil had told them. One witness, Mr R.D. Neish, the deputy editor, was British. Bassett first had to get a subpoena from the British Supreme Court to compel Neish to give evidence. Neish refused to produce documents. He said he had only received a subpoena from the British Court to give evidence. Bassett went back to the British Supreme Court to get an order that Neish produce the notes that he had been given by De Menil.

Once this order was obtained, the editor of the *Shanghai Mercury*, John Clark, came to court to say that despite a search having been conducted, the notes were missing. Neish then told the court that he could not remember what had been written. He then gave such evasive answers that Bassett took the extraordinary step of asking that the evidence of his own witness be struck out. Wilfley decided to take matters into his own hands and cross-examined Neish himself. At the end, Wilfley said that Neish had changed his answer on a key question. Bassett said he would not rely on Neish's testimony. He said: "I don't care to offer this testimony to the Court. I would not ask for a man to be convicted on the evidence of such a witness."

Neish was most likely being evasive because he did not want to see De Menil convicted on what he had told him. De Menil had effectively admitted to manslaughter in his diary where he had written: "I have killed a Tibetan warrior, partly carelessness, partly accidental."

This was damning evidence. Fleming tried to exclude the diary on

John Clark, editor of the Shanghai Mercury

the basis that it had been taken off De Menil by the American Consul in Chungking after an improper search. After an argument about whether US constitutional or English common law protections against illegal search applied in China, Wilfley ruled that the diary was admissible.

With the diary in evidence, De Menil had no choice but to testify in his own defence. He said he had been arrested in Artunza in Tibet. The Chinese authorities there had found the killing to be accidental. He denied seeing the bullet in the Tibetan's eye and any suggestion the shooting was not accidental. To explain away the diary, he suggested it was an embellished account he had written after the fact with the intention of getting it published. Wilfley was not impressed. He said that De Menil's testimony was "peculiar to say the least." De Menil was asking him to believe all the statements that showed he did not intend to kill. But on the other hand he had made statements that were "highly improbable and lacking in frankness."

Nevertheless, after reserving judgment for three weeks, Wilfley acquitted De Menil. He accepted that De Menil was in a bad physical condition at the time. He also accepted that De Menil had not intended to kill anyone when shooting; the question was: was what he did so careless to be criminal in the eyes of the law? Wilfley found that, given the area was sparsely populated, it was not so careless. He, therefore, acquitted De Menil.

Wilfley then said that De Menil had already suffered much inconvenience and pain in the case, including being detained by the Chinese authorities, and he "did not feel the ends of justice would be subserved by imposing further punishment on the accused." This was a strange point to make. The question of the deprivations De Menil had suffered before his trial should not have affected his guilt or innocence. It may have been relevant as to what punishment to impose if he found him guilty but not as to whether he was guilty or not.

One can only suspect that De Menil's station in society and the fact he was from the same home town swayed Wilfley's judgement.

It was an unsatisfactory conclusion to an unsatisfactory case. The Chinese authorities certainly thought so. A full report on the case was prepared by Magistrate Li, which was passed on by the Taotai to the Superintendent of Trade. In August 1908, the Chinese Ministry of Foreign Affairs sent a formal protest in the name of Prince Ch'ing over the acquittal to the American Minister, W.W. Rockhill. The protest complained that in shooting at his guard, De Menil clearly "had murder in his heart" and as such should be liable for the killing of Pu and that "the great wrong done the murdered man is not in the least atoned for … In this case justice does not shine, and the good name of America suffers."

Then, in a direct challenge to the independence of the US Court for China, Prince Ch'ing wrote to Rockhill that he "must refer this case to your excellency that your excellency may think of a way to straighten this affair out, determining the crime of which the aforesaid criminal is guilty, or the fine which he ought to pay, so that angry passions may be calmed and justice displayed."

The note's request that the American Minister overturn the verdict was not made due to a lack of understanding of the American concept of judicial independence. On the contrary, it is clear that the Chinese had studied in detail the law establishing the United States Court. The Chinese protest noted that the act that had created the court had granted the court the powers "now exercised by consuls and ministers" and that the judge was appointed at "the pleasure of the President."

"From this it appears that the status of the court is different from that of an independent judiciary. Although the term 'judge' is employed it is evident that he is only an official of the executive department appointed for the conduct of foreign relations."

Because of this, the Chinese note concluded:

> "The American minister at Peking will be regarded as having ultimate appellate jurisdiction in all matters concerning the exercise of judicial power over foreigners within Chinese territory."

This was a very sophisticated analysis and in many ways correct. The act did not create an independent judiciary. The independence only came from the common law and the practice of the judges and lawyers.

The State Department could not let this direct challenge to the independence of the court pass. Secretary of State Root in early 1909 replied to Rockhill that the note from Prince Ch'ing "uses certain language in expressing its understanding of the functions and status of the court which is so incorrect that the department deems it advisable not to allow these observations to pass." Rockhill was instructed to explain the independence of the court and that the act establishing it had created appeals to the Ninth Circuit in San Francisco. The treaties with China and the act establishing the court required trial "according the laws of the United States" and that both statutory and common law rules should apply.

Rockhill was also instructed to inform the Chinese that De Menil could not be retried under American rules and that the lama's family could bring a claim for compensation in the court if they wished.

The Chinese complaints about the handling of the De Menil case went no further. However, Wilfley was at the same time facing serious complaints by American lawyers about his handling of other cases.

The original courthouse of the Supreme Court for China and Japan

The British Consulate in Yokohama – Home of the British Court for Japan

The Capture of Chusan during the first opium war

Some of the destruction of the Yuanmingyuan looted by British and French troops in 1860 after the second opium war

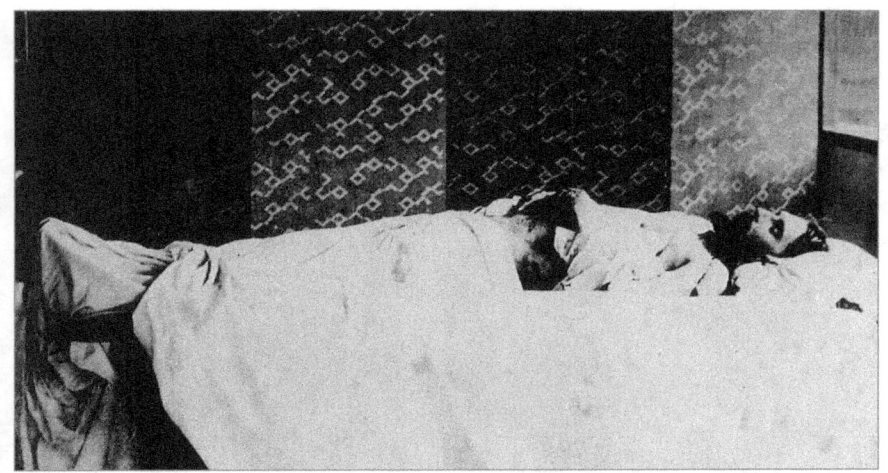

The body of Charles Richardson. His death at the hands of a samurai triggered the bombardment of Kagoshima in 1863

British, American, French and Dutch forces capture Japanese cannon at Shimonoseki in 1864

Sir Edmund Hornby, founder and Chief
Judge of the British Supreme Court for
China and Japan

Sir Nicholas Hannen, Crown
Advocate, Judge for Japan, Chief
Justice and Consul-General in
Shanghai

Prince Kung, founder of the Tsungli Yamen

Victor Deacon who acted for the Chinese
government in the Canton claims commission. His firm, Deacons, still exists today.

Robert Hart, Inspector-General of the Imperial Maritime Customs, who challenged the authority of the British Courts a number of times.

John Richard Wolfe, Head of the Church Missionary Society in Foochow, defendant in the Wushishan case

John Lowder, prosecutor of John Hartley; Edith Carew's defence Lawyer

John Hartley, opium importer to Japan. His acquittal led to a major diplomatic incident.

Sir Nicholas Hannen's Funeral Cortege on the Maloo in April 1900.
The Town Hail is in the background.

Troops of the eight nation alliance that occupied (and then looted) Peking in 1900. Note the British solider is a Sikh. Sikhs underpinned British military power in China

Li Hongzhang in 1900. Called on, yet again, to negotiate an unequal treaty

The Entrance to the British Minister's palatial residence in Peking; restored after the siege of the legations.

US Court for China

The US Court for China in 1906. Left to right: Arthur Bassett, District Attorney, Hubert O'Brian, US Marshal, Lebbeus Wilfley, Judge, Frank Hinckley, Clerk of the Court

The US Consulate on Whangpoo Road. The first home of the US Court for China

Sir HS Wilkinson

HP Wilkinson

Milton Helmick

Stirling Fessenden

HENRY D. O'SHEA,
Proprietor and Editor.

Henry O'Shea, Plaintiff in the Shanghai Liar
case; Defendant in R v O'Shea for defaming
Judge Wilfley of the US Court for China

Dr Henry DeMenil, acquitted of killing a
monk in Tibet in 1907

Ernest Bethell, Korea's hero. Imprisoned
in 1909 for inciting sedition against the
Japanese Government of Korea

Yang Ki-Tak, Betthel's Korean co-pub-
lisher in 1918. He is carrying a sign stating he is prohibited from living in China

The Shanghai Club building opened in 1910 .The home of the British elite in Shanghai. Lawrence Kentwell was refused membership due to his mixed race

The entrance to the former American Club in Shanghai. DA Leonard Husar received his bribes here. The author is at the bottom right corner.

Lawrence Kentwell – Rebel with a Cause

The US Court for China sitting in the American Legation in Peking in 1935.
The judge Milton Helmick. Norwood Allman is second from left. R.T. Evans is far
right and British Barrister, Percy Kent, appearing by courtesy, is far left.

The British Supreme Court for China in the 1930s

Sgt Ernest Peters and Sumiko. Peters was accused of throwing a Chinese beggar in a river.

Frank Jay Raven, fraudster

A beggar boat on a river in Shanghai. Peters claims to have placed the beggar on a boat like this.

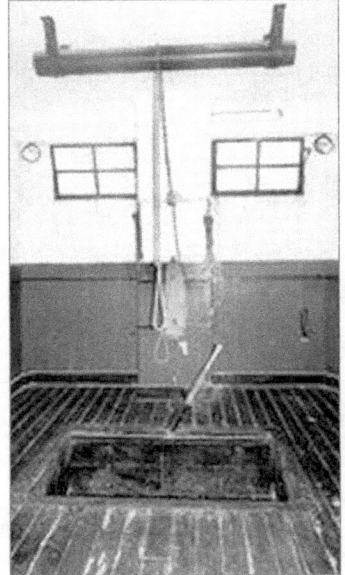

FOREIGN SECTION, MUNICIPAL GAOL, WARD ROAD (3rd Floor, Interior)

The gallows at Ward Road Gaol

A warder looks through the hole made by Japanese shelling of Ward Road Gaol in 1937

HJIMS Idzumo in Shanghai in 1937. The China Printing and Finishing Factory where Maurice Tinkler was bayonetted is top left on the Pudong side.

Bombing and death on Nanking Road (1937)

A bomb-damaged house, flying the German Swastika, on Hungjao Road (1937)

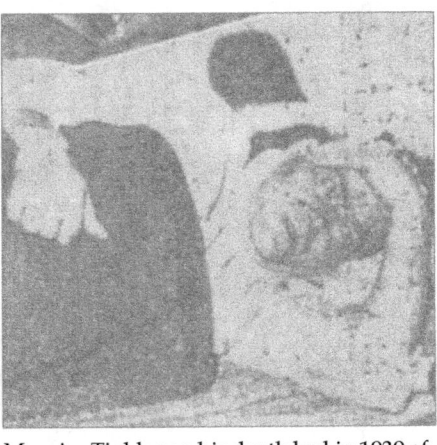

Kenneth Piper and his wife, Jane, ordered to pay rent for a house of Hungjao Road despite the danger of war.

Maurice Tinkler on his death bed in 1939 after being bayonetted by Japanese soldiers. 76 years before when Charles Richardson has been cut down by a samurai, British gunboats bombarded Kagoshima.

Japanese electric fences surround the Tientsin British Concession in 1939

The very last British or American court hearing in China. The US Court for China in Kunming which tried Boatner Carney in January 1943.
Top row, left to right: Captain Edwin Kessler, US Attorney; Major Bertrand Johnson, Special Judge; Lieut. Lincoln C. Brownell, Defense Counsel; Raymond P. Ludden, US Consul, Kunming. Bottom row: Stanley A. McGeary, Marshalll; Mrs L.D. Tayler, Recorder; Alfred T. Wellborn, Clerk of the Court

CHAPTER 15

The Wild East Fights Back

WILFLEY IN HIS TIME on the bench had made a lot of enemies. Lorrin Andrews, in particular, was not going to take Wilfley's refusal to admit him and treatment of his client, Mr Price, lying down. In the Price case Andrews filed a writ of *habeas corpus* in San Francisco. He was quoted in the press as calling Wilfley a "czar," suggesting he was like a king controlled by no one. He then went on to Washington DC where, on November 17, 1907 he filed a petition to President Theodore Roosevelt seeking to have Wilfley removed from office.

Andrews' charges against Wilfley were a bucket list of complaints. He alleged that Wilfley had prevented six lawyers in Shanghai from practicing before the court by requiring them to take an examination; that he allowed Bassett, as Attorney-General, to practice without taking an examination; that Wilfley had libeled those who had failed the exam; that Wilfley had commenced proceedings to disbar Andrews; that Wilfley abused his power in certain cases by ordering an American to appear before the British court and refusing to grant adjournments in two cases; and, finally, that he refused to grant Price bail.

Secretary of State Root sent a formal opinion to the President on February 29, 1908, rejecting all the charges as ill-founded and explaining the difficult situation that Wilfley had found in Shanghai. Root concluded:

"My opinion is that Judge Wilfley is entitled, not to

condemnation but to commendation and high credit for his conduct in office, and that the charges against him should be dismissed."

Roosevelt replied on March 2, 1908 agreeing with Root's recommendations, adding:

"I cordially concur in your finding, which is to the effect that Judge Wilfley is not only innocent but is attacked solely because of the fearlessness and integrity with which he has stamped out vice and crime in Shanghai."

Roosevelt attached to his letter a letter from Robert E. Lewis, the secretary of the International Committee of the YMCA praising Wilfley. Roosevelt added after reading this letter that "it is clear that Judge Wilfley has been attacked not because he has done evil, but because he has done good," and that "if the attack were to succeed, the beneficiaries would be every keeper of a house of prostitution, every swindling lawyer, every man who lives by blackmail and corruption, in the cities of the Far East." Roosevelt concluded that: "It is not too much to say that this assault on Judge Wilfley, in the interest of the vicious and criminal classes, is a public scandal."

Perhaps suspecting that he would not get very far with his petition to the President, Andrews through Congressman Waldo filed a further petition seeking that Wilfley be impeached directly to the Senate Judiciary Committee. This petition, in addition to the charges put to President Roosevelt, included an allegation that Wilfley was anti-Catholic. The petition was signed by Andrews and eight other Shanghai residents including W.W. Dowdell, the President of the Catholic Sodality of Shanghai and, the "Shanghai Liar", Henry O'Shea, the proprietor of the *China Gazette*.

Wilfley's anti-Catholicism was alleged to have been shown by a decision he had made in a probate case involving a Captain J.P. Roberts. The petition alleged that "in violation of the duties and oath of his high office, he has condemned the Catholic clergy as the Popish clergy, guilty of robbing the poor, the widows and the orphans under the name of the Church, which slanderous statements, if made in print, other than in a decision of one of the court of the United States would be a criminal libel." He was also alleged to have applauded at a conference when a Protestant priest made an attack on the Catholic Church and to have also have made public statements questioning Catholicism.

Wilfley was required to give evidence before a small subcommittee of three. He arrived in Washington in mid-January 1908. Andrews was there as well as some members of the press. In the course of the hearing, Wilfley was asked about the *China Gazette* which Henry O'Shea, one of the petitioners, published. He responded that it "did not enter the best homes in Shanghai."

The committee found that there was no case for impeachment but after doing so delivered what Wilfley later described as "hypothetical rebuke." The committee that even a totally uncorrupt judge could by entirely legal acts may "convert the machinery of justice into an engine of despotic and autocratic power."

"Terror to evil-doers, if purchased at the price of judicial fairness and overstrained legal authority, is achieved at too great an expense, for it defeats its own high aim and warps the very fabric of the law itself.

"The temptation of an honest judge to 'Bend once the law to his authority: To do a great right — do a little wrong,' is fraught with such danger to our whole system of remedial justice that it merits the condemnation of every legal mind."

The sub-committee continued that "such acts of legal oppression and of abuse of judicial discretion" lay at the base of the charges against Wilfley, but said they were dismissed because they fell short of an impeachable offence.

Then, in a strange passage, the sub-committee first noted that because of the dismissal of the petition Wilfley did not have an opportunity to defend himself:

> "he can file no answer; make no denial; nor explain to the House the legality or necessity for his action."

Wilfley returns from Washington, vindicated

All fair enough and a worthwhile point to make. The subcommittee report then undid the fairness of this comment, by adding that:

> "if Judge Wilfley's judicial acts in the future are marked by the rigorous and inflexible harshness imputed to him they will hang as a portentous cloud over this new Court, impairing his usefulness, impeding the administration of justice, and challenging the integrity of American Institutions."

The report was sent to the full committee, made up of 24 members, who in the normal course would have adopted the recommendation of the sub-committee. However, given the clear rebuke in the report, the committee asked for all the evidence to be published. Ultimately, the Committee issued a final report stating:

"Adopted unanimously that no impeachment proceedings be instituted at all."

The Shanghai Liar attacks

Henry O'Shea was outraged by Wilfley's evidence before the sub-committee and published a number of articles attacking Wilfley, each article becoming more and more virulent. O'Shea admitted later that he published the reports because "I wished to expose Judge Wilfley. I did not consider that he was a proper man to be head of the American Court. In the public interest I thought Shanghai deserved a better judge and one who made fewer blunders."

O'Shea's attacks culminated in an article in the *China Gazette* on August 4, 1908 that was scathing in its comments on Wilfley. The attack read:

"An exhibition of greater indecency, of more venomous mendacity, of meaner innuendo, a greater contempt for the truth and justice, and a wilder desire to simply revenge himself by besmirching the name of everyone who dared to criticize his methods, has surely never been presented in any country by a Judge than has been given in this case by this coarse, unscrupulous, ignorant and vulgar mountebank, whom the grim irony of corrupt American politics has entrusted with the discharge of judicial functions - functions that he is intellectually, mentally and morally unfitted for and incapable of exercising. The miserable tactics of Mr. Wilfley while before the Committee remind us only of the tactics of the squid, the creature which when pursued hopes to escape by darkening and poisoning the waters all round it by the discharge of the noxious fluid concealed in its glands. When Mr. Wilfley made the above statements he not only was lying, but we say it deliberately, he knew at the time he was lying, his only object being to mislead the members of the House Committee as to the standing and record of his critics in Shanghai. It was surely a poor role for a Judge to plead in order to excuse his own protection of notorious swindlers, that the British Court and British Law in China are parties to like swindles under the Hongkong Ordinances as Mr Wilfley falsely and audaciously pleaded."

The British authorities could not let such a venomous attack on the Judge of the court of a friendly power go unnoticed or unpunished. O'Shea was prosecuted for criminal defamation. The trial commenced in November 1908 before Frederick Bourne sitting with a jury of five. Crown Advocate, Harrie Wilkinson, prosecuted the case and F. Ellis, J. Hays and C.W. Godfrey appeared to defend O'Shea.

O'Shea, from his own experience in the Shanghai Liar case, knew how hard it was to prove that defamatory words were true. However, he also knew how damaging a defamation case could be for a plaintiff's reputation even if he won. After all, after the case against him, who could think of O'Shea as anybody but "the Shanghai Liar"?

O'Shea therefore pleaded "Not Guilty" to the charges and sought to justify the words that had been written. He

Wilfley reading the China Gazete and asks "What is a Squid?"

sought to prove that Wilfley was a liar, was "intellectually mentally and morally" unfit to be a judge and that he protected notorious swindlers. For good measure O'Shea in his pleadings added that the holder of a judicial office such as that of Judge of the United States Court for China should "is one which should in the interests of the whole community, both Chinese and foreign, of Shanghai, be filled by a person of integrity, of unbiased mind, of scrupulous fairness, truthfulness and honesty, and of unquestioned legal ability."

This, as can be imagined, made for a sensational trial. Because O'Shea had admitted the defamation and sought to justify it, the normal order of a criminal trial was reversed. O'Shea was required to call his witnesses first to justify the statements with the prosecution witnesses to be called afterwards.

Mr Ellis opened O'Shea's case. He framed it is a question of the liberty of the press and the responsibilities and duties that members of the press have in society. O'Shea, he said, was attempting to fulfill these responsibilities and duties in publishing the article.

O'Shea called seven witnesses on his behalf, including himself, Dr Hinckley, the clerk of the United States Court, Mr Trissel, Mr Davis, the manager of the Astor House Hotel and Mr Holcomb and Mr Brooks, two of the lawyers who had been refused admission by Wilfley.

O'Shea gave evidence about his background and how he had been surprised by the results of both the McCord and Biddle cases and that the appeal court had overruled Wilfley in the Biddle case. He gave other evidence regarding Crozier, Trissel and Black and a "pyramid scheme" known as the Shanghai Watch Club, of which Black had been a part.

He was particularly upset that Wilfley had stated that the *China Gazette* did not enter the best homes, saying he took it that Wilfley was seeking to infer it was a paper of "inferior character".

Mr Hays asked O'Shea if he was an intimate friend with anyone in Shanghai. O'Shea was able to pull an ace from up his sleeve. He had been a good friend of one of the leading members of the British community in Shanghai for many years. He answered: "Mr. Wilkinson's father was one of my oldest friends, and best friends, and I hope he is still." He

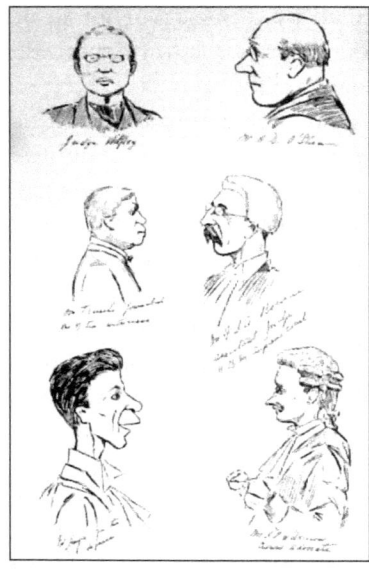

Sketches from the O'Shea trial

then added, referring to the Crown Advocate, "I even consider Mr. Wilkinson as one of my friends." Wilkinson immediately confirmed this to the court with a "That is so." In fact, Wilkinson and O'Shea had been in business together trying to set up telegraph company to send messages from Shanghai to Europe via Russia.

Despite this friendship, Wilkinson was willing to cross-examine O'Shea aggressively. He put it to O'Shea that he had been willing to change sides whenever it suited him: that back in Dublin he had switched from the Nationalist to Unionist sides as a journalist; and, then during the Russia-Japan war he had switched from supporting the Japanese to supporting the Russians. O'Shea said that as a working journalist he was like a barrister. He had to do what it took to make money. One newspaper in Dublin was paying better so he switched. With regard to the war he said he was "tired of supporting the Japanese," because it was clear they were feeding his reporters propaganda. He added later that it was also partly "because I did not desire to support Asiatics against a European Race." As to the British court protecting notorious swindlers, O'Shea pointed to a passage in Wilfley's evidence before the sub-committee where he suggested it was hard to prosecute Americans involved in companies set up under the Hong Kong ordinances.

With regard to the McCord case, Trissel said that Wilfley

had lived in a boarding house with McCord for some time in the Philippines. Frederick Davis, the manager of the Astor House Hotel was then called and said he saw McCord come to the hotel the night he had been convicted and send his card up to Wilfley's room. Wilfley had then come down and talked to McCord briefly.

For the prosecution, Wilkinson said that he proposed to call, Mr Bassett, the US District Attorney and then Wilfley. He asked that Wilfley leave the court while Bassett gave evidence. Bassett said that he was in charge of instituting prosecutions in the US Court and that when he came to Shanghai he found the problem of prostitution by Americans was very serious. He said that the McCord case was the first criminal case to come before the United States Court for China. The sureties had forfeited the bail they had put up.

The final witness was the star of the show, Judge Wilfley. The court was packed. Many spectators had to stand outside to get a view of the court. Wilfley said that he had come to Shanghai from Manila where he had been briefly a judge, then Attorney-General. With regard to the admission of lawyers, he said that as there were no rules governing admission, he, as the judge, had the power to make them and he wanted to ensure a high standard of professional ethics.

Wilfley was asked to explain the circumstances of McCord's escape. He said that the offence was a common law offence and there was no schedule of penalties so he took the case under advisement to consider the penalty. He did not know how easy it was to escape from Shanghai and that it was not possible to extradite people back to Shanghai. He had, therefore, continued McCord's bail. He had known McCord in the Philippines and that he had met McCord in the lobby of the Astor House Hotel after convicting him. He said that it was a "matter of great chagrin" that McCord had escaped. As to Price, he said he refused bail pending an appeal being filed but Price's appeal had never been perfected.

Early on in his evidence, Wilfley made reference to his speech to the American Association where he promised to clean up American Shanghai and said that he had no fault with that. Later, he flip-flopped saying that work done by the court had:

"not been undertaken with any view to reforming the Shanghai or any other community. The purpose, the policy of the Court is simply this: to hear cases which are brought before it and determine them according to the facts and the law, and that is all."

He added that "the general policy of the Washington Government—the reason for the creation of the Court—is a different thing."

Wilfley turned to the Roberts case and said that the offending passage had been directly copied from a law reference book, Blackstone, and there had been no attempt to doctor the judgment.

Then Wilfley, obviously deciding that he needed to get in front of the jury that the Catholic representative in the US had said he understood Wilfley's position and accepted the matter fully, decided to sneak some inadmissible evidence in.

This led to some fireworks in the court.

Wilfley first said that "I called on the Papal delegate and discussed the matter with him for a few moments. He understood the matter fully."

O'Shea's counsel, Mr Hays, immediately leapt out of his seat to object. Wilfley, as he well knew, was breaking all the rules of evidence by trying to put in hearsay evidence as to what the papal delegate said.

Wilfley, ignoring Hays, went on: "The Papal delegate seemed satisfied and dismissed the whole matter as amounting to nothing at all. He recognized this, that it was an attempt on behalf of rejected lawyers in Shanghai ..."

Bourne intervened: "No, we cannot have that," he admonished Wilfley.

Hays speaking directly to Wilfley also sought to chastise him, saying: "I object to you going on this way trying to shoulder in evidence which you know must not go in."

This led to Hays himself being reprimanded by Bourne who warned him: "You must not address the witness. If you object, you must say so."

Wilkinson intervened to seek to calm the situation by asking Wilfley if he "would be on his best behaviour?"

"Yes. I shall be very glad to comply with the ruling of the Court ..." Wilfley responded. Then, presumably smiling like a Cheshire cat and just to show that he had known exactly what he was doing, he added, "... and the rules of testimony." Turning to the lawyers who had been refused admission, Wilfley said that Brooks had not been admitted because of the Grand Jury indictment in Hawaii. Holcomb had failed the exam. He said Andrews had also failed, and that he had offered him a new examination in 30 to 40 days but instead Andrews had chosen to go to Washington and "made war on the Court." Andrews then asked for admission without an examination, which Wilfley refused, but he did offer to allow Andrews to practice until he passed. He then said that he had later sought to disbar Andrews because he had made a false affidavit in the Price case.

With regard to O'Shea, he said he had been asked questions regarding the China *Gazette* and had made the comments he had. He had no personal animosity towards O'Shea. Wilfley denied protecting swindlers or suggesting that the British Courts had done so. On the contrary, with regard to the British Court, he said that its structure and decisions had been a model for the US Court.

Wilfley was cross-examined by Mr Godfrey. When the questioning turned to the McCord case Godfrey landed some solid punches. Wilfley had said in his evidence that "McCord was one of the worst criminals who ever vexed the China coast." Picking up on this, Godfrey went on the attack:

Godfrey: When did you find out that McCord was one of the worst criminals who ever vexed the China coast?

Wilfley: I had known that for a long time. I had not a particle of doubt about it.

Godfrey: Yet when you had convicted McCord of embezzlement, knowing him to be one of the worst characters who ever vexed the China coast, you allowed him out on the same bail?

Wilfley: I had no idea that he would escape (Laughter) I had not the slightest apprehension that he would leave the jurisdiction of the Court, or I should have put him in gaol.

Godfrey: I should think it would be a temptation to a man who was not a very black scoundrel to run away?

Wilfley: Possibly.

Godfrey: How much more is it a temptation to a man who is the worst character who ever vexed the China coast?

Wilfley: Yes.

Godfrey then turned to the meeting at the Astor House Hotel. Wilfley agreed that it was indiscreet and admitted: "I made a mistake in not putting him in gaol at the time. I made a mistake in talking to him afterwards, or rather, in permitting him to attempt to talk to me."

Wilfley was then cross-examined on the admission of lawyers and asked a number of questions as to whether he looked at the certificates as to morals first or the results of the examinations. He gave very poor evidence, stating a number of times that he did not remember and asking if he needed to answer questions.

There were some further questions regarding the Price and Biddle cases and then Godfrey finished his cross-examination. Wilkinson had no re-examination and the court adjourned to the next day for closing submissions which repeated the evidence that had been called. The prosecution argued that the evidence did not prove the statements in O'Shea's article to be true the defence argued that it did.

Bourne then summed up the case. He emphasized the importance of the jury's role in a case such as this by first saying the case law was clear that:

> "An Englishman was free to publish anything he chose so long as a jury of his countrymen found it to be blameless. Thus there was nothing between the irresponsible, unconscientious abuse of the Press and men's sacred right to their good name and reputation but a jury."

He then went through the charges one by one. He said he would treat Judge Wilfley as a private person and that "he had every respect for the sister Court in this place, but what he thought it necessary to say he would say without the least compunction." Without dealing with every issue, Bourne told the jury that the areas where Wilfley could be criticized were in relation to the admission of lawyers where they had clearly been given "a run for their money," but even here O'Shea's criticism may have gone too far. With regard to the McCord case he said it was "quite true that he could have been more discreet," but there was no gross indecency in this. The Price and Biddle cases seemed to be purely questions of law and all judges were overturned on appeal from time to time. He finished up, with a fairly clear direction to convict, saying that the criticisms seemed to go far beyond what was required by the public interest.

The jury retired and returned with a verdict of guilty. O'Shea did not have anything to say. Wilkinson, addressing Bourne on sentencing, said that the purpose of the case was to put an end to "libels on a judge of a friendly power" and he was not pushing for a heavy sentence.

Bourne turned to O'Shea saying he agreed entirely with

the verdict and then sentenced him to two months in prison.

Farewell to Wilfley

O'Shea was, however, to get satisfaction from his prison cell. Just like O'Shea's victory in the Shanghai Liar case, Wilfley's victory was a Pyrrhic one. His support in Washington was waning. Root cabled Wilfley requesting he calm things down, saying "the President and the State Department have been much disturbed by the strife and recrimination which have attended the conduct of affairs in Shanghai since you returned." Wilfley made the mistake of telling Root that he would resign whenever the President felt it necessary. Root accepted this as a resignation. Wilfley lobbied to keep his job, particularly with the incoming President-elect, William Taft, who had recommended his appointment in the first place. Root's decision, however, stood and Wilfley's resignation became effective on January 1, 1909. Wilfley wrote to Taft twice, denouncing his forced removal as "a brutal act and a crime against the case of Decency and Good Government in the Far East," and the "most colossal blunder our nation has ever made in the Far East." Pitifully, he pleaded that he had been left like "a homeless dog … seeking shelter."

Wilfley returned to practice law in New York. Publicly he stated that "his resignation was neither asked nor suggested, and that he told President Roosevelt in September last that he intended to resign." He added that "Shanghai rogues" had no reason to celebrate his departure because his successor would continue his work. Wilfley was also not "a homeless dog seeking shelter" for long. In 1917, he married Ms Belle Zabriskie, the widow of Alonzo Zabriskie, the "capitalist", in Greenwich Connecticut. The ceremony was followed by lunch at the new Mrs Wilfley's country estate in Connecticut.

A new judge

Rufus Thayer was appointed very quickly to replace

Wilfley. President Roosevelt signed Thayer's commission on December 16, 1908 and Thayer took the oath of office on December 23, 1908. But despite the quick appointment, it took him three months to get to Shanghai. He arrived in Shanghai in March 1909 and re-opened the court.

Thayer had been a lawyer in private practice in Washington DC in his own firm, Thayer & Rankin. He also served part-time as a Judge Advocate General in Washington. Thayer had not applied for the job. The main thing that appeared to recommend Thayer to the President was that he was the brother in law of the head of the New York Republican Party. Norwood Allman, an American consular official and later lawyer, described Thayer as "a man of much calmer temperament than his predecessor, and being a likable and kindly soul, he soon established himself in the confidence of the better element of the American community without all the pyrotechnics that characterized the Wilfley regime." He was also "extremely popular with the British, probably because he wore a Vandyke and bore a striking resemblance to King Edward VII."

Thayer would later hear some tricky cases in his time on the bench in Shanghai, however, at the time of his arrival it was his brother judge on the British Supreme Court, Frederick Bourne, who had to deal with some politically sensitive cases in Japanese occupied Korea.

CHAPTER 16

Korea's Hero: Ernest Bethell

THE UNITED STATES HAD, when establishing the United States Court for China in 1906, clearly foreseen that extraterritoriality would not last long in Korea. Unlike Britain, they had not included Korea (or Corea) in the court's name. The act creating the court provided that the United States Court for China would only have appellate jurisdiction over Korea "so long as the rights of extraterritoriality shall obtain in favor of the United States."

They were correct that extraterritoriality would not last long. Two years before the court was created, in 1904, Korea and Japan signed an agreement whereby Korea agreed to look to Japan for advice over its administration. By a protocol to this agreement, they agreed to appoint a Japanese as adviser to their Finance Ministry and a foreigner as an adviser to their Foreign Ministry. Korea also agreed to consult with Japan before signing any treaties with other powers. In November 1905, a further protocol was signed making Korea effectively a protectorate of Japan and Japan took over foreign matters for Korea. Hirobumi Ito, the former Prime Minister of Japan, was appointed Resident-General in Korea. Ito, as Resident-General, effectively ran the country. He was assisted by a Resident, Mr Yagoro Miura, and other Japanese officials. Given that Korea was now effectively run by Japan, in 1905 and 1906, America and Britain withdrew their legations from Seoul leaving consulate-generals in their place. In 1907, Ito engineered the abdication of the Korean Emperor in favour

大韓每日申報

대한미일신보

The Korea Daily News

Hirobumi Ito (right) feigns surprise at the Korean emperor's decision to abidcate

of the, presumably more malleable, Crown Prince.

The Japanese occupation of Korea led to three cases in the British courts all involving Ernest Bethell, the proprietor of the *Korea Daily News* and its Korean sister *Daehan Maeil Sinbo*. Bethell, who had been in the export business in Kobe and Yokohama, had first come to Korea as a correspondent for a British newspaper, the *Daily Chronicle*, during the Russo-Japanese war. He had stayed on to found his newspapers. The newspapers were pro-Korean which upset the Japanese. However, because of Bethell's extraterritorial rights, the Japanese dominated government of Korea could not directly take legal action against Bethell.

As a result, Bethell had the singular honour of having an Order in Council enacted specifically to deal with him. In 1907 an OIC was issued which prohibited the publication of seditious materials or matters "calculated to excite tumult or disorder, or to excite enmity between His Majesty's subjects and the Government of China or Corea." The Supreme Court for China and Corea was given sole jurisdiction to try cases under this provision. The Order in Council, known locally as the "Bethell Clause", was posted at the Supreme Court in Shanghai on September 5, 1907 and came into effect on the same day.

Bethell found himself in court soon after this. In October 1907 he was prosecuted in the British Consular Court in Seoul before the Consul-General, Henry Cockburn. He was not charged under the "Bethell Clause" but for breach of the peace for publishing articles that were "likely to produce or excite a breach of the public peace given in that there was an armed movement in Korea and conflict had taken place between Korean and Japanese troops." The charge added, "there was a considerable number of Japanese residents in Seoul [and] that there was a feeling of dislike and hatred on the part of Koreans against the Japanese."

At the hearing, Bethell asked who his prosecutor was. Mr Cockburn told him that Mr Holmes of the Consulate was his "nominal prosecutor" indicating that the prosecution was, in fact, instigated by the Japanese authorities. Bethell was convicted and required to enter into a six-month good behaviour bond.

The following year, he found himself charged, on the complaint of Mr Miura, the Japanese Resident in Korea, with the more serious crime of publishing seditious matter under "the Bethell Clause." The charge related to three articles published in Korean in the *Korea Daily News*. One article referred to the murder of Durham Stevens, a foreign affairs advisor to the Korean government who had been appointed at the suggestion of the Japanese government. The article called Stevens' assassins patriotic, loyal and righteous gentlemen because they had murdered a man who supported the Japanese protectorate over Korea. The second article was entitled "A hundred Metternichs could not keep one Italy in bondage," where Korea was compared to Italy in the middle of the 19th century and then went on to describe how the Italians rose up and fought for their independence. The third, "Flowers of the Educational World," about the death of 17 student activists said: "We will certainly recover out Korea ... What heroes have left glorious monuments in history except through blood?"

Frederick Bourne, as Judge, and Harrie Wilkinson, as Crown Advocate, travelled to Seoul from Shanghai, in June 1908, to try the case. A British lawyer from Kobe, Mr Charles Crosse, represented Bethell. The Japan Chronicle arranged for a special correspondent to attend. Seoul at the time was still a backwater. The Japan Chronicle's correspondent noted that although the Japanese had issued an edict that top knots, the traditional form of hair style for married men in Korea, should be removed, "the tumbledown streets of this quaint city are as full of tall-hatted and top-knotted men as they were long before they were policed by the Japanese."

The trial was conducted in the hall of the former British Legation Guard's barracks and attracted considerable interest amongst foreigners, Koreans and Japanese. The Japan Chronicle's correspondent said that the hall made an excellent court room, "though it was almost unbearably hot this afternoon towards the conclusion of the day's proceedings." The room got so hot that at one point Crosse asked Bourne for permission to remove his wig, to which Bourne "perspiringly acquiesced, at the same time removing his own."

The first witness was the Japanese Resident, Yagoro Miura, who gave evidence in English. Miura explained that the prosecution had been brought because the "actual Government of Korea was under direction of the Residency-General according to treaty." About half the country was affected by armed disturbances and many Japanese soldiers and police had been sent to quell the disturbances. Under cross-examination by Crosse, he explained the relationship between the Japanese and Korean governments in very tortured logic:

"The Korean Government was under the direction of the Japanese Government where Government business was concerned. Japan had a protectorate over

Korea but there was nothing like annexation in the
relationship between the two countries."

He said there were disturbances in many parts of Korea
but not in any organized way. There had even been fighting
in August 1907 at the South Gate of Seoul. He admitted that
"unfortunately there were many cases of disorderly conduct
committed by Japanese in Korea and there were some
instances in which Japanese had been guilty of misconduct
towards foreigners."

Mr Crosse opened the defence for Bethell, with an
impassioned plea, which showed, at the least, despite the fact
that Crosse lived in Japan where extraterritoriality had ended,
he was not frightened of upsetting the Japanese authorities.
Crosse argued that the Japanese Government of Korea was
not in fact the Government of Korea. He said that as far as he
understood the case for the British Crown was:

> "That there was only one government here; that the
> Korean Government did not exist for all practical
> purposes; that the Korean Government was, so to
> speak, in the fatherly or grandfatherly care of the
> Japanese Government, which could tuck it up and put
> it to bed, or take it out again at pleasure."

He said that it appeared there were two governments,
Japanese and Korean. The Japanese had chosen not to occupy
Korea so that "it did not lie in the mouth of Mr Miura or
anyone else to say Mr Bethell had excited enmity between
the Government of Korea and its subjects, posing as the
representative government of Korea."

The charge he argued, should be dismissed on the ground
that the Government of Japan was not the Government of
Korea.

Bethell was then called to give evidence. He said he did

not read Korean but that he had given strict instructions to his staff of the Korean editions not to publish seditious materials and that he "had never in any way taken advantage of [his] extraterritorial privileges." He also deeply regretted the opprobrious terms used in relation to Mr Stevens, who was a personal friend. Bethell was then extensively cross-examined by Wilkinson. Bethell's Korean editor, Yang Ki Tak, also gave evidence on Bethell's behalf. However, most of Yang's evidence only confirmed that Bethell was responsible for all the publications. A number of other Korean opponents of the Japanese regime were also called to explain their opposition to Japanese rule; their experiences in prison and, most importantly, that the articles that had not incited them to violence.

Bourne was very concerned that the Korean witnesses not incriminate themselves and thereby be exposed to punishment by the Japanese. Wilkinson assured him that Mr Miura had agreed that no steps would be taken against the witnesses no matter what they said. Bourne insisted this be interpreted to the witnesses and that a similar assurance be given to the Korean interpreter.

In closing, Crosse said that he had been left to prove a negative. That is, that the articles did not incite people to violence. The Order in Council was a muzzling of the press. The proceedings were only to safeguard the interests of Japan in Korea. In conclusion, he submitted, the articles did not cause any tumult in Korea and the charges should be dismissed.

Wilkinson, in response, insisted that the British Government was not acting as a "cat's paw" for the Japanese government. He assured Bourne that he himself, as British Crown Advocate, had decided to bring the prosecution. The articles were clearly "calculated to excite" enmity against the Korean government and Bethell should be convicted.

Bourne said immediately that he would convict Bethell,

but deferred giving his judgment until the next day.

The following morning, Bourne delivered judgment. He said the articles were clearly seditious particularly given the current state of affairs in Korea. Sitting as an extraterritorial judge, he must take notice of the situation. With regard to Crosse's argument that Japanese Government was not the Government of Korea, Bourne gave the only decision he could in the diplomatic and political situation:

> "But, if the Government of the existing Emperor, protected by the Government of Japan is not the Government of Korea, who is governing the country? Nations sometimes fall into a wretched state of organized rebellion when a de jure and de facto government, are existing in the same national territory at the same time, for instance in England in 1645 when the King ruled at Oxford and the Parliament in London. Here there is no existing body that can be called a government but the Emperor under the protection of Japan."

He then formally convicted Bethell. As to punishment, Bourne noted the mitigating factors that Bethell's intentions were fair and honest. But he had to take account of the fact that Bethell's paper was a recognized mouthpiece of Korean disaffection and that "under the shelter of our ex-territorial rights" the newspaper escaped Japanese censorship and its staff escaped the arm of Japanese law. Bourne sentenced Bethell to three weeks in prison. Because, there was no British consular jail in Seoul, he granted him bail until a suitable place could be found to imprison him.

Many Koreans had gathered outside the court to hear the verdict. When it was found out that Bethell had been sentenced to jail "there were some signs of active resentment, but Bethell and his friends urged them not to create any disorder." One of the Koreans in the crowd had brought Y4,000 to pay any fine which was imposed.

It was decided to imprison Bethell in Shanghai and he was taken there by British Navy ship.

Two and a half weeks after his arrival in Shanghai, on July 11, 1908, Bethell was brought before Bourne in the Supreme Court in Shanghai and was released on a 6-month good behaviour bond.

The case attracted attention worldwide and particularly in England. Questions were asked in the House of Parliament to the Secretary of State to Foreign Affairs as to why Bethell was being prosecuted. The Secretary of State answered, in effect, that it was what the law required. The *London and China Telegraph*, itself, ran an editorial on June 22, 1908 supporting the prosecution and conviction while lamenting that the Japanese may have ill-treated many Koreans, but it was no worse than what their own government had done to them. In any event, the Japanese were clearly there to stay and "no amount of kicking against the pricks will alter the main fact."

Bethell back in court

Bethell was back in the Supreme Court in Shanghai before Judge Bourne, exactly six months and one day after his release, but, thankfully for him, not for breach of his good behaviour bond. This time, he was there as a plaintiff suing the *North China Herald* for defamation. Bethell's claim related to a report published in September 1908, two months after he had been released from prison. The report, which had been sourced from Japanese newspapers, said that Bethell had confessed to misappropriating money from the Korean National Debts Redemption Fund. This was a fund created by Koreans seeking to collect enough money to buy back Korean debts owed to Japan in the (mistaken) belief that this would lead to Korean independence.

Without ever having said that it would receive such money,

funds were being sent
to the *Korean Daily News*
because it was considered
to be independent of the
government. Bethell had
at first passed Y400 on to
another organization but
found they were not the
proper recipients. In total,
the *Korean Daily News*
had received Y60,000 that
Bethell decided to invest
until a proper recipient
could be found. Bethell's
Korean partner, Yang Ki
Tak, was investigated,

The main characters in Bethell's case against the North China Herald

prosecuted for and acquitted of embezzling some of these
funds in the Japanese controlled courts in Korea. In the course
of the investigation of Yang, Bethell provided the authorities
with information on Yang's behalf. This was misreported in
Japanese newspapers as Bethell having made a confession.
The *North China Herald* carried this report without checking.
The *Herald* article was subsequently repeated in numerous
English language papers in Asia.

After a short trial, Bourne summed up for the jury. Bourne
had only recently found Bethell guilty of sedition against the
Japanese government of Korea. Now, he had to address the
jury as to whether the conviction reflected that Bethell had a
bad character. He went as a far as a judge could to indicate to
the jury that this particular conviction should not go very far,
if at all, to do so. Bourne said that he "could not say that those
proceedings had in any way affected the plaintiff's character
for the purposes of this suit. His conduct might have made
him an unsuitable member of a 'peace at any price' Society or
of a Quaker body', but nothing more."

Even though Bourne, as a judge, had convicted Bethell, it did not mean that Bourne, as a man, disagreed with him. Judges have to uphold the law. It is rare that they get a chance to subsequently comment publicly on a case. Bourne made it clear, as clearly as a judge can in any event, what he thought. The jury returned with a verdict for the substantial sum of $3,000 for Bethell plus his costs.

Bethell did not, however, enjoy his money for long. Soon after returning to Korea, in late April or early May 1909 he died of cardiac enlargement in Seoul at the age of 39. He was given the largest funeral ever for a foreigner in Korea and thousands of Koreans joined the cortege. The only good to come from his early death was that Bethell was not alive to see the dream of Korea independence die.

The following year, in 1910, Japan completed its accretion of power in Korea. On August 22, 1910, Japan and Korea signed a Treaty of Annexation that was approved and promulgated on August 29, 1910. From that date, Korea became an integral part of Japan and remained so until the end of World War II.

When the treaty came into force, Japan issued a declaration that treaties by other powers with Korea were abrogated and that extraterritoriality in Korea was abolished. The British Government formalized this by an Order in Council dated January 23, 1911, whereby the jurisdiction of the Supreme Court over Korea was formally abolished and the court was renamed the Supreme Court for China.

The Bethell cases were not the only difficult cases Bourne and Wilkinson handled in 1908. They both had to deal with a difficult case where a Briton had killed a Chinese in Shanghai. The result attracted a vehement protest from the Chinese authorities.

CHAPTER 17

The Ricshaw Coolie and the Sampan Man

IN THE SPACE OF LESS than a year both Frederick Bourne in the British Supreme Court and Rufus Thayer in the United States Court had to try cases where a Briton and an American were accused of killing Chinese: one a ricshaw coolie; the other a sampan man. Both cases attracted strong attention from the Chinese authorities and in the case before Bourne a blistering protest at the decision.

Both dead men were, of course, more than a mere ricshaw coolie or a mere sampan man. They were Zung Zu-fung and Kong Shing. Zung had a father, mother and pregnant wife: his death caused them great distress. Kong's background is not available from the records but he was, at least, someone's son.

Their deaths were taken seriously.

In Shanghai, Thomas J. Stevenson was ordered to stand trial in the British Supreme Court for murder for the killing of Zung. The 1904 Order in Council had allowed for juries of between five and twelve jurors with the number for each case to be set by rules of court. In this case a jury of twelve was empanelled. Harrie Wilkinson, the Crown Advocate, prosecuted and Mr F. Ellis and R.E. Gregson defended.

Stevenson, 40, was a marine engineer by trade but his current job was as a travelling cinematographer. He had been in China for 17 years. He travelled on a houseboat around

A Ricshaw coolie drives into the night with a foreign customer

China and showed movies to audiences. While in Shanghai,
his wife had become ill and was convalescing in the Victoria
Nursing Home, the leading hospital in the city at the time.
Stevenson visited his wife daily. On the evening of Saturday 8
August 1908, he had been to the Astor House Hotel where he
had had two or three gin and sodas before visiting his wife.
After seeing her, he had gone drinking at the Metropole and
Globe hotels. He had then gone back to his boat around 11pm.
After getting some cigarettes he had then strolled down to
the Bund. He ended up eating at the Grill Rooms in the early
hours of the morning leaving around 4.00 am, about half an
hour before dawn.

According to Stevenson, he then hailed Zung and got in
his ricshaw. He was very sleepy and "remembered seeing
Range Road … When he took notice again he was in an
entirely strange locality." Zung kept on going and then
stopped on top of a culvert over a creek. He then went down
a plank towards the creek. Stevenson told Zung to return to
the road and Zung made as if he was doing so. Stevenson

fearing Zung was planning to rob him, grabbed Zung and they both ended up in the creek. Stevenson said that Zung tried to hold him under water, so he grabbed his queue and twisted it around his neck. Stevenson then passed out and woke up with his mouth just above water. Zung was lying nearby, apparently dead. After crawling out of the creek, Stevenson asked passers-by to call the police.

Zung's father, elder brother and cousin attended the trial of Stevenson for the murder of their son. Despite being in their own country – and the judge speaking fluent Chinese, the trial was conducted solely in a foreign language, English. Magistrate Li, who had also observed the trial of Henry De Menil, was sitting on the bench. As he was there only as an "observer" under the Chefoo Convention, he had no power over the conduct of the case. Zung's father tried to speak at the trial to demand justice. He was silenced and removed from the court by the Marshal. Zung's cousin was allowed to remain but was not allowed to speak.

Wilkinson prepared a very strong case against Stevenson. A full post mortem had been conducted on Zung which Wilkinson said in court was a "great step in advance." Dr C. Davis gave evidence that from his post mortem there were no signs or strangulation. Numerous Chinese and western witnesses were called to give evidence as to what they had seen including bar boys from the hotels Stevenson had been drinking at. Dr Davis who had also examined Stevenson after he had been arrested gave evidence as to Stevenson's injuries. One Chinese witness from village just near were Stevenson and Zung had fought said she saw Stevenson throw the ricshaw from the road into the river.

Stevenson gave evidence on his own behalf recounting his evening out and how Zung and he had ended up in the river. Bourne in his summing up told the jurors that they could convict of murder or manslaughter or acquit Stevenson. They came back twice saying they could not reach a verdict.

Bourne considered ordering a mistrial but asked the jury to try one more time. The jury finally returned a verdict of guilty of manslaughter but "with a strong recommendation for mercy."

Bourne then sentenced Stevenson. He said that he agreed with the verdict, but that while he believed Stevenson did not intend to kill the coolie, Stevenson had done so with a "great deal of ferocity." Other than the recommendation of mercy, he would have passed a harsh sentence. But, given the jury's recommendation, he sentenced Stevenson to one year's hard labour from the date of his arrest.

Magistrate Li wrote a report to the Taotai on the case, which included a petition from Zung's father complaining about the lack of justice in the British courts. Zung senior complained that he had been removed from the court by the Marshal and that his cousin had not been allowed to speak. Most importantly, the penalty imposed was nowhere near harsh enough to reflect that a pregnant wife had lost her husband and a father and mother had lost their only son and source of sustenance in their old age. He said:

> "It is my opinion that the British Judge reckons a Chinese life of little worth when he inflicts a sentence no severer than that of one year on a man guilty of killing another."

He then pointed to the unequal treatment of Chinese and foreigners in China:

> "Were a Chinese to accidentally kill a foreigner would this case be taken as a precedent? If not (I would remark that) the principles of justice are one, though mankind may be divided into Chinese and foreigners."

Magistrate Li was also not happy with the result. He commented harshly on Stevenson's plea of self-defence:

"Who can believe prisoner's crafty allegation that
he was acting in self defence and not of design? (To
account for the mud on his clothes) he says they came
to blows (in the course of which they fell into the
creek) because the ricshaw man tried to rob him – but
brings forward no witness to prove it. But his muddy
garments and money may just as well show that he
took the victim's life by pressing him down in the mud
when he could not possibly have kept on dry ground.
Or alternatively he may have purposely besmattered
himself with mud to divert suspicion."

Li went on to compare British justice unfavourably with
Chinese justice. He found it difficult to hide his sarcasm:

"Such a story would not carry credence in Chinese law
and I am surprised that foreign jurisprudence, which is
of such high repute, should adopt the view it does … It is
not surprising that the deceased relatives smarting under
a sense of injustice should address me as they do."

The Taotai wrote a protest to Sir Pelham Warren, the
British Consul-General, in October 1908 requesting the
case be re-considered and compensation paid to the family.
There is no further correspondence on the Foreign Office file,
but as the case had been finalized by a jury verdict, under
English law there was nothing that could have been done
to re-try the case. The family could have brought an action
for compensation but again would have to do so in a foreign
language in a foreign court.

Another killing in Chefoo
The next year Rufus Thayer, in one of his first cases as
Judge of the United States Court for China, also had to try

an American for killing a Chinese in Chefoo. The case there had echoes of Hornby's Shantung lighthouse case, which had also been tried in Chefoo. A local American, Thomas Jones, had shot a sampan man, Kong Shing, at the Kaiping jetty. Times had, however, moved on since Hornby's day. The Qing Emperor and the Empress Dowager had both just died and the government was in the process of its own legal reforms and there was far less opposition to the extraterritorial courts. Jones had not been put in chains and no gunboats were necessary to protect Thayer or his court.

Nevertheless, the case attracted a lot of local attention. The local Taotai and six other Chinese officials attended the trial. The Taotai had also instructed a foreign attorney, Mr Rice, to observe the hearing on his behalf.

District Attorney Arthur Bassett travelled to Chefoo to prosecute the case. Reprising his role from defending Henry De Menil, William Fleming, acted for Jones. There was no

A sampan man

doubt that bullet from Jones' gun had killed Kong. Jones had been trying to hail sampans to get out to an incoming steamer. Two sampans had not stopped and, according to the Chinese witnesses, Jones, getting angry, had pulled his gun and fired it. The bullet had hit Kong, killing him instantly. Jones' evidence was that he had been about to board a sampan and had taken his gun out to make it safe for the trip when a bullet had discharged, struck the water, ricocheted and killed Kong. Fleming arranged for Mr Kierie, a former officer in the Italian Navy, and W.E. Fairburn of the Shanghai Municipal Police, who was a qualified gunner in the marines, to give evidence about the carrying power of the Browning pistol Jones had been holding. Fleming in a closing argument of three hours "in the course of which he went into the minutest details of the evidence" strongly attacked the evidence of the Chinese witnesses. He suggested that they had colluded in their evidence to try to defeat Jones' story that the shooting was accidental. He then made the startling submission, that of course Thayer could not accept, that "the Court must not treat the Chinese evidence as it would treat that given by foreigners." Bassett summed up in a short half hour speech.

Thayer did not have the problem that Hornby had of having to direct a jury that could deliver a "mischievous" verdict. There was no jury in the US Court. Thayer made it clear that he believed the Chinese witnesses and did not believe Jones' story. Responding to Fleming's argument he added that "while there were racial differences in the manner of giving testimony, still the Court had little doubt in accepting the evidence as a whole of the Chinese witnesses."

Nevertheless, this did not mean that Jones had intended to kill Kong and thus was guilty of murder. The Chinese witnesses may have thought that he intended to kill Kong, but he had no reason to. Thayer said that he had to give Jones the benefit of the doubt. He found Jones guilty of manslaughter for his criminal neglect in the handling of the weapon and sentenced him to three years imprisonment to be served in Shanghai.

Fleming made an application for a new trial and after "some conflict of opinion" Thayer agreed to Fleming making an application back in Shanghai.

The *North China Herald* reported that Thayer "seemed to find difficulty in repressing the emotion he felt when he was about to pronounce judgment." Thayer later conceded privately that he had imposed the harsh penalty to satisfy public opinion. No doubt Magistrate Li's protest in the De Menil case and the diplomatic furore the case had just caused were to the forefront of his mind when deciding Jones' sentence.

Thayer did support an application by Fleming for a pardon by President Taft. It seems this would have been forthcoming on the basis that Jones serve six months in jail and leave China for three years so as to not antagonise Chinese sentiments. Jones, however, died in prison, so was never released.

CHAPTER 18

The Law of the Land

JUST BEFORE THE END of the Qing Dynasty, Frederick Bourne and Rufus Thayer had to deal with complex cases involving land law both of which showed the complexities arising from conflicts of laws and practice that inevitably occurred in an extraterritorial jurisdiction where the law of one land was applied in the other.

The corrupt Tipaos

The ownership of land created a special problem in China: What law should be applied to a case involving land; the law of the defendant's country or the law of China?

This question was even more complex in the international settlements where Chinese were not allowed to own land held under consular title deeds. This problem was overcome by having a foreigner hold the land on trust for a Chinese landowner. Chinese would even seek to have land they already owned registered with a consular title, because it gave greater security of tenure and accordingly increased its value.

They would transfer the land to a foreigner and then get a trust deed back.

In a case just before the end of the Qing Dynasty, Thayer had to deal with the difficult and vexed question of who owned land registered under a US Consular title deed that had been fraudulently taken from its Chinese owners with the assistance of a corrupt "Tipao." In order to understand the issues Thayer faced and who a "Tipao" was, it is best to backtrack to two cases involving Frederick Bourne some years before.

Land law was an area of expertise for Bourne. When he had first been appointed Judge in 1898 he had also been appointed Consul in charge of the Land Office and had served in that position until 1901. Because of this, in one case in the late 1900s he gave an expert deposition on the process by which British citizens and other foreigners could acquire title to land in China. Bourne described two systems for acquiring title. In certain concessions, such as Shameen Island in Canton, the Chinese government had leased the entire concession to the British Government, which then sub-let to tenants. However, in most concessions this had not been done and land was acquired under native title deeds. In order to give security of title to British, "who were authorised under the Treaty to lease land for certain purposes" a system of registration of title was established. In Shanghai, a formal set of instructions had been drafted covering how to register title. Bourne said, however: "Originally there was no instruction. It grew up. The Consul had to exercise his functions of protecting British property as best he could. He did it sometimes in a rather extraordinary way."

The system in Shanghai was that the British applicant for registration would bring in his native title deeds, or fangtan, to the British Consulate. The fangtan deeds would then be sent to the Land Deputy of the Chinese Land Office, part of the Taotai's administration. There had also previously been another land office, the Shengko office, which by the early 20th century was amalgamated with the Taotai's land office. The Land Deputy would then appoint a date for meeting on the land with the local Tipao, or if the land abutted different districts, the local Tipaos. A Tipao was a lower level official chosen annually "from amongst the people. He is generally of what we should call the middle class, who is living in the particular lot." Generally, his family will have been living in the area for some time. It is the Tipao's "duty to know everybody's property and what everybody is doing as far as possible."

The Tipao took responsibility for ensuring the measurements, boundaries and ownership of the land. If the land abutted another piece of land registered to a foreigner, the Tipao would not involve himself with this because, as Bourne put it, "he regards the foreigner as a different sort of being with whom he is not concerned." Instead, a deputy from the British Land Office would go to check the measurements. In order to ensure that he does his job properly, the Tipao was required to give a bond. Bourne commented that if he did not do his job properly, "he used to be bambooed, but they have gone beyond that now."

Anybody else with an interest in the land was allowed to attend the meeting. The Deputy would then conduct an investigation through the Tipao as to whether the seller had the right to sell and whether there were any rights over creeks or roads. Then, the Deputy would report to the Taotai who would write directly to the British Land Registry enclosing two sealed copies of the title deed. A plan of the land would also be sent, which would be traced, reproduced, agreed and signed. The Vice-Consul dealing with the registration "looks upon himself practically as counsel" for the British purchaser and "endeavours to protect his interest." If he is not satisfied with what the Chinese Land Office says, for example that there is a right of way, he may write that he has been informed there is no right of way. There would often be long correspondence before the title deed came out.

When the title deed did come out, Bourne said, "we regard it as an indefeasible title from the Chinese government; that, the Chinese Government has cancelled the native title of the Chinese seller and has given out to the British subject who bought the land, another title, in a different form altogether, known as the Taotai's deed." Bourne explained that by issuing this deed, "the Chinese Government being the Supreme Power has destroyed all other titles to that land and given a new title in a new form to the British subject."

If British subjects then agreed between themselves to a right of way over the land, this would be noted in the Consulate records without reference to the Taotai.

Other consulates registered lands for their citizens in much the same way. If the land registered with the British Consulate was sold to another foreigner, the owner's and the office copy of the title deeds would be sent to that person's consulate. The old Chinese title deeds would remain with the British Consulate but be open to inspection.

Bourne was quite proud of the system, which he said had originated from a "running fight" for years between "the Vice Consul, the Taotai, the Land Deputy, the Lawyers and the Land Agents." The result, he said, "was that a very ingenious system of registering land had evolved." While conceding that the area was relatively small, he added that the system depends "on the excellent cadastral survey which the Council has made and is always improving." He concluded, proudly, "I believe a better system exists nowhere in the world. One can transfer land here as readily as Consols in London."

The question remained, however, as to which law applied to this particular title. George French had decided that Chinese law applied to leased land in the *Wushishan* case. But later in 1899 Nicholas Hannen in the case of *Hanson v Watson* ruled that English land law should apply to land leased from the Chinese authorities in Shanghai (or apply the law of the forum, called in Latin, *Lex Fori*).

Soon after stepping down as Consul in charge of the land office, Bourne decided a case *McDonald v Anderson* involving land in Tientsin which the *North China Herald* described as "a landmark in the history of the Law administered by the British Courts in China." Bourne decided that Chinese land law applied to all transactions in land in China and the British courts should apply Chinese land law (or apply the law of the location, called in Latin, *Lex Loci*). Bourne wrote a long and extremely well reasoned judgment to show that *Hanson v Watson* had been decided wrongly. Legally he pointed out that "to apply the law of English realty to land under the sovereignty of China is to disregard the distinction between the real and personal statutes—a fundamental principle of Private International Law," and the legislation could only overthrow this with "irresistible clearness." Practically, it produced absurd results. Land owned by British in Tientsin (and Shanghai) often abutted land owned by Germans, French and other citizens of treaty powers. If the laws of each country applied, then different land laws could apply to the same land, particularly in claims of adverse possession where German land law required 30 years possession but British only 12.

Bourne said that despite all this he should bound by Hannen's decision in *Hanson v Watson*, having been made by the Chief Justice. Bourne, however, was not going to let things go there. He found a higher authority in a recent decision of the Privy Council from Zanzibar that held that the *Lex Situs* (another term for *Lex Loci*) applied in extraterritorial courts there. The only difference between the cases was that in Zanzibar there was a written land code, whereas matters "in China are thrown back on a very few written rules — the Penal code — the greater part of which cannot be applied to a Christian community—upon local customs and upon the Judge's conscience." But he emphasized, that this "is not a legal reason for applying the English feudal tenures to land in China." He therefore decided that Chinese land law was to be applied to the case.

The question then became, where to find Chinese land law? In a final paragraph to the decision, he set out that Chinese land law was made up of local customs that would need to be proved by evidence. Where there was no clear rule, a Chinese judge was required to apply "good conscience," and he suggested a British judge should apply civil law from continental codes and text writers. He added that: "If a land law so derived is thought too uncertain to support the large foreign commercial interests now in China" then "the Land Regulations would need to be amended."

The *North China Herald* praised Bourne's decision while noting that it removed the security of tenure British had felt to date in their land, the questions of land law now to be decided by Chinese Custom and that the "familiar figure of the oldest inhabitant will doubtless amuse the Courts with his personal narrative of what he remembers of local custom." However, the newspaper said Bourne was bound to decide the law as he found it and leave it to the authorities to remedy any problems if necessary.

In the case before Thayer, Mr Barchett, who had recently died, held U.S. Lot No. 1102 in his name. However, he had in fact received the land from a person named Hsu Pei Chi to hold on trust. Another Chinese, Koh Chee Wen also known as Koh Kwei Foh, challenged the title arguing that the property was his. The executrix of Barchett's estate admitted the land was held on trust and stood neutral.

Koh relied on a judgment of the Mixed Court that had found in his favour. The Mixed Court had ruled that he had not sold he property and had been defrauded by corrupt

Tsipaos who had deceived the authority to "have the land in question shenkoed in Hsu's name."

Koh sought a declaration from the US Court that the land belonged to him.

Thayer found that the land belonged to Koh because he could produce the fangtan title deeds and the tax receipts for the land. He also accepted that the judgment of the Mixed Court between the two Chinese parties was binding and ordered the land be transferred. Hsu Pei Chi had by then transferred his interest in the trust to a Woo Zung Seng.

Woo was not satisfied by the decision and instructed Shanghai's two leading American lawyers, Thomas Jernigan and Stirling Fessenden. Koh was represented by another leading lawyer, William Fleming. Jernigan and Fessenden filed a petition to have Thayer's judgment set aside on the basis that as it was a dispute between two Chinese and, therefore, the US Court had no jurisdiction. Secondly, they argued that the Mixed Court was below the Taotai in the Chinese hierarchy. The Taotai was also a judicial officer. The Mixed Court could not, therefore, make a decision contradictory to what was shown on the Taotai's deeds.

Thayer accepted on the basis of the decision in *McDonald v Anderson* that Chinese law must be applied to questions of land law. He agreed the US Court had no jurisdiction and granted the petition to set aside his earlier judgment. He noted that the Mixed Court themselves had held that:

> "In the settlement the title deed is a good and sufficient proof as to the ownership of any lot. It could not be cancelled at anytime. Otherwise, the foreign land owners in the settlement would create a serious diplomatic dispute."

He said that this must mean the Mixed Court had recognized that it had no power to enter any judgment that affected the integrity of the Taotai's deed.

All very well, but what was Thayer and the executrix to do? Thayer did the best he could in the circumstances. In order to get the land out of the executrix's hands, he ordered that the title be transferred to a third party nominated by the parties. He then ordered the parties to submit a full statement of the case to the US Consul-General with a request that he submit it to the Taotai for appropriate action.

There is no record of whether this was done. Revolution was just around the corner and the Taotai would only be in office for a few more months before the founding of the Republic of China and the abolition of the office of Taotai.

CHAPTER 19

The Republican Revolution

THE QING DYNASTY ended very much with a whimper. The reforms that had been introduced following the Boxer Rebellion had weakened the power of the central government substantially. Yuan Shikai controlled the strongest army in the country, the Beiyang army, and Sun Yat-sen, from his base in Canton, was travelling the world looking to raise funds for a revolution.

Numerous small-scale uprisings occurred around the country, with the largest at Hankow in mid-1911. Yuan Shikai, who had returned home nominally on sick leave, was prevailed upon to return to office and put down the revolt. After one battle where he soundly beat the revolutionaries, he changed sides to support them. He then convinced the Emperor to abdicate with promises of security for the Imperial families.

Other Manchus were not so lucky. In many cities, the Manchu Garrisons fought to maintain Qing rule and in some, such as Nanking, they were overwhelmed and killed by the Chinese. When the Qing finally fell, many Manchus were massacred around the country.

The Republic of China was declared on January 1, 1912 and Sun Yat-Sen was appointed Provisional President. He only served in the role for three weeks before yielding to Yuan Shikai and his greater military power. Sun was appointed the Minister for Railways and set about a program to build large numbers of railway lines around the country. Initially,

THE

NATIONAL REVIEW

報 西 論 公 國 中

CHINA
21 OCTOBER 1911.

20 Cents.

AT LAST!

The National Review welcomes the rise of Yuan Shikai.

democratic elections were held for a parliament. Yuan however, by a series of maneuvers including the assassination of the Nationalist Prime Minister at the Shanghai Railway Station in 1913, aggregated power in his hands.

Yuan served as President until 1916 when he made himself Emperor, although he was not coronated. This was the last straw for many of his supporters who still believed in a republic. Yuan only served as Emperor for three weeks before abdicating. He died soon after of renal failure.

Due to Yuan's machinations, Sun's Nationalist Party, or

the Kuomintang as it is often referred to, split with the central government and formed their own government in Canton, which existed as a separate government through to 1927. The government in Peking remained the recognized government of the China but held little power over large parts of the country. Many provinces were ruled by warlords who fought for control of different areas of the country. It was not until 1927 that a unified government under the Nationalist Party was formed. The intervening 15 years gave foreigners large freedom to exercise and extend their extraterritorial rights.

The Revolution and the treaties

The Revolution brought before both British and US courts the important issue of whether the treaties granting extraterritoriality were still in force.

During the Revolution, foreigners were on high alert for attacks. On Shameen Island in Canton, Indian troops built sand-bagged defensive lines and were readied to fight. One of these soldiers, Ibrahim, an Afghani soldier serving in the 126th Regiment of Baluchistan Infantry shot and killed his superior officer. His immediate superior, the Subadar, had disciplined him for gambling and had confiscated his money. Ibrahim got his gun and killed the Subadar. The commanding officer of the unit, Major Barrett, was called. He arrived 10 to 15 minutes later. He went up to Ibrahim and asked him: "Why have you done such a senseless act?" Barrett's told the court later that he said nothing else; did not threaten him in any way. Barrett said that when he spoke to Ibrahim, he was sorry for him because he had killed the Subadar. Ibrahim replied: "Some three or four days he has been abusing me; without a doubt I killed him."

The British Consul in Canton considered it would be better for the case to be tried in Hong Kong. This was presumably because of the unstable situation in Canton at the time and because all the witnesses were in the British army. There would be no problem with compelling their attendance to give evidence. The 1904 Order in Council allowed for trials to be conducted either in Hong Kong or in Mandalay, Burma, provided the Judge of the Supreme Court for China agreed. Havilland De Sausmarez signed a warrant transferring the case to the Supreme Court of Hong Kong.

Ibrahim's first trial was aborted when the jury could not reach a verdict. He was convicted after a second trial. The case ended up in the Privy Council and remains a leading decision on the question of voluntariness of a confession to a person in

A soldier of a Baluchi regiment

a position of authority. At the trial, the Chief Justice of Hong Kong, William Rees Davies had reserved questions of law to the Hong Kong Full Court (then like the Shanghai court made up of two judges). The questions were whether the court had jurisdiction to try Ibrahim even though he was not British and, more interestingly, whether the treaties giving extraterritorial rights were still in force? Ibrahim's counsel argued that the treaties were no longer valid following the Republican Revolution.

With regard to the first point, the Hong Kong Supreme Court and Privy Council accepted that Ibrahim as an Afghani was an alien. However, by enlisting in the Indian army, he was subject to British military law while in Shameen. The British army required service, loyalty and allegiance from its soldiers. In return, it extends to all soldiers the protection of the army. Ibrahim "enjoyed His Majesty's protection in China" and was therefore "a British protected person" subject to the jurisdiction of the Supreme Court for China.

With regard to the Republican Revolution, the Hong Kong Supreme Court took a relatively easy way out, holding that the onus was not on the prosecution to prove the validity of the treaties. No evidence had been put in to show the treaties were not valid, and thus the court would presume they were. Chief Justice Rees-Davies added that as a practical matter, the onus could not be on the Crown to prove the validity of treaties in every case saying this would be a "course pregnant with difficulty and inconvenience."

The second member of the Hong Kong Full Court, Henry Gompertz agreed in full with Rees-Davies. He added that in any event, there was no suggestion the new Chinese Government did not accept the treaties were valid:

"Treaty or no Treaty, the evidence is that the British Consular officials do assert jurisdiction at Canton over British subjects, including soldiers of the Indian Army, without apparently question or protest, from the Chinese Government."

Very soon after this, the constitution of the Hong Kong Full Court was changed by an amendment to the law that allowed a judge of the British Supreme Court for China to sit on the Hong Kong Full Court – an arrangement that continued until 1941.

The question of whether the treaties were still valid was also raised in the United States Court for China in Shanghai in the prosecution of a Mr J.F. Jordan. In that case, Jordan's counsel argued that because the Emperor had abdicated and the United States had not recognized a new government, there were no treaties that the court could rely upon to exercise jurisdiction.

Thayer, in fact, did not have to answer the question. Jordan jumped bail and fled China. Thayer nevertheless, considered it proper to issue a decision on the point so as to put the matter to rest for once and for all.

His first answer was that the question was a political question to be answered by the executive and not a legal one to be answered by the court. He held that the making and termination of treaties and the recognition of new governments belong to executive and that:

"It is a well established doctrine that until the recognition of a new government by the political department, courts of justice are bound to consider the former state of things as remaining unaltered."

Despite this, he then cited a British authority on international law, Sir Sherston Baker, who had written that international law provided that following a revolution the state took on all the debts and obligations of the previous states. Therefore, whatever, the form of government in China at the time the treaties were still in effect.

Nevertheless, at least one American lawyer practicing in Shanghai, Mr Frost, thought that the end of the Qing Dynasty would mean the end of extraterritoriality. In 1912, in a letter to a former fraternity brother he wrote, "the revolutionists had left no court to practice in."

In fact, the collapse of the Qing Dynasty meant the Shanghai Municipal Council was able to take control of the International Mixed Court. From 1911, the council employed the Chinese magistrates directly. This gave foreigners control of the court and greatly increased the power of the consular assessors.

While the United States Court and the British Supreme Court did not disappear with the Republican Revolution both of them saw some major changes after the Republic of China was established.

Thayer Resigns

In late 1913, Judge Rufus Thayer resigned under a cloud after George Curtis, a Shanghai attorney, brought complaints against him to the US Congress. The main complaints were that Thayer had been away from Shanghai for many months but certified he was in China and that he had abused his expense account for trips to Canton and Hong Kong. There was probably an element of truth in the charges of being absent from office. Thayer's wife had left Shanghai in 1911, not being able to withstand the climate. Thayer was very often not in Shanghai.

Rather than face an investigation, Thayer resigned with effect from December 31, 1913. In mid-November, a private ceremony attended by most members of the American Bar was held in the Judge's chambers where the members of the bar presented Thayer with a silver tray. This was followed by a reception which Frederick Bourne as Acting Judge and W.C. Platt as Acting Crown Advocate also attended. Frank Hinckley, now District Attorney, and Bourne both made speeches farewelling Thayer, who responded in kind. He left a few days later on the PMS Mongolia. He died suddenly of apoplexy four years later in 1917 in Kingston, New York.

Charles Lobingier

The new judge appointed to the US court was Charles Lobingier. Lobingier from his record is the man who should probably have been appointed the first judge. He was revolutionary in his zeal, very much in the mold of Edmund Hornby. He had already been a judge of a colonial court, the

Philippines Court of First Instance, for 10 years. He was a good administrator, hard-working and had a passion for setting the US Court on the right footing to overcome the various legislative and administrative problems it faced. He was also well-educated, holding a PhD (and three other degrees) from the University of Nebraska.

Lobingier had been born in Lanark, Illinois in 1866, making him 48 at the time of his appointment. He had practiced as a lawyer in Omaha for 10 years from 1892 to 1902 and had also been a professor of law at the University of Nebraska from 1900 to 1903. While in the Philippines, he had been on the Commission to codify Philippines law and a member of the law faculty of the University of the Philippines. He had written nine legal books including books on Stocks and Stockholders, Constitutional Law, Equity, Foreclosure, Insurance and Evidence. When he left the Philippines, Chief Justice Arellano wrote him a letter of praise commending his

Charles Lobingier

"zeal, intelligence and rectitude".

From his arrival in February 1914, Lobingier set out to get the United States Court for China on as strong a legal footing as possible. He also wanted to make it clear that he was getting straight down to business. There was no formal opening of the court, as he considered this unnecessary.

In a number of early cases, he also made it clear that he would give the court the broadest legal authority as possible under the statutes that had created it. The first case where he did this was an application for the annulment of a marriage which was opposed that the court had no jurisdiction to deal with annulments. Using logic which he would employ in a number of cases in the future, he went back not only to the original treaties and acts establishing the consular courts but deep into the history of English common law to show that the United States Court for China had jurisdiction over almost any civil dispute. In the specific case, he held that the court had jurisdiction under the treaties; under the acts of Congress that gave power to handle cases "in regard to civil rights"; under the inherent jurisdiction of equity inherited from England; and, under the "reversionary jurisdiction" of the English Ecclesiastical Courts which had been passed to US Chancery courts.

Lobingier also quickly took steps to improve the functioning of the United States Court for China. He commenced work on a bill to be put to Congress. The bill provided for, amongst other things, codification of the decision in *United States v Biddle* that the court could apply Alaskan and District of Columbia law; the appointment of a Special Judge to act when the Judge was absent; the transfer of consular jurisdiction in Shanghai to the US Court; the appointment of a Commissioner to hear smaller cases; and, for the Consular Jail to be supervised by the marshal of the court. Lobingier also sought to make the court self-funding by following the example of the British Court and charging probate fees based on 3% of the value of the estate.

As well as proposing new legislation, Lobingier took matters into his own hands as far as he could. He reached an agreement with the Government of the Philippines that longterm prisoners be transferred to Bilibid Prison in Manila. The prisoners were normally transported on US Navy ships travelling between Shanghai and the Philippines. He also established the Far Eastern Bar Association in Shanghai and the Philippines for American lawyers.

Bourne retires

Soon after Lobingier was appointed, in mid 1915, Frederick Bourne went on pre-retirement leave. He formally retired on February 18, 1916 after 46 years service in China. There was no special hearing to mark Bourne's retirement in the Supreme Court. Indeed, this had not been the custom when an assistant judge retired. Bourne was, however, Judge of the High Court of Weihaiwei. He had been appointed in 1904 after the British had taken over the territory. Harrie Wilkinson as Acting Judge in the High Court of Weihaiwei gave a farewell speech. He said that Weihaiwei and the British in China that had suffered a loss by the retirement of Bourne. He described Bourne as a "courteous gentleman, a just judge, a man with a deep and kindly knowledge of human nature and of Chinese law and custom" adding, that it would be difficult to find anyone to "fill his place, especially in this Court where the special knowledge referred to and his insight into the ways of the inhabitants of the Territory."

The Colonial Office did not have to look far for a replacement in Weihaiwei. Wilkinson was now offered his first substantive judicial appointment in China. He was appointed Judge of the High Court of Weihaiwei, the position to be held concurrently with his role as Crown Advocate for China.

Just prior to his formal retirement, Bourne was knighted on January 1, 1916, making him the only Assistant Judge of the court to be knighted. Sir Frederick Bourne died on August 23, 1940 in England.

To replace Bourne as Assistant Judge, the Foreign Office looked outside China. Skinner Turner, a judge in the Foreign Office Legal Service then based in Bangkok, was appointed in Bourne's place. Turner was born near Tonbridge, Kent on June 2, 1868 to Frederick and Marsha Turner, the eighth of nine children. Turner was educated at King's College School, Strand, and at London University. He was called to the Bar at the Middle Temple in 1890, and for some years afterwards practised on the Western Circuit and at the Hampshire Sessions.

He joined the Foreign Office Judicial Service in 1900 and served in Africa until 1905 when he was appointed Judge of the British Court for Siam. In 1909, on conclusion of the treaty partially bringing extraterritoriality to an end between Siam and Great Britain, he was lent to the Siamese Government as legal adviser. In this role, he sat on the Siamese Court of Appeal.

All of these appointments had been made in the shadow of World War I which was raging in Europe and which had brought a number of conflicts to China.

CHAPTER 20

World War I

WORLD WAR I HAD STARTED for the British in Shanghai in late 1914. While there was no fighting in Shanghai, the war had a large impact on the British Supreme Court. Most immediately, a number of the lawyers practicing before the court signed up to join the army. Others in Shanghai also wanted to go to the front, but were not allowed to. Captain Barrett of the SMP applied to be allowed to go to fight but his application was rejected. Both of Frederick Bourne's sons had signed up and were serving in the army, one in France and the other in India.

War also came home to the court when news was received at least twice of the death of members of the Shanghai bar, the first being Loftus Jones, an Australian who had been Crown Advocate Harrie Wilkinson's best man. In late 1915, news arrived of the death of John Douglas, the former Registrar of the court. Douglas was killed in action in France just before Christmas in 1915. Court hearings were held to remember Douglas with Allan Mossop his former partner telling the court that he had died a "glorious death in the cause of righteousness and of the King and his Empire."

It was into this environment of fierce patriotism that defendants accused of disloyalty came. The war had also encouraged rebellions in other parts of the British Empire. In 1915, de Sausmarez ordered the deportation of Kesar Singh and Ganda Singh for being members of the Sikh Revolutionary party.

In early 1916, the most serious case involving the war

came before de Sausmarez. Wilkinson had charged Sidmond Abbas and his son Oswald under the Defence of the Realm Act, or DORA. DORA was enacted to allow the government to investigate and punish crimes that would affect the war effort. The Abbases, were apparently well known in the Shanghai community and, while it was not stated directly in the case, were of Middle Eastern descent. The case gathered a large amount of attention because Wilkinson applied for it to be heard in secret. The Defendants pleaded not guilty and a jury was empaneled. After hearing the secret evidence, they found the father guilty of the offence and the son guilty of aiding and abetting his father.

In sentencing, de Sausmarez stated for the first time publicly what the case was about. Abbas had sold 15,000 rifles, 1,000 revolvers and about a million and a half rounds of ammunition to be delivered to India, Ceylon and the Straits Settlements to be used in a rebellion against the British Government. The sentence for this was death or whatever lesser penalty the court thought fit. In sentencing de Sausmarez gave the elder Mr Abbas a tongue-lashing:

"you allowed an utterly despicable desire for gain to overcome the sentiment of loyalty to your country which ought to have inspired you and, which, whatever your origin, were due to a country under whose government you were born, which had protected you and under whose protection you carried on a profitable business."

He then passed a very harsh sentence of 15 years imprisonment. He turned to the son and said that he appreciated that he had not been involved in the sale but had helped him to collect payment, or as de Sausmarez put it, assisted "him in obtaining the price of his villainy."

De Sausmarez was much gentler on the son, sentencing

him to two years in prison.

Dealing with the enemy

The outbreak of war brought a number of tricky cases before the British courts. First, there were cases that came about from a short war which Japan, with the assistance of Britain, fought to capture Tsingtao, a Germany colony, and then take over other German interests in Shantung Province. During the fighting, British Navy ships captured two ships: the *Hanametal* and the *Paklat*. Both had been taken to the British territory of Weihaiwei where the crews were interned. They were then sailed to Hong Kong where the Supreme Court of Hong Kong was asked to rule on whether they should be seized. In the case of the *Hanametal*, the court ordered the ship returned its American owner on the basis the Crown had not proved the Hanametal was engaged in non-neutral activities. In the case of the *Paklat*, Chief Justice Rees-Davies ordered the ship condemned on the basis that it had been bringing non-combatants out of a war zone. This was not a humanitarian mission unless permission has been granted by the besieging power in advance. He concluded with a statement that today would be considered the encouragement of war crimes or terrorism:

> "Although such permission is sometimes granted,
> it is in most cases refused because the fact that
> noncombatants are besieged together with combatants
> and that they have to endure hardships, may and
> very often does exercise pressure on authorities to
> surrender."

The Japanese, after capturing Tsingtao, in early January 1915 made a set of 21 demands to the government of Yuan Shi-Kai. These sought to confirm the Japanese occupation of Tsingtao and other German concessions, railways and mines in Shantung as well as Japan's special position in Manchuria. More aggressively, the Japanese wanted China to allow Japanese advisers be appointed to its government ministries. The demands were bitterly opposed by the Chinese people who boycotted Japanese products. After negotiations, a watered down treaty was signed in May 1915 giving Japan some of its demands.

Away from the zone of actual war in Tsingtao, the British also had to deal with a number of tricky cases regarding trading with enemy nationals and what to do with enemy property in Shanghai. Things were made difficult because China did not join the war immediately meaning that, other than in Tsingtao, Germans were not considered enemy nationals and British and Germans continued to live side by side.

As soon as war was declared regulations were promulgated prohibiting trading with the enemy. These regulations had been designed to stop money from England and its colonies and territories being sent to fund the German war machine. In England itself, this was a relatively easy process. Enemy property was vested in the Custodian of Enemy Property who held the property and any profits until the end of the war. Depending on the treaties signed ending the war, the property would be returned or dealt with according to the treaties. But in an extraterritorial jurisdiction, this was much more difficult.

In 1915, regulations were passed requiring any British subject in China to pay any interest, dividends or profits due to an enemy national into an Enemy Dividend Account. The difficulty was that while China remained neutral, Germans could freely reside and do business in China. The British Consulate in Shanghai was bombarded with questions from British banks and companies who owed money to Germans or were planning to pay dividends. In most cases, they were allowed to pay the money.

The first set of regulations issued had prohibited trading with people based in enemy countries. This did not apply to Germans and other enemy nationals in China because China was neutral. New regulations were then introduced preventing trading with enemy nationals. The new regulations also, on a strict interpretation, forbade any dealings with Germans, even, for example, retail purchases from your local butcher. De Sausmarez wrote a note recommending that such transactions not be the subject of prosecution.

In 1917, when China formally entered the war, the regulations prohibiting dealing with enemy property were extended to cover any balances and deposits in banks. Anyone managing property owned by an enemy was also required to report this to the Consul.

The *Peking Post* prosecuted

The war also brought into the US Court for China a case that caused far greater anger amongst the public and foreign officials than the ownership of enemy property.

The ongoing civil wars in China meant that the central and regional governments in China had an insatiable need for money. Customs and salt revenue was already pledged to pay back previous loans and the Boxer Indemnity. Since 1911, the foreign-run Chinese Customs had taken over collection of customs revenue and started paying the money directly to foreign governments and bondholders. The collection of other taxes was difficult due to the unstable situation in most of the country. All regional governments and particularly the central government had to resort to taking loans from foreigners to fund their operations and ongoing civil wars.

In 1917, after America had entered the war, the Chinese government in Peking appeared to be arranging for a loan from American bankers with the assistance of the American Minister, Paul Reinsch. Gilbert Reid, the editor of the *Peking Post*, was outraged by this, particularly because President

Wilson had denounced the
giving of loans to China of
a political nature. Reid had
received a personal letter from
Wilson thanking Reid for his
support in this policy. In an
article entitled "Are Chinese
Loans made in the Open,"
Reid questioned the legality of
the loans that were not being
submitted to the Chinese
parliament for approval and
the role of Reinsch in arranging
the loans.

*Gilbert Reid, Missionary and
publisher of the Peking Post:
Accused of sedition*

Reid, who was American,
was a missionary and had been
in China for many years. He
had founded the Mission for the Upper Classes. When World
War I first began he had been based in Shanghai. There were
allegations at the time that at his mission he was showing
young Chinese people films favourable to the German cause.
In 1917 he had moved to Peking and taken over the *Peking
Post*. The newspaper had taken a very pro-German stance
and grown from a four-sheet paper to an eight-sheet paper
in a very short period of time. Allegations were made that the
paper was being funded by Germany as a propaganda paper.

When President Wilson decided to enter the war against
Germany in early 1917, Reid published a scorching editorial
denouncing the decision. Reid said that the majority of the
American people were not in favour of joining the war. He
attacked Wilson personally:

"And the Kaiser of Germany showed no more
symptoms of autocracy in getting Germany into the
Great War than has President Wilson in getting the

United States into the war."

He continued that the majority of the American people may, in order to appear patriotic, acclaim the war. Only a small minority will insist on their constitutional rights to "do their own thinking."

Reid was arrested and charged with seditious libel against Mr Reinsch and the American President. He was first brought before the American Consular Court in Tientsin, granted bail and ordered to appear for trial before Lobingier in Shanghai.

At the first hearing in Shanghai, the US District Attorney, Chauncey Holcomb told the court America was at war. It is not patriotic to question the American government when the country is at war. Reid pleaded not guilty and said that he would make a formal objection to the charges, presumably on constitutional grounds that his right of free speech should be protected. He was ordered to appear for trial on Monday morning, June 11, 1917.

The weekend gave Reid time to reflect and to find himself a lawyer, Dr Hua-chuen Mei, a Chinese-American. Mei, a graduate of Columbia University with high honours, was one of the first, if not the first, Chinese-Americans admitted to practice before the federal courts in America. After being admitted in 1915, he practiced in New York for a short time before moving to Shanghai.

Dr Mei gave Reid some wise counsel. He advised Reid to make a statement apologizing. So, on Monday morning, Reid appeared with Dr Mei and read a statement that accusations he faced meant he was not in a pleasant position, particularly at war time:

"What I wish to say, and I say it with all sincerity, is that I have never experienced a feeling of disloyalty to my country, and I do here in open Court unhesitatingly profess my loyalty and devotion to my country, to its great constitution, and to the high ideals for which our Republic has stood and still stands."

He continued that he never intended to libel either President Wilson or Mr Reinsch and that "if, in expressing myself on current events, in the hurry of an editorial room, I appear to have stepped beyond the bounds of propriety, I express my honest regret and desire that what has been written may not be construed to possess any offensive meaning."

When Reid was finished, Holcomb asked for an adjournment so he could consider the statement. It was agreed the court would reconvene the following day. The next day, Holcomb said that taken at face value, Reid had "purged himself of the charges filed against him." Under American law, great latitude was given to newspapers to comment on governmental affairs and in times of peace much, even if illegal, will go unnoticed. However, in times of war, "articles of the same kind do, and it is properly so, merit and receive the attention of the prosecuting officers of the Government, especially under conditions existing in this jurisdiction."

Holcomb then asked for leave to withdraw the charges. If charges are withdrawn, they can be refiled. Dr Mei questioned if withdrawing the charges was fair on his client because the charges would "leave an axe suspended over Mr. Reid's head" that may prevent him from reporting legally. Lobingier responded that the motion was to withdraw and that was all he could deal with. He made an order that the charges be withdrawn.

Reid did not stay quiet. Once China joined the war later in the year, the Allied Powers put pressure on the Chinese not to deal with Reid. In November 1917, Reid reported in the *Peking Post* that he had been received at the Chinese Foreign Ministry on his birthday. This resulted in a strong public protest from the Allied Powers signed by John Jordan, the

British Minister to Lu Chiang Hsiang the Chinese Foreign Minister noting that it was "strange that a person notoriously working in the interests of the enemy" should be entertained by Chinese officials.

In very direct language he added:

"I have been requested to warn Your Excellency against the renewal of such incorrect conduct, which, can only cause the most unfavourable comment in allied countries."

The Chinese got the message loud and clear. Within the month, they "requested" that Reid be deported. Coincidentally or not, Major Holcomb happened to be in Peking at the time and obtained an order from the Tientsin Consular Court deporting Reid. Reid was placed on the Chingwantao and sent to Manila.

Versailles Peace Conference

World War I ended in November 1918 with an armistice and in 1919 a peace conference was held in Versailles, France. China joined as a party. As part of its requests, China sought an agreement to end extraterritoriality once China had prepared and passed new legal codes and established a new system of Western courts in all districts where foreigner resided. China undertook to have these reforms in place by 1924. It asked for an agreement that extraterritoriality would be abolished if China achieved these goals.

The Versailles Conference was, however, more concerned about sharing the spoils of victory and punishing Germany than with freeing China from the chains of extraterritoriality. China did receive some benefits under the final treaty. Germany gave up all extraterritorial rights in China; agreed to return the German concessions in Tientsin and Hankow; returned to China all buildings and lands (other than diplomatic premises) it owned in China; waived claims for any more payments under the Boxer Indemnity; and, agreed to return astronomical instruments looted from Peking following the Boxer Rebellion.

There was, however, a kicker. Under the treaty, all German rights and properties in Shantung (Shandong) were to be transferred to Japan. This was totally unacceptable to the Chinese government and people and triggered the first largescale nationalist demonstrations in China. These commenced on May 4, 1919 with demonstrations by Chinese students in Peking. The protest spread nationwide. In Shanghai boycotts of foreign and, particularly, Japanese goods were organized. The movement, called "the May 4th Movement", is now considered the starting point of Chinese national awareness. Protests were also held in France by Chinese students including, it is claimed, Zhou Enlai and Deng Xiaoping to stop the Chinese negotiators signing the treaty. The movement did not stop Japan from taking over the German rights in Shantung. China refused to sign the Treaty of Versailles, becoming the only country to not sign. The US Senate also refused to ratify the treaty. Both China and the United States therefore remained technically at war with Germany.

Right for an enemy to sue
The lack of a peace treaty between Germany and America brought a case before Lobingier in 1920 where he had to decide whether a German, technically still an enemy national, was allowed to bring an action in the US Court for China. The German was a partner with two Chinese in the firm Hai-Chong Hong. Hai-Chong Hong had sued the Consolidated Steel Corporation for breach of contract. Stirling Fessenden on behalf of Consolidated Steel argued that Hai-Chong Hong could not sue them, relying on a principle of common law that enemy nationals could not sue in American courts. Lobingier

reviewed old English decisions as well as US decisions that had considered the common law rule during the Anglo-American War of 1812. Lobingier found that the principle relied upon by the defendant was good law. However, he also found that there was a principle that if enemy aliens were residing "peaceably" within the United States and no steps were being taken to remove them, then they were allowed to bring actions in court.

The problem that Lobingier faced was that the German partner was living in China. The United States government had no jurisdiction over him and could not force him to leave. The Chinese were now allowing him stay. He was therefore residing "peaceably" in Shanghai but not because the US government allowed him to. Given that the war was long over, Lobingier most likely felt that this was a technical point which it would not be a good policy to enforce. He therefore held that the burden was on the American defendant to show that an enemy national was not residing peaceably in Shanghai. Consolidated Steel had not produced any evidence to show this and accordingly the case was allowed to proceed.

De Sausmarez retires

In the British courts, the end of World War I brought an end to Havilland de Sausmarez's long career as a judge. All long leave had been cancelled during the war. De Sausmarez was granted one of the first long leaves available commencing from March 1920. It was expected that he would not return. He did not.

Skinner Turner was appointed as Chief Judge in de Sausmarez's place and Peter Grain, a member of the Foreign Office Judicial Service and at the time British Judge in Egypt, was appointed as the new Assistant Judge. Grain was 56 at the time of his appointment. He was the son of John Peter Grain, a well-known criminal barrister in London. He was called to the bar of the Middle Temple in January 1897. In 1906, at the age of 42, Grain commenced a career that followed a very similar path to that of Havilland de Sausmarez. He went from Africa to Turkey, to Egypt and finally to Shanghai.

De Sausmarez did not completely forget China when he retired. Five years after retirement, he gave a talk to the University of London on "The Extraterritorial Court and China." A note of his talk reported he considered the courts to be invaluable and China was not in a position to establish a legal system that would allow their abolition. De Sausmarez, not surprisingly, thought that the British courts in China would be a necessity for a long time to come. This was not a view shared by the Chinese. The next decade was to see massive changes in China that brought the British and American governments to agree, but only to agree, that the time for extraterritoriality to end had come.

CHAPTER 21

Attacks from Inside and Out

JUDGE CHARLES LOBINGIER faced some challenging cases in the early 1920s. First, an American lawyer, William Fleming launched a campaign against the clear structural weakness of the United States Court for China the over concentration of power in the hands of one man, the Judge. Later, Lobingier had to decide some murky cases involving arms smuggling into China.

Fleming's campaign resulted in Fleming being jailed by Judge Lobingier for six months, a decision upheld on appeal and a subsequent review by the United States Supreme Court. As a result of his complaints, the United States Court was shut down for almost a year in 1922 while his allegations were being investigated. It nearly led to Lobingier's forced resignation and almost certainly resulted in Lobingier not getting the reappointment as Judge he clearly desired.

Fleming's campaign started after he lost five cases in a row before Lobingier. Fleming published a paper "The United States Court for China as an Institution." The paper was highly critical of how so much power had been given to one man, the judge of the court, and advocated for a jury system, as was used in the British Supreme Court, to be introduced, or, at the least, for trials with assessors. He argued:

"The Judge of the United States Court for China
exercises a jurisdiction, power and control over the
affairs of his fellow American citizens in China, greater

than any civil judicial officer ever appointed under
our system of Government, and greater even than that
exercised by the Chief Justice of the United States."

He compared the system unfavourably to the Chinese
legal system; challenging the very basis of extraterritoriality.
He wrote that the practices of the court were:

"consistent with the practice under the barbarous
system obtaining in China, against which we
were attempting to guard when we demanded
our extraterritorial jurisdiction and at a later date
established this Court."

Fleming brought his allegations to a head when a
prosecution was brought against him for defamation. In
response, he filed an affidavit accusing Lobingier of bias and
conspiring against him.

Lobingier found Fleming's accusations to be a "direct
contempt committed in the face of the Court, deliberately,
knowingly and with premeditation," by a lawyer who
knowing the law who "proposed to violate the law as he
apparently thought with impunity." Lobingier sentenced
Fleming to six months imprisonment and ordered the
Marshal take him into custody immediately. But later granted
bail pending appeal.

Fleming filed a complaint against Lobingier to President
Harding who passed it to the Department of Justice to review.
The review was completed by February 1922 and a report was
completed. It was however, decided to wait until the decision
of the Court of Appeal in San Francisco on Fleming's appeal
before making a final decision.

The Court of Appeals heard Fleming's appeal in March
1922 and immediately handed down a decision supporting
Lobingier in all respects and upholding the conviction and

sentence. The Department of Justice then issued its decision. Out of all the allegations, the DOJ found that Lobingier had not properly handled a case where his clerk, Earl Rose, had stolen a client's assets and had created an "unfortunate situation which ... which weakened the prestige" of the Court. The report stated that Lobingier had "lost his usefulness in China and [was] not conducting his office to the best interests of the Government." The Department of Justice wrote to Lobingier, with President Harding's consent, suggesting that he resign "for the good of the service in China and in order to establish that atmosphere that is so essential to a Federal Court, especially in a Foreign Country."

Lobingier refused to resign. There was not enough evidence to justify dismissing him; nor to deal with the political fallout. On June 21, 1922 Lobingier met with President Harding and no doubt impressed on him the fact that the court had not been functioning for almost 10 months; that the Chinese were already questioning whether America was complying with its treaty obligations by failing to provide a forum for Chinese to bring cases against Americans; and, that the appointment of a new judge would need Senate confirmation and could take some time. He also seems to have assured Harding that he would make peace with Fleming and that quiet would be restored to the court.

The meeting was a success for Lobingier. Two days later on June 23, 1922, Harding issued an executive order completely clearing Lobingier and ordering him to return to work. It read:

"A full investigation of the charges preferred by W. S. Fleming against the Judge of the United States Court for China having been made, the charges are determined to be unfounded and are, therefore, dismissed.

Fleming then made an apology in court to Lobingier. He,

however, also sought leave to appeal to the US Supreme Court. After this was dismissed, Lobingier had to decide whether to send Fleming back to jail.

Taking into account the suffering further imprisonment would cause on Fleming's wife and daughter, he gave the family a late Christmas present. Lobingier reduced Fleming's sentence to time served.

Lobingier's next challenge on the bench was to deal with some very complex cases against alleged gun-runners feeding China's insatiable appetite for foreign weapons.

Gun Runners

The 1920s had begun with some hope for China that the treaty powers might finally take steps to bring an end to extraterritoriality. The Washington Conference that was agreed as part of the Versailles Peace Treaty convened in 1922. The United States, Britain, Japan, China, Italy, Belgium, Netherlands, and Portugal all took part. The Soviet Union was not invited. The conference reached agreement on the substantial reduction in sizes of the United States and British navies and limits on the growth of the Japanese navy.

No agreement was reached, however, on an end to extraterritoriality. Instead, it was decided that a Commission on Extra-Territoriality should be established to consider and report on steps for the abolition of extraterritoriality. The commission was meant to be established immediately, but China at the time was still very unstable. No one faction ruled for any length of time in Peking. The Nationalists had established themselves firmly in Canton but had not yet expanded their power to the rest of the country.

There was one glimmer of hope for China from the conference. All countries participating agreed that that they would ban the import of arms into China. In 1922, the US Congress had passed a "Joint Resolution to prohibit the exportation of arms or munitions of war from the United

States to certain countries and for other purposes."

In the US Court, the resolve to stop the smuggling of guns to China led almost immediately to two prosecutions for smuggling munitions into China. In the first case, James Slevin was prosecuted for bringing 14 cases of airplanes into China. He was acquitted because there was no evidence the planes were for military use.

The second case was bizarre. It involved a Russian Admiral, Cossack soldiers, Chinese warlords and a sea captain with two wooden legs.

In early July 1923, the new District Attorney, Leonard Husar gave newspaper interviews to say he was investigating the activities of alleged gun-runners. He estimated that guns and shells worth millions of dollars were being sold in China. Husar believed that Shanghai was "the center of a gigantic organization carrying on an illicit trade in arms and ammunition throughout the Far East."

Husar's investigations, he said, had found 12 prominent Americans actively involved in contraband operations and that up to 30 Americans were involved as well as British, Chinese, Japanese and Russians. He identified one deal with a Chinese warlord Chang Tso-lin as being worth US$3 million. According to Husar, one prominent American running guns was Captain Lawrence D. Kearny.

By mid-July 1923, Husar was ready to take action. He issued warrants for Kearny's arrest: one for the sale of weapons to the governor of Chekiang Province, and one for the sale of Russian ships to Kiangsu province. Kearny had one distinguishing feature that meant it would be hard for him to hide out anywhere in China. He had two wooden legs, one going above the knee; the other being shorter and joining the leg below the knee.

In preparing the warrants, Husar faced a big problem: what to charge Kearny with? There was no law of the United States of America, or of Alaska or the District of Columbia, that prohibited the import of arms into China. There was no common law crime either. Husar had to fall back on the US treaties with China, all of which had prohibited the importation of weapons into China in some form. The Federal Penal Code made it an offence for persons to conspire to commit an offence against the United States or to defraud the United States. Husar framed his charges on the basis that Kearny had conspired with others to import weapons into China in contravention of the Treaty of Wanghsia and the Treaty of Tientsin.

This was a stretch and Husar probably knew it. However, with Charles Lobingier on the bench Husar would have known he had a judge who would do his best to stretch the law to prevent activities that harmed US relations with China.

Kearny's lawyer, Cornell Franklin, was prepared to fight the charges and fight hard. He filed a demurrer to the charge, which Lobingier acknowledged to be "exhaustive and ingenious." Franklin argued that the treaties were not in force, or went beyond the treaty-making power of the United States. The first argument, on the face of it, seemed weak. If the treaties were not in force, then the Court itself would not have jurisdiction indeed, it should not exist. The argument was a little more sophisticated. The argument was that each treaty had been cancelled by the succeeding one and thus ultimately the joint resolution of Congress following the Washington Conference had cancelled any parts of the treaties that prohibited arms

Judge Cornell Franklin, Kearny's lawyer and later Chairman of the SMC

smuggling. Lobingier made short work of this, pointing out that in international law, one treaty did not supersede the other, unless the treaty specifically stated it did so. This had been confirmed by the Supreme Court in the Ross case. In any event, the joint congressional resolution had nothing to do with smuggling arms into China but with exporting arms from America.

Franklin's second argument was much stronger. Treaties are made by the executive branch with the consent of the Senate. Laws should only be made by Congress, that is, the House of Representatives and the Senate together. The argument was that the President, by signing a treaty, could not create an offence without Congress enacting a law to support it.

Lobingier, in an exhaustive analysis, held first that the acts establishing first Consular Courts and later the US Court had been passed to enforce the treaties. Under the act establishing the US Court the court had been:

> "'expressly empowered to arraign and try ... all citizens
> of the United States, charged with offenses against
> law,' in China, and this grant of jurisdiction is made
> for the express purpose of carrying 'into full effect the
> provisions of the treaty.' Then, as if to meet just such a
> situation as this, the Court is authorized to supplement
> the treaty by imposing penalties at its discretion."

Secondly, Lobingier, relying on various Supreme Court decisions interpreting Article 6 of the United States Constitution, provided that treaties were self-executing, meaning they became part of United States law once ratified even if the treaty proscribed an offence. He concluded that only an appellate court could find otherwise, saying: "If this record is to be broken it should be by some higher tribunal." Kearny's objection was therefore overruled and his cases came on for trial.

The two cases against Kearny were tried separately but the judgments given together. The first case heard in September 1923 related to dealings with Russian navy ships that had landed at Woosong to the north of Shanghai in December 1922 with over 3,000 Russian refugees on board. The second case was heard in October and related to an attempt by Kearny to sell a Russian ship, the *El Dorado*, that was in Korea to Governor Chang of Chekiang Province.

The ships in the first case were the remnants of a flotilla that had left Vladivostok in October 1922 when the last resistance to the communist revolution in Russia had ended. The flotilla was led by Admiral George Stark, a 72-year-old retired admiral who had been called back into service at the beginning of World War I to be based in Vladivostok. With the communists approaching Vladivostok, Stark put together a flotilla of 30 boats, some of them very old, to evacuate the armed forces and all other refugees they could take.

Kearny made deals with Admiral Stark to sell weapons from the ship to Admiral Tu of the Chinese Navy. In total 50 guns, 160,233 rifles, 564,492 rounds of ammunition and 26 field telephones were transferred from the Russian boats and taken to Nanking.

The second case involved the purchase of a ship and weapons from Gensan on the east coast of Korea from Ural-Cossack soldiers who had also retreated from the Far Eastern Provinces with the communist victory. Kearny, through intermediaries, had approached the men to buy the boats and offered them passage to southern China. He had said he was acting on behalf of the governor of Kiangsu province, Chang Tsai-yang. One group of about 800 men had agreed and the boat the *El Dorado* had sailed for Chekiang Province. On the way, arms had been off-loaded in the "Saddles" a set of islands off the coast. The Chinese authorities refused to allow the men to land and stationed a police boat to ensure they did

The Saddles a popular recreation area and site of a Russian arms transfer

not leave their ship. In total, it was alleged that 6,000 guns, 21,000 rounds of ammunition, 28 machine guns and one field gun were sold in this transaction.

A number of witnesses were called in each case to show Kearny's involvement in the deals. Kearny did not challenge this evidence strongly and at the end of the prosecution case in each case sought a dismissal because the prosecution had not proved that the arms were not for the Chinese government. Lobingier overruled the applications on the basis that on a reading of the treaties and the law, it was incumbent on Kearny to prove that the arms were for the Chinese Government. This Kearny then attempted to do. Kearny was not embarrassed about being an arms dealer. He had obtained legal advice, most likely from Franklin, that stated there was nothing illegal in selling arms to the Chinese, and he had been happy to do so.

Kearny's main witness was Mr Chang Nieh-yun who said he was "adviser to the Commissioner of Foreign Affairs in Shanghai, Counselor to General Lu Yunghsiang, adviser to the Chapei Tax and Works Department and adviser to the Chamber of Commerce." Chang gave evidence as to what powers a Civil Governor had. Chang said that before the Republican Revolution, a civil governor had a bodyguard and a regiment of soldiers that he armed. There was no written law providing for this, but it had been the custom for a long time. Chang said that the Civil Governor of Chekiang was, in addition to that role, the commander of a division, the largest military unit in the Chinese army. As such, and unless there was an express prohibition, he was entitled to purchase arms and if he was bringing them into his own province, he had complete power to do so.

Husar cross-examined and asked what provisions of the Provisional Chinese Constitution gave the Governor the power to purchase arms. Chang said that not all powers were express; some came from custom. Husar then asked how Kearny would be appointed to purchase arms. Chang said that he should receive an appointment with a seal on it. Mr Chang said that he did not know how the governor had been appointed but said he had not been governor for very long. Husar then asked point blank: "There exists a state of war between Peking and Hangchow?" Mr Chang replied, to laughter in the court, "I wouldn't say that, but relations have been strained for some time."

Franklin tried to get evidence from both Governor Chang and Admiral Tu, but both being Chinese, the United States

Court had no power to compel them to give evidence. After a number of hearings where it was explained it was impossible to get evidence from the Chinese witnesses, Husar and Franklin agreed to admit the letter from Admiral Tu explaining the deal with him and the letter from Governor Chang giving his explanation. Admiral Tu's letter took full responsibility for the deal and confirmed he had engaged Kearny to assist him. Governor Chang's letter on the other hand, denied all knowledge of the deal. He said he had met with Kearny once and said "My conversation with L. D. Kearny on that date, being confined to the subject of purchase of ship, had absolutely nothing to do with any other question."

Lobingier gave his decisions in both cases on November 30, 1923. Not surprisingly, given the content of Admiral Tu's letter, he acquitted Kearny of the charge relating to Admiral Stark. Also, unsurprisingly given Governor Chang's letter, he convicted Kearny on the second charge. As to punishment, Lobingier said that, "we must consider on the one hand the gravity of the offence from the public standpoint and the menace to life and property in China, from the illicit important and consequent reckless distribution of arms, and munitions" but because this was the first case under the treaties he would impose a heavy fine of $2,500 rather than imprisoning Kearny.

After Lobingier had convicted him, as Kearny left the court, a free but poorer man, he turned to Lobingier and said "Thank you, Judge."

Lobingier retires

Lobingier retired soon after this. The only blot on what was otherwise a very successful term of office for Lobingier was William Fleming's attack on him and the subsequent Department of Justice investigation. He stabilized the court after a very difficult beginning and developed the court's jurisprudence fully, putting it on par with the British

Supreme Court. He retired to well-deserved accolades from the American bar and others.

Perhaps the highest praise for Lobingier came one month later from the man sent to replace him, Milton Purdy. Purdy was effusive in his praise of Lobingier's decisions saying:

"His decisions show a remarkable clarity of legal vision and precision, all the more significant because he had no precedent to fall back on. It is his interpretation of treaties, thought out with a marvellous clearness that has advanced the Court to its present status, ranking as it does, above the similar bodies in America."

Lobingier's replacement, Milton J. Purdy, had served briefly as a federal judge in Minnesota from July 1908 to May 1909 having been given a recess appointment, but had failed to obtain confirmation in the Senate. The President had appointed him without consulting the senators from Minnesota and they had killed the nomination by sending it to sub-committee from which it never emerged. Before that, Purdy had been a special assistant Attorney-General in the Roosevelt administration to handle anti-trust actions. He had become well known as "the chief trust buster." Purdy took office on April 11, 1924 and was welcomed by all members of the American Bar Association in Shanghai.

Purdy took a practical view to extraterritoriality. Very soon after his appointment, he had to decide whether the Municipal Council bye-laws could be enforced in the US Court. This was a particular problem because the statute establishing the US Court made no mention of them or the Land Regulations they were made under. A Mr Fuller was prosecuted for carrying ammunition in the settlement contrary to municipal bye-laws. His lawyer, Nick Char, argued the Court had no power to try any cases under the bye-laws. Purdy did not bother with fine legal reasoning to deal with the issue. He said that the court had not only the authority, but also the duty to enforce municipal regulations. To not do so would create a condition of chaos, if "any one government [held] it cannot enforce the bye-laws against its own citizens." He therefore held that under the Court's common law power, it could enforce the bye-laws of the municipality in which it was existing, particularly when the Land Regulations had been enacted with the consent of the American Minister. He added that all the courts of other countries in Shanghai enforced the municipal bye-laws and that the US Consular Court and Commissioner had also done so over the years. He said that if he was wrong, the Court of Appeals in San Francisco could correct him.

CHAPTER 22

Rebel with a Cause: Lawrence Kentwell

OUT OF THE MANY extraordinary judges and lawyers of the British and American Courts in China, Lawrence Klindt Kentwell, a British barrister of mixed Hong Kong Chinese, Hawaiian, American and British heritage was perhaps the most extraordinary.

Kentwell arrived in Shanghai during World War I after graduating from Oxford. He built himself a successful practice representing mainly Chinese and but also lower to middle class Westerners and Indian moneylenders in a number of the courts in Shanghai. His Eurasian blood probably made him attractive to Chinese seeking a British lawyer. It certainly made him unattractive to the upper class British society. Despite being a barrister and Oxford graduate, he was refused membership of the Shanghai Club which until the mid-1920s did not admit Chinese.

Throughout the 1920s, Kentwell was in and out of the numerous courts in Shanghai not just in his professional capacity as a barrister but personally suing and being sued in the British and American courts. The British Crown Advocate, Harrie Wilkinson, accused him in one case of being a criminal mastermind.

Kentwell was born in Hong Kong in 1882 to a Hong Kong Chinese mother and an English ship captain, Robert Kentwell, who it appears were not married. He migrated with his mother to Hawaii when young and grew up there. His mother, who taught him Cantonese, either subsequently married into or came from a wealthy family. Kentwell attended the exclusive Oahu College in Honolulu and graduated in 1897. He then attended Columbia University in New York and, later, Oxford University in England.

Despite his success in life, Kentwell's Chinese blood led him to face active official discrimination in both America and Britain. This was, justifiably, to taint his view of the world for the rest of his life.

In the early 1900s, he was working as Manager of the Hawaiian Realty and Maturity Company. Hawaii had been annexed in 1898 and become part of the United States. Under the Chinese Exclusion Act, Immigration Inspectors could bar Chinese from entering the United States even if they were US Citizens.

Kentwell often made trips abroad, travelling first class. He returned many times to mainland USA ports without trouble, most likely because he was travelling first class and because his skin colour was relatively fair. However, in 1904, after returning to Hawaii from a trip from the Philippines, an immigration officer singled him out for investigation under the Chinese Exclusion Act. Kentwell protested his treatment all the way up to President Theodore Roosevelt saying that he should not be treated as Chinese because he was English, having been born in Hong Kong to an English father. The Immigration Officials in Hawaii did not agree and in their correspondence simply referred to him as the "Chinaman."

Once in 1905, returning to San Francisco on board the *China*, he actively sought to be excluded on arrival. The San Francisco Chronicle reported that as the ship docked:

"He walked the decks of the *China*, waiting anxiously for some Chinese Bureau official to treat him with discourtesy. He wanted to be insulted. He would have welcomed an assignment for the night to the meanest bunk in the detention shed, and would have greeted as brother the Government official who asked."

He also gave speeches, in Cantonese, to the Chinese community encouraging them to fight discrimination.

Kentwell did later become an American citizen. However, by 1911 he had moved to Oxford in England with his wife and four young children and in 1915 re-naturalised to become a British subject. At Oxford, he also faced discrimination because of his race and was refused entry to the Officer Training Corp because he was not of pure European descent. The English Bar did not discriminate on the basis of race and he was admitted to practice as a barrister in England in 1916.

Soon after his admission in England, Kentwell moved to Shanghai. He left his wife and six children behind in Oxford. Upon arrival in Shanghai, he was admitted before the Supreme Court for China by Havilland de Sausmarez, and quickly built up a substantial practice appearing in many cases in the British Supreme Court, the US Court for China, the Mixed Court and other consular courts.

During the course of his practice, Kentwell locked horns with the Assistant Judge, Peter Grain, on many occasions. It appears Grain did not like Kentwell, possibly because of his mixed race. Kentwell directly suggested this was the reason in one case. The Chief Judge, Skinner Turner, on the other hand, appears to have been more sympathetic.

Kentwell defamed

Kentwell did not just get himself into trouble with judges. Kentwell's practice of law, or probably more correctly the supervision of his practice, got him into trouble with clients on a number of occasions.

In one case, newspapers reported he was a co-defendant with his interpreter, Mr G.R. Grove, in a lawsuit relating to the sale of some properties by a client, Mr H.B. Clough, to Grove. The writ said that Clough "was induced to sign the deed by the false and fraudulent misrepresentation of the defendant and Lawrence K. Kentwell, counsel for both parties to the deed." This resulted in Kentwell being subpoenaed as a witness in the British Supreme Court and in Kentwell bringing an action for defamation in the United States Court for China.

Kentwell had represented Clough in the Mixed Court in a claim against a Mr Sia and obtained judgment for $5,944. Sia owned 17 houses on Avenue Road (now Beijing West Road). They were sealed by the Mixed Court to satisfy the judgment. Some mortgagees had come forward, reducing the value of the properties. Kentwell told Clough that his interpreter, Grove, was interested in purchasing the properties. Clough agreed to this and signed a deed, drafted by Kentwell, giving up his right to claim the $5,944 in return for a payment of $3,000. Clough later found out that Grove had then quickly on-sold the properties for $3,300 making a tidy profit of $300. He brought action in the British Supreme Court to rescind the deed on the basis of misrepresentation by Grove and Kentwell. Clough, however, only sued Grove and not Kentwell.

When the action was commenced in 1923, it first came before Gilbert King, the Registrar. Kentwell had protested against the publication of the writ mentioning him and asked that the press be directed not to print his name. King left this to the discretion of the reporters. The British-run *North China Herald* and *North China Daily News* did not mention Kentwell's name, but two America-run newspapers, the *China Press* and *Evening Star* did. The *Evening Star*'s headline was:

"Fraud Charge made against Atty.
Kentwell: British Lawyer is co-defendant in action by
Mr Clough"

The *China Press'* headline was:

"Charge of Fraud is brought against Local Attorney:
Mr. L. K. Kentwell is made defendant in British Court
Suit"

Both headlines were inaccurate and clearly defamatory. Kentwell had not been made a Defendant to the action. Kentwell filed a suit in the US Court for China seeking damages.

Clough's action against Kentwell's interpreter, Mr Grove, was heard first before Judge Skinner Turner without a jury.

Clough said that it was Kentwell who had dealt with the matter, not Grove. Kentwell had told him he had an offer of $2,500 and was trying to get a better offer. Eventually, Kentwell had told him $3,000 was the best he could get and he had better accept it. Clough said he had signed the agreement with Grove not realizing that he was giving up his rights under the judgment.

Turner stopped Clough there. He had had enough: "The difficulty about this case is, that it is a fierce attack on Mr. Kentwell who is not a party to the proceedings. It is nothing but an attack on Mr. Kentwell. Nothing whatever is said about Mr. Grove, the actual defendant."

Turner pushed Clough who eventually admitted he had no complaint against Grove but that he thought Kentwell and Grove had colluded together to cheat him. His lawyer, Mr P.W. Goldring, called this an "accumulation of suspicions."

Grove's lawyer, Ranald McDonald, argued there was no case to answer. Turner agreed and dismissed the action with costs.

Kentwell proceeded with his action for defamation in the US Court against the *China Press* and the *Evening Star*. Charles Lobingier heard the case just a few weeks before the end of his term in office. The only defamatory part of the article was the heading that described Kentwell as a co-defendant. One witness called by Kentwell, Mr R.C. Faithfull, said that after seeing the report he had contacted Allan Mossop, the Acting Crown Advocate to make enquiries about Kentwell. He also said he had been told by one member of the press that "something ugly was coming against Kentwell in the near future."

In his decision, Lobingier clearly had some sympathy for Kentwell, but said that if any damage had been done to Kentwell it was from the report of the writ, not the use of the words co-defendant. He therefore decided not to award him any damages but did award him his costs on the basis that Kentwell was "not unjustified in bringing the action."

Kentwell the criminal mastermind?

Kentwell did not stay out of trouble for long. As Mr Faithfull had been told, there was indeed "something ugly coming against Mr Kentwell." He was charged by the British Crown Advocate, Harrie Wilkinson, as a criminal mastermind. On March 21, 1925, Detective Sergeant Maurice Tinkler of the Shanghai Municipal Police arrested Kentwell on charges of possession of and uttering (that is, making use of) counterfeit banknotes.

Wilkinson, in prosecuting the case, made it clear that although the charges were only for possession and uttering of counterfeit bank notes, his case was that Kentwell was most likely the mastermind of the operation. Or, as Wilkinson put it: "he must have known of the forgeries and he might or might not have been the intellectual head in the matter."

These were very serious allegations to make of a member of the British Bar. However, the reasons to suspect Kentwell were damning. Kentwell, who obviously was doing well, had three premises in Shanghai. He owned or rented a house at 1 Soochow Road (Suzhou Road) along Soochow Creek, a house "in the country" at 200 Warren Road (now

Gubei Road in Hongqiao) which he leased and had another house in Nanziang (Nanxiang), in Putong far out of town. At the Warren Road house, Chinese men had been arrested photographing genuine banknotes. At the house in Nanziang, printing presses were found which were being used to print counterfeit banknotes.

Kentwell's Chinese assistant, Johnson Dzung, had at one time owned the property in Nanziang. But by either a lease or mortgage Kentwell had claimed the house was his. Kentwell had applied to the British Consulate-General for an official notice declaring that a British subject who was protected by extraterritorial rights occupied the house. This would ensure that the house would not be interfered with by Chinese soldiers or others. The notice had been given to Kentwell and it was placed outside the house.

Kentwell had not been arrested in possession of any counterfeit banknotes. The evidence against him came from two Chinese men who had been caught by the French police with fake currency. The French police investigations had led to the searches of Kentwell's houses and the discovery of the counterfeiting operation. The French police had then requested the SMP to arrest Kentwell and search his Soochow Road premises, which were in the International Settlement. The case was passed to Detective Sergeant Tinkler who arrested Kentwell. Nothing was found at the Soochow Road premises. Kentwell told Tinkler "Well, I think you will find all this is false." He soon after added that he thought the case might have a connexion with him having unsuccessfully defended some Chinese in counterfeiting cases.

Kentwell was released on bail. At his committal hearing, Kentwell reserved his defence and he was committed to trial in the Supreme Court.

Between the committal and the trial, the case had an extraordinary twist. Kentwell had employed another British lawyer, Mr M.L. Heen, to assist to run his practice while he was being prosecuted. Heen had come into Kentwell's office on Szechuan Road (Sichuan Road) to find a Chinese assistant in conversation with some Chinese men. Heen asked what the men wanted. He was told that they were Chinese police from Nanziang who had in their possession a document that Mr Kentwell may wish to buy from them. The document was a letter signed by Kentwell addressed to the Chief of Police in Nanziang confirming the house in Nanziang was his and asking the police to leave the house alone because it belonged to a British national who was protected by extraterritorial rights.

The Chinese police thought they were sitting on a gold mine. And, in Chinese courts, where documentary evidence is king, they would have been. They however, did not appreciate that in British courts where oral evidence can be decisive, Kentwell may be able to explain the letter. The Chinese police put a very high price on the letter: $25,000.

Heen told Kentwell of the Chinese police's offer. Kentwell's response could have come out of a bad American detective novel.

"Collar them."

The SMP were called and a sting operation was set up. Two foreign detectives and two Chinese detectives hid behind a partition in Kentwell's office while Kentwell met with his visitors. The Chinese said the French police had offered $50,000 for the letter but they were willing to offer it to Kentwell for $25,000 because they wanted to help him out.

The SMP detectives pounced and arrested the Chinese men who

Judge Skinner Turner presides over the prosecution of Kentwell

turned out to be the Chief of Police at Nanziang, Po Sa-tien, his secretary and a man who was said to be the teacher of Kentwell's interpreter, Johnson Dzung. Kentwell had them prosecuted them in the Mixed Court before Magistrate Zau and the British Assessor, Mr A.J. Martin, on blackmail charges. The case was adjourned until after the case in the British court against Kentwell was finished.

Kentwell's counterfeiting trial started before Skinner Turner and a jury on March 23, 1925. Harrie Wilkinson prosecuted together with R. N. Macleod. Kentwell had three defence Counsel, Mr K E Newman, Mr Heen and a French lawyer, Mr R Cremieux.

Wilkinson called numerous witnesses including Tinkler and Detective J. C. Giuuhs of the French police who had raided the house in Nanziang where two printing presses and numerous other printing equipment had been found. Kentwell and Dzung's professional letter paper had also been found there. The French police had also obtained a warrant from the Chilean Consul to arrest Dzung but could not locate him. He eventually surrendered himself when the police found he was no longer Chilean and then obtained a warrant from the Mixed Court. Other detectives from the French Police also gave evidence.

The key witnesses for the prosecution, Kentwell's alleged accomplices in counterfeiting, were then called. The first was Tsu Sing Tseng who said he was an insurance broker. He said he had overheard Kentwell and Dzung talking about getting a proclamation for the Nanziang house and hoisting the British flag to keep Chinese soldiers away. He said he had met Kentwell at Kentwell's office where Kentwell had told him that banknotes were nearly ready. He and Kentwell had negotiated a price for the counterfeits.

Wilkinson's next witness was Tsang Zien-sung who had given information to the French police about the operation. Tsang had been employed by Tsu as a cook at the house. Tsang said that he had seen Kentwell at the Warren Road house and that Kentwell had been on a launch near the Nanziang house when counterfeiting equipment was loaded. Notably, he did not say he had seen Kentwell in possession of counterfeit bank notes. He said that there were seven forgers at work at the house. Turner asked Tsang if he had been paid his wages. Tsang responded: "Tsu is my relative." Turner could not resist. Showing that he had come to understand the Chinese he said, amidst laughter: "That means you didn't get them." Tsu confirmed this, saying, "I didn't get cash. Arrangements were made."

Wilkinson's final witness was Kentwell's interpreter, Johnson Dzung, who said that he had arranged with Kentwell to get the proclamation for the Nanziang house and that he had been to the Warren Road house and seen men working there. He did not know anything about counterfeiting activities.

In defence, Kentwell gave evidence on his own behalf and put the blame firmly on Dzung. He said that Dzung had been his interpreter but that he had realized later that "he was a bad lot." Asked why he had not dismissed Dzung, Kentwell responded that "he had to act carefully, that he could not dismiss the man at a day's or a month's notice, and that unless he acted diplomatically in the matter it was possible that Dzung, who knew a great deal about his practice, might do damage to it if he thought he had ground for complaint." He added in response to a further question that "the greater part of my business was Chinese business, and if I had dismissed him instantly he might have done me an injury."

Carmen Roderique, who was described as Kentwell's "lady friend", told the court she lived at 1 Soochow Road and had been to the Nanziang house but had never seen any counterfeiting paraphernalia. She said the Warren Road house was used for riding and tennis. A number of office staff were called to say they had seen Tsu who had spoken to Dzung but never spoken to Kentwell. Finally, Mr Heen was called to recount the blackmailing incident.

Turner summed up to the jury with a very clear direction to acquit. He said the real evidence against Kentwell came from Tsu and Tsang. A jury could rely on the evidence of accomplices, however they should be very careful if they wished to do so. Kentwell was a very well known legal practitioner and that there was no evidence that he had actually ever slept at either of the houses where the counterfeiting was occurring.

Not surprisingly the jury returned in 35 minutes with a verdict of Not Guilty. Turner agreed, saying: "I think, gentlemen, it would have been dangerous to have convicted on the evidence brought before you."

Kentwell defends himself
Soon, Kentwell was again fighting for his professional life in the British Supreme Court. By this time, reflecting the current mood of Chinese generally, he had become a shrill Chinese nationalist.

In July 1926, Grain heard a case against Kentwell brought by one of his former clients for professional misconduct. In 1921, Kentwell had assisted a Chinese businessman, Chow Kwei-Ching, to register a Spanish company at the Spanish Consulate under the name of "Chinese Coal Produce and Stock Exchange Co." In order to do so, Kentwell had registered Chow as a Spanish subject, born in the Philippines. Chow said that he took no part in the registration, save giving Mr. Kentwell his photograph and paying to Mr. Kentwell's office $380 as the registration fee.

Chow said at the trial that he never went to the Spanish Consulate, that he was a Chinese subject, born in China, and had never been to the Philippines. He said he had never claimed to be Spanish. Kentwell knew he was a Chinese subject. Kentwell did not deny that he carried out the registration, stating, "I effected the registration of Chow

Kweiching;" and that he had "probably attended at the Spanish Consulate to do so."

Chow paid in total $46,650 to establish the company. The company was soon after put into liquidation with Kentwell as the liquidator. Mr Chow only received back $26,000 of the money he put in. Of this, he paid more than $10,000 to Kentwell in fees.

The initial registration at the Spanish Consulate was not a direct issue in the case. Chow had not claimed that this was improper. Grain, however, thought it was grossly improper and said so in his judgment:

> "It is most distressing and regrettable that a man who has been called to the English Bar for about 10 years and has practised as an admitted legal practitioner before this Court for about the same time, should have lent himself to obtaining a false and fraudulent registration. This registration is only a side issue, but it is part of the history in the case and also, as it concerns a legal practitioner in my Court, I felt bound not to pass it by without some comment."

Grain then said that Kentwell's various defences were not believable, but more importantly:

> "There is a rule among members of the English Bar which is highly prized. Namely, that one's first duty is to consider and protect the interests of one's client. I regret to say that in this case that rule does not seem to have been adhered to."

He concluded by ordering Kentwell to give the account requested by Chow showing the money he had received from Chow and how he had spent it. To punish Kentwell further, he ordered that Kentwell pay Chow's costs on the highest scale.

Kentwell was not going to take this lying down. After the judgment was delivered, Kentwell stood up and accused Grain of being "hostile to him throughout the proceedings." Then he accused him directly of racism:

> "the whole atmosphere was so hostile that at I considered it was bordering on racial prejudice."

Judge Peter Grain
Accused of bias by Kentwell

Grain tried to call Kentwell to order but Kentwell refused to stop. The *North China Herald* reporter noted that, "it was difficult to follow his remarks, but he was heard to say: 'This country is my motherland.'"

When Kentwell finally stopped, Grain reprimanded him: "I cannot have platform speeches. I am under the impression that you are a countryman of mine. You are a member of my own profession and a British subject, aren't you?"

"Yes, I am," replied Kentwell.

Grain had had enough and lectured Kentwell:

> "I am satisfied that anybody who listened to the proceedings during the many days that the hearing of this case occupied will agree that I exercised the most extraordinary patience. I don't mind saying on my own behalf that if you had not been the defendant there were many things I should have objected to you saying, and the case, instead of lasting 13 days, would have lasted six. You have the right of appeal and you can

state as the grounds of your appeal that the Judge was prejudiced."

He then asked if Kentwell wanted leave to appeal. Kentwell replied in the affirmative. Grain granted him leave.

Kentwell disbarred

Kentwell did not appeal. After the appeal period expired, the British Crown Advocate Allan Mossop, applied for Kentwell's disbarment on the basis Grain had found that Kentwell had fraudulently assisted Chow to register as a Spanish national at the Spanish Consulate so he could register a Spanish company.

Skinner Turner was out of Shanghai so the application came before Grain. Because the reasons for seeking disbarment were based on Grain's findings in the Chow case, Grain recognised in his judgment that he was not the most appropriate person to be dealing with the case.

This time, Kentwell was smart enough to get another lawyer to represent him, Tyco Wing. While Kentwell had admitted registering Chow as a Spanish national, all was

Tyco Wing attempts to defend Kentwell

not lost. The Privy Council had, many years before, overturned a decision to disbar an attorney who had put a false recital in a contract. The effect of a false recital is that the other party would sign the contract believing something to be true when it was not. The Privy Council had found "the reason assigned for the false statement, though unsatisfactory, had any fraud whatever followed upon the transaction, was not inconsistent with the possibility of honest motives." More importantly, the document had not been used fraudulently. Wing argued that the facts were similar in Kentwell's case. The Spanish Consulate had not been deceived and, in fact, the "the Spanish Consulate was ready to accept registrations without inquiry."

Grain took a very dim view of the practice of obtaining false registrations. He emphasized the need for British lawyers to maintain the highest possible standards while practicing in an extraterritorial jurisdiction:

> "Even if this particular Consulate did at that time give great facilities for the registration of Chinese subjects, there was all the more reason for Mr. Kentwell as a member of the English Bar and a legal practitioner in this Court to do nothing that might in any way directly or indirectly encourage this irregularity.
>
> "Foreigners in China by Treaty are in possession of extraterritorial rights and it is most essential at all times, and more especially at the present period, that foreigners should not abuse those rights. It is still more essential that a trained lawyer, a member of the English Bar and a legal practitioner in H.B.M. Supreme Court for China, should do nothing in any way to abuse those Treaty rights which he in the course of his profession does so much to uphold, and administer."

Grain acknowledged that disbarment would be the end of Kentwell's career as a barrister. However, he said "it is the duty of the official presiding over these courts to do all in his power to maintain the high standard of integrity and honesty."

He ordered that Kentwell be permanently disbarred. When Grain had finished reading his judgment, Kentwell leapt to his feet to protest. His lawyer, Wing, "made an ineffectual attempt" to restrain him. When this failed he walked out of the court leaving Kentwell arguing.

Kentwell complained that the decision was politically motivated because of his support for Chinese nationalism. Grain said that he had no knowledge of Kentwell's political views. But, that if Kentwell objected he could appeal to the Privy Council. Kentwell retorted that this would be futile.

Kentwell did not appeal. He did, however, write a stream of letters to the British judicial and political authorities in Shanghai and London denouncing the decision and British imperialism. He took particular pleasure in attacking Grain personally.

Grain in his own defence, some years later, wrote to the British Minister:

"L. K. Kentwell usually states that he was disbarred merely because he caused a Chinese subject to be registered as a Spanish subject. But the facts against him were far more serious than that. L. K. Kentwell constantly speaks of China as his 'Mother Land' or some title, but the grave charge against him when the court was moved to disbar him was that he had taken large sums of money from one of his Chinese brothers."

Kentwell returns

Kentwell was back in the Supreme Court two months after his disbarment. He was now a journalist having founded the *China Courier*, "an anti-British Journal" with another Eurasian, G.R. Grove, his former interpreter. Needless to say, the Municipal Police were keeping a close eye on him.

He had been summonsed for payment of the money he had been ordered to pay Mr Chow in the case he had lost the year before and for payment of back rates to the Shanghai Municipal Council. He had by this time become a fervent Chinese nationalist and a strong supporter of the Nationalist Government in Canton.

In the council rates case, Kentwell had written to the Municipal Council Inspector, Mr Inwood, stating he would "not pay the above taxes until Shanghai is handed back to the Chinese people, whose sovereignty the imperialistic countries of Europe have continually infringed."

When summonsed to appear in the British Supreme Court, he responded in a letter to the court stating: "I have taken steps to become a citizen of the Republic of China, my motherland, and I throw myself heartily into the fight to recover her rights." Kentwell did not appear in court. Judge Peter Grain, however, agreed that if Kentwell had taken Chinese nationality then his British nationality would go, leaving the British Supreme Court without jurisdiction. But, until satisfactory evidence could be produced to show that he had become Chinese, Kentwell would be considered British. Because Kentwell had not appeared, Grain issued a warrant for his arrest.

Kentwell was arrested by Plain Clothes Constable Rhind on Sunday, January 31, 1927 outside his Chinese lawyer's house on Burkill Road (Fengyang Road), just behind Bubbling Well Road. Kentwell had been expecting to be arrested. He had in his pocket a letter he had pre-written addressed to the *North China Daily News*, which read:

"I am aware that the local British Supreme Court has issued a warrant for my arrest. I am advised not to surrender myself, being a Chinese citizen. The local British court has no jurisdiction over me. I can only be brought before the British Court under duress, that is by being arrested wherever I happen to be."

Kentwell was brought the next day before Registrar Gilbert King. Watching Kentwell in court must have been great entertainment. Many of the British lawyers in Shanghai had found that they had business in court that day and the legal benches were "closely packed."

Kentwell said to King:

> "I told the policeman that I would appear under duress and would only appear here by force. I am a Chinese citizen and do not recognise this court."

Registrar King does not want to be a "judicial gunboat""

King said that there were judgments against him made when he was registered as British subject. He was asked how he was going to prove he was Chinese.

Kentwell responded:

> "I renounced my allegiance to Great Britain because of the snobs who have brought disgrace to Great Britain. I am ashamed of them as my nationals and I renounce my allegiance. This is the class of people who have brought on the disgrace. They are snobs and proud people who are looked upon with shame by the Chinese. I did not register this year at the British Consulate."

He and his Chinese lawyer gave evidence that he had applied to become a Chinese citizen but could not produce evidence that it had been granted. His lawyer said it was possible for foreigners to naturalize to become Chinese if they had lived in China for more than five years or if their father or mother were Chinese. Kentwell interjected:

"And my mother was Chinese."

At one point Kentwell said in an outburst:

"I demand my immediate release as a Chinese citizen. This is the Gunboat Policy again."

A heated outburst followed and waving his hand over the legal benches he shouted:

"These snobs also secured the rendition of the Mixed Court"

King, exasperated, retorted: "Oh Mr Kentwell, please!" "That's right," continued Kentwell, "Snobs all of them! The Shanghai Club and Country Club! I am ashamed of their behaviour as Englishmen!"

King responded:

"I do not propose to act like a judicial gunboat, but I have to obey the law."

King required Kentwell to prove he was Chinese. Kentwell said that if he was not granted Chinese citizenship he would be stateless, to which King said, that no, he would be British. Kentwell said, "I don't recognize the Crown." King as a judge of the court could only reply, "But I have to."

Kentwell was cross-examined as to his assets. He said he had none. He had invested all his spare cash in the *China*

Courier and had sent any other cash back to England to support his six children. King asked him if he had any money now.

"I have money which I put into a newspaper," replied Kentwell, "but that is just like throwing it into the Huangpu River. I put in $50,000 to fight this arrogant British snobbery." King's famous patience was wearing thin. "Perhaps that shows the futility of fighting the arrogant British snobs," he suggested facetiously.

Kentwell then gave evidence concerning his businesses. Then, as the *North China Herald* court reporter put it, he made "an uncomplimentary remark about Judge Grain which had been made several times previously."

This brought a quick and strong reproof from King: "I have great admiration for Judge Grain and I will not allow you to speak evil of him. What he did was not a personal matter but as Judge of the Court."

Kentwell said his wife had means and property in Honolulu and that he had wired her for some money, but added, "If I get the money from her, I am willing to put $50,000 more into the paper to exterminate this British snobbery."

The case was adjourned soon after this for two months with Kentwell being granted bail. The *North China Herald* has no record of the case being heard again. Presumably Kentwell, in a moment of rationality, paid his rates and reached a compromise with Chow.

Kentwell's British nationality was, four years later, revoked for "disloyalty and disaffection."

Kentwell wants to come back

Ten years later, Kentwell sought to be allowed to practice before the British Supreme Court. Kentwell had continued to practice law in Shanghai at some point qualifying as a Chinese lawyer, but, he could not appear in the British courts.

Kentwell wrote a very polite letter to Penrhyn Grant Jones

who at the time was Acting Judge, requesting the right to appear before the British courts. He based his application on the fact that he was a practicing member of the Chinese bar as well as still being admitted as a barrister in England. He noted that:

> "Your Honour are no doubt aware that the Chinese Government extends to all British legal practitioners the courtesy to practice in all Chinese Courts where British interests are involved and in return it seems only fair that the British Government extends the same courtesy to qualified Chinese legal practitioners to appear in H.B.M. Courts in China."

Grant Jones, passed the letter on to the Registrar who responded in a terse letter on his behalf that "as you were struck of the Roll of this Court on the 24th November, 1926, he is precluded from hearing you."

Kentwell replied in a less polite letter complaining his disbarment was a "travesty of justice and a terrible reflection on the integrity of H.B.M. Supreme Court." He said that Judge Grain had been motivated by political considerations related to Kentwell's "extreme political views on Anglo-Chinese relations." Many American lawyers and a British law firm had all obtained similar registrations at the Spanish Consulate. Kentwell asked for reconsideration of the Grain's decision on the basis that "assuming that I did advise the Chinese to obtain registrations," the penalty of permanent disbarment did not fit the crime:

> "It is too drastic and too severe. It is like cutting off both my hands and my feet with the removal of my eyesight. I cannot endure it any longer."

A dramatic plea that may have had a chance, but, Kentwell

surely did not help his cause when he wrote: "I did intend to shoot Judge Grain and his co-conspirator" presumably referring to Allan Mossop who as Crown Advocate had applied for his disbarment "but the thought of my six young children and wife restrained me from transplanting my wish into action. As each year rolls by, my desire for revenge the injustices and wrongs done me by Judge Grain grows stronger and stronger." He called Grant Jones' attention to the famous case of Captain Dreyfus who had had wrongful convictions annulled against him. He then begged: "I implore your Honour to assist me to redress the wrongs and injustice done to me by reviewing my case. Please do so for you have the power."

The Registrar closed the correspondence with a short letter that followed instructions written by Grant Jones on the top margin of Kentwell's letter. The reply to Kentwell stated, simply, "the Acting Judge has no power to review the decision of Sir Peter Grain in this matter."

What drove Lawrence Kentwell?

Kentwell had faced institutionalized racism all his life: in America as a Chinese; in England when he was refused a military commission because of his mixed blood; and, most certainly for the whole time he was in Shanghai. He was refused admission to the Shanghai Club despite being a barrister and an Oxford graduate as he was to repeat on many occasions in his own form of snobbery. It is impossible now to say whether Grain disbarred him because of racism as Kentwell alleged. Nevertheless, there can be no doubt he genuinely felt that many of his problems were caused by his mixed heritage.

Kentwell wrote plaintively to the British Ambassador to China in 1940:

"There is no doubt that I was regarded as a despised Eurasian, a half-caste outcast with all sorts of hidden indignities heaped upon me like Hitler by the people of my fatherland as unworthy of their association in spite of the fact that I was British born, a gentleman, an Oxford graduate and a member of the English bar and father of six wonderful children, two of whom are Oxford graduates. The golden portals of the Shanghai Club dubbed the 'home' of British snobs and racial prejudice may not be soiled by my unworthy feet because I am not a person of 'pure' European descent. Do you think any human being with any spark of self respect and pride in him will take such outrageous treatment lying down? Never!"

Reading these words almost three-quarters of a century later, it is impossible not to have complete sympathy for Kentwell. He was, of course, right. But, he was also a man before his time.

As we will see in the next chapter, the British system (as well as those of other countries) was not quite ready to treat other races as equals.

Chapter 23

The Rise of Nationalism

LAWRENCE KENTWELL WAS NOT the only nationalist to appear before the British Courts in the 1920s. The world was changing quickly. The new socialist Soviet Union offered hope of change to the down-trodden around the world. Nationalist movements were established around the world. In 1920, Gandhi had taken over the leadership of the Congress Party in India and was agitating strongly for independence agitation that spilled over to Indians in China. A decade after the Qing Dynasty had fallen, Chinese were becoming more and more conscious of their rights and willing to take steps to protect them.

This rise of nationalism brought a number of cases before the British courts, a riot in Shanghai and, at last, to the formation of the long promised Extraterritoriality Commission.

The Indians revolt
Throughout the 1920s British authorities were very concerned about sedition being spread amongst Indians in China. In late 1920 an Order in Council was enacted specifically prohibiting the publication of seditious materials in China.

In the spring of 1924, Sikh disaffection, led to one of the most extraordinary scenes ever to occur in any British court in China.

At 10am on Tuesday, April 22, 1924, the trial of Harbak Singh on charges of sedition was due to resume in the

Police Court which was located on the ground floor with a door opening directly to the consulate gardens. The case had started the previous Saturday morning before Registrar Gilbert King. The public gallery of the court was packed with Sikhs, all wearing black turbans. Another hundred or so black-turbaned Sikhs, who could not fit into the court, were in the garden of the Consulate, surrounding the court on two sides.

Singh had been charged with sedition for publishing several pamphlets, including "British Barbarism in India" and "British Justice gone Bankrupt." A few months before, King had convicted Singh after a trial on a similar charge and released on giving two recognisances in the amount of $250.

After publication of the new pamphlets, a warrant was issued for his arrest. This was passed to Detective Sergeant Tinkler of Central Police Station to execute. While Tinkler was looking for his man, Singh went to Central Police Station on Foochow Road (Fuzhou Road) to ask if there was a warrant out for his arrest. He waited for Tinkler to return. Tinkler searched Singh's shop and found nothing. But pamphlets ready to be printed were found at a printing company. It appears that Singh wanted to be prosecuted. Captain Barrett, Superintendent of Police, testified that he had received a copy of the pamphlet through the post addressed to him in Singh's handwriting.

When first brought into the court on the Saturday, Singh had adopted a policy of strict non-cooperation with the court. He refused to plead or to recognise the court. When asked by King if he objected to Tinkler's evidence concerning his arrest he merely said: "I don't object to anything. You can do as you like." He similarly refused to question witnesses from the printing company. When the prosecutor, Mr Maitland, asked for an adjournment until Tuesday, Singh said: "I am a strict non-cooperator. I do not recognize your court. You can do what you like." King told Singh that he wished to see the case against him proved to the hilt and ordered that the case continue on Tuesday. Singh was ordered to be held in custody.

The adjournment gave Singh's supporters the opportunity to attend the trial and, although they were there in large numbers, they were relatively well behaved. The *North China Herald* reported:

> "Remarkable scenes were witnessed in the grounds of H.B.M. Consulate and in H.M. Police Court on Tuesday morning at the termination of the trial of Harbak Singh. The court room was filled with Indians and the grounds outside harboured some fifty to a hundred others."

On the Tuesday, one more witness for the prosecution was called who confirmed receiving the pamphlet in Nanking Road.

Singh then asked if he could make a statement. King said that he could. Singh produced a number of pages of closely written words, which he read out in "quite good English." Singh started by saying that Shanghai was part of China. He had done nothing seditious against the Government of China. The International Settlement was not a British colony so he could not therefore be charged with sedition against the British Government.

He went through Indian history, covering various injustices and broken pledges by the British government. He complained about the treatment of Sikhs in Shanghai; how there were special registration rules for them, and, that many had been deported by Captain Barrett during World War I. Captain Barrett and the Jemadar of the Sikh Police Sirdar Sahib Budda Singh were singled out for their abusive treatment of Sikhs and personal persecution of Harbak Singh.

He said that in India sedition was not a crime. He knew he was about to be deported to India but did not care. "He would only be one of many innocent Sikhs sent out from Shanghai." Then in a flourish of rhetoric he added:

> "What did it matter? By sending me to gaol you do but send me from a large prison to a smaller one. You can imprison my body, but not my soul."

He emphasized that he did not hate the English.

> "I love all men as my brothers. All men are my brethren. I hate the system of Government by the British in India."

But, he said, he would fight for the freedom of India, even if it "led him to the gallows." King, has been born in India and spent his early years there, went through the statement with Singh to try to convince him of the errors of his ways. Singh asked King why he was being prosecuted for sedition when most of what he printed had passed the censor in India. Some of the papers in India had even described "the British Government as the Government, not of His Britannic Majesty, but as the Government of His Satanic Majesty."

At this point King broke protocol and asked Captain Barrett directly if that was true. Barrett responded: "I believe that is so, Sir. Some of them I know are very hot stuff." Singh then tried to produce the papers, but King said he would take his word for it.

Mr Maitland prosecuting then said there was nothing really to say. Singh had admitted everything and "was so bigoted in his ideas he could hardly be considered a reasonable being."

King, was not having this and dressed down Maitland telling him:

> "Every British subject had a right to hold any opinions he wishes, no matter how much anyone else differs

from him. He can only be stopped when the expression of those opinions is likely to cause trouble."

King clearly did not want to convict Singh, at least not without hearing a defence. He made one last exhortation to Singh to "make some plea on his own behalf." Singh refused. King said he had no choice but to convict Singh and sentence him to the maximum sentence of two months imprisonment. At the end of his term of imprisonment he would be bound over to keep the peace on his own surety and that of three others for $250.

At the end of the hearing and before King could leave the bench, "the crowd broke into loud cheers for the prisoner, which were taken up by their fellows outside — cheers which could not be suppressed by the police." A rush was made for the doors, which King ordered to be closed but the mob was too strong for the police. Some of the crowd was arrested and the rest of the crowd then "cheered more and threw flowers and confetti over them." King ordered that they be released and the crowd moved towards the Bund Gardens before being headed off by the police. They then marched to the Sikh Gurdwara on North Szechuen Road.

The *North China Herald* published a hand-wringing editorial, headed the "Sikhs and Sedition", about the case. And they were right to wring their hands. The Sikhs had always supported the British. They had put down the Indian mutiny; they had formed the backbone of the British army in the Opium Wars; and, they served as the muscle of British power in the treaty ports. Without the Sikhs, Britain would not have been where it was in China.

The editorial acknowledged that "in the history of India, we find much to feed our pride, great deeds of endurance and feats of courage and in nearly all we find the Sikhs fighting side by side with our soldiers, sharing in our victories, bearing with us the burden of our defeats... In the Indian Mutiny the

Sikhs stood by us to a man, and it was largely due to their aid we soon turned the dreadful tide which threatened to engulf us." The editorial firmly put the blame for the disturbance on the lower levels of the Sikh community and expressed the "hope that the saner and more educated Sikhs will have done something to calm their brethren and show them the foolishness of their ways."

After Singh completed his sentence, having failed to find sureties, he was brought to court for deportation. Normally, a judge would hear such an application, but both Turner and Grain were absent from Shanghai and Singh came before King as Acting Assistant Judge. King ordered Singh be deported.

The Chinese fight back

Chinese were not subject to British jurisdiction, so normally protests by Chinese would not find their way in front of the British courts. However in 1923, in a very high profile case, Chinese in Shanghai decided to use the British justice system to fight back against a gross injustice.

That year, a Ningpo native, Loh Tse Wah, 43, had found himself in serious trouble with the Shanghai Municipal Police. He had joined Hongkew Police Station on February 2, 1923 as the "boy" of Inspector Prosser. He resigned three days later on February 5, 1923, very soon after $400 had been stolen from a new recruit to the force, John Gavan. Detective Superintendent J.F. Gabbutt was determined to get the money back; it was too much loss of face for money to be stolen from a police station. He was certain he had his man; the only problem was how to get him to confess.

Loh was subjected to "intensive questioning" by Gabbutt, Sergeant Alfred Balchin, a Japanese detective Sergeant Okajima and two Chinese detective constables Woo Zer-yung and Yang Tse-shang. Plain and simple, he was tortured. He confessed at least twice but the confessions were not considered satisfactory because he could not produce the money. Okajima had been brought in at midnight after two other interrogation sessions to see if he could extract the location of the money from Loh. Loh was finally brought before the Mixed Court, which acquitted him despite his confessions.

Loh's injuries were horrific. He had been hung by his thumbs, garroted, hung from a ladder with his hands behind his back, had lit opium pipes put up his nostrils and been stripped and beaten on his genitals. Loh said Gabbutt had personally beaten him with a leather belt and had told him in Chinese that he would hang him from a ladder until he died. Following his acquittal by the Mixed Court, his former employer, Mr Chang took him to a doctor, Dr Stafford Cox, for treatment. Chang was a leading member of the Chinese community, fluent in English and a director of the Commercial Press. Dr Cox said Loh was extremely exhausted when he came to him. He had a black eye, wounds on his ears, hands and elbows. His right side had significant swelling from the kidneys to the hip caused by deep injuries. He had blood in his urine. His feet were badly injured and the right foot looked like gangrene was starting. Dr Cox immediately sent Loh to hospital for treatment.

The injuries to Loh caused outrage in the Chinese community. Circulars were issued denouncing the torture of Loh and demanding an end to extraterritoriality. The Ningbo Guild went one step further. They determined to use the extraterritorial system against the foreigners. The Guild decided to bring a private criminal prosecution against Gabbutt and Balchin in the British Supreme Court. Okajima was also prosecuted in the Japanese Consular Court and Woo and Yang in the Mixed Court.

The Ningpo Guild instructed a senior British barrister R.N. MacLeod to bring committal proceedings in the Police Court. The hearings were held before Peter Grain sitting as magistrate. MacLeod appeared with a Chinese barrister,

Mr MacLeod prosecuting on behalf of the Chinese

Reader Harris

Y.S. Ziar, who had studied in England. MacLeod asked for leave for Ziar to appear because there was considerable Chinese evidence. This was granted. R.F.C. Master represented Gabbutt and Balchin. After the evidence was heard, Master suggested that there were political motives for the prosecution and argued that there was no direct evidence against either Gabbutt or Balchin. Grain disagreed saying: "It would be proper for me not to make any comment now, and I shall say I consider this is a case which should go before a jury."

The jury trial started two weeks later before Skinner Turner. The prosecution was taken over by the Crown Advocate, Harrie Wilkinson. Reader Harris defended. The jury was an all-white panel of Britons. The court was packed the entire time, mainly with Chinese who had come to see if the British courts would deliver justice. Turner found the entire case extremely distasteful. When Harris tried to suggest that there was some political motive for the prosecution because the Guild had paid for the committal proceedings, Turner made it clear he saw nothing improper with this and pointed out that for the trial, the case was now in the hands of the Crown Advocate, Harrie Wilkinson.

Major Hilton-Johnson seeks to justify "intensive questioning"

It appears, however, that Wilkinson did not prosecute the case with any "perceptible zeal." On a visit to the Hongkew Police Station, he was recorded as telling the police: "you had better keep the ladder out of the way." Perhaps because of Wilkinson's lack of zeal, Turner on many occasions took over the questioning of witnesses himself. He wanted to know if they approved of "intensive questioning" and why Okajima had been brought in at midnight. When the Deputy Commissioner of Police, Major Hilton-Johnson, tried to justify "intensive questioning" as being an acceptable investigation method, Turner almost exploded saying in open court, "Well, I don't think you will find many people will agree with you."

Gabbutt and Balchin both gave evidence in their defence denying being involved in any assault on Loh. Turner summed up as fairly as he could. He made it clear he considered the Ningbo Guild had been acting entirely properly in assisting Loh. The one weakness in the case against Gabbutt was that Loh had not picked him out in an identity parade.

The jury retired for 50 minutes and returned with a verdict of not guilty on all charges.

They did, however, add an important rider:

"We are convinced that Loh received his injuries while in the hands of the Police."

The two or three hundred Chinese watching the proceedings retired quietly but certainly not happy. Gabbutt and Balchin did not get off scot-free; they were both dismissed from the SMP.

Following the acquittal in the British court, the charges against Okajima in the Japanese Consular Court and against Woo and Yang in the Mixed Court were withdrawn. In withdrawing the cases in the Mixed Court, Mr MacLeod on behalf of Loh said that he had been "instructed to withdraw the charge on the ground that the evidence must be the same as that in the British Court. The most serious charges were against Det-Insp. Gabbutt who had been acquitted." He did not wish to see subordinates convicted when Gabbutt had been acquitted. William Fleming who was appearing for Woo and Yang consented to this. The British assessor, Mr Mead, with perhaps deference to Chinese sentiments, said that the Mixed Court "knew nothing about the British Court or any other court, and was not bound by decisions of such courts. If counsel did not wish to put in evidence and wished to withdraw the charge, the case would therefore have to be dismissed."

All police in Shanghai knew that the result of the case had deeply upset the Chinese. Detective Sergeant Maurice Tinkler, a good friend of both Gabbutt and Balchin, wrote that as a result of the case, "the feeling amongst the Chinese was at fever heat."

More trouble in Canton

The situation in Shanghai was nevertheless better than that in Canton. The British and other foreign powers still controlled Shanghai and the area around it. This was not the case in Canton. The Nationalist Government there had grown militarily very strong. They did not have the power to throw foreigners out. They did, however, have the power to make life for them very difficult.

The British and French concessions in Canton were located on Shameen Island, a Manhattan shaped island separated from the Chinese city of Canton by a narrow river about 10 metres wide. Aerial photos of the time show it as an oasis of green with grand European style buildings protuding through the tree cover surrounded by the large grey city of Canton.

Numerous anti-foreign protests were held in Canton in the 1920s. In 1923 the British and French authorities had tried to limit Chinese access to Shameen Island leading to an antiforeign strike.

That year the Bank of East Asia (BEA), a bank incorporated in Hong Kong, bought some land on Shameen Island in the British Concession. BEA was one of the first banks established in Hong Kong by ethnic Chinese soon after the end of the Qing Dynasty.

BEA applied to register the transfer of land at the British Consulate in Canton. The registration was refused on the basis that the Land Regulations for Shameen forbade the sale of land on the island to Chinese. BEA brought an action in the Supreme Court seeking an order that Sir John Jamieson, the Consul-General, and the Mr Frank Wallis, the Vice-Consul, register the transfer.

The case brought before the court vexed question of the status of Hong Kong Chinese. Normally, the British considered them to be British, and the Chinese considered them to be Chinese. In this case, the roles were reversed, the British (or at least the Consul-General in Canton) wanted to treat them as Chinese. The Hong Kong Chinese wanted to be treated as British. Such dual nationals had been a problem since the British first entered China. Some Hong Kong Chinese would claim to be Chinese when it suited them, for example to live in cities not opened to foreigners and buy land; and, to be British when it suited them, mainly to avoid the jurisdiction of the Chinese courts.

The BEA case was heard by Skinner Turner in late October 1924 in Shanghai rather than in Canton. That may have been because only two months before Canton have been blockaded by Chinese protesters for five weeks and the presence of HMS *Tarantula* had been necessary to "dissuade Sun Yat-Sen from bombarding Shameen, which is protected at all times by American, French, Portuguese, and Japanese gunboats." Both sides instructed high-powered lawyers. The Bank brought up Eldon Potter KC from Hong Kong. Harrie Wilkinson, the Crown Advocate, and his assistant, Victor Priestwood, represented Jamieson and Wallis.

In evidence, Consul-General Jamieson said that even though BEA was incorporated in Hong Kong, the owners were Hong Kong Chinese. The Chinese government and, particularly the Nationalist government in Canton did not recognize the British nationality of Hong Kong Chinese and he was obliged to refuse registration. He described the very difficult situation that the British faced at the time in Canton. He had had to deal with a case in 1921 where a Hong Kong Chinese was due to be executed. Jamieson had contacted the Chinese authorities to demand the man's release on the basis he was a British national. This was refused. After considerable correspondence, the man had been dropped at the bridge near the British Concession. Jamieson was told by the Nationalists that he had better get him far away from Canton as soon as possible.

Jamieson said the partial closing of the Shameen in 1923 had been necessary due to the "overwhelming numbers" of Chinese who had been coming on to island. Jamieson said that the presence of Chinese on Shameen could lead to great difficulties:

"No purely Chinese institution, no association of
Chinese, can at the present day dissociate itself from
politics and in the course of the various political

disturbances that
arise, one can never be
sure which particular
party may want to
persecute another
particular party, and
at no time can one be
certain what steps a
man's enemies may
take to arrest him or
assassinate him."

He came to the real
objection in the case. He
wanted to keep things
quiet on Shameen:

MR. E. P. ELDON POTTER, K.C., ELOQUENTLY DEMONSTRATES THAT A
HONGKONG COMPANY CANNOT CONCEIVABLY BE "A NATIVE OF CHINA."

*Eldon Potter KC from Hong Kong argues for
BEA that it is British*

"Were Chinese or British subjects of Chinese descent, to
reside on the island, there would be danger of attempts
being made against them on political grounds, and
thus the government would be hampered and the
inhabitants involved in trouble."

He said the nature of BEA's business was different to other
British banks such as the Hongkong & Shanghai Bank or the
Chartered Bank. BEA dealt solely with Chinese, implying that
BEA did not need to be on the island. Then, in a bombshell
that would be widely reported in the newspapers, Jamieson
said: "If I am correctly informed they are associated with the
opium trade."

Turner, the following day, said that he "regretted the
statement had been reported in the newspapers. There was
no suggestion in the pleadings or elsewhere that the Bank was
not conducted in all respects as a perfectly proper banking
business."

Potter, on behalf of BEA, made a simple argument. The bank was incorporated in Hong Kong and was a British subject. It should be entitled to have the transfer of title registered. Wilkinson, on the other hand, argued BEA was "an artificial person of double nationality," and it should not be the responsibility of the British authorities to protect "the bank from Chinese authorities across the creek."

Turner, in a long judgment, found in favour of the bank. He ruled that a corporation's nationality is derived from where it is incorporated and not from the nationality of the shareholders. The bank was therefore British and was entitled to register the land. As to the policy that the British Government was trying to enforce, Turner said:

> "I am only concerned with the law. If the law has not provided for that policy, it is the fault of the legislature. I can only administer the law as I understand it, irrespective of the views of the Executive as to what the law ought to be."

Jamieson and Wallis filed an appeal but this was later withdrawn. They had decided to deal with the case another way. Rather than fighting in the courts, they amended the Shameen Land Regulations to provide that "British Companies" did not include companies controlled by persons of Chinese race. They also told BEA they would refuse to renew their lease. BEA never built its new premises, but did keep the land.

The May 30 Movement

Turner handed down his decision in the Shameen case at the end of December 1924. This was probably the high water mark for foreign judicial power in China. Foreign courts could deal with issues involving foreign and Chinese nationals with limited concern for Chinese interests. But within one month

Kitaro Suga   *Finley Johnson*   *Henry Gollan*

this was to change.

May 30, 1925 marked what Professor Robert Bickers has called "Britain's single biggest disaster in China." On this day, Shanghai Municipal Police officers at Louza Police Station on Nanking Road shot and killed Chinese protesters outside the station. The day had been marked by protests around Shanghai against the killing of a Chinese worker at a Japanese mill. Inspector Everson in charge of the station had arrested 15 protestors. A large crowd of protesters gathered outside the station seeking their release. Everson, fearing the station would be overrun, ordered Sikh and Chinese police to fire into the crowd. After the shooting subsided, 12 Chinese lay dead in Nanking Road for all of China and the rest of the world to see. Numerous others were injured.

The shootings sparked furious protests. They were a propaganda godsend to the Chinese authorities. The Ministry of Foreign Affairs published photos of the dead and injured, as well as photos of clothing they were wearing at the time. Two days later, on June 2, some of the survivors were tried in the Mixed Court and given very light sentences. The fact that protesters were prosecuted further enraged Chinese sentiment. Attacks on foreigners continued for days after the hearings.

In part, to try to quell the Chinese rage, the foreign

powers set up an International Commission to investigate the killings. The Chinese were invited to participate but refused to. The foreign Commissioners were: from Britain, Sir Henry Gollan, the new Chief Justice of Hong Kong; from the United States, Judge Finley Johnson, Chief Justice of the Philippines; and, from Japan Judge Kitaro Suga, Chief Justice of the Hiroshima Court of Appeal. The Commission sat in October 1925, with Judge Johnson presiding, at the Shanghai Town Hall. It heard evidence from the police officers involved and other foreigners. Chinese had been encouraged to boycott the Commission and no Chinese gave evidence.

The three commissioners could not agree on a joint report so all three issued their own findings in January 1926. They essentially cleared the Municipal Police of misconduct. Johnson was the most critical in his report. He set out his views of what caused the disturbances. These included the Municipal Council control of the Mixed Court and the inherent unfairness of extraterritoriality. Perhaps most importantly, he listed as a cause:

> "The failure on the part of the foreigners in China to realize that the Chinese people have made greater advancement during the past 10 years in civics, in the fundamental principles of government and in the better understanding of individual rights under the law than they have made in any 100 years during their entire history."

China was to keep on advancing and the killings put much more pressure on the Municipal Council to return the Mixed Court to Chinese control; something that Chinese lawyers had already been pushing for a number of years. By the end of 1926, the Mixed Court was abolished, to be replaced by a Provisional Court.

Extraterritoriality Commission

For Chinese, there was further hope for change. The Extraterritoriality Commission, promised since the end of World War I, had finally been formed in late 1925. It was made up of representatives from each of the treaty powers and a Chinese representative. Turner, as Judge of the British Supreme Court for China, was appointed the British representative. The United States Representative was Silas H. Strawn of Chicago, an "eminent attorney" and personal friend of President Coolidge and the Secretary of State, Frank B Kellog. Strawn was elected Chairman of the Commission and Dr Wang Ch'ung-hui, the Chinese Minister of Justice and Chinese Commissioner, Honorary President. This position of Honorary President had no powers but was created to save face. The Chinese had previously insisted that a Chinese be Chairman.

The members of the commission first reviewed the development of the new Chinese legal system. Then, from May 1926, a travelling committee went around China for more than 4,200 miles (6,700 kilometres) to study the implementation of new codes and to inspect the new courts and Chinese prisons. As can be expected, on many occasions, the courts and prisons had received special treatment to improve facilities before the arrival of the Commission. The report was finalized in September 1926 and, not surprisingly, did not recommend an end to extraterritoriality. The report effectively put off any promise of an end to extraterritoriality until China had developed a fully functioning Western legal system. The key recommendations were that China must develop an independent judiciary and that there should be further reforms of the judicial, police and prison systems. Numerous laws were required to be completed or put into force, including civil and commercial codes; a revised Criminal Code; Banking and Bankruptcy laws; a patent law; and a land expropriation law. In addition, the report required that a uniform system for enacting and publishing laws should be enacted and that the modern system of courts, prisons and detention houses should replace all Magistrate's courts and old style prisons and detention houses.

If, and only if, these reforms were carried out, then the extraterritorial powers said they may consider the abolition of extraterritoriality on a progressive basis.

"May consider" on a "progressive basis." This was a procrastinator's charter and fell far short of what the Chinese people and government expected. Dr Wang, the Chinese representative of the Commission, added a disclaimer to his signature that "by signing this report my approval of all the statements is not implied."

Turner retired soon after the Extraterritoriality Commission delivered its report. Harrie Wilkinson also retired as Crown advocate in late 1925.

On Turner's retirement, Peter Grain was promoted to Judge of the Supreme Court. Gilbert King was appointed Assistant Judge. King, who was originally a solictor had joined the court in 1903 as a clerk and had been promoted to Registrar in 1908. He qualified as a barrister during the war. Allan Mossop, who was from South Africa and had come to Shanghai in 1908 was appointed to replace Wilkinsnon as Crown Advocate.

These changes were uneventful. In the United States Court a scandal of immense proportion which led to the demise of the US District Attorney was unfolding.

CHAPTER 24

The Dirty DA

MILTON PURDY ON HIS arrival as the US Judge in Shanghai at the hearing to welcome him commented on "how fortunate had been the U.S. Government in getting men of such excellent quality and ability as the officials of this court."

At the very end of 1926, he learnt how wrong he had been. The US Court for China saw the trial of two of its officials for engaging in serious criminal misconduct.

First, Purdy had the sad duty to pass sentence on the former Clerk of the US Court, William Chapman, who had pleaded guilty to embezzling G$15,000 from the court. He had originally fled to Seattle, but was caught on arrival in the US and was brought back to Shanghai for trial. Purdy sentenced Chapman to three years and five months imprisonment. Having arrived in Shanghai to be sentenced, Chapman was then put back on the same boat, the President Roosevelt, heading back to Seattle. Long-term US prisoners were now imprisoned at the federal penitentiary on McNeil Island in Puget Sound just near Seattle.

At that very same time that Chapman arrived in Shanghai to be sentenced, a scandal of far greater proportions, in fact the largest scandal to occur in the 37-year history of the US Court for China, was unfolding. Leonard Husar, the United States District Attorney, was arrested for corruption. The allegation was that he had solicited and taken a G$25,000 bribe to hand over to Tracy Woodward, an opium smuggler, a file detailing Woodward's dealings in opium. Woodward's file had been

HON. JUDGE MILTON PURDY.

DR. GEORGE SELLETT, U.S. DISTRICT ATTORNEY.

LEONARD G. HUSAR, THE ACCUSED.

MRS. PORTER, COURT STENOGRAPHER

U. S. v. HUSAR: THE CHIEF PERSONALITIES

sent to Shanghai from the US Consular Court in Persia. A few month's earlier, Husar's wife, Mary Jo Grubb Husar, had filed for divorce in California. As part of her divorce petition she alleged that Husar had taken the bribe.

As soon as the allegations were made, Husar resigned as District Attorney. He also decided to hit back, filing his own divorce proceedings in Shanghai, accusing Mary Jo of drunkeness and infidelity. He later filed a cross-complaint in the US proceedings where he "named 10 men with whom she openly consorted" and called her a "vulgar-minded woman without any sense of decency, pride or shame." He added she habitually drank to excess and danced nude at a party. All terribly scandalous, but the best was yet to come.

The new, very young, District Attorney, Thomas Sellett, prosecuted Husar. Sellett, who held a PhD, had been appointed to replace Husar. Sellett had been born in November 1898 making him 28 at the time of his appointment. He had graduated from the University of Michigan in 1923 and come to Shanghai where he commenced practice as an attorney. He also taught at the Comparative Law School of China for a year before becoming Dean of the school.

The allegations against Husar were that he had arranged for another American lawyer, Neil Heath, to approach Woodward who was at this time running a successful business. Heath blackmailed Woodward by telling him that Husar intended to prosecute him for his dealings in opium unless Woodward paid a bribe of G$75,000 to get the file back. This was bargained down to $25,000. Woodward then said that he had arranged to meet Husar and Heath at the Shanghai American Club on Foochow Road (Fuzhou Road) where Husar handed over the file. He had arranged to pay $25,000 Mexican, but Heath told him it was Gold Dollars, take it or leave it. Woodward paid and then took the file home and with the assistance of his chauffer burnt it.

Sellett decided that he would only be able to get a

conviction against Husar and Heath if he offered Woodward immunity from prosecution.

Heath's trial started first before Purdy with Sellett prosecuting. Heath was represented by a phalanx of Shanghai's leading American lawyers, including William Fleming, Cornell Franklin, P. Faison and Norwood Allman. Heath also represented himself. Surprisingly, given the allegations that were to be made in both trials, Husar also appeared to defend Heath. Heath was charged with two counts of receiving and taking government property and one count of larceny of US property.

Woodward was the main witness and gave evidence of how Heath had contacted him to shake him down and how over a course of four meetings he had negotiated a price of G$25,000 plus a 2,000 taels commission for Heath. He said that he had not met Husar when he came to club to hand over the file, but had instead stood with his face to the window so he did not see him. However, as he left the club he had seen Husar standing outside of the bathroom.

A letter Heath had sent to Woodward when the case was being investigated was the most damning evidence. The letter read:

> "The situation is serious for both you and I, it is dangerous… The Secret Service in Washington obtained our names some way … they are looking for me now, I feel that they will get me … I am using a false name … You know that the U.S. Government will not let drop a case as this … Husar thinks that I had relations with his wife, this is not true, although he alleges it … I would spend a year in prison to see him get the limit … he will be begging me on bended knees to save him. I am going to write to Dr Sellett … I'm busted, this worry is driving me crazy. I am etc., Neil McKay Heath."

Detective Inspector Tinkler of the SMP who had been sent by his superiors to inspect the file was called to give evidence what he had seen on the file. He said the SMP had decided to take no action against Woodward because they believed the US authorities would prosecute him. He said that about eight charges had been brought against Woodward in Persia and he had pleaded guilty to about half of them. Tinkler added, mysteriously, that, "certain foreigners were mentioned, including Father Costello, Mr Kentwell and Lissie Bell."

Detective Inspector Maurice Tinkler tells the court L. K. Kentwell was mentioned in the opium files

Even in such an important case as this, the mention of Kentwell's name was too good an opportunity even for the erudite and serious Dr Sellett to resist. He asked Tinkler, who of course knew Kentwell well having arrested and given evidence against him two years before in the British Supreme Court:

"Do you know Mr Kentwell's nationality?"

"No", deadpanned Tinkler to laughter in the court.

One suspects that even Purdy was forced to have a chuckle at this entirely irrelevant question and answer. After the prosecution closed its case Franklin and Fleming argued that Purdy should dismiss the charges on the basis that Woodward was a co-conspirator and that the law required that his evidence be corroborated by other evidence. Purdy agreed that much of the evidence was not corroborated. But Purdy considered the Heath's letter to Woodward to be totally damning. He said: "I cannot imagine a letter being written more clearly linking the author with a crime. You would have a hard time convincing any jury in Christendom that this letter did not refer to this case." He dismissed the application.

Heath chose not to give evidence. His only defence was to attack Woodward's credibility by calling a number of witnesses to testify as to his bad character.

At the close of the case, Franklin applied for a dismissal of the charges on the basis that there was no evidence the file was US Government property and that Woodward's evidence was not corroborated. Purdy held that two of the counts had not been properly proved and acquitted Heath. However, he found Heath guilty on one count, larceny of government property. He then, over the objections of Heath's lawyers, put off sentencing of Heath until after Husar's trial.

Husar's trial commenced on April 20, 1927. He was also represented by Fleming, Franklin, Allman and Faison. He pleaded not guilty. Much of the same evidence that was called in the Heath trial was given again. There was also evidence from the Consul-General and other consular and court officials and staff as to how the Woodward file had gone missing. It was also formally admitted that Husar had been District Attorney at the time.

Woodward gave additional evidence of how he had met with Husar a few times after the bribe had been paid and that Husar had told him that he believed Heath had had an affair with his wife. Woodward said Husar told him of Heath that, "after giving him $17,000 in the book deal the sneak and dog had the impudence to eat at my table and conduct himself in a shameful way with my wife." Woodward also said Husar told him Heath was blackmailing him over the payment of the bribe.

The most damning evidence against Husar, however, was that on the day after the alleged bribe had been paid, December 16, 1925, Husar had opened a safety deposit box at the Hong Kong & Shanghai Bank. He had visited the box eight times until it was closed a little over a year later in mid-January 1927. There was also evidence that Husar had made other transactions at other banks.

Husar had two defences. The first was an alibi. He called witnesses and gave evidence himself that he could not have been at the American Club at the time in question. The first witness Cornell Franklin tried to call on behalf of Husar was Heath. Heath had been subpoenaed. Heath had not yet been sentenced so the case against him was still pending. He had a right not to answer questions that might incriminate himself. He answered a few questions before Purdy warned him of his right against self-incrimination. He was then withdrawn as a witness.

Husar's second defence was absolutely startling.

He claimed he had made the money in his safe deposit box from dealing in guns!

He said that in 1924 he had befriended Colonel Hsu, the intelligence chief of a Chang Tsung-Chang who was then in charge of the defence of Shanghai. He said he had received $6,000 a year paid in cash. This had been increased to $750 per month (or $9,000 per year). From December 1925 he had acted as a go-between in an arms deal between an Italian named Parlani and Colonel Hsu. A total of 6,000 rifles with bayonets and ammunition had been sold and Parlani had offered him a 5% commission on the deal. He had introduced Parlani and Chang and then told them he would look to Chang for the commission because he was not familiar with Parlani. The sale price had been agreed at 500,0000 taels giving Husar a $37,000 commission.

Colonel Chang paid the commission, he said, on December 15, 1925. Husar had asked for cash payment because he did not want to be identified with the deal "as anything that has arms connected with it in China carries a stigma." He, of course, knew this because two years before this purported deal he had prosecuted Kearny and his "gigantic organization" for gun running. Despite this he said, "at the same time, however, I did not feel I was doing any wrong. General Chang was the accredited militarist of this area at the time. I was simply offered a commission by his agent and took it." Husar then said he took the bulk of the money and put it in the safety deposit box at the Hong Kong & Shanghai Bank.

The next day, Sellett cross-examined Husar. He first asked about Husar's domestic difficulties and Heath's relationship with his wife. Husar said that he had beaten Heath once Heath had denied any relationship with his wife, but Husar said he was convinced they had committed adultery. He also admitted that having prosecuted Captain Kearny for arms smuggling he had, only two years later, turned around and made money the same way. He had interviewed Woodward when he had come to Shanghai and obtained a lot of useful evidence from him about opium smuggling. He had decided, however, not to prosecute him. Husar said that Parlani was in Europe and he could not get Colonel Hsu to give evidence due to the political situation in Shanghai. This was, in relation to Hsu at least, probably true. Shanghai was at the time surrounded by Nationalist troops. Hsu had most likely long since vanished.

Sellett then changed tack completely to attack Husar's credibility. He suggested that the amounts of $500 and $750 that Husar had been paying into his bank account were, in fact, protection money he had extorted from two American prostitutes, Virginia Nelson and Blanche Bennett. Husar responded sarcastically: "That's the best insinuation I have heard you make today." Sellett pushed Husar to answer as to whether he had met Blanche Bennett.

Husar's response was telling in terms of showing the divisions in the American community in China and, given Husar's own admissions in the trial, how the old District Attorney and new one were like chalk and cheese. He said:

"The only business I ever had with these unfortunate women was when some of your people – missionaries – came to me with an affidavit that they had gone into some of the houses and spent money and asked me to help get them out of town."

Even from the written page, you can almost hear Husar spitting the word "missionaries" out.

This closed the case. Both prosecution and defence agreed to make limited arguments in closing. Sellett said the case was clear and Husar's own admissions about the money in the safety deposit box made his defence impossible. Cornell Franklin, for Husar, asked simply, who would you believe, "a useful citizen, a man honoured with a responsible position of high trust and a man with an unblemished record" or a convicted opium smuggler of low character.

Purdy gave a very short judgment saying that after hearing all the evidence he believed the convicted opium smuggler, Woodward, and that Husar was guilty.

The next day, saying "it pained and grieved him" to be in the position of sentencing a government official he had been associated with since he occupied the bench, he sentenced Husar to two years in McNeil Island in Washington State. He also sentenced Heath to 18 months in McNeil Island.

Husar appealed to the Ninth Circuit in San Francisco and the case was heard a year later in June 1928. Husar had three grounds of appeal. The first was that the United States Court for China did not have jurisdiction over him. The second that Purdy had improperly not allowed Heath to give testimony and the third that the letter from Heath to Woodward sent in 1926 should not have been admitted in evidence.

The first ground, lack of jurisdiction, was the only one of real interest and was not raised by Husar until the oral argument before the appeal court. The charge against Husar had not stated that he was a United States citizen. The US Court for China only had jurisdiction over United States citizens. This needed to be stated in the charge.

Husar "freely admitted" that he was a US citizen but argued that the charge was technically defective. The Ninth Circuit dealt with this neatly by relying on the Supreme Court decision in the *Ross* case that gave the court jurisdiction over any seaman on a United States vessel. Husar had been prosecuted as the United States District Attorney for China, had been appointed as such by the US President and had taken an oath of office. This was more than enough to give the US Court jurisdiction. The other points were rejected on the basis that Purdy had been right to caution Heath and that Husar had only objected to the evidence later. The Ninth Circuit therefore upheld the conviction. Husar was paroled in December 1929 after serving a year and a half in McNeil Island.

After Husar's appeal had failed, Heath also filed an application for habeas corpus against the warden of McNeil Island on the ground that the charge had not stated that he was a United States citizen and the court therefore did not have jurisdiction. This was successful and Heath was released. The government appealed. The Ninth Circuit allowed the appeal on the grounds that in a habeas corpus applications are treated differently to appeals. On appeals the record must show there is jurisdiction. In habeas corpus applications it must appear affirmatively on the record that the court did not have jurisdiction. Heath's conviction was restored and he was ordered to be returned to prison.

The prosecution and convictions of Chapman, Husar and Heath were a very bad start to 1927 for the United States Court for China. For China, on the other hand, 1927 started with the hope for the first united government of China in more than a decade.

PART THREE

Revolution, Resistance and
Resurrection
(1927 to 1943)

CHAPTER 25

The Rise of China

1927 WAS A WATERSHED year for China. Sun Yat-sen had died in 1925 and Chiang Kai-shek, the commander of the Whampoa Military Academy, had taken over as the leader of the Kuomingtang (Nationalist Party) in Canton. The Whampoa Military Academy had been set up by Chiang in 1924 to train, with Soviet assistance, an officer corps for the Nationalists. It had been a great success. In July 1926, Chiang launched a Northern Expedition from the Nationalists' base in Canton to take over the country. The warlord armies in the south of China were no match for the Nationalist Party's modern and well-trained army. By September 1926, the Nationalists' troops had captured Hankow on the Yangtze River and were poised to drive north onto Peking. In Hankow, the Nationalists took over the Hankow foreign concession. Other smaller concessions throughout the country were also occupied. The Nationalists captured Nanking in March 1927 and attacked the concessions there, causing outrage amongst the treaty powers.

Soon after, the Kuomingtang forces reached Shanghai where at one stage, given what had happened in Hankow and Nanking, there were serious concerns they would try to take over the foreign concessions. The British Cabinet in London met on numerous occasions to discuss the crisis. Unlike in the past, there was no clear consensus on what could be done to stop a Chinese advance. Gunboats were still an option. Two proposals were made to seek to force the Nationalists to agree

Sapajou does a round of the boundaries

to leave foreign concessions alone. First, was a blockade of the Bogue at Humen sealing off the Pearl River and Canton's access to the sea. The second was to use the British naval power on the Yangtze to prevent the Nationalist armies crossing the river in their advance northwards.

One thing that was agreed was that Shanghai had to be defended at all costs. The treaty powers including Britain, America, Japan and France all sent substantial numbers of troops to defend the concessions. Britain alone sent 20,000, mainly Sikh, troops to Shanghai. The political branch of the Shanghai Municipal Police was particularly concerned that the Nationalist Party's North Expedition forces contained "subversive foreign agents" who would seek to propagate communism and nationalism amongst the Indian population in Shanghai. This was not just paranoia. Numerous Sikhs were arrested and tried in the British Police court for sedition for trying to convince Sikh soldiers not to fight.

Even more alarmingly, political assassination came to British Shanghai. In early April 1927 in broad daylight, Harbant Singh, walked up to the most senior Indian policeman in Shanghai, Senior Inspector Sirdar Sahib Budda Singh, at the gates of the Central Police Station on Foochow Road (Fuzhou Road) and shot him twice in the back and once in the chest, killing him almost instantly. Budda Singh lying on the ground was able to call out to another Sikh policeman, Bhan Singh, "Call for help, I am dying." Bhan Singh grabbed Harbant Singh from behind and sub-inspector Phillips, who had rushed from the police station, gun in hand, disarmed

Harbant Singh. The SMP raided the Sikh Gurdwara soon after this and arrested 10 other Sikhs for being part of the conspiracy to kill Budda Singh.

Sirdar Sahib Budda Singh: Assassinated

Harbant Singh was put on trial for murder before Peter Grain and a jury of 12. Singh made his pro bono defence counsel's job very hard. He refused to cooperate with him and did not give him any instructions. When asked to plea, Singh responded coolly: "I did murder Sirdar Sahib Budda Singh, so I must plead guilty." His lawyer asked, in accordance with the custom that a defendant could not plead guilty to murder, that a plea of "Not Guilty" be entered. Grain agreed to this. After the prosecution evidence was called, Harbant Singh made a statement from the dock admitting the crime and saying that he killed Budda Singh because "I wish he die and no make more trouble." After closing submissions and being instructed by Grain, the jury took only five minutes to find him guilty. Before sentencing Singh, Grain asked if he had anything to say. Singh replied: "I kill him because he was a bad man." Grain, without putting on the traditional black cap, then sentenced Singh to death. Grain, who was "visibly affected," then told the court:

"Mr Crown Advocate, this case being concluded, I desire to pay a tribute to memory of the murdered man. Sirdar Sahib Budda Singh was a gentleman. He was brave, loyal, generous, courteous and kind hearted. He served his sovereign bravely and loyally. He carried out his duties in Shanghai conscientiously, courteously and with kind-heartedness. I knew him personally and it was with great sorrow that I heard of his death."

Harbant Singh became the martyr he obviously wanted to be. He was executed by hanging at Ward Road Gaol on June 18, 1927.

The Municipal Council in its Annual Report for 1927 made specific mention of Singh's murder stating that he "was a most loyal officer and his death was directly attributable to his unceasing efforts against disaffected Indians in Shanghai."

The Shanghai Municipal Police believed that the assassination was part of the Nationalist-inspired move to instigate a strike amongst Sikh policemen supported by Russian agents. While this may have been true, Chiang Kai-shek had by this time decided to rid the Nationalist Party of leftists and to break with the Russians. Rather than agitating inside the concessions or seeking to occupy them, instead, in the same month that Budda Singh was killed, April 1927, Chiang launched a purge of the Nationalist Party to remove Communist Party members. This was tacitly supported by the foreign powers. In Shanghai, with the consent of Stirling Fessenden, now the Chairman of the Municipal Council, armed Chinese troops moved through the International Settlement to be in a position to attack communists who were on strike in Shanghai. A bloody purge followed in which many communists were killed. Eight months later, in December 1927 the Nationalists severed relations with Soviet Russia and sent away its Soviet advisers.

By 1928, the Nationalist Party had relatively firm control over the country from Canton up to Peking and was formally recognized as the government of China. A system of District and High Courts headed by a Supreme Court was introduced to handle legal cases. Additionally, military and naval courts, an administrative court, magistrate's courts and police tribunals were all established. In areas where there were foreigners without treaty rights, special courts were introduced with foreign advisers, interpreters and special prisons. The first place such courts were introduced was in

Harbin in Manchuria where a large number of Russians, who had lost extraterritorial rights in 1922, lived.

A provisional farewell to the Mixed Court
In Shanghai, as well, new Chinese courts were established. As a result of the Shanghai riot in 1925, the treaty powers agreed with the local government of Chekiang to abolish the Mixed Court in the International Settlement at the end of 1926. It was replaced with effect from January 1, 1927 by a Provisional Court with a Chinese Judge sitting alone for most cases. A deputy foreign consul was allowed to sit with the judge to watch proceedings where the case involved municipal regulations or the accused was an employee of a foreigner enjoying extraterritorial rights.

Sapajou on the rendition of the Mixed Court

The judges of the Provisional Court were more than willing to exercise their newly returned sovereignty and power. One judge in particularly, Judge Ziar, refused to follow the old way of doing things. Y.S. Ziar had been a practicing lawyer in Shanghai for many years, had been educated in London and had qualified as a barrister in England. He had at times appeared in the British Supreme Court, in particular, it will

JUDGE ZIAR
Of the Shanghai Provisional Court

Judge Ziar, British barrister, now a Chinese Judge of the Provisional Court

be recalled, in the private prosecution of Superintendent Gabbutt for torturing Loh Tse Wah. In one case before Ziar, a destitute Russian, Mr Leontieff, was brought before the court on vagrancy charges. The prosecutor, Mr Maitland on behalf of the Municipal Council, sought a fine and expulsion order. Ziar responded, over protests from Maitland, that he did not have the power to make the order. He said to Leontieff:

> "That you are poor does not necessarily mean to say we can deprive you of your liberty as this Court will make no distinction between the rich and the poor. You may go."

In another case, when a British barrister, Mr Covey, appeared in a suit, Ziar told him he could not hear him unless he wore Chinese robes. Covey said he could not because British Bar Association rules prohibited him from "appearing in other courts than our own in the dress a foreign court may have laid down as to be worn by its nationals," nor was he allowed to wear his wig and gown in a foreign court. Covey pointed out that all recognised practitioners of other nationalities did not appear robed in the British courts. Ziar

Sapajou on Judge Ziar's ruling that barristers appear in Chinese robes.
R.N. MacLeod is in the centre. Reader Harris is to his right

responded that he could not do anything about that. After consultation with the clerk of the Provisional Court, Covey returned to say he would need to withdraw from this and all other cases. After negotiations, British barristers were allowed to appear in a normal business attire.

Recognizing a rebel government

The Nationalists' rise to power created a new problem for both the American and British courts. In the US Court, the question was whether the Nationalists had the right to sue as the Government of China and when did they acquire it? In the British Court the question was: should edicts of the revolutionary army be binding?

Since 1924, the United States had not recognized any government of China. In February 1926, a fire had destroyed the Chinese Government Telephone Administration Exchange buildings in Wuchang next to Hankow (both cities are now part of Wuhan). Merchants Fire Assurance Corporation of New York and the Great American Fire Assurance Corporation of New York had insured the building and equipment. The Nationalists captured Wuchang in 1926 and took over the property.

By early 1928, the Nationalists had occupied most of China, but had not yet captured the capital, Peking. They wished to bring an action under an insurance policy against the insurance companies claiming $135,000 Mex. They instructed H.D. Rodger and Nick Char to bring proceedings in the US Court for China. In April 1928, Rodger first asked the US Consulate for a certificate "stating when the United States Government ceased to recognize the Chinese Government either the present so-called Peking Government or the Nationalist Government at Nanking." This was passed on to the State Department. The legation was instructed to reply that since the previous administration had collapsed, the American government had not dealt with any regime as the Government of China but had dealt with "certain authorities on the basis of regional jurisdiction." The US authorities declined to give Rodger a certificate.

Two months later, after the Nationalists had captured Peking, Rodger wrote again asking if the Nationalist government could now sue as the de facto government of China. He got a pass-the-buck reply that while the US government now dealt with the Nationalists as the de facto government, the question of whether they could sue in the US Court was a question for the US Court for China. Rodger, therefore, then filed suit in the US Court. Judge Purdy declined jurisdiction on the basis that the Nationalist Party was not the recognized government.

Rodger with his partner, Nick Char, appealed to the Ninth Circuit in San Francisco, who had an easy decision to make. By the time the appeal was heard in early 1929, the US had recognized the Nationalist Party as the government for China and entered into a Treaty of Commerce, although it had not yet been ratified by the Senate. On this basis, the Ninth Circuit ruled that the US Court for China now had jurisdiction. It did add that Purdy's original decision was correct but the change in recognition now meant the Nationalists had taken over the rights of the Chinese government.

Norwood Allman acted for the Merchant Fire Insurance Company. In his memoirs he wrote that:

"Our client was perfectly willing to pay. There was no question about that. The sole problem was to pay whom."

Not true. Allman was suffering from selective memory.

The case came back to the US Court for China, where both insurance companies first sought to have the case dismissed because the fire had happened before the Nationalists had captured Wuchang. When they had taken Wuchang, the "incoming forces got only the partially burned buildings, and acquired no capital in the insurance policy." Purdy dismissed these arguments without giving detailed reasons.

The cases were then tried in June 1929. The insurance companies made some of the usual arguments about there being no proper evidence of loss and that the claim had not been made in time. Purdy rejected these and gave judgment against the Great American Insurance Company.

The Merchants Fire Assurance Company, Allman's client, however, had an interesting defence which caused Purdy considerable difficulties. This was that the former Chinese Government had reached an agreement on March, 27 1928 to settle the claim. A judgment had been granted by consent in the US Court for China on April, 23 1928 recognizing this agreement. Rodger attacked the agreement as having been made by a government with no legal capacity to sue in the court, for the same reasons that the Nationalist government had not been able to sue at the time. Purdy agreed. He said that the agreement and the judgment had clearly been entered into by collusion between the parties. If the judgment had been an act of the purported Chinese government he would have been able to treat it as having no effect.

He faced a difficulty, however. The judgment was not an act of the Chinese government; it was an act of the United States Court for China. He had to give it effect until it was formally set aside. Purdy said that he was satisfied the Nationalist Government should recover on the policy, but very reluctantly concluded that until the previous judgment was set aside, he would have to give effect to it. He was forced to dismiss the claim, but did so without prejudice to the Plaintiff bringing a new claim once the previous judgment had been set aside.

The devalued tael

The Nationalists capture of Hankow in 1927 produced another insurance case, this time in the British Supreme Court for China. The issue in the case was a very important one that produced a rare occasion where the Full Court - which had been established in 1925 with the two Shanghai judges and the Chief Justice of Hong Kong sitting as a full bench - overturned a decision of the Judge of the Court.

The issue was relatively simple. Wo Ho Tong Co in Hankow bought insurance from the Commercial Assurance Co Ltd in March 1927. The policy provided that any payments under the policy would be paid in Hankow Taels. Hankow Taels did not, in fact, exist as a unit of currency but were used as an accounting unit. When payment was to be made, Hankow Taels were converted into silver dollars at the daily rate of exchange.

THE FULL COURT IN SESSION
Judge Sir Peter Grain, Judge Sir Henry Gollan (presiding) and Judge G. W. King

Soon after the contract was signed, the Nationalists captured Hankow and on April 18, 1927, Mr T.V. Soong the Nationalist Finance Minster issued regulations fixing the exchange rate of Hankow Taels at 71 taels to $100. On June 30 there was a fire at Wo Ho Tong's premises. The damage was assessed and agreed at 4,006.16 taels. The new Nationalist regulations provided that only the notes of three banks at Hankow, the Central Bank, Bank of China and Bank of Communications were allowed to be in circulation. The effect of these regulations was to depreciate the value of the Hankow Tael by 80%. That is, it was only worth 20% of its previous value. The insurance company paid the claims with the notes of one of the approved banks. Wo Ho Tong rejected the payment on the basis that the payment should have been in silver dollars, the currency of China. Wo Ho Tong argued that the Nationalist Government was not the legitimate government of China or Hankow at the time of the fire and payment. The British Supreme Court should not give effect to the regulations, which were those of a rebel government. At the trial, Peter Grain agreed with this argument and ordered that the money should be paid in the legal silver currency of China.

The insurance company appealed to the Full Court, made up of Sir Henry Gollan, the Chief Justice of Hong Kong, presiding, Grain, and Gilbert King. The decision of the Full Court was given in January 1929. Because Gollan had returned to Hong Kong, Grain read out Golan's judgment. This must have been hard for him, because Gollan disagreed with Grain entirely. Gollan considered that the Nationalist Government was at the time in de facto control of Hankow and therefore entitled to issue the regulations. Payment in the notes of the Hankow banks was acceptable.

Grain wrote a powerful dissenting judgment. For him, the question was not whether the Nationalist Party was in de facto control of Hankow, the question was "were they the government of the country with the power to alter the currency of the Nation?" He said that at the time the Government of the Republic of China was still in existence and functioning. The Nationalists had occupied Hankow by force, but their power "did not run beyond the places they were holding by force."

"They were in fact at that moment rebels, as a rebel is an individual who rises against and rebels against constituted authority of the nation. No doubt rebels do often in due course become the constituted authority if successful in defeating the authority in being."

He concluded that the Nationalist Party was at the time not the lawful government of China and had no power to alter the national currency. He added that "as it happened the Nationalist Party have become successful" and become the lawful government. But, it may have been that they had not become successful and been "turned out of Hankow shortly after the regulations in question were promulgated." He then asked what would have happened should the court have then been asked to decide if the bank notes were legal tender.

Chinese Americans

By 1928, the Nationalist Chinese authorities around Shanghai started taking a stricter interpretation of extraterritorial rights, especially in relation to Chinese Americans, whom in many cases they considered to be Chinese. In some cases, Chinese Americans brought problems upon themselves by trying to have the best of both worlds and be Chinese or American when it suited them. In other cases, Chinese authorities asserted jurisdiction over Chinese Americans solely because they had failed to take appropriate steps to renounce their Chinese nationality.

This new reality was brought home to Chinese American lawyer Nick Char who had with H.D. Rodger represented the Chinese government in the Wuchang Insurance cases in the US Court. He was not able to attend court when Purdy gave his judgment because he was sitting in a Chinese jail serving a three months sentence for assault.

Char had been born in Hawaii to Chinese parents. At a baseball game at Pioneer Field in the southeast corner of the French Concession in June 1927, he assaulted a Chinese, Jui Hsoh-hsien. The attack had been quite vicious and two years later, Jui was still confined to his bed. Jui filed a complaint against Char in the Provisional Court. Char originally did not object to this and appeared to defend the charge. Char and his partner, H.D. Rodger, thought, correctly, that the Provisional Court would treat Char lightly. Char also wished to represent Chinese clients before the Provisional Court. Under the new rules applying in there, foreigners were not allowed to represent Chinese. He therefore chose not to assert his American citizenship.

Even though they could clearly see that Char was seeking to take advantage of his dual nationality, the US Consulate in Shanghai took steps to assist him. A consular official told the Provisional Court before the trial that Char was American and that he could easily be prosecuted in the US Court for China because he lived in the International Settlement. However, the judge said that in his application to the Chinese authorities for the right to appear in the Provisional Court, Char had described his origin as "Canton Province." The court considered this sufficient evidence to hold he was Chinese. In October 1928, Char was fined $300.

Jui was not satisfied with the light penalty and appealed the decision to the Chinese Court of Appeal. In early February 1929, Char was arrested in the International Settlement on the orders of the Chinese Court of Appeal and was detained by the Shanghai Municipal Police. The US Consulate suggested to the President of the Court of Appeal that Char be granted bail so that an agreement could be reached on his citizenship status. This was rejected.

Rodger then appeared in the Provisional Court seeking Char's release. Rodger said that Char was an American citizen not subject to the jurisdiction of the court. He produced a US army discharge certificate showing Char had fought in the US Army in World War I. Judge Shen said that the matter was before the Court of Appeals and he could not deal with it. Mr H.E. Stevens, the US Vice-Consul and the Senior Consul's deputy at the Provisional Court, made a formal statement that Char was a United States Citizen and could not be prosecuted in the Chinese courts. The Chinese authorities could arrest him but he must be handed over to the American authorities if a request was made. Mr Bryan, the prosecuting solicitor appearing on behalf of the Police said that the Police would hold Char until they received information from the United States Consul-General that Char was American.

The United States Consul-General, Edwin Cunningham, felt strongly that if action was not taken in this case, the Chinese government would seek to assume jurisdiction over all Chinese Americans. First, the consulate sought to achieve a diplomatic resolution. Cunningham wrote to the Commissioner of Foreign Affairs, Mr Wunsz King, seeking Char's release. Mr Stevens and Mr C.D. Meinhart, American Vice Consuls, went on appointment to see Mr King. King snubbed them. When they arrived they were informed he was not in. The US Consulate then felt that it had "no alternative" but to ask the SMP to release Char on the grounds he was an American. Cunningham reported to the Secretary of State that: "This request the police complied with as is the usual custom in Shanghai when a Consul of an extraterritorial power makes a request." On his release, Char was advised not to leave the International Settlement.

Char's appeal hearing was scheduled the following day, on February 8. Char had already been released and did not appear. The Court of Appeal waited one hour for Char to appear and then handed down a judgment in his absence. The court said that "to a poor man" a fine of $300, "would be a heavy punishment, but as the accused is a rich man this fine is no punishment so he is sentenced to imprisonment." The court then imposed a sentence of three months imprisonment. Thomas Sellett, the US District Attorney, was asked for his opinion on the case. He advised that because Char was a dual national, he could be tried in the Chinese courts or the US Court. Consul-General Cunningham disagreed with this. He held to the view that Char could not be prosecuted in a Chinese court as long as he lived in a treaty port and had not "expatriated" himself; that, is done things inconsistent with his status as a US citizen. Cunningham reported the case to the US Secretary of State, Henry Stimson, asking for guidance as to how to handle cases of this type in the future.

Sellett, despite thinking Char had been properly tried in the Chinese courts agreed to try Char in the US Court. A letter was sent to the Commissioner for Foreign Affairs requesting this to be done. The Commissioner for Foreign Affairs, or more likely his superiors, had other ideas. Char had been friends with the Commissioner for many years. Char had been discussing some matters concerning his clients with the Commissioner on the telephone. The Commissioner invited Char to come to his office in the Chinese part of Shanghai outside the International

Settlement. Once there, he was promptly arrested. He was allowed to telephone the US Consulate General but was subsequently placed in a Chinese jail outside the Settlement. The US Minister in China, John MacMurray, on July 15, 1929 immediately cabled Washington for instructions on what to do, adding that the case was "attracting considerable attention locally." He said that the imprisonment of Char outside the Settlement was a breach of the Mixed Court rendition agreement that required imprisonment in the Settlement. The next day before he received a reply, he sent another cable requesting "early action," and that there was "an important principle involved which will affect large numbers of Sino-American citizens if the Chinese authorities are permitted without prejudice to arrest and arbitrarily detain Char without judicial authority." Secretary of State Stimson was in no mood for "early action" or to save Char. He cabled back one month later, essentially agreeing with Sellett's earlier opinion that Char had brought the issue on himself and instructed the US officials in China to take "no action looking for Char's release from the custody of the Chinese authorities." Cunningham, on being informed of this, still wanted to make the best of a bad lot and obtained MacMurray's approval to tell the Chinese authorities that they were not requesting Char's release because of his past actions and so to avoid "silence on our part [being] interpreted to mean that we acquiesce in the Chinese view on the question of jurisdiction over persons of dual Chinese and American nationality."

New Chinese Courts
The agreement to establish the Provisional Court in place of the Mixed Court only had a term of three years. In 1929, negotiations began with the Chinese government over the establishment of new courts in Shanghai, leading to an agreement in February 1930 signed by Britain, the United States, Brazil, Norway and Holland establishing a District

Court and a branch High Court in Shanghai. Appeals from the High Court lay to the Supreme Court of China.

Any Chinese arrested in the International Settlement were, at least, to face a preliminary hearing in the District Court to determine if they should be transferred to another court. Foreign lawyers were allowed to practice before the court when a foreigner was a party, but only to act for the foreign party. The Municipal Council was allowed to nominate policemen to serve as judicial police and "as far as practicable" they should be Chinese. The court took over all cases pending before the Provisional Court and all judgments of the Mixed Court and Provisional Court were agreed to remain binding.

The agreement provided that the practice of consular assessors sitting on the bench be abolished in all cases. However, a declaration annexed to the agreement provided that the foreign parties did not give up any rights under existing treaties, meaning that under the Chefoo Convention, a consular official could still attend cases as an observer when a national of their country was a party.

The Shanghai Special District Court was opened in the old Provisional Court Building (which was itself the old Mixed Court building) on April 1, 1930 in a very impressive ceremony. A total of 26 judges were sworn in beneath a portrait of Dr Sun Yat-sen. Dr Sun's will was read, followed by three minutes silence. Dr Showin Wetzen Hsu the new Judge of the 2nd Branch Kiangsu Provincial Higher Court said that "he would ensure impartial administration of justice by those under his control." He

Dr Showin Wetzen Hsu, former President of the Provisional Court, new Judge of the Kiangsu Higher Court

then added a very serious note that it was clear "that the reputation of China and her diplomatic future, was in the hands" of the judges who had all been sworn in this morning.

There was no immediate purge of foreigners involved with the court. Mr R.T. Bryan, who had served as "Police Advocate", remained on as "Municipal Advocate" and the Judicial Police remained a foreign domain with Chief Inspector W. Whiting appointed as head, assisted by Inspector N. White and two foreign sergeants.

Gilbert King retires

At the same time, British Assistant Judge Gilbert King retired due to ill-health. Two men were appointed to take over from him. In 1930, Cyril Henry Haines, from the Foreign Office Judicial Service, was appointed Registrar and in 1931 Penrhyn Grant Jones was appointed Assistant Judge. Grant Jones had been in consular service in China for 30 years, including eight years as an assessor on the Mixed Court in Shanghai and as Acting Judge of the High Court of Weihaiwei in 1919.

Grant Jones was not a pleasant man. While sitting as an assessor in the Mixed Court in the 1910s and 1920s, Grant Jones was quoted on a number of occasions commenting on the lack of civil and moral standards in Shanghai. In 1914, he said that flogging should be brought back as a punishment. In 1915, he called Shanghai a "festering sore" on the body politic of China and: "What should be the habitat of a peaceful commercial community has become an Alsatia of rogues and vagabonds, native and foreign." The same year, he said that Shanghai must not become a place of asylum for Chinese and all acts of rebellion against the Chinese government must be firmly suppressed. In 1920, he said on the bench of the Mixed Court: "I have sat here for eight years, listening to lie after lie."

At the time of Grant Jones' appointment, negotiations were proceeding that may have meant his time on the bench would be very short.

CHAPTER 26

Extraterritoriality to End

IN 1928, WITH THE Nationalist Party now firmly in power, Britain commenced negotiations on ending extraterritorial rights. In a Memorandum in December 1926, Britain had already urged the extraterritorial powers to institute a policy of "readiness to negotiate on treaty revision and all other outstanding questions as soon as the Chinese themselves have constituted a Government with authority to negotiate."

By the end of 1928, China had entered into agreements with most treaty powers giving it tariff autonomy (that is, allowing China to set its own import and export duties). This prompted the Chinese Government to issue a note signed by Foreign Minister, C.T. Wang, to all the treaty powers on April 27, 1929 seeking an end to extraterritoriality. After pointing out that China had now been unified under one government, the note said:

> "It goes without saying that extraterritoriality in China
> is a legacy of the old regime, which has not only ceased
> to be adaptable to the present-day conditions, but
> has become detrimental to the smooth working of the
> judicial and administrative machinery of China that her
> progress as a member of the family of nations has been
> unnecessarily retarded."

Wang pointed out that China had now drafted Criminal and Commercial Codes that would come into force before

C.T. Wang, The Chinese Foreign Minister who almost brought an end to extraterritoriality

January 1, 1930 and that numerous foreigners were now subject to the jurisdiction of Chinese courts in China their governments had not had cause to complain. Wang finally sought agreement that extraterritoriality be abolished at the earliest possible date. Miles Lampson, the British Minster, replied on August 10, 1929 setting out the historical reasons for extraterritoriality in China and stating that since 1902 Britain had committed to relinquishing extraterritoriality at an appropriate time. These had been repeated in 1926. He then said C.T. Wang, The Chinese Foreign Minister who almost brought an end to extraterritoriality that establishing of legal codes was an important step, but that it was necessary that the new laws be enforced in practice and not just on paper. He said:

"In order that those reforms should become a living reality, it appears to his Majesty's government to be necessary that Western legal principles should be understood and be found acceptable by the people at large no less than by their rulers, and that the courts which administer these laws should be free from interference and dictation at the hands not only of military chiefs but of groups and associations who either set up arbitrary and illegal tribunals of their own or attempt to use legal courts for furtherance of political objects rather than for the administration of equal justice between Chinese and Chinese and Chinese and foreigners."

Lampson continued that until these conditions were

fulfilled any agreement to relinquish extraterritoriality would be a paper agreement and that extraterritoriality would therefore need to continue for a time.

Unsatisfied with this, the Chinese government took unilateral action. On December 28, 1929, the State Council of the National Government issued a Mandate Abrogating the System of Consular Jurisdiction to take effect from January 1, 1930. The mandate first set out that China had been subject to extraterritoriality for more than 80 years. It the provided:

"It is hereby decided and declared that on the first day of the first month of the nineteenth year of the Republic (January 1st, 1930) all foreign nationals in the territory of China who are now enjoying extraterritorial privileges shall abide by the laws, ordinances, and regulations duly promulgated by the central and local government of China. The Executive Yuan and the Judicial Yuan are hereby ordered to prepare as soon as possible a plan for the execution of this mandate and to submit it to the Legislative Yuan for examination and deliberation with a view to its promulgation and enforcement."

Read carefully, this mandate did not immediately abolish extraterritoriality. It provided that foreign nationals should abide by Chinese law, but did not announce immediate enforcement of laws against them, rather that a plan would be introduced to bring an end to extraterritoriality. Nevertheless, the mandate clearly laid down China's strong intention to abolish extraterritoriality.

Dr Wang confirmed himself that the mandate was a first step in bringing an end to extraterritoriality. In a discussion with a Chinese writer Edward Bing Shuey-lee, Wang appeared optimistic about a new era of foreign relations coming in 1930. Bing reported that Wang "realized the many difficulties that

stood in the path of immediate abolition of extraterritoriality."
But Wang said that if the Nationalist government's foreign
policy was to be carried out "he must act like a man who is
determined to reach his destination."

The mandate certainly got the powers' attention.
Amid reports that the Judicial Yuan had drawn up plans
to implement the mandate, the British Minister, Sir Miles
Lampson, arrived in Nanking by gunboat on January 9, 1930
for discussions with Wang on the extraterritoriality. The US
State Department issued a statement that US Government did
not consider extraterritoriality had been abolished.

*Sapajou questions whether China will ever reach a final
agreement with the foreign powers*

Following the issue of the mandate, there were a few scattered incidents where local Chinese authorities took the mandate as the end of extraterritoriality. In Wuchow, Chinese authorities refused to hand over the pilot and coxswain of a British launch on the basis that extraterritoriality had ended. In Hankow, Commander McBride of the British Navy while driving home hit and killed a Chinese boy riding a bicycle, resulting in a dispute over who had jurisdiction to hear the case. The Chinese authorities eventually released him.

By 1931, things moved on quickly, China had completed enacting almost all their legal codes, including a Civil Code made up of 1,225 articles providing detailed regulation of civil and commercial relationships. Not only had the Nationalist government completed the drafting of laws, they had extended their control to most of China. Even in Manchuria, which for a long time had only paid lip service to the government of China, an agreement had been reached with the warlord in control, Chang Hsueh-lian, that recognised the Nationalist Party as the Government of China. Chang had extracted some big concessions for this. He had been allowed to take over the Customs revenue in Tientsin as well as been appointed to Deputy Commander of the Chinese armed forces.

By April 1931, the British Secretary of State for Foreign Affairs, Arthur Henderson, told Cabinet that it would be impossible for Britain to fight against a unilateral abrogation of the treaties by China. The force which would be needed would not be acceptable to either domestic British or Chinese public opinion. The threat of strikes and boycotts against British interests in China, which had been successful in the past, loomed large in deciding that it was better to negotiate the best deal that was possible rather than have one imposed unilaterally.

The world economy also must have had a big influence on British and American decision makers. The Great Depression was biting hard in Britain and even more so in America. Both economies had shrunk by at least 25% and unemployment was a serious problem. No one would have supported going to war, or even deploying troops, as had been done in 1927, to fight to protect rights of foreigners far away in China.

Britain was willing to accept Chinese jurisdiction over British subjects in the new Modern Courts with promises that for at least five years assessors could sit on the courts. The key issue for them was progressive reduction of extraterritoriality so that Chinese would only assume jurisdiction over British subjects in the key treaty ports of Shanghai, Tientsin, Canton and Hankow some time after they had assumed jurisdiction in the rest of China. Two important considerations in relation to Shanghai and Tientsin, in particular, were that if they were to pass immediately under Chinese jurisdiction, there would be a financial panic. Further, it would take some time to unwind the systems of municipal government that had been put in place in those cities. Canton and Hankow were considered of secondary importance and the negotiators were authorized to give up rights there if necessary.

The Shanghai Municipal Council in 1929 greatly worried by the developments decided to appoint a South African judge Mr Justice Richard Feetham to prepare a report on extraterritoriality in Shanghai. Feetham was very highly regarded and had already been chairman of three international commissions, the Feetham Function Committee on constitutional reform in India, the Irish Boundary Commission and the Kenya Local Government Commission.

Feetham came to Shanghai in early 1930 and over a period of 18 months prepared a very comprehensive and thorough report which noted the extraordinary position of Shanghai and the Council. The Council relied on independent courts to enforce its bye-laws. It also relied on the continued protection of troops and ships of foreign powers to maintain its authority. Feetham proposed that extraterritoriality continue in the International Settlement until China could form a united and pacified government with a constitutional government of checks and balances.

Feetham had also expressed this view to the British authorities before issuing his report saying that a "fixed time limit puts a rope around the neck of the Settlement." However, a fixed time limit was all that Henderson thought they could manage to agree with the resurgent Nationalist

Justice Feetham of South Africa - appointed by the SMC to report on extraterritoriality

Government, noting that "estimating the strength of China political forces" was "a matter which the opinion of Judge Feetham, for all his great ability, is not likely to be of great value."

Henderson explained, in contorted diplomatese, that extraterritoriality could only exist where one side had the political and military power to impose it on the other:

> "His Majesty's Government, however, believe that the true criterion is not whether the Chinese are fit to assume jurisdiction over foreigners, but whether the Chinese are politically sufficiently stabilised to give effect to their determination to put an end to the extra-territorial system. When that time has arrived, the choice that lies before foreign nationals in China is submission to Chinese jurisdiction with reasonably adequate safeguards duly negotiated and embodied in a treaty or submission without any safeguards at all."

The Americans who were working closely with the British, in principle, agreed with the British position. The French and

Japanese were slower in the uptake. Henderson commented they were "somewhat disquieted, their own inclination being to go more slowly." With regard to the French, Henderson view was that their "dilatory policy exposes them to smaller risks." With regard to the Japanese, Henderson said they were less willing to compromise due to their physical closeness to China and the fact that they were "perhaps less averse to the use of force in defence of the existing position" as well as having "special interests of their own, notably in Manchuria." Moreover, they were "apt to flatter themselves that they can manage the Chinese in a way impossible to western Nations."

Cabinet approved Henderson's approach and by June 1931, a draft treaty was finalized. The draft specifically excluded Shanghai for a period of 10 years to allow time to work out special arrangements. The treaty, in the end, was not signed due to the internal break up of the Nationalist Party. In May 1931, Wang Ching-wei and other left wing members of the Nationalist Party had split from the party and formed a new government in Canton opposed to the Nanking government.

In a memo to Cabinet dated June 2, 1931 Henderson said that Foreign Minister Wang had "made it plain that he is not in a position actually to sign the Treaty at this moment in view of the political situation in China and the revolt of the Cantonese." Wang feared that the offer regarding Shanghai would be used "as a weapon against the Nanking Government." Wang was however ready to agree on the text between himself and Lampson "for the consideration of the Chinese Government and His Majesty's Government." Henderson recommended following this course because it would have the "advantage of having reached a complete agreement with the Chinese Minister for Foreign Affairs," so that Britain "shall be in a strong position to hold the Chinese Government to the terms negotiated with him."

Cabinet agreed this approach and Foreign Minister Wang and British Minister Lampson signed an agreement between themselves. Britain had agreed, in principle, to bring an end to extraterritoriality in China.

The United States also on July 14, 1931 submitted a draft text with very similar terms to the British agreement, save that it included a five-year period where extraterritoriality would continue in Tientsin. Negotiations had then broken off for the summer. On September 15, 1931, Wang invited the US Minister, Nelson

Miles Lampson, British Minister to China who signed a treaty with C.T. Wang to end extraterritorially

Johnson, to return to Nanking to finalize negotiations and on September 18, Johnson received instructions to proceed to Nanking but not to mention negotiations on extraterritoriality pending further instructions.

Exactly on the day Johnson was directed to go to Nanking, an event occurred that meant the meeting was never to happen and the end of extraterritoriality was not formally discussed again between China and the United States or Britain until 1942.

CHAPTER 27

Major Battles

SEPTEMBER 18, 1931.

September 18, 1931 must go down in Chinese and world history as one of those great "What if?" days. If the events that occurred on that day had not happened, would China have abolished extraterritoriality and recovered its sovereignty? Would the Nationalist Party have been strong enough to defeat the communists? Would Mainland China today be as vibrant a democracy as Taiwan is today?

We will never know, for on that day, Japan invaded Manchuria. The pretext for the invasion was an alleged attack on the Southern Manchurian railway by Chinese troops. It is generally now accepted that the attack was set up by the Japanese army to justify their invasion. Chiang Kai-shek ordered Chang Hsueh-liang not to fight the Japanese and Chang pulled back his troops. The Japanese quickly occupied the whole of Manchuria. As part of a peace treaty, they also obtained the agreement of the Chinese to demilitarize Hopei (Hebei) Province surrounding Peking, or Peiping as it was now called.

The effect of the Japanese action in Manchuria, and later actions in and around Shanghai was to bring to a close to all formal negotiations on the end to extraterritoriality. The Chinese government was not in a position to force the foreign powers to agree to an end to extraterritoriality, and, in fact, the foreign powers' presence in China helped to temper Japanese actions.

Extraterritoriality in Manchuria

After the Japanese occupied Manchuria they set up the "independent state" of Manchukuo on March 1, 1932 with its capital in Changchun. This state, despite its alleged independence, Britain and America had, however, pledged not to recognize the existence of Manchukuo either de facto or de jure. So while both sides acknowledged that extraterritoriality remained in place, it was for different reasons.

The first major test of extraterritoriality in Japanese occupied territories came in 1933 when the Japanese authorities, ordered Mr E. Lenox Simpson, editor of the *Harbin Herald* to leave Manchuria. The Japanese said the *Harbin Herald* was publishing pro-Soviet propaganda. Simpson had given an undertaking to cease to do so. When he failed to abide by the undertaking the Japanese sought to deport him. On May 22, 1933, Mr Lun asked the British Prime Minister, Ramsay MacDonald, in the House of Commons if this was true and, if so, what the government was doing about it.

MacDonald replied that it was correct Simpson had been asked to leave. The Consul-General in Harbin had already protested against this breach of British extraterritorial rights and that he had been "instructed to continue to protest strongly, if necessary, against the breach of treaty rights involved." The Prime Minister continued that the "Charge D'Affaires in Tokio has also been instructed to ask the Japanese Government to use their influence to prevent this threatened violation of treaty rights, and the matter is being inquired into by them." Ultimately, a compromise was reached where Simpson moved to Dalian, but the *Herald* was closed down. This was a fudge on the British side. Dalian was still a Japanese colony at the time, so Simpson would have then fallen under the direct jurisdiction of the Japanese authorities there.

Sino-Japanese war in Shanghai

Soon after invading Manchuria, in January 1932, the Japanese launched an attack on Chinese forces around Shanghai seeking to create a cordon sanitaire around the city. The main goal was to protect the Japanese businesses and Japanese people in and around Shanghai.

To the surprise of the Japanese, the Nationalists committed a large number of troops, over 50,000, to the defence of their positions around Shanghai leading to massive battles. At one point a shell fell in the back garden of British Judge, Peter Grain. The situation was so tense that the Municipal Council issued an Emergency Proclamation imposing a 10pm to 4am curfew, prohibiting public gatherings and banning the publication and distribution of any document "calculated to cause alarm of a breach of the peace."

While the foreign powers had opposed the invasion of Manchuria, they were much more ambivalent about the battle for Shanghai. In private, many supported the Japanese action. If the Japanese were successful in driving the Chinese army back from Shanghai, the situation where foreigners had a free hand in and around Shanghai prior to the Nationalists' successful Northern Expedition in 1927 would in many ways be restored. Soon after the war started, Stirling Fessenden, as Director General of the Shanghai Municipal Council, sent a cable to the *New York Times* explaining that the Settlement could not be neutral in the battle because the Japanese were one of the treaty powers. It was "almost impossible" to get the Japanese to cease landing troops in the International Settlement because their reason for doing so was to defend the Settlement.

The China Association sent a telegram to the British Secretary of State "which contained a confidential passage commenting adversely on the anti-Japanese sentiment as expressed in certain British newspapers and in the communications of the Council of the League of Nations to

Japan. These, according to this communication, tended to stiffen the Chinese and to prolong the trouble, and indicated a misunderstanding of the situation."

In the end, the Japanese committed over 100,000 troops to the offensive around Shanghai and forced the Chinese army back. A truce was signed in April 1932 providing that Chinese troops would not be stationed within 20 miles of Shanghai. The Chinese civil government stayed in place. But without the Chinese military to back it, they were in a much weaker position to enforce Chinese rights or challenge extraterritoriality.

Battle for the Hardoon millions

Japanese shelling was not the only thing to disturb Grain's slumber in mid-1932. Two major legal battles also came before the British Supreme Court in 1932 and 1933.

From mid-June, Grain was required to try a case of mindboggling complexity brought about by the question of the status of Jews from Iraq who had made their way to Shanghai over the years, usually by way of India. Silas Hardoon, a Baghdadi Jew, and one of the richest men in Shanghai, died in June 1931. He owned numerous properties around Shanghai including a massive estate on Bubbling Well Road. His will left all his property to his wife, a Chinese who had converted to Judaism, Liza Hardoon. He left a large personal fortune amounting to at least GBP4,000,000 (or US$20,000,000) – some reports say it was much higher.

The trial was extremely high profile in Shanghai and Hong Kong. Ezra Hardoon wanted the best. He convinced Harrie Wilkinson, now a Northern Irish King's Counsel, to come out of retirement to represent him.

Liza Hardoon also wanted the best. She hired Mr Eldon Potter KC of Hong Kong with Mr G.H. Wright. The key issue in the case was whether Hardoon was a British subject under the Orders in Council. Potter argued that he was. Wilkinson argued that as a British Protected Person, Hardoon was not a British subject and that his estate should be dealt with under the law of Iraq or the Ottoman Empire.

Grain handed down his judgment in late July on an extremely hot day. The *North China Herald* in a front page editorial saluted the judgment and Grain's stamina. One can almost imagine sweat dripping down his face from under his wig. Wilkinson KC had argued that special nature of the International Settlement – effectively an extraterritorial enclave – meant Hardoon could not have become domiciled in Shanghai. After considering a number of cases, Grain found that a domicile could be established in Shanghai saying: "This court has now since 1923 been continually finding that British subjects have acquired a Chinese domicile in the Settlement."

Turning to the law to be applied, he then found that the law of the court determined the law of the domicile and accordingly he would apply English law and not Iraqi law. This meant that the case was dismissed and Mrs Hardoon allowed to inherit the fortune. So, Harrie Wilkinson's last case in a court he had first appeared in 42 years before ended with a loss. He died the following year and was buried in Bubbling Well Cemetery in a grand funeral.

Luna Park – Racing around the Court of Consuls

While the plaintiffs in the Hardoon cases had been trying to get the case out of the British courts, in another case, the plaintiffs were trying to get themselves before the British courts.

As part of a concerted anti gambling campaign the Municipal Council, in 1931, resolved to close Luna Park, a greyhound racing track opened on the eastern outskirts of the International Settlement in Hongkew. The Municipal Council's attitude to Luna Park had, as the *Shanghai Evening Post* put it, been "ambiguous and vacillating." The Council had originally approved the opening of the park. But the increasingly influential Chinese community in Shanghai felt that greyhound racing was a particularly bad form of gambling because it attracted poor Chinese to waste their money. Partly due to Chinese complaints but probably more because of pressure from some consulates, the Council determined to close the park. Rather than taking on the difficult task of working out who to sue and in which court, the Municipal Police took a simple approach. They barred access to the track by placing large numbers of policemen and an anti-riot van at the entrance, a trick they had taken to use when shutting down gambling establishments in Shanghai.

The closing of Luna Park led to a closely watched case in the British Supreme Court. The owners of Luna Park sued General Macnaghten, the Chairman of the Municipal Council, and Captain Martin, the head of the Municipal Police, for damages for illegally shutting the park.

The novel feature of the case was that as a claim against the Municipal Council, the case should have been brought in the Court of Consuls. But according to Luna Park's Counsel, Reader Harris, "action had not been brought in the Court of Consuls because, for one reason, there was no appeal from that court ... It was known that the British Consular authorities ... were supporting the Council and it would be very difficult for the British Consul to say the Council should not have done so and so."

THE GREYHOUND RACING CLUB

LUNA PARK

8.30—SATURDAY NIGHT—8.30

14 RACES—3rd Meeting (1930)—14 RACES

The George Sadler Stakes—500 Yards Flat

Welfare	Barron's Toss
Nightshade	Black Sheik
Union Lady	Burn Black
Fresh Fancy	Esmeralda

On same card:—

Four 285-yard Flat Races
Two 500-yard Hurdle Races
Seven 500-yard Flat Races

(See News columns for entries)

Race-cards on sale from 10 a.m. on Saturday at:—

The G.R.C. Offices, No. 2 Canton Road
Messrs. Kelly & Walsh Ltd., 24 Nanking Road
Messrs. H. E. Brewer, 39 Kiangse Road
Mercantile Printing Co., Ltd., A321 Szechuen Road
Asanol Stores, 52 Woosung Road
Ah Fong, Photographer, Nanking Road
E. Tai Liang Kee Garage, 58A Hupeh Road
May Wah Garage, Cr. North Szechuen Road and Tiendong Roads
Lee Lee Garage, all stations
Breehuen Road Garage, 98A North Saichoen Road
Park Garage, 187 North Szechuen Road
Far Eastern Garage, 1605-4 Yangtszepoo Road
Wing On Garage, 106b North Szechuen Road.

BAND OF THE 2nd Bn. THE GREEN HOWARDS, by kind permission of Lt.-Col. F. F. I. Kinnman and Officers.

TRAFFIC NOTE.—No cars will be allowed to make a right hand turn off Ward Road. Will those using the Members' Entrance co-operate by proceeding via Baikai (or Pingliang) and Whabshing Roads.

Members wishing to make dinner reservations are requested to communicate with the undersigned, No. 2 Canton Road, Tel. 19397, 10330, 10331, before NOON on Saturday.

DUNCAN E. CAMPBELL,
Secretary & General Manager.

6282

The case was founded on the argument that the Council did not have extraterritorial jurisdiction over a British company. The only authority with powers over a British company was the British Supreme Court. The Municipal Council should have come to the British Supreme Court to seek to close Luna Park and not take the actions it had done. As the heads of the Municipal Council and the Municipal Police, Macnaghten and Martin were liable.

Grain had originally dismissed the case in 1931 on the basis that there was no good cause of action but this had been overturned on appeal by a majority decision of the Chief Justice of Hong Kong and Skinner Turner who found it was possible to challenge the executive acts of British individuals on the council in the British courts.

Grain then tried the case with a jury of five in February 1933. The damages claimed were for, at the time, an astronomical sum of $2,500,000. The plaintiffs gave evidence regarding the shutting of the Park by the Police and the damage that had been suffered. During the course of evidence, Mr Buyers of the accountants Thomson & Co gave evidence that a 1% "stamp duty tax" had been paid to the Chinese authorities. This immediately elicited the question:

"A British company paying a stamp duty tax to the Chinese government! What for?"

"This payment was paid confidentially and is somewhat of a political matter."

Grain intervened to save Mr Buyers: "I will not compel you to answer."

Relieved, Buyers responded: "I would rather not answer." The Chinese government would have liked an answer. They immediately wrote to the Greyhound Racing Association asking to whom and how much had been paid.

In response to a no case submission, Grain dismissed the case against McNaghten but allowed the case against Martin to go to the jury.

Grain summed up for the jury, virtually directing them to find for Martin. He referred to Luna Park as a "huge gambling club." He said:

> "The Council had to decide how they could stop this intolerable nuisance as soon as possible...I feel with the evidence before me, and also on the facts, that I cannot find that the Council has no power to order their police to take the action that they did ... I find they had the authority to take the course they did to prevent this huge gambling centre being a public nuisance in this Settlement."

Not surprisingly, after an hour's deliberation, the jury returned with a verdict that Martin had been acting bona fide and that there were no damages caused by his actions.

Grain retires

Soon after hearing the Luna Park case, Peter Grain decided to retire. He left Shanghai in May 1933 on pre-retirement leave.

Unlike de Sausmarez's or Turner's retirements, Grain's retirement left the Foreign Office with no obvious internal choice for successor. Given the Japanese attacks the year before and the uncertainty over the future of extraterritoriality, it would also have been difficult to convince any practicing barrister from Home to come out to China. Grant Jones had only just been appointed Assistant Judge and had never practiced as a barrister. Allan Mossop, the Crown Advocate, was, therefore, appointed Judge of the British Supreme Court for China with effect from December 24, 1933. Victor Priestwood, who had worked as Mossop's assistant for eight years and been Acting Crown Advocate for eight months in 1930 when Mossop was on leave, was appointed Crown Advocate. Priestwood was born in May 1902 in Lancashire. He studied at Keble College Oxford and was called to the bar of the Inner Temple on January 29, 1920. He passed his bar exams in April 1922. He was the second son of John George Priestwood, a solicitor who had practiced in Shanghai and regularly appeared before the courts.

Changes in the US Court

At almost exactly the same time Mossop was appointed Judge of the British Supreme Court for China, down the road in the United States Court, Milton Purdy's term of office came to an end in February 1934.

At the time, Purdy was no longer an employee of the State Department. About half a year earlier, the United States Court for China and its staff had all been transferred from the State Department to be under the Department of Justice as part of a re-organisation of government services that had been mandated by Congress. For the State Department, this meant that the court's roles as "a part of the machinery for conducting foreign relations of the United States" and "indirectly an agency of the Government of China" had come to an end.

Purdy's successor, Milton Helmick, had been a judge in New Mexico since 1925. He had graduated in law from the University of Denver in 1910 and at one time had served as the Attorney General for New Mexico. Helmick had been appointed the new Judge by President Franklin D. Roosevelt six days before Purdy's term of office came to an end. The Senate, however, delayed confirming him for two months, giving "law breakers in China a field day," according to an Associated Press report. The AP report continued:

"For the last two months American legal machinery

throughout China as been paralysed. Lawyers say the situation is unparalleled in American jurisprudence. The court docket is choked with civil and criminal cases, awaiting a judge to hear them."

While the situation was not without parallels – Lebbeus Wilfley and Charles Lobingier had both been away for longer periods – there were probably now many more cases that needed to be dealt with so that the absence of a judge was more keenly felt.

Helmick also recommended the appointment of a young lawyer form his home tow, Felthan Watson, to replace Thomas Sellett who had resigned as US District Attorney.

After their arrival in Shanghai, Helmick and Watson were soon in the thick of things.

CHAPTER 28

Predators

MILTON HELMICK, the new Judge of the United States Court for China, was called upon to deal with three very complex and difficult cases in 1935 and 1936. The first two were brought about by a financial crash; the third, it seems, by a desire to remarry. In one of the cases, Helmick had to answer the tricky question of what was an American corporation. In the other two cases leading American citizens of Shanghai and Tientsin were on trial.

Attack on a Russian American bank
In Harbin, an American registered bank, the Thriftcor Bank, became insolvent in October 1935. The Thriftcor Bank was incorporated in Nevada. It had its headquarters in Harbin with a branch in Shanghai. The bank had been founded by a Russian whose daughter had been born on an American boat while crossing the Pacific Ocean, making her American. The bank, whose main customers were Russians, flew an American flag on top of its offices in Harbin. Directly above the main door the name was written in Russian with English being written much higher up above the second floor windows. It had been refused registration as a United States company by the American Consulate in Harbin.

Thriftcor was one of the few remaining independent banks in Manchukuo. The Japanese had since 1931 been tightening their hold on Manchuria. Pressure was being put on foreign companies to sell out or to take on Japanese partners. Almost all other banks in Manchuria had effectively been forced to bring in Japanese partners.

In October 1935, Thriftcor became insolvent and needed to be put into liquidation. On October 5, 1935 Walter Adams the US Consul-General in Harbin telegrammed the US Ambassador in China, Nelson Johnson, saying that there was "much excitement in Harbin over the suspension of Thriftcor Bank which remained closed yesterday." He said that appointment at once of a liquidator by the US Court for China was necessary and asked if the US Court wished him to take any action.

Ambassador Johnson reported to Secretary of State Hull that Helmick had said to him on October 4 that he had already told H.D. Rodger, the lawyer for Thriftcor (and its vice president), that there was no American interest in the bank, registration with the Consulate had been denied and Helmick saw no reason for the US Court to be taking action. Johnson said he agreed with Helmick's view and asked for confirmation from Department of State that he should proceed in this way. Hull wrote back stating that the State Department "was doubtful whether American authorities in China could properly refuse to recognize the jurisdictional status of the bank as an American citizen if the question were submitted for judicial determination." However, this was a matter for the court and if Helmick was willing to maintain that the court did not have jurisdiction, then Johnson could proceed to tell Harbin to take no action.

Rodger telegrammed the bank in Harbin to say that the court had declined jurisdiction. Consul General Adams in Harbin was very concerned that this would look like weakness on the part of the Americans by allowing the local courts to take over the liquidation. He asked for permission to put out a statement that America had declined jurisdiction. Helmick agreed to this. Adams put out the statement in eight Harbin newspapers and told Thriftcor to stop flying the US flag.

Frank Raven – A bird of prey

Back in Shanghai, the attacks on American finance companies
were not coming from outside. Rather, they were rotten to
the core from within. In May 1935, in what was described as
"the most severe blow to American business prestige in the
Far East since the beginning of Chinese-American business
relations," four finance companies, all under the American
Oriental Banking Corporation, and all controlled by Frank
Jay Raven, closed their doors. Bewildered investors, many
who had lost their life savings, milled outside the doors of the
companies. Affixed to the doors was a simple sign "Closed by
Order of the Board of Directors."

The closure of the finance companies was bad for its
investors and did, indeed, deal a serious blow to American
prestige. It was, however, a bonanza for lawyers. As soon as
the companies shut almost every lawyer in town filed claims
against them. At the time, Helmick was in Peiping trying
a case. Norwood Allman was also in Peiping appearing
before Helmick. Allman's office in Shanghai telegraphed
him to obtain various
restraining orders from
Helmick against the bank
officers and to start some
claims. Allman was able
to do this, "sitting right in
the lap of the court, as it
were."

Helmick wanted to
appoint an American
lawyer as the liquidator
of the group, but could
not find a lawyer who
had not either acted for
the Raven Group or was

Mr. F. J. Raven

Frank Raven, fraudster

not now acting against them. Finally, he appointed Mr Frank Hough of the R.C.A. Victor Company and a "prominent and reputable businessman" to liquidate the Raven Group. On taking over the companies, Hough found that the Raven Group had been effectively insolvent since 1932 and Raven and the top management had known about it. He later estimated that the companies would only pay seven cents in the dollar on liquidation.

This prompted a criminal investigation by Felthan Watson, the new US District Attorney. The investigation revealed a scandal on a grand scale. Frank Raven, a church-going municipal councilor and hero of the American community was, quite simply, a fraudster. The fraud was very simple. The Raven Group and in particularly the American Oriental Finance Corporation (AOFC) would use client money or shares to gamble on the stock market. When customers bought shares fully paid, they would be issued notices confirming their holdings of fully paid stock. AOFC, however, would not necessarily buy the shares. When they did, they would buy through a margin account held with their brokers in San Francisco, E.A. Pierce. With a margin account, you do not have to pay the full price to buy shares. For AOFC, Pierce allowed them to purchase shares with a 25% margin. This meant they needed only to have funds available to cover 25% of the value of the shares. In addition to this, there were occasions when AOFC received orders to buy shares and instructions from other clients to "short" shares. They would just offset the orders in their books, meaning there were no actual shares purchased for the customers who were long.

Raven, J. Warner Brown, the President of the companies, and Alfred Driscoll, the Company Secretary, were all charged with numerous counts of embezzlement, theft and related charges. Halfway through the case, Watson dropped the charges against Driscoll in return for him giving evidence against Raven and Brown. The case commenced straight after

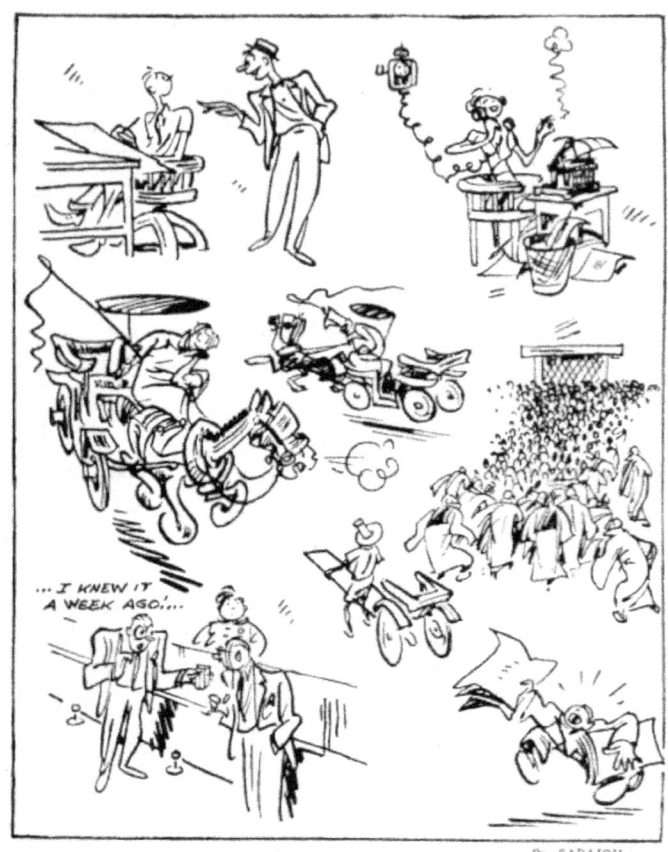

THE NEWS THAT ROCKED THE MARKET   *By SAPAJOU*

Sapajou on the collapse of AOCB

New Year in 1936.

More than 30 witnesses were called and over 300 exhibits prepared. Before the trial commenced, Raven and Brown made an application for a jury trial. Helmick refused the application. He said that if he "had been the first judge of the US Court for China he would, of course, have made the matter the subject of exhaustive study. But after 29 years of established policy, he did not feel he could make any rule offhanded or lightly

which would establish the
precedent set up."

The trial itself was a grueling
four-week slog, as any white-
collar crime trial is, particularly
where there are well-paid
defence attorneys. Numerous
witnesses were called to give
evidence about paying money
to buy shares through AOFC;
that they received statements
that the shares were "fully
held" and that they had never
approved any margin trading.
In addition to Driscoll, who
was testifying under immunity,
the three main witnesses for

Mr. R. T. Evans

Mr R.T. Evans of Tientsin, Warner Brown's defence attorney

the prosecution were the liquidator, Mr Frank Hough, Mr
CC Curtis of E.A. Pierce & Co who came from San Francisco
to give evidence, as well Cletus Joseph Haley, who had been
treasurer of AOFC in 1932.

Hough gave evidence about the dire financial situation of
the entire Raven group of companies with numerous cross
loans between the companies. Mr Curtis from E.A. Pierce
was brought from San Francisco. He confirmed that almost
all trades were done on margin and if required, E.A. Pierce
would call on other shares held on behalf of AOFC to cover
any margin losses. Driscoll, the insider, gave evidence as to
how secret codes were used to identify accounts held by Raven
and his family for trading as well as by other businessmen
who used the trust to hide their deals. He said that Raven had
attended many meetings regarding the financial situation
of the companies. Haley, who had only been treasurer for a
short time, told the court that he had been given the title of
treasurer but no real authority to act as treasurer. He was not

allowed to sign documents. All he had received was a name card. His evidence was, however, vital. He said that when he was at AOFC, he had written a report setting out his concerns about how the company had been margin trading with client shares. He had given a copy of the memorandum to Brown and, he said, discussed it directly with Raven.

Brown chose to give evidence in his own defence. Raven, claiming ill health, did not. Brown may have been better off if he had followed Raven's lead. He ended up giving evidence for a total of 22 hours over five days. Watson grilled him in cross-examination. Brown made a very poor witness and ensured his own, as well as Raven's, conviction. Raven was furious with Brown. During a break in the trial, Raven accosted Brown in the coffee shop downstairs demanding to know why he had said they had discussed the incriminating memo. Back in court, Watson asked Brown if, in fact, he was angry with Raven because Raven had decided not to give evidence. He asked Brown if he had told Raven: "I am not going to take the damn brunt of this affair myself." Brown effectively convicted Raven there and then with his answer by saying that other than "that bad word," yes, this is what he had said.

After closing submissions, Helmick took a short break and then gave a very short judgment convicting both Raven and Brown of a number of offences. He adjourned sentencing until the next day. At 10 am the court was packed with a large crowd outside trying to peer in. The US marshal sat between Raven and Brown. Helmick asked Raven if he had anything to say.

He did. He showed just what a scoundrel he was.

Despite, having chosen not to give evidence – where he would have faced cross-examination - he now wanted to get even with Brown. He said that Brown was "a man of average ability, fundamentally and basically honest." He had made many mistakes, as they all had, but, Raven claimed, Brown had never told Raven of any of the matters that he said he had. He said he had never seen the Haley memorandum or spoken to Haley, finishing: "if you convict me on the two reports and the evidence of those two witnesses, which I know, and they know, to be entirely untrue, you are sentencing, me an innocent man to the penitentiary." Raven sat down but stood up again when he saw Helmick was about to address him.

Helmick sentenced Raven to five years in McNeil Island. Brown had nothing to say. Helmick sentenced him to two years in McNeil Island.

Doctor, poison thy wife?

Just after the Raven trial, United States District Attorney Felthan Watson, travelled to Tientsin to investigate a case that also involved a leader of the American community and also made international headlines. He returned in May 1936 with Judge Milton Helmick for the trial.

Dr John Colbert, a medical doctor, was accused of attempting to murder his, much younger, fourth wife. Colbert was a leading member of the Tientsin foreign community and a member of the Rotary Club. He was also deeply involved in getting medical treatment for poor Chinese children. His prosecution was a great surprise to many.

His third wife had died in Tientsin six years earlier in suspicious circumstances. Colbert had been very friendly with the fourth Mrs Colbert just before the third Mrs Colbert died. Before the fourth Mrs Colbert became ill, Dr Colbert had a very close relationship with a Grace Thomas, a teacher at the Tientsin British School. The question left unanswered in the court was: was Grace Thomas meant to become the fifth Mrs Colbert?

The alleged poisoning, as would be expected from a trained doctor was cleverly carried out. Mrs Colbert was an avid tennis player. Her husband had started treating her for exhaustion, which he diagnosed as anemia. A British doctor,

Dr J. W. H. Grice, became suspicious of the treatments and after an inspection of the pills Colbert had been giving his wife, it was revealed they contained pure acetanilide, a poison. Mrs Colbert refused to believe her husband had poisoned her and gave evidence at the trial that: "I am convinced of my husband's innocence and am backing up for all I am worth."

After a four day trial Helmick gave his verdict. He first said that he was in the "unenviable position of sole juror." He considered that Dr Grice had been fully justified in his suspicions and the prosecution had been fully justified in bringing the case. He said that while he harboured a "strong suspicion" of guilt of the defendant, he must give the defendant the benefit of the doubt. He acquitted Colbert saying, however, he did so "with some misgivings, but realizing that if an infallible decision cannot be reached the law holds that it is better to make a mistake in favour of the accused than against him."

Five days later, Colbert was attacked in his office. A foreigner "with a hat lowered to cover his forehead and a handkerchief covering the lower part of his face," walked into his office and tried to stab him in the heart. Colbert warded off the blow and then the foreigner struck him in the head, knocking him out. Mrs Colbert, who had heard about the incident by phone, accompanied her husband to the hospital. A very strange conclusion to a very strange case. Who was this assailant? Mrs Colbert herself? Someone she paid? Someone else all together?

Change in DA

Soon after the Colbert case Felthan Watson was called to Washington to serve as a special assistant to the Attorney General in 1936. To replace him, Leighton Shields, from Missouri, was appointed the last US District Attorney for China. Shields had already practiced law in St Louis for 28 years. He had graduated from Harvard College in 1903 and

Washington College of Law at St
Louis University in 1905. He was
a political player in Missouri.
He had attended Harvard with
President Franklin D. Roosevelt
and been a member of the
Glee Club with him. In 1934,
Roosevelt appointed him counsel
of the Reconstruction Finance
Corporation in Washington DC.
He then appointed him District
Attorney for China.

*Leighton Shields, New US
District Attorney for China*

Shields was luckier than Watson and did not have to
handle a major case for some time. In the British courts,
however, Crown Advocate Victor Priestwood had to deal
wiith a number of high profile cases.

Chapter 29

In the Shadows

IT WAS NOT ONLY murder cases in Tientsin that attracted international attention in 1936. In Shanghai two murder cases in the same year were extremely high profile both in China and worldwide. Both cases involved British policemen. The first drew attention for the almost unbelievable nature of the crime; the second for its equally almost unbelievable conclusion.

Throw the beggar in the river?

Before and during their trial in early 1936, Frank Raven and Warner Brown had been held in the foreigners' section of Ward Road Gaol. Newspaper reports at the time said that Raven and Brown were in very comfortable rooms with private bathrooms allotted to them.

Ernest Peters, a British sergeant of the Shanghai Municipal Police debunked this. Raven and Brown were in very uncomfortable cells with a shared communal bathroom. Peters knew the cells were uncomfortable because he, along with British Probationary Sergeant William Judd, had occupied the very same cells for some time while awaiting trial for murder of a Chinese beggar, Mau Te-piau. Peters and Judd had allegedly thrown Mau in a river in Hongkew at 3.30a.m. on a cold winter's night of December 1, 1935.

It was an extraordinary case for many reasons. First, the prosecution had not been initiated by the British authorities because of any complaint by Chinese officials. The Municipal

Police themselves had moved quickly to prosecute Peters and Judd as soon as allegations were made against them. Even before Mau had died, Assistant Commissioner Kenneth Bourne (son of former British Judge Sir Frederick Bourne) authorized an investigation and prosecution. Second, the prosecutors really believed in the guilt of both men. Victor Priestwood, the Crown Advocate, assisted by John McNeill, prosecuted the case with great vigour, clearly believing Peters and Judd were guilty and doing all that he could to get a conviction. Third, the case does not seem to have raised any particular anger in the eyes of Chinese officials, perhaps because the victim was on the lowest rung of society. (There were a number of complaints and protests in the Chinese press relating to the case, Shanghai's extraterritorial status and the arrogance of foreigners, particularly foreign policemen.) Fourth, unlike all other cases, we have a long account written by one of the accused, Peters, giving his side of the story. Fifth, Peters had a Japanese girlfriend, Sumiko, who he planned to marry. This last point was never mentioned by Peters to anyone so never came out at the trial. It is an interesting fact. He cannot have been a complete racist; yet perhaps he never mentioned it because having a Japanese girlfriend would have played out badly before an all-white upper class Shanghai jury.

The evidence against Peters and Judd was damning. Peters was assigned to the charge room of Kashing Road Police Station on that night. Kashing Road Police Station was located just off Kashing Road (Jiaxing Road) right on the border between the International Settlement and Chinese Territory in Chapei. This was a tough area to police. Since 1932, the Japanese controlled the Chinese territory and foreign police were sometimes detained by the Japanese military for seeking to enforce the law against Japanese.

Peters was required to report for duty at 12 midnight, but had arrived late at 2.30 am because, he was to admit later in court, he had been with a lady friend. When he arrived on duty, he was told that two Chinese constables had called in that a Chinese beggar was sick on Point Road (Zhoujiacui Road) where it met Shinkeipang Road (Xinjiang Road). Judd had just come in for a coffee break half an hour before he was meant to. Peters told him to warm up with a coffee and then told him to go with a Russian sergeant, Boris Makovetsky, to see if there really was a sick beggar. Peters said later that he was concerned that in other cases he had called an ambulance and the call had turned out to be a false alarm. Peters then countermanded his order to Makovetsky and told him to look after the charge room while he and Peters went to check on the beggar. He ordered up the station car and the Chinese chauffeur, Doo Sung-foo, came along and took them. They found the beggar who was foaming at the mouth.

They decided to take him to the hospital and put him on the running board, the step that was built outside the doors of many cars in the 1930s. As Peters put it, "anyone who has seen and smelled a Chinese beggar will realize why we did not put him inside the car. Diseased and filthy, it was bad enough having to handle him, and anyway we made him quite comfortable."

Judd got in the car while Peters stood on the running board and held on to Mau. When they reached Fearon Road (Jiulong Road), according to Peters, Mau appeared to be in a better condition and began to move about. Peters told the chauffeur to turn around and drive along Fearon Road. The road ran along the west side of Hongkew Creek and led to Chapei back near Kashing Road. According to Peters and Judd, they intended to take Mau outside the International Settlement to drop him off. The police practice of the time was to "deport" beggars back to Chinese territory. When they reached the Yuhung Road (Yuhang Road) Bridge they told Doo to stop.

Up to this point, the evidence of the prosecution witnesses and Peters and Judd essentially matched. After this, the stories differed. The chauffeur, Doo, told the court that Peters and Judd then threw Mau directly into Hongkew Creek. Doo physically demonstrated in court how Mau had been thrown and how he heard the water make a noise which sounded like a "wah" or a "piah." Another Chinese witness, Zung Ching-sung, a Chinese hawker who lived across the creek, said that he had seen a man struggling in the river and had called for help. He had taken down the number of the car he had seen leaving the scene. This matched the number of the police station car. Mau was fished from the river but died six days later from pneumonia.

Peters and Judd were very ably defended by two British barristers: Ranald McDonald for Peters and Hugh Reeks for Judd. The defence faced a serious challenge. There was a very strong case against Peters and Judd. When first challenged about what had happened that night, they did not say what they had done with Mau. Peters had also committed a serious breach of regulations by leaving the charge room. The evidence of Doo, the police chauffeur, could not really be challenged. The evidence of Zung who admitted to an opium habit was easier to challenge. Be that as it may, Mau had been fished out of the river soon after Peters and Judd were alleged to have thrown him in. Mau had been in their charge and very soon after he had been found in a freezing river.

On the other hand, Priestwood and McNeill also faced a serious challenge. One of the great difficulties in prosecuting police officers is that they know how the system works. They have seen numerous people they considered guilty get off because they have worked the system. They also know that the smaller the lie the better the lie. If you lie about what happened, make sure that it is only a small lie. You can tell the truth about everything else and appear credible and can more easily remember the details of the small lies. With competent lawyers, and Peters and Judd had very competent lawyers, this can get you an acquittal.

So what was Peters and Judds' story? It was very simple,

and for that reason it was very effective. They said that having
decided to return Mau to Chinese territory when going along
Fearon Road, they had seen a beggar boat. Peters in his book
described the creeks of Shanghai as "being infested with
beggar boats. The Police near the waterways go off duty at
night and the beggars seize the opportunity to bring their
boats close to the shore, tying them along the embankments
even in the most central parts of the city, and then going off
to do their begging." The beggar boat that Peters and Judd
had seen was "about 20 foot long, dilapidated, cloth covered
in the centre." While the streets were part of the International
Settlement, the rivers were Chinese territory. This seemed the
simplest way for them to resolve the problem of what to do
with Mau. They told the driver to stop. Peters told the jury:

> "We then both walked to the creek, looked at the boat
> and decided that it was quite safe to put him there.
> We then went back to the beggar. I held his left arm
> and Judd his right and we walked him to the railing
> alongside the creek. There we sat him down … We then
> lowered him on to the rear portion of the boat."

They said nothing more. They made no suggestion that
perhaps someone else had then thrown Mau off the beggar
boat or that Mau was not the beggar they had picked up.

Priestwood attacked Peters aggressively in cross
examination firing off question after question at him. As he
later explained to the jury, "questions must be put as quickly
as possible, otherwise witnesses will have time to think up
another lie." The questions came so fast that McDonald
objected that he "could not take down the answers."
Priestwood retorted: "I am not interested in that." Mossop
told Priestwood to slow down enough that Mossop could
take notes.

McDonald and Reeks then took over. They put the jury

between a rock and a hard place. McDonald and Reeks had already met with Peters and Judd in prison and made the very tough decision on tactics. Peters recounts telling McDonald that he had nothing to hide and MacDonald telling him he would try all out for an acquittal. Peters recalled:

> "I agreed with everything that he said, because I knew that I had not done this thing, and I did not want to cringe behind any pleas of manslaughter. So after a long talk about my character in the Royal Tank Corps and the case in general, he left me, and I returned to my cell with the words 'Murder or nothing' ringing in my ears."

This was the tactic in court. In both their closing speeches, Reeks and McDonald made it clear it was an all or nothing verdict. Murder and the gallows. Or, acquittal and freedom. On the evidence, there should have been no question of manslaughter or any other verdict arising. Peters and Judd either threw Mau in the river and killed him or they did not. McDonald emphasized that if the jury was satisfied beyond reasonable doubt, they had to convict but if they had any doubt they should acquit. He then suggested that "there were sinister figures behind the prosecution." Priestwood leapt to his feet to challenge him on this. McDonald quickly said that no foreigner was involved. McDonald went on that Peters had covered up to seek to protect himself because "like Samson of old he had dallied with Delilah" but this did not amount to murder. He concluded by leaving the "issue of life and death" in the hands of "good men and true."

Reeks, on behalf of Judd, took another tack, appealing at first to logic rather than emotion. There was no reason to believe the accused had any malice towards Mau. A crime of this nature could only be "committed by a man or men deprived of all sense of social justice and a total disregard of the laws of humanity." The Crown case was that they had committed the crime before the eyes of a Chinese policeman, yet afterwards had never said anything to him to seek to silence him. He then turned to emotion, referring to Judd's father and mother in England "and possibly a little friend at the back of the court" were awaiting a verdict.

Judge Allan Mossop then directed the jury, emphasizing the importance of reasonable doubt. He took them through all the evidence before reminding them that it was for the prosecution to prove the defendants guilty and not for the defendants to prove their innocence.

The jury retired.

Peters and Judd, who were being guarded by SMP policemen and were being given relatively special treatment, were taken out of the court to the top of the steps facing Yuenmingyuen Road. The steps led down to the consulate gardens. McDonald said nothing to them and only "made some encouraging signs." Reeks told them that he thought the judge had "dwelt rather too much on manslaughter" and that "although we should be alright in the end, it was always best to prepare for the worst."

Peters did not want to hear this. "I began to realize the grim reality of all that I had been through. And still the issue was uncertain. My great fear was manslaughter and a sentence of imprisonment ... I can not describe my feelings as we waited. [Judd] and I kept out thoughts to ourselves and spoke encouraging words to one another."

The jury returned after 41 minutes. Anyone who has seen a jury trial knows this is one of the tensest moments anyone can experience. The questioning to the jury seems to take an eternity. The accused must sit there while the question is put to the jury as to whether they are guilty or not guilty. Time seems to stop still.

Peters and Judd sat impassively waiting for the verdict. Mossop asked first what was the verdict for Peters. "Not

Guilty" replied the foreman to cheers from the 150 so people in court. The clerk had to shout "Be Quiet" three times before the verdict for Judd could also be read with the same result. Mossop then discharged both men and excused the jury from service for 10 years. As soon as they left the court, Judd and Peters were surrounded by wellwishers congratulating them and celebrations continued into the night.

They both, however, faced disciplinary charges for their admitted breaches of discipline during the trial. Both resigned from the force. They were able to collect their own superannuation contributions, but the Council did not pay them the Council's contributions. Peters returned to England after the trial. Judd stayed on working as a clerk at Clarke's Detective Agency.

The trial and the verdict did not attract any protest from the Chinese authorities. There were two letters to the editor of the *Shanghai Evening Post*. One from "Anglo-Saxon" bemoaned the weakness of the jury system and, in particular, noting that Frank Raven had been convicted by the United States Court in a trial without a jury. This drew a response from "A Chinese" who said that he or she had been "agreeably shocked" by the fact that Peters and Judd had been prosecuted and had during the trial told his Chinese friends that what China needed was English-style justice where policemen would be prosecuted for killing a beggar. Then came the anticlimax and the judge's caution about "malice" and intentions. The writer went on that of the Chinese papers only the *Shunpao* had carried an article critical of the acquittal. No other paper even mentioned it because:

"we Chinese are accustomed to this form of English justice as we accept the Sun rising from the East."

This was not entirely correct. Some of the Chinese press had been scathing. The *Modern Daily News* noted that victim was a "beggar of a semi-colony, while the culprits [were] policemen of a great power." The editor of *Lung Yu* wrote sarcastically that he expected the verdict contained the expression: "The deceased lost his life because he could not swim."

John Brenan, the British Consul General was also dismayed saying in a note to the Foreign Office that British juries were most reluctant to convict a white man on Chinese evidence.

On a cold December morning, I retraced the route Peters and Judd had followed that fateful night. The bridge near to where Mau was found is still there. On three corners, the same buildings that were there in 1935 remain almost exactly as they were. Standing there, it was hard to believe that Peters and Judd (or any other human being) could have, in cold blood, thrown Mau in the river. Chapei, which was Chinese territory, was only a short drive away a couple of hundred metres. On the other hand, Peters in particular was in a foul mood. He had had a fight with his girlfriend. He had travelled on the running board of the police car in the freezing cold keeping a dirty filthy struggling Mau in place. Peters may have wanted to kill him; but why Judd? In any event, I am certain that he and Judd did not gently lower Mau onto a beggar boat as they describe. They had most likely manhandled him roughly over the side.

What was the truth? It is hard to say. What can be said is that three questions went unanswered during the trial, because neither side wanted to ask them.

First, Doo said that he heard a splash. Did he? It was a cold night. He had most likely left the car engine running and had his window closed. Priestwood did not ask how he heard the splash. Doo said he had heard the splash – it was for the defence to challenge this. McDonald and Reeks did not want to challenge him by asking a question they did not know the answer to. Perhaps he had, in fact, switched off the engine and wound down his window.

Second, was there a beggar boat there? Was there anyone

else on that beggar boat who might have thrown Doo off or forced him to leave? Beggar boats were not charities. Mau may have been asked for money if he wanted to stay or been told to get off. In his weakened condition he could have been thrown off easily or, if he tried to stand up, fallen into the river. Again, neither side needed to know the answers. For Peters and Judd in particular, going for "Murder or Nothing" they could not suggest that Mau had not been made safe. This would open the door to the jury to consider manslaughter.

Third and most confusing, Zung, the hawker, at the committal hearing before Registrar Haines had said he had seen two foreigners in uniform shining torch lights on the creek before the police car had driven off. This did not come out at the trial. But, as evidence coming soon after the incident, it was probably true. What were Peters and Judd doing shining their torches on the river? Zung did not mention this in his evidence at the trial; there was nothing Priestwood and McNeill could do about it. They were not allowed to ask leading questions to get the evidence from him. Reeks and McDonald could have cross-examined on it, but again it did not support a "Murder or Nothing" case. Reeks had, in fact, cross-examined Zung strongly on the point in the committal hearing, so it was not something he would have forgotten. If Mau had been safe, why would Peters and Judd have needed to shine their torch lights on the river?

Divine intervention?

Later the same year, Priestwood and Reeks were back in court in another high profile case where a policeman was accused of murder. This time, Priestwood had a much easier case to prosecute; Reeks had it tough. The policeman was not white, but Sikh, and there was no doubt that the victim had been killed by the accused. Atma Singh hacked another Sikh policeman, Bawa Singh, to death in the bathhouse of the Pootoo Road Police Station (on the corner of Pootoo Road

(Putou Road) and Gordon Road (Jiangning Road)) in the northwest of the International Settlement.

The killing was especially vicious. Sergeant Simms and Sergeant Peterson had heard terrible screams coming from the bathhouse. They went inside and found Bawa Singh lying on the floor. The floor and walls were splattered with blood. Bawa Singh had a deep chopper wound in his forehead and both his forearms had been almost severed. Bawa Singh was taken to hospital where he had both arms amputated and an eye removed. He died soon after of hemorrhage and shock.

Atma at the time was 32. He had been in the Shanghai Municipal Police for 12 years and had a clean record. He was put on trial before Penrhyn Grant Jones, as Acting Judge, and a jury of twelve Englishmen.

Atma had attacked Bawa because Bawa had disturbed his wife at home and then when confronted by Atma suggested he had had improprer relations with Atma's wife.

Grant Jones in summing up said that the presence of a person in a man's house is certainly sufficient to arouse justifiable indignation: but was it sufficient provocation to justify murder? He then reviewed the law and, taking advantage of the fact he had a jury to decide the case, said: "Well, Gentlemen you are men of the world, men of common sense, and I prefer to leave it – possibly you may call it shirking on my part – but I propose to leave the matter to you." After five minutes deliberation, the jury convicted Atma of murder. Before passing sentence, Grant Jones said to Singh:

> "You will recognize, I think, the righteousness of the saying contained in an old Book: 'Who-so sheddeth man's blood, by man shall his blood be shed'."

Grant Jones put on the black cap and sentenced Singh to death telling him in the time-honoured words that he would be "hanged by the neck until he was dead."

The British Ambassador, Sir Hughe Montgomery Knatchbull-Hugessen, confirmed the sentence just before Christmas 1936. Singh was scheduled to be hanged on December 29, 1936. Mr H. Plumb, a hangman with 12 years experience, was brought from Hong Kong.

Hanging is a complex business. The executioner must work out the exact length of rope to be used based on the prisoners weight and height. This is modified depending on the physique and muscularity, particularly of the neck. The goal is for the fall to break the prisoners neck; killing him instantly. If the calculation is wrong, the prisoner can either be slowly strangled or decapitated.

Darshan Singh, Singapore's former Chief Executioner, in order to calm those he was about to execute, would quietly say to them just before hanging them: "I am sending you to a better place than this." Darshan Singh had been trained by Singapore's last colonial hangman, Mr Seymour. Presumably this was the formula that had been passed down by all British hangmen to each other.

Plumb brought a rope with him from Hong Kong. In order to try out and stretch the rope, he conducted a test the day before the hanging using a sandbag attached to the rope. The sound must have been chilling to Atma Singh who had been placed in the condemned man's cell directly next door.

We can imagine the scene in Ward Road Gaol on that fateful day. Singh is pinioned by Sikh guards and brought into the small execution chamber. The rope is in position hanging above the trapdoor over a steel bar. The trapdoor had been specially designed to open directly into the prison's mortuary below. Plumb orders Singh to stand on the trapdoor. He places the noose around Singh's neck, firmly fixing the knot next to his ear. Singh, as a good loyal Sikh, presumably takes this all stoically, accepting it as God's will. The witnesses must have felt sick to the pit of their stomach. When everything is ready, the executioner tells Singh the last words he will ever hear: "I am sending you to a better place than this."

The next words from Plumb were an anguished cry: "My God! That's a Terrible Thing."

Atma Singh woke some time later in the police hospital. The rope had broken. Singh was still breathing and had been rushed for medical treatment. His neck had been stretched two inches (six cm) by the hanging and he had suffered a concussion. His first words were to ask for some water. He then said: "I thought you were going to hang me." Due to the damage to his throat he was kept on a liquid diet for over two weeks.

Sir John Brenan, the Consul-General, as Sheriff, immediately convened an enquiry. Cyril Haines, the Registrar of the court, assisted Brenan. Plumb, the Governor of the prison and a number of other witnesses were examined. Two ships' captains also gave evidence as experts on ropes.

The explanation was, in the end, remarkably simple. In Hong Kong, the rope was thrown over a round wooden girder when a prisoner was hanged. In Ward Road Gaol, a steel "I" shaped girder had been installed. This was intended to be used with a specially designed shackle. Plumb was not provided with a shackle, so he followed the procedure he had always used in Hong Kong.

The enquiry found that the edge of the beam had cut the rope. Fragments of rope were found on the beam and the place the rope had broken matched where the rope had passed over the beam. The ships' captains confirmed that they considered this was the cause.

British officials now had to decide whether to hang Atma again. One suspects many of them would have believed in divine

Sir John Brenan, asks, why did the rope break?

intervention. Grant Jones, having quoted the Old Testament when sentencing Singh, must surely have had doubts. Brenan and the British Ambassador were against carrying out a new execution. Grant Jones supported a reprieve. Singh's sentence was commuted to life imprisonment.

Problems after Midnight in Peking

In the mid 1930s, tensions were very high in North China. Peiping (as Peking was now known) was almost completely surrounded by Japanese troops. Since occupying Manchuria, the Japanese had slowly been extending their control of provinces north of Peiping. Using their rights under the Boxer Protocol, they had also stationed large numbers of troops on the railway line between Tientsin and Peiping. A large legation guard was stationed in Peiping. The foreign powers also had substantial troop presences in Peiping. Tensions between Japan and China and Japan and foreign powers were high.

In June 1936, in the badlands in Peiping – a strip of virtually unregulated bars and entertainment venues near the city wall – the actions of three British soldiers heightened the already high tensions between Britain and Japan. The soldiers, Herbert Cooke, T.D. Parrish and Ralph Hunt, from the embassy guard were accused of killing a Japanese officer, Kisaku Sasaki, in the street, and assaulting another Japanese, Mr Onishi, in a Korean bar, The No. 27.

Given the importance of the case, Victor Priestwood, the Crown Advocate, flew from Shanghai to Peiping to prosecute at the preliminary inquiry. He dropped the case against Parrish. Japanese officials, including Mr Okamura, second secretary of the Japanese embassy, were present. British Vice-Consul, Nicholas Fitzmaurice conducted the enquiry.

The hearing went on for two weeks and numerous Japanese, Chinese and Koreans were called to give evidence, all needing translation into English. One particularly testy exchange showed the tensions at the time between the Japanese and British. When a barboy from the Korean bar was giving evidence in Chinese, the British interpreter, Mr G.W. Creighton, the Assistant Chinese Secretary at the Embassy, motioned him to silence.

Mr Okamura said loudly, "Let him speak."

Priestwood chastised Okamura: "Excuse me, Mr Okamura, I am in charge of this examination and intend to conduct it."

Okamura responded "Please let the Chinese Chief of Police interpret. Mr Creighton is interrupting the witness and I object. I have the right."

"You have no right," retorted Priestwood coldly.

At the end of the hearings, Fitzmaurice held that there was insufficient evidence to try Cooke or Hunt for the killing of Sasaki. Cooke was remanded for trial for assault and causing bodily harm of Onishi. As the charge no longer was that of unlawful killing, which would have required a trial in the Supreme Court, Priestwood withdrew from the case, leaving the prosecution to the local British consular staff. Cooke was tried in the British Magistrate's Court in Peiping, but acquitted on the basis that the magistrate believed he had not been present when Onishi was attacked.

The Japanese Residents' Association organized an "indignation meeting" and asked the British Embassy for a "just solution." They also telegraphed to the Japanese Army headquarters in Tientsin and the Ministries of War and Navy in Tokyo. Three British soldiers were fired at in a drive-by shooting on their way back from the cinema.

A spokesman for the Japanese Embassy criticized the verdict, resulting in a question in the British Parliament as to what was being done about it. The Secretary State for Foreign Affairs, Mr Eden, replied that the matter had been brought to the attention of the Japanese government.

Not long after Cooke's acquittal, in January 1937, a 19-year-old British schoolgirl, Pamela Werner, the adopted daughter of Edward Werner, a former British consular officer (and barrister) was brutally murdered in Peiping. Her body was found beneath a watchtower of the city wall. Her stomach had been sliced open and all her internal organs removed. Her death was investigated by the British authorities and a number of hearings were held into her death in the British Consular Court in Peiping without reaching any satisfactory conclusion. No suspect was prosecuted, although a number of Americans suspects were identified.

The same year, a British army officer, Lieutenant Wilson, attacked a 19-year-old French girl on the roof of the Peking Hotel. He was charged with rape in the British Consular Court, the same court that was also responsible for the coronial inquests into the killing of Pamela Werner and had tried Cooke and Hunt. After a preliminary hearing, Consul Archer dismissed the case against Wilson on the basis that a jury would not have convicted.

Archer, nevertheless, sent a detailed report on the case to Judge Allan Mossop in Shanghai. He wrote that he would not normally send a long report with the case record. However, the French girl had after the acquittal, for reasons Archer attributed to "youth, French nationality, and ignorance of British judicial procedure," accused him of letting Wilson off because he was a British army officer. Further, and probably the true reason, he said he was sending the report because the Consulate and Court was "under criticism for alleged lack of energy and even integrity in connection with the still unsolved murder of Pamela Werner." Archer lamented "the singularly unfortunate accident that I should have been called upon to hear and decide another serious case affecting safety of young women in Peking."

Archer and his Vice-Consul, Nicholas Fitzmaurice, who was sitting as coroner in the Pamela Werner case may have been singularly unlucky. Their handling of the Sasaki case may have been the cause of Pamela Werner's death. A year

later, Sir Edmund Backhouse, a noted China scholar, wrote
to the British Embassy that he had received information the
murder of Pamela Werner had been carried out by the Japanese
as revenge for the acquittal of Cooke and Hunt. Backhouse
may have been a fantasist. He wrote memoirs where he
claimed to have engaged in sex orgies in the Forbidden
City and even to have had sex with the Empress Dowager
herself. Nevertheless, his story is given some credence by Mr
Creighton who interpreted at the trial of Cooke and Hunt.
Many years later he wrote that the killing of Pamela Werner
was a "Japanese revenge act" against the British consular
authorities for the acquittal of Cooke and Hunt. He continued:
"After all they easily could have found out that Werner was
still living in Peking, was a former British Consul, so if they
couldn't get Fitzmaurice's hippopotamic wife, then why not
get the Werner girl?..."

Extraterritoriality tested: The China Eastern Railway Zone

The Japanese were certainly, at the time, aggressively
asserting their rights in Manchuria where two British subjects,
both Indians, suffered the wrath of the Japanese police in the
China Eastern Railway Zone. The railway had originally been
built by the Russians from east to west across Manchuria to
connect Vladivostok to the rest of Russia. A spur line, the
South Manchurian Railway had been built from Harbin to
Dalian.

The Japanese had taken over most of the South Manchurian
Railway following their victory over Russia in 1905. The
Railway Zone was a sixty-metre wide strip of land on either
side of the railway line. The zone had been created when the
line was built to allow for effective management of the line
and to provide security. In cities, this meant that properties
built near the railway fell within the zone.

The Japanese were prepared to allow extraterritoriality
to continue in Manchukuo. But they took a different view in

relation to the CER, asserting that they had sole jurisdiction over all people in the zone. Despite this, in most cases, they allowed other powers to exercise jurisdiction in the zone over their own subjects as well.

In mid-1937, the difficulties of this *modus vivendi* came to the fore in a case where two Indian employees of a British shopkeeper in Mukden (Shenyang), Motwani and Lahkati, were arrested for suspected arson by the Japanese police. After numerous protests by the British, they were released. The British Consul in Mukden, P.D. Butler, wanted to put them on trial in the British Consular Court and issued a warrant for their arrest. In order to avoid "political complications", Butler ordered the warrant only be executed outside the zone.

Butler faced the difficulty that the Japanese police would not assist the prosecution in the British court. Butler had written to the acting Japanese Consul-General in Mukden, C. Yoshimura on June 7, 1937, requesting Japanese police and fire brigade officers to give evidence in court. In a formal letter to Butler the next day, Yoshimura rejected this request stating: "I regret that I am unable to comply with this request, as a question of principle is involved."

Butler had no evidence on which to base a prosecution. Foreseeing this possibility, he had telegraphed the Supreme Court in Shanghai asking if he could rely on a letter "from the Japanese Consul embodying an outline of the Japanese police case against the men who have been examined by them and of whose guilt they profess themselves convinced."

Mossop immediately responded that the "letter from Japanese Consul would not be admissible as evidence," and that any preliminary examination must be held in "strict compliance with provisions of China Rules of Court, 1905." Butler had to release the men who, though under no immediate threat of arrest by the Japanese, chose to leave Mukden to avoid further problems. Butler in a letter to the British Charge d'Affaires in Tokyo described the outcome of the case as "highly unsatisfactory" as the attitude of the Japanese authorities had made a proper judicial investigation of the case almost impossible.

Even after this, the Japanese police continued to exercise their claimed rights in the zone by arresting and beating the Chinese employee of the British insurance company who had come to investigate the fire.

These difficulties of protecting extraterritorial rights in Japanese-occupied territories were only a very small taste of what was to come.

Chapter 30

Dark Days

THE YEARS FROM MID-1937 onwards were dark days in extraterritorial China. In the late summer of 1937, Japan occupied the whole of China's eastern seaboard leaving foreign concessions completely surrounded by Japanese-controlled territories, making them, as they were called at the time, "solitary islands."

In Shanghai, there was intense fighting throughout the Chinese part of the city between Japanese and Chinese troops outside the International Settlement and French Concession that went on for five months. The Japanese battleship the HJIMS *Idzumo* shelled Chinese positions from its position in front of the Cathay Hotel (Peace Hotel) on the Huangpu River. The Chinese returned fire with their shells often missing and falling on the International Settlement. During the war local papers all carried reports on difficulties for travel out of Shanghai; battles all around the city; and, Japanese victory parades through the streets of the International Settlement. One foreign newspaper carried a map of the city under the heading "Shanghai Doomed City."

Officials of the courts evacuated their families from Shanghai. United States District Attorney Leighton Shields, who was in Japan at the time with his family, was advised to stay there. This was not due to over-cautiousness. British and Americans were attacked during the fighting. On August 26, the official car of the British Ambassador, Sir

DESTRUCTION IN SHANGHAI.—Land, air and sea fighting by Japanese and Chinese in Shanghai, China, is fast reducing the "Paris of the Orient" to ruins. This map shows location of (1) Cathay and Palace hotels, (2) Japanese cruiser Izumo, (3) Japanese Consulate, (4) Pootung, with American and British warehouses, and (5) Japanese barracks at Hangkew. All were bombed.

2. Is in fact the location of the hotels, and
3. Is the location of the Idzumo and consulate

Hughe Montgomery Knatchbull-Hugessen, was strafed by two Japanese fighters between Nanking and Shanghai and the Ambassador shot through the chest. He survived but was evacuated to Hong Kong after being hospitalized for a month. Two months later in October, a British Embassy car with the Union Jack painted on its roof was attacked by Japanese fighters, but no one injured. In December 1937, the

USS *Panay*, a Yangtze River gunboat, anchored near Nanking was attacked and sunk by Japanese warplanes.

In order to reduce attacks on Japanese nationals by Chinese fighters, the Japanese took complete control of the Hongkew and Yangtzepoo sections in the north of the International Settlement. They installed barricades on the bridges across Soochow Creek and refused access to the area to all citizens of other nations, including the non-Japanese police of the Shanghai Municipal Police. Police officers and firemen who tried to enter the area were repeatedly attacked by Japanese troops.

The Japanese were not yet ready to fight the other foreign powers and made no attempt to occupy the International Settlement as a whole, but from time to time, they sealed off sections of the city after attacks on Japanese nationals. On December 7, 1937, the Japanese army closed a large section of the Nanking Road area following an attack on a victory parade on that road.

The Japanese occupation of Eastern China meant that life became harder for foreign policemen in Shanghai. Guidelines for the Shanghai Municipal Police issued in 1938 required that a Japanese police officer should be present at all raids where Japanese may be arrested and, chillingly warned that the "officer in charge of the raiding party is responsible for any unlawful entry into the houses of innocent persons." Helpfully, the Guidelines stated that "Japanese residences may be easily distinguished by the painting of a cherry blossom on a wooden block at each doorway."

End of extraterritoriality off the table

In December 1937, Japan captured Nanking, the Chinese capital, and massacred over 100,000 civilians in what has become known as the Rape of Nanking. The Nationalist Government moved to Chungking. The Japanese established a "Provisional Government of China" in Peiping in December

1937, but moved the government to Nanking the following month as the "Reformed Government of the Republic of China." The Chinese courts outside the foreign concessions all came under control of this puppet government. However, in Shanghai, still under British and American control, the Special District Court remained independent from the Japanese-controlled Chinese government of Kiangwan (Jiangwan) and continued to be loyal to the Nationalist Government.

The Japanese attacks meant that the question of ending extraterritorial rights in China was taken completely off the table. United States Secretary for State Cordell Hull said the invasion made it necessary for American armed units to remain in China and that to pull them out would look like weakness. He added, "the Chinese themselves, although previously eager to have extraterritorial rights annulled were anxious for us to stay, since they felt that withdrawal of our troops would appear like abandoning China to her fate..."

Nor did the Japanese seek to abolish extraterritorial rights in China for foreign nationals. In 1938, the British Prime Minister, was asked in the House of Commons "whether his attention has been drawn to the official declaration by the Japanese spokesman in Shanghai that the Japanese Government intends to abolish extra-territorial rights in those portions of China which are in Japanese occupation; and whether he is in a position to make any statement on the matter?" Mr Butler responded on behalf of the Prime Minister that the Japanese government had advised that the Japanese spokesman was misunderstood:

"The Japanese Government had no intention of using the present situation in China as a pretext for denying the extra-territorial rights enjoyed by Great Britain and other Powers vis-á-vis China. They consider that this is a question which solely concerns the Powers and China."

The spokesman's statement was explained as meaning that:

"should individual foreigners contrive to endanger the safety of the Japanese forces or to impede the conduct of their military operations, these forces will naturally take the necessary actions against them."

The Sino-Japanese war and the courts

The war brought a number of problems to the British and American courts. The United States Court faced the particular problem of how to deal with companies that were incorporated as American companies but were in reality Chinese owned and controlled. This was less of a problem in the British courts because of a 1919 Order in Council that required the senior management of a British company to be British.

Things became particularly problematic when Chinese sought to transfer their interests in properties to American companies so as to put them out of reach of the Japanese. Soon after occupying the area around Shanghai, the Japanese military authorities announced that they would not recognize any transfers of properties by Chinese to foreigners after August 13, 1937.

Under the principles of extraterritoriality, this declaration should not have been binding on foreign courts. No foreign power could tell another what to do. However, Milton Helmick, Judge of the United States Court for China, later explained that "there was such supine acceptance of the Japanese fiat in all quarters that conveyances from Chinese to foreigners were regarded as transfers in fraud of creditors." Helmick explained this supineness as being based on "the earnest wish of the United States not to risk the lives of its sailors and marines or maybe provoke a war with Japan by assuming protection of property ostensibly American but actually Chinese."

One transfer that was effected and that particularly annoyed the Japanese was the transfer of the *Shunpao* (*Shenbao*), a Chinese language newspaper, from its owner I.K. Shih to American lawyer Norwood Allman. Shih, who was only 20 years old, had inherited the paper from his father Shih LiangTsai who had been assassinated in 1935, most likely on the orders of Chiang Kai-shek. The *Shunpao* had been founded by a British tea merchant, F. Major, in 1872 and had always had an independent editorial policy. After the Japanese invasion, the younger Shih, as Allman put it, "wanted to keep it that way. He did not want to capitulate to the Japs, nor was he ready to die." He shut the paper down for a while but this put the employees out of work. Shih came to Allman for advice. Allman told him that "it would be the better part of valour for him to leave Shanghai until conditions change." Allman agreed to take over the newspaper. He set up an American company to do so and, as he put it, "neither I nor this American company ever advanced any claim to owning the paper, it was well known to everyone in Shanghai that I was publishing and editing the *Shunpao* for the Chinese owner, but on my own responsibility." These actions led to the *Shunpao* being bombed on a number of occasions and to Allman being placed on a Japanese blacklist.

Most cases where a company was transferred from Americans to Chinese were dealt with by the consular authorities, who usually refused to recognise the transfer. However, one particular tricky case came before Helmick in the US Court. William Hunt, a former consular officer and entrepreneur, had entered various debt guarantees with China Merchants Steam Navigation Company. China Merchants was largely owned by the Chinese government and operated vessels along the coast or on the inland waterways of China. After the war with Japan started, Hunt announced he had taken over all the assets of China Merchants because it had defaulted on its debt. Many suspected that the transactions were a sham designed to keep the shipping company out of Japanese hands. The US consular authorities refused to recognize the transfer.

Helmick said he never dreamed that the issue would end up in his court. But in 1938, China Merchants filed an application for an injunction to prevent Hunt from seizing their ships in areas of China the Japanese did not control. Helmick noted drily: "Apparently China Merchants had no objection to Hunt taking over in areas where the Japanese were menacing." To Helmick, it was clear "that both sides wanted the same decision – an adjudication that Hunt was the lawful owner of China Merchants," made by the United States Court for China.

The application for an injunction was a neat trick to give the US Court jurisdiction. Normally, Hunt would have been required to bring a case in court to have his ownership under the contracts confirmed. However, this would have required him to bring a case in a Chinese court. The Special District Court in Shanghai was still under Nationalist control so he could have filed there or in a part of China the Nationalists controlled. Or he could have also brought a case in a court in Japanese-controlled China. A judgment from a Nationalist-controlled court would be useless against the Japanese. The outcome of an application to a Japanese-controlled court could be easily predicted.

A way had to be found to make Hunt a defendant so that the US Court could have jurisdiction. This was done by seeking an injunction against him. Helmick suspected collusion, but "it would have been a painfully delicate thing to suggest to the Chinese Government, which was the virtual plaintiff, that the United States Court for China would not hear its suit and action on moral grounds, and besides I had no evidence of collusion."

Helmick confessed to doing the "unusual thing of

conferring with Consul General C.E. Gauss about it." Gauss was not particularly shocked and suggested that the parties were entitled to bring some kind of test case. Helmick allowed the case to proceed and both parties produced their contracts which were dated in 1936 and 1937. It was suggested, of course, that they may have been backdated, but one of the contracts was also with Hong Kong & Shanghai Banking Corporation whose manager confirmed the date of the contracts. Helmick, in his judgment, held that Hunt was entitled to do what he wanted to enforce the contracts and refused the injunction. He doubted, however, "whether the decision did anyone much good." He did not make a finding that Hunt now owned the ships, nor did the decision get the State Department to offer Hunt extraterritorial protection. It did, as he wrote later, show the dates on the contracts were not backdated.

Does Piper have to pay?

One case in the British Supreme Court related directly to the fighting between the Chinese and Japanese. Kenneth Piper had rented a large house at 21 Granada Estates on Hungjao Road (Hongqiao Road) intending to live there with his wife and two children aged seven and two. Hungjao Road was located outside the International Settlement boundaries but was treated as part of the Settlement by the Municipal Council because it was an extension of a road from the Settlement. Such niceties did not impress the Japanese and Chinese armies which fought pitched battles from August to December 1937 in the area. The area was sealed off with barricades and residents were refused access by the Settlement authorities.

Houses owned by foreigners were not immune from attack. This was partly due to a Chinese anti-aircraft battery being located near to the Granada Estates attracting Japanese fighter planes trying to destroy it. On 14 October, one house at 140 Hungjao Road owned by a German, Mr Wilhelm Moller, and flying the German Swastika on its roof, was directly hit by a bomb. Piper moved out of his house when the war started in August 1937. By February 1938 the fighting had died down, but the British Consul-General still warned that it was not safe for British subjects, particularly women and children, to live in the area. In June 1938 Granada Estates, the landlord, sued Piper for rent for February to May 1938. No claim was made for rent for November 1937 to January 1938.

Piper defended the claim on the basis that the premises were unsafe to live in and that "occupation and or enjoyment of the premises has been and still is further prevented by the restriction of normal access to the Hungjao area, including the closing of all access by the Japanese authorities on various occasions, curfew regulations, lawless acts and looting, guerrilla fighting and lack of any normal policing or maintenance of order."

All good reasons, one would think, not to pay rent. But when the case came before Judge Allan Mossop in the British Supreme Court, Mossop disagreed. English law had always given strong protection to landlords. Relying on a 300-year-old case from 1647, *Paradine v Jane*, Mossop held that even if a tenant was expelled by a trespasser, the tenant had to pay rent.

British spies for Japan?

The Sino-Japanese war also brought espionage cases before the British courts in China. In two cases, the Chinese government requested British citizens, Miss Kathleen Weston and Peter Prevot, be arrested and tried for spying on behalf of the Japanese against China.

Weston was accused of working with a German, Karl Rein, to gather information about Chinese troop movements. Weston and Rein had travelled from Canton to Hankow by car, leaving on May 8, 1938 and only arriving on 21 May, taking almost two weeks to complete a trip that should normally take three days. Upon their return to Canton, Rein and Weston were arrested by the Chinese police. Weston agreed to be detained at the British Consulate until evidence to support a charge could be brought. In the end, the Chinese authorities said they believed that Weston did not have knowledge of Rein's activities and allowed her to be released.

Prevot was arrested by Chinese military police as he tried to leave Hankow by plane to Hong Kong, where he had been born. He had posted a letter addressed to himself in Hong Kong that discussed the relations between the Nationalists and the Communists; troop movements; and, the war between China and Japan. After interrogation by the Chinese police (which he had strongly objected to as a breach of his extraterritorial rights), he was taken to the British Consulate. The Chinese pushed for him to be prosecuted, but the Consul in Hankow could not find an offence to charge him with. He cabled Victor Priestwood, the Crown Advocate, for advice. Priestwood advised that a charge under Article 89(1)(a) of the Order in Council for committing acts likely to breach the peace would be appropriate. Prevot was charged and pleaded guilty. He was ordered to be deported to Hong Kong by plane, which he was.

Spying was not the only activity that could get foreigners in trouble with the Japanese or Chinese authorities. In June 1939, the British in Shanghai and Tientsin were to find out exactly what was meant by the explanation given in British Parliament as to the Japanese position on extraterritoriality:

"should any individual foreigners contrive to endanger the safety of the Japanese forces or to impede the conduct of their military operations, these forces will naturally take the necessary actions against them."

In Shanghai, it was one individual who would suffer; in Tientsin, it was the entire British community.

Tinkler, failure, soldier, spy

Former Inspector of the Shanghai Municipal Police, Richard Maurice Tinkler, was by 1939 a failure in life. He had resigned from the police force in 1930 after having been demoted back to be a sergeant in the uniformed division for various misconduct offences. He had drifted for the next nine years before washing up ashore on the Putong side of the Huangpu River as the Labour Superintendent of the China Printing and Finishing Company's Lun Chong Mill. The mill was owned by a British company and workers came over to the plant from the Shanghai side by boat. The land gates, which led on to Japanese-occupied territory, were locked. Tinkler stayed at the plant and kept detailed notes on Japanese ship movements which he passed on to the British consulate.

The mill was facing serious communist agitation. As a result of a labour incident, Tinkler ended up in an altercation with Japanese troops. This brought him back into a British court in Shanghai for the last time, as a hero.

A dead hero, but nevertheless a hero.

And, Tinkler did, literally, appear in court. Following his death at the Shanghai General Hospital, Registrar Cyril Haines, as coroner, convened an inquest at the hospital to identify his body. Mr Robert Cowan, director of the China Printing and Finishing Co formally identified him. Haines then ordered an autopsy.

Earlier the previous day, Japanese troops had been called to the mill due to labour unrest. Tinkler had met them with a loaded revolver which he had waved around. He also fired one warning shot into the ground. His colleagues had tried to get him to go back indoors and to put the gun away. Tinkler had been a solider in World War I, and had killed many men. As a former soldier and policeman, he well knew that the only thing that can happen from challenging a superior force was that, at the very least, you would get a beating. He had certainly given out some beatings when he was in the police force.

The Japanese soldiers knocked the gun out of his hand. They then gave him his beating. Unfortunately, they did this with rifles to which bayonets had been fixed. Tinkler was bayonetted three times in the stomach. He was first treated by a Japanese naval surgeon at a Japanese military hospital, but when his condition worsened he was transferred late at night to the Shanghai General Hospital where he died after emergency surgery.

His death caused an uproar in the British community and the British Government ordered their Ambassador in Tokyo to take the matter up with the Japanese government.

A Japanese spokesman, explained that the Japanese military respected extraterritorial rights but in diplomatese conveyed the clear message: "Keep out of our way." He said:

"in any case of a person threatening the safety of the Japanese forces in occupied territory it was only natural that his extraterritorial rights would be limited ... It would not be a question of application to the law but of direct action necessary to maintain the safety of the Japanese Forces. It would be an act of law but a summary act."

The spokesman continued that after investigations, a treaty foreigner would be handed over to his consular authorities. The inquest into Tinkler's death reconvened on June 15, 1939 at the Police Court before Coroner Haines. The hearing continued for five days with evidence from his colleagues who had been at the plant and the doctors at the General Hospital who had treated him. No Japanese came to give evidence at the inquest, despite being invited to. Haines delivered his verdict on June 21. He made brief findings saying that the evidence disclosed "a most deplorable story" and that the "bayonetting of Tinkler after he has been disarmed" was "entirely unnecessary and unjustifiable." He criticized the Japanese Naval Surgeon for failing to appreciate the gravity of Tinkler's injuries.

He then gave his verdict. Almost 80 years previously when Charles Richardson had been killed by a Japanese samurai outside Yokohama, British gunboats had shelled and almost destroyed Kagoshima to obtain justice.

Times had changed.

The extraterritorial boot was now well and truly on the other foot. Haines could only find that Tinkler had died:

> "as a result of injuries inflicted on him by persons not subject to the jurisdiction of this court."

He dared not even state that Tinkler had been killed by Japanese soldiers.

Produce the bodies

In Tientsin, things were getting far uglier between the British and Japanese than a dispute over the death of a labour supervisor. During the year, in both Tientsin and Amoy, the Japanese had

Japanese troops blockade the British Concession in Tientsin

blockaded the British Concessions to force the British to agree to hand over Chinese silver that had been stored in banks in the concessions. In Tientsin, the Japanese also demanded the right to supervise criminal trials against Chinese.

By June, things had heated up. Four Chinese who were suspected by the Japanese authorities in Tientsin of having assassinated, on April 9, 1939, Cheng Shi-kang, manager of Tientsin branch of the Federal Reserve Bank and Customs Commissioner. The Chinese suspects had fled to the British Settlement in Tientsin and were detained by the British at the Municipal Council gaol.

For the Japanese it was very important that they punish the alleged killers. The Japanese were intent on establishing Chinese-led governments in the areas they controlled. Cheng had come over to work for the Japanese puppet government in Tientsin. At the time Cheng was killed, the Japanese were assiduously pursuing Wang Ching-wei, the major rival to Chiang Kai-shek in the Nationalist Party to lead their reformed government. They had to do everything in their power to show Chinese they were wooing that they would be protected.

The Japanese-controlled government of Tientsin made a request to the British authorities for the suspects to be handed over for trial. Evidence was provided to show their complicity in the murder but the British did not think it sufficient. The Japanese became frustrated at the refusal of the British to hand over the suspects and in early June 1939 the Japanese consul at Tientsin demanded that the suspects be delivered to the Japanese authorities by June 6, 1939.

The suspects were not handed over and the Japanese started to enforce a blockade of the British Concession as well as the French Concession which was next door to the British Concession. The Japanese stated that it was necessary to blockade the French Concession to ensure the British concession remained isolated. The British and

French concessions were completely surrounded. Barbed wire was put up in the streets around the concessions and electrical fences placed around the non-urban areas.

The matter was dealt with at the highest levels between the British and Japanese governments. The British Prime Minister even faced intense questioning over the affair in the House of Commons.

A Dutch cartoon shows British Prime Minister Chamberlain in a Japanese headlock

By August, after receiving further evidence from the Japanese, the British authorities made a decision to hand the suspects over to the puppet authorities for trial. This was met with an immediate protest by the Nationalist government in Chungking that the suspects should only be handed over to Nationalist Chinese authorities.

Seeking to save the suspects, Professor Norman Bentwich, Professor of International Law at Jerusalem University and the former British Attorney General of Palestine, and Marjory Fry, a human rights campaigners based in London, instructed British barrister Hugh Reeks to make an urgent application to the British Supreme Court in Shanghai for a writ of habeas corpus to be issued against the British municipal gaol in Tientsin for the prisoners to be brought before a judge of the British Court. A first hearing of the application came on before Allan Mossop on August 12, 1939. He ordered that the application be heard later in the week.

Grant Jones heard the application. On August 17, 1939 he handed down a decision rejecting the writ. In his decision, he did not consider any of the political aspects of the case, but relied on case law that the person making the application must have some standing and that a "mere stranger or volunteer could not do so." He also said that there should have been an affidavit from the Chinese prisoners or someone with authority to act on their behalf. There was no such affidavit in this case. The applicants had relied on the case *Re Gooloo and Invokwana* where the British and Foreign Anti Slavery Society had been able to bring an application. Grant Jones noted that no similar society had made an application in China.

Professor Bentwich and Ms Fry were, however, not going to give up so easily. They made an immediate application to the High Court in London for a writ of habeas corpus against Lord Halifax, the Foreign Secretary, the British Consul-General at Tientsin, the chairman of the British Municipal Council, and the gaoler of the municipal prison. This time the application was made on their behalves and, presumably to avoid the standing issue, on behalf of the "China Campaign Committee." Justice Cassels granted leave for the summons to issue and a full hearing was held a few days later with Sir Walter Monckton KC appearing for the applicants and the Solicitor-General, Sir Terence O'Connor KC, for the Foreign Secretary. The Solicitor-General pointed out the absurdity of the idea of the four Chinese suspects being brought to London to determine the question of the legality of their detention saying:

> "The application for the production of these four men here is very little short of a fantasy ... I cannot say what percentage of the Home Fleet might be necessary to secure such production."

Cassels decided that, under Britain's treaties with China,

the court had no power to make an order for habeas corpus when the suspects were not British citizens and had never resided in the British Settlement. They were being detained for the purposes of handing them over for trial in the Chinese District Court and this could not be considered illegal. He therefore dismissed the application.

Bentwich and Fry would not give up, and on September 1 they made a new application to Grant Jones having obtained the authority of the Chinese suspects. Grant Jones ordered there be a full hearing on September 11. Unfortunately for the Chinese, they were handed over and executed before the final hearing could be held.

The Japanese blockade was lifted.

Change in Crown Advocate

The pressures of being Crown Advocate in Japanese-occupied China also appeared to have got to Victor Priestwood. Soon after the Chinese suspects were executed, he was terminated. The Consul-General, Herbert Phillips, and other officials had felt uneasy for some time with Priestwood's performance, and particularly that he was prone to excessive drinking.

It was the view of all concerned that John McNeill, who had acted as Crown Advocate in 1937 when Priestwood was on leave, was the best man to replace Priestwood. McNeill, like Priestwood and Wilkinson before him, had a father who had practiced before the court. John McNeill was the younger son of Duncan McNeill who was a barrister who practiced in Yokohama and then Shanghai for more than 30 years from the early 1890s to 1926. Duncan McNeill had also acted as Crown Advocate between 1902 and 1903.

McNeill took over as Crown Advocate at a time when things were going to get even tougher than they had been for Victor Priestwood.

CHAPTER 31

Live by the Gunboat…

THE LAST TWO YEARS of the effective exercise of extraterritorial rights in China by Britain and the United States were a very difficult time in China. War had broken out in Europe at the end of 1939. It was clear that war between Japan and the Western powers was coming to China sometime soon. The foreign settlements saw an exodus of foreign residents.

In Shanghai, this exodus had an immediate effect on the Municipal Council's revenues, the finances of which were also being stretched by retirements by officials keen to cash out their superannuation while they could. The Council started trying to collect rates from Chinese residents who continued to hold land in the settlements under fangtan title deeds. Approximately one-fifth of the land in the International Settlement was owned under such deeds. Mr Justice Feetham when he had prepared his report on extraterritoriality had expressed surprise that Chinese owners were not taxed by the Council. When the Council tried to tax them, Chinese landholders brought a suit against it in the Court of Consuls to determine whether owners of land under fangtan title deeds could be taxed. The Council was also forced to levy a 40% surcharge on rates with effect from 1 January 1940. This upset the Japanese residents in particular and at a special meeting convened to pass the resolution W. J. Keswick, the Chairman of the Council was shot and wounded by a Japanese, Mr Y. Hayashi. Despite all this, the British and American courts continued to function handling many dark cases that came about from living in the shadow of impending war.

Soldiering on

Perhaps the people with the most difficult job in Shanghai during this time were soldiers in the British and American military forces stationed in Shanghai, purportedly to defend the International Settlement. This must have been a soul-destroying post. Even though the Japanese had relaxed some of the pressure they had put on in 1937 and the situation was less tense than it had been then, the only enemy the British and American soldiers could possibly be fighting was the Japanese. It was clear that they were outgunned and outmanned. What made matters worse is that they did not even have a defensive line. The Japanese were just as entitled to enter the International Settlement as the British and Americans. Fully armed Japanese troops regularly passed by British and American soldiers on guard duty.

This pressure led to a number of tragedies. On November 4, 1939, Private David Eckford of the Seaforth Highlanders was on sentry duty with Lance Corporal Davis and three other privates in a blockhouse on North Thibet Road on the edge of the International Settlement. Eckford had drunk about six bottles of beer and was drunk. Davis told Eckford he was placing him on report for being drunk on duty. Soon after this Eckford shot Davis. Eckford admitted that Davis had been killed by a shot from a gun that he was holding but denied that he had intended to kill Davis. He said that he merely intended to scare him. The British Army could have court martialled Eckford, but instead chose to hand him over to the Supreme Court for trial.

The case was the first case to be prosecuted by John McNeill after his formal appointment as Crown Advocate. After hearing the evidence, the jury returned a verdict of guilty of murder but with a recommendation for mercy. Judge Allan Mossop then, for the last time, in the British Supreme

Court for China, passed a sentence of death. He was however a vocal local campaign reprieved and sent to England to be imprisoned for life.

The last British troops were pulled out of Shanghai towards the end of 1940. The British government knew that it was impossible to defend Shanghai against the Japanese and that the Settlement was only allowed to survive because the Japanese were not yet ready for war with the Western powers.

Marine kills baby

US Marines, however, remained until almost the end of 1941, bringing a very sad case before Milton Helmick in the US Court. Private Gerald Casement was charged with the murder of his stepson, Floyd "Skipper" Sebastian. Casement, who was from Nebraska, was only 22 at the time. He had studied at high school for one year and joined the marines at 17 or 18. He had already served in North China and recently been transferred to Shanghai. Against regulations, he had married in Shanghai. Skipper had been born some time earlier to another man. Casement was normally required to live on base, but when he got leave he would return home to the one-room apartment he shared with his wife and Skipper. They had a Chinese maid who stayed overnight if necessary.

Casement was given liberty on March 12, 1941 at 1.45pm. He first went on a drinking spree with his buddy, Homer Triplet. The Chinese Amah said that Casement came home drunk that evening. "Missie" was in hospital, but Casement told the amah she could stay and sleep on the floor if she wanted. She went home, planning to come back in the morning.

The next thing anyone saw of Casement was when the watchman of the compound where they lived saw a marine leaving the compound on Seymour Road (Shaanxi North Road) before sunrise with a package under his arm. The badly beaten body of Skipper was found and Casement was put on trial for murder.

No motive was offered for the killing, a point Casement's attorney was to make in his closing speech, but perhaps unspoken in the court was the suggestion that Casement had killed the baby in a fit of jealous rage when he found himself home alone with the child of his wife's former lover. The frustrations of being a soldier in a city everyone conceded could not be defended must have contributed to his anger.

The District Attorney, Leighton Shields, summed up saying the case against Casement was damning and concluded that the only thing to do with Casement was to "send him to the chair."

Helmick adjourned the trial until the next day. The next morning, before a packed courtroom in a very short judgment, Helmick convicted Casement of second-degree murder and sentenced him to imprisonment for the term of his natural life on McNeil Island.

The sad case of Mr Turner and Mr Kau

In the last unlawful killing case to come before the British Supreme Court, Mr E.C. Turner was prosecuted for the accidental killing of Kau Kwang-sung, a coolie working at his house. By 1941, western Shanghai faced a serious law and order crisis. The overlapping jurisdictions of the SMP, Chinese police and Japanese police made proper policing almost impossible. In 1940, an agreement had been reached to improve policing, but still with the ever-declining economy and war ravaging China, crime was at an all-time high. Turner had lived in Shanghai most of his adult life and had been senior architect with the Shanghai Municipal Council for 22 years from 1904 to 1926 when he had retired. By May 1941, his house was being regularly robbed by thieves. In response, Turner set up .22 calibre rifles as booby traps in his garden to keep away marauders. On May 18, Kau Kwang-sung, a grass cutter's coolie working at his property was shot and killed by one of the booby traps. Turner was arrested and committed for trial before Grant Jones in July 1941. Turner pleaded guilty to unlawfully killing Kau. Mr Jones appearing for Turner then spent close to a day pleading for a light sentence. He told Grant Jones that Turner had already paid $1,500 for Kau's burial and to buy his eldest son a larger plot of land so he could provide for the family. A trust fund had also been set up for the family and in total $7,000 had been paid.

Jones closed his mitigation by saying that Turner was in the "autumn of his life" and "was a man who had been in retirement for 15 or 16 years and who had occupied himself with gardening and music – that is not the stuff that a criminal is made of."

All very true, but Turner had caused the death of a man. Grant Jones taking into account all the factors, including his plea of guilty; the compensation paid; that Turner's house had been "infested by a plague of thieves;" and, his unblemished record, sentenced Turner to four months imprisonment. Not a long sentence, but still the British courts had moved on from the days when Captain Drake was sentenced to three months imprisonment for the manslaughter of 23 Japanese.

One final scandal for the US Court

Having started life with a number of scandals, it is perhaps fitting that the life of the United States Court for China ended with a scandal. Mr Sam Titlebaum, the deputy Marshal of the court was charged with a number of counts of embezzlement in August 1941. Titlebaum, who was 32, had only been appointed Deputy Marshal at the beginning of 1941. He was a close friend of the Marshal, Mr Charles Richardson Jr, who had recommended him for the job. He had previously worked as an announcer and radio commentator on a local radio station.

Titlebaum was accused of 12 counts of embezzlement, including taking six .38 Colt revolvers and 1,500 rounds of

.38 pistol ammunition. He had been caught because he sold two of the guns to a Chinese policeman who immediately tried to register them in the International Settlement.

The case was heard by Nelson Lurton sitting as a Special Judge of the court. Titlebaum pleaded not guilty to the charges. The *North China Herald* reported that at the hearing, mention had been made of "two undisclosed counts which were expected to be of a sensational nature." And indeed they were. Titlebaum was most likely not even "Sam Titlebaum." He had tricked a friend, Mr Eric Shekury, into placing his fingerprints on the fingerprint card needed for the application form on the pretence that he could get Shekury the job. He had also concealed he had a seven inch scar on his body, apparently from a gunshot, and that one leg was shorter than the other. He was charged with two further counts of concealing his identity, to which he also pleaded not guilty.

Titlebaum was convicted on all counts by Lurton. Lurton did have to deal with one question. Was Titlebaum American? There was no evidence of who he was. However, Lurton just said simply that he was "satisfied that Titlebaum was an American citizen within the court's jurisdiction." Lurton then gave Titlebaum a tongue lashing:

> "You are responsible for these things which are not in accordance to law and order which an American should uphold here, in China. We are not at Home, we are guests here by courtesy of Congress and the Chinese Treaties which are sacred. You have brought

shame upon yourself and imposed on the dignity of
your country, betrayed men who have recommended
you and heaped humiliation on yourself."

He sentenced Titlebaum to two years imprisonment on
all of the embezzlement counts and one of the false identity
counts and five years on one of the false identity counts, all to
be served concurrently at McNeil Island.

A lucky embezzler
One British embezzler, Patrick MacKellar, was to be slightly
luckier than Titlebaum. The last appeal ever before the Full
Court of the British Supreme Court for China was heard in
August 1941. By this time, the threat of war in the Pacific
loomed over Shanghai. America had imposed sanctions
on Japan over its occupation of China and incursions into
Indochina. Local newspapers were full of articles about
the break down in relations between the US and Japan. By
mid-1941, the British Prime Minister, Winston Churchill,
announced that if Japan went to war against the United
States, then Britain would join the war "within an hour."
MacKellar had worked for American Express since 1935,
starting out as a stenographer. He had been promoted to be a
travel clerk in 1937 and was a trusted employee. However, by
1940 he was suspected of embezzlement for pocketing some
of the money clients had paid to him for travel bookings.
The only real defence MacKellar could offer was that it was
a conspiracy amongst the other employees to set him up.
The jury took an hour to return a verdict of guilty. The trial
judge Penrhyn Grant Jones sentenced him to five years hard
labour saying in true Grant Jones fashion: "Embezzlement is
a particularly despicable crime for it involves the betrayal of
a fiduciary relationship," and adding "there may have been
temptations in the conduct of the American Express Company
but temptation is no excuse."

MacKellar appealed against his conviction and the sentence of five years. However, before the Full Court he only maintained his appeal against conviction. The appeal was heard by Chief Justice Atholl MacGregor of Hong Kong, Mossop and Grant Jones in August 1941. In their decision, the Full Court quickly disposed of the appeal against conviction holding that the conviction was safe. But in an extremely rare move, the court decided to review MacKellar's sentence even though he had not provided any grounds for doing so. British

Atholl MacGregor, CJ of Hong Kong, presided over the last appeal hearing in Shanghai.

appellate courts normally do not do this. If a prisoner has chosen not to appeal against sentence, that is their choice. The court will not interfere. However, citing a recent case where the English Court of Appeal had allowed an appeal against two out of four convictions and then reduced the total sentence imposed, the judges held they did have the power to review the sentence. They said that it was unusual to send a first offender to jail and reduced MacKellar's sentence to 18 months.

Grant Jones did not write a separate opinion or dissent from this despite having been the sentencing judge. The only explanation for this unheard-of generosity must be that the judges could clearly see that war was coming, Shanghai would be occupied by the Japanese, and they did not want to leave MacKellar in prison under Japanese occupation.

Out with a bang

It was clear to everyone that war was coming soon, it was

Tenser And Tenser !

BY SAPAJOU

US-Japan tensions mount in November 1941

just a question of when. In mid-November 1941, President Roosevelt ordered all remaining US Marines, 750 in Shanghai, 165 in Peiping and 55 in Tientsin to leave China. Roosevelt could see war was coming and stated the reason for the order was because the garrison "offered protection to comparatively few Americans." Seeking to avoid war, the Japanese had arranged for a special envoy, Saburo Kusuru, to fly to Washington for talks. Due to this, American lawyer,

Norwood Allman, arranged a business trip to Hong Kong saying he was "lulled into a temporary sense of security by the knowledge that Japan's special peace ambassador, Kusuru, was already on route to Washington." He thought that he would have time to get back to Shanghai before war started.

Allan Mossop, on December 1, 1941, seeing that war with Japan was approaching fast cabled the British Ambassador at Chungking saying that in the event of war, he and Grant Jones would both be "incapacitated" and that an Assistant Judge should be appointed to fill their place.

The courts kept on functioning until the last. The last full reports of cases before the British and American courts in China were carried in the *North China Herald* of Wednesday, December 3, 1941. The largest case was a probate action over Liza Hardoon's estate. She had died during the previous year and, not surprisingly, a number of her and her husband's relatives were again fighting over her fortune. Mossop adjourned the case and it was never to be heard again in a British Court. Grant Jones heard a case where a Russian, Mr Kobeneff sued the Cathay Laundry for losing a coat. The laundry relied on a limitation of liability clause. Kobeneff said he could not read English so the laundry could not rely on the clause. Grant Jones found for the laundry. He also made a decree absolute for a divorce between Mr and Mrs Smoleff. In the United States Court, Judge Helmick, who had returned from leave a few weeks before, granted Mr and Mrs Condon a decree nisi for their divorce. He also granted Mrs Sadie Wilholt a divorce decree nisi by default against her husband, Mr Harry Wilholt.

The Judges' notebooks record one of the very last criminal cases in the British Supreme Court as the prosecution of Charles Percival Archer, a former member of the Shanghai Municipal Police, for false pretences. Archer was accused of passing bad cheques in a number of shops in August 1941. He had then left Shanghai but had been arrested when he arrived back in town on a steamer from Singapore in November. He was convicted on December 2, 1941 and sentenced to six months imprisonment.

Norwood Allman had been wrong that he would have time to get back to Shanghai. Mossop had been right that he and Grant Jones may soon be incapacitated. On Monday, December 8, 1941 (Japan and China time), Japan declared war on Britain and the United States. By this time, Britain and America had only two navy ships in Shanghai. The HMS *Peterel*, a former Yangtze River gunboat, was moored off the Bund near the consulate and was being used as a communication station. Its larger guns had been removed and it only had machine guns on board. The USS *Wake*, also a Yangtze River gunboat, was tied up at a pier. The ship was also being kept in Shanghai to also act as a communications station. Most of its crew had been ordered to the Philippines 10 days before and it had only a skeleton crew of 14.

In the early morning of December 8, a Japanese navy party from the Japanese battleship HIJMS *Idzumo* boarded the HMS *Peterel* under a flag of truce and demanded its surrender. Her commander, Lieutenant Polkinghorn, even though completely outgunned, in the best British tradition of not going down without a fight, refused and ordered the party to "get off my bloody ship." Having boarded under a flag of truce, in accordance with the rules of war, the party left. Approximately 15 minutes later, the *Idzumo* opened fire with its powerful guns assisted by artillery from the Bund. The *Peterel* returned fire with its Lewis machine guns. After a short fight, the *Peterel* was sunk with the loss of six sailors. Many other sailors were saved by Chinese sampans that came to the rescue. The USS *Wake* had been rigged with explosives to be scuttled in the event of war but was captured without a fight.

With this warning of the commencement of hostilities, the

staff at the British Consulate and Supreme Court commenced destruction of confidential materials. At 10 o'clock that morning, the British Consulate received a phone call from the Japanese Navy stating that the operations of the Consulate and Court were to be suspended, and at 11 o'clock in the morning the premises were occupied. Allan Mossop reported that the Japanese "posted sentries, cut-off all telephones, and sealed up all safes, cupboards and rooms."

The US Consul in Shanghai, Mr Edwin Stanton reported that the US Consulate General was closed up at 1pm and sealed by the Japanese authorities who had said that "[a]ll the officers of the American Consulate General will be treated in accordance with international law and the principle of reciprocity.'"

The judges and the other staff of the courts were interned at the Cathay Hotel (for the British), the Metropole Hotel (for the Americans) or their homes. Both hotels were top hotels in the city at the time and internship in them cannot have been too much of a hardship.

Following negotiations with the Japanese, an exchange of consular officials was agreed. The British officials were taken aboard a Japanese boat, *Kamakura Maru*, to Lorenco Marques (now Maputo) in Mozambique, then a Portuguese colony and neutral territory. They travelled from there to Cape Town in South Africa, and then on to England aboard the P&O ship, the SS *Narkunda*.

The Americans were also evacuated to Lorenco Marques where they were transferred to a Swedish ship, the *Gripsholm*. The *Gripsholm* arrived in New York in late August 1942 with over 1,500 diplomatic and consular staff from China and Japan. Judge Helmick took charge of keeping morale up. Just before the ship arrived in New York, he organized a party for all those who had been interned in China and somehow managed to collect baseball caps and jockstraps all adorned with the Chinese characters for the prisons that they had been

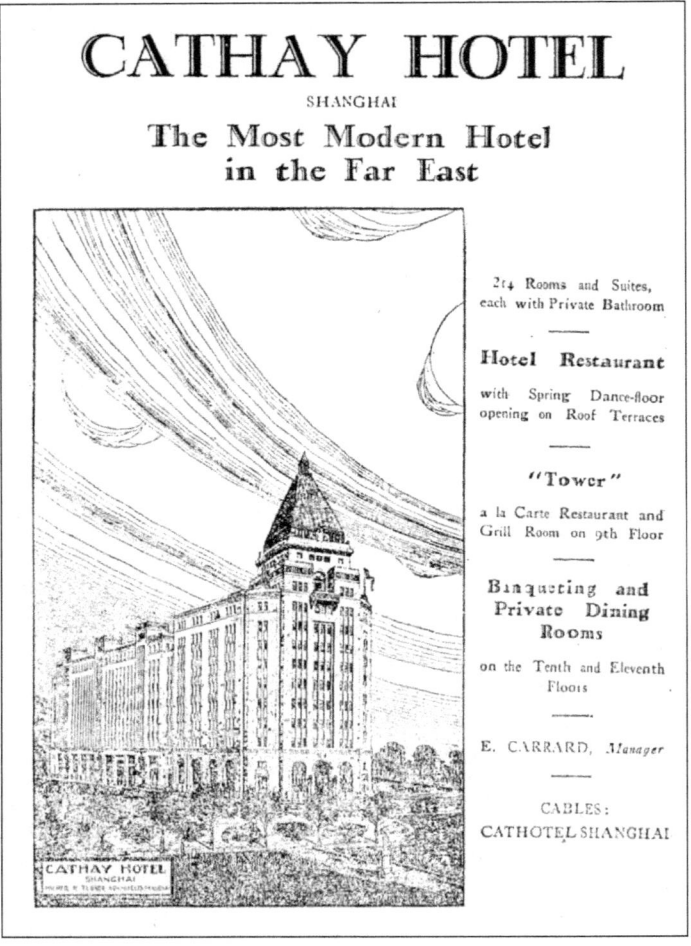

CATHAY HOTEL
SHANGHAI
The Most Modern Hotel in the Far East

214 Rooms and Suites, each with Private Bathroom

Hotel Restaurant

with Spring Dance-floor opening on Roof Terraces

"Tower"

a la Carte Restaurant and Grill Room on 9th Floor

Banqueting and Private Dining Rooms

on the Tenth and Eleventh Floors

E. CARRARD, *Manager*

CABLES:
CATHOTEL SHANGHAI

The Cathay Hotel (now the Peace Hotel). One of Shanghai's luxury hotels where Judge Mossop and others were interned.

interned in.

Mossop reported that there were eight British prisoners in Ward Road Gaol at the outbreak of hostilities. All of the prisoners, other than two who had been convicted of murder, received "Get Out of Jail" cards from Mossop. Mossop had obtained advance permission from the British Ambassador to cut their sentences if hostilities broke out. On the morning of December 8, 1941, Mossop signed orders to allow them to be freed and they were released some days later.

Casement wants out

The commencement of the Pacific War did not bring a complete end to cases before the American courts. Gerald Casement, now imprisoned on McNeil Island, filed a writ of habeas corpus against the Warden of McNeil Island, Mr Squier. His sole appeal ground was that he had been denied a jury trial. This was rejected at first instance and then on appeal by the US Ninth Circuit relying on the Supreme Court decision in the Ross case. District Judge Black in his first instance decision added, in the understated tone of many judicial opinions, a very practical reason why a new trial should not be ordered:

> "By reason of recent and present historical events involving Shanghai, the witnesses necessary to another trial for this petitioner could undoubtedly never in the future be presented before any court."

Extraterritoriality was not, however, dead yet. Agreements still needed to be reached to bring it to an end.

CHAPTER 32

The End of Extraterritoriality

WITH THE WAR RAGING against Japan in Asia and Germany in Europe and Africa, America wanted as many friends as it could get. With most of China occupied by the Japanese, agreeing with the Chinese to end extraterritoriality was a good way to keep the Chinese government on side without creating any immediate practical difficulties.

On September 1, 1942 the United States Secretary of State, Cordell Hull, wrote to the British Foreign Secretary, Anthony Eden, saying that he considered that it was an opportune time to raise the question of the end of extraterritoriality with the Chinese government with the view of reaching the most favourable agreement possible. He therefore suggested a confidential approach by the Americans and the British to the Chinese government offering to bring to an end extraterritoriality.

The British Cabinet considered this and concluded that it was an opportune time to take the initiative to contact the Chinese, but with the caveat that some agreement should be reached regarding Shanghai. They appreciated that the Chinese government would demand the return of Shanghai, but suggested that a special status be granted to Shanghai "to enable the development of the port to continue with the co-operation of foreign commercial interests."

Hull later wrote that he pushed the British to give up all rights saying:

"I stated that what we had in mind was the complete wiping out of all rights of a special character. Any holdover from the existing anomalies would be a further problem and the cause of continuing friction. Britain agreed."

On October 9, 1942, one day before the Chinese National Day, the British and American governments approached the Chinese ambassadors in London and Washington to let them know that they were willing to begin negotiations to end extraterritoriality. These went on over the next few months.

The British and Americans negotiated the treaties in tandem and attempted to keep the terms (and Chinese versions) of the treaties as consistent as possible, which the British described as seeking to make the "signing of the treaties an Anglo-American-Chinese act of political solidarity." The basic terms of the treaties had been agreed by the end of December and the original plan had been to sign the treaties on January 1, 1943. However, the need to finalize translations and prepare formal versions for signature pushed the date back.

The formal end to Extraterritoriality in China
On January 11, 1943, China signed treaties for Relinquishment of Extra-Territorial Rights in China with both Great Britain and the United States. The British treaty was signed in Chungking (Chongqing) between the British Ambassador Sir Horace Seymour and Dr T.V. Soong, the Chinese Foreign Minister. The American treaty was signed in Washington by Dr Tao-ming Wei, the Chinese ambassador, and Cordell Hull.

To celebrate the signing of the treaties, the Chinese Government proclaimed January 11 as "Justice Day" and February 5 to 7, 1943 as a three day national holiday. The Chinese Foreign Ministry later claimed that "throughout the country people could be heard singing the 'Song in Celebration of the New Equal Treaties.'" The song went (in translation):

> "50 years of revolutionary bloodshed,
> Five and half years of fighting and sacrifice,
> Struggle to break the chains,
> Bring back the Chinese soul,
> Bury the burden of history,
> Launch a national renaissance,
> Justice has been won,
> Our divine land has seen the light......"

Both treaties contained essentially the same terms. Article 1 of the US treaty and Article 2 of the British treaty both provided that all of those provisions or treaties or agreements in force between Britain or America and China which authorized Britain/America or their representatives to exercise jurisdiction over nationals or companies of Britain or America were abrogated. Then, most importantly, bringing an end to almost 100 years of British and American extraterritorial rights in China, the treaties provided that the nationals and companies of Britain or the United States:

> "shall be subject in the territory of the Republic of China to the jurisdiction of the Government of the Republic of China, in accordance with the principles of international law and practice."

Cases that had been decided were to be enforced by the Chinese courts and pending cases could be transferred to Chinese courts if the parties chose to do so.

The very last case
Fittingly, perhaps, given it was the military who brought the courts to life, the very last trial in a British or American extraterritorial court in China was before a court where the

judge, prosecutor and defence attorney were all in active military service. Three days after the signing of the US-China treaty on 14 January 1943, in Kunming, the United States Court for China heard its very last case. The treaty had not yet been ratified, so extraterritorial rights were still in place.

A year and a half before, on August 16, 1941, Boatner Carney had shot and killed another American, Sgt W.R. Reichmann during a poker game. Carney was an American Aviation Instructor with the Chinese Air Force, or as they were usually referred to, a Flying Tiger. The Flying Tigers was a group of former US military pilots who had come to assist China in its war with Japan, under the command of General Claire Chennault. As a Flying Tiger, Carney was not part of the US military and could not be tried by a military court. The US Consular Court in Kunming held a preliminary hearing and on August 31, 1942 committed Carney to trial before the United States Court for China.

This created a difficulty. There was no United States Court for China to try Carney in. Helmick had only just arrived back in the US following his internment and would have no inclination to immediately turn around to try a case in Kunming. The Department of Justice and the Judge Advocate General agreed to appoint two military officers to be judge and prosecutor for the case. Major Bertrand E Johnson with the Judge Advocate's department of the US Army Air Corps, then based in India, was appointed a special judge to try the case. Johnson had been a judge in Tulsa, Oklahoma, before joining the military. Captain Edward Kessler, an Air Corps supply officer, prosecuted. Lieutenant Lincoln C Brownell defended. The case was heard at the US Consulate General in Kunming with the US Consul, Raymond P Ludden, in attendance.

Despite the judge and prosecutor and defence attorney being military officers, the case was tried as a civil case and all the proper forms were observed. Carney pleaded not guilty on the basis of temporary insanity. Witnesses said that during a friendly poker game, Carney, who had been drinking, waved a pistol and said: "I am taking over." The gun discharged killing Reichman. Carney exercised his right to silence. Johnson convicted Carney and sentenced him to two years imprisonment and fined him $10,000. Carney returned to the United States to be imprisoned but on the special request of General Chennault, the head of the Flying Tigers, Carney was pardoned by President Roosevelt in June 1943.

There appears to be no surviving transcript of the final hearing. However, almost certainly Johnson sitting as the last special judge of the United States Court for China would have noted the end of extraterritoriality and that the hearing was the last-ever sitting of the Court.

No formal steps were taken to close the US Court for China, presumably because under American law the treaty ending extraterritoriality, once ratified on May 20, 1943, was self-executing. The act creating the United States Court for China was repealed in 1948.

Formal closing of the British Supreme Court for China

The British did take steps to formally close the British Supreme Court for China. On March 22, 1943, an Order in Council, which came into effect on May 20, 1943, was issued. The Order repealed 20 other Orders in Council; ordered that companies that had not already moved their registered offices from China were now deemed to be registered in Hong Kong; and, for any divorces where a decree nisi had been granted, deemed that a decree absolute had been granted. The records of the Supreme Court were ordered to be kept in China for at least 10 years so that Chinese courts could take over pending cases or refer to judgments that had been delivered.

Most importantly, and formally closing the British Supreme Court for China, S.3(1) provided:

"All courts established under the principal Order shall be closed on the date of the coming into force of this Order and the appointment of the Judge, Assistant Judge, Acting Judge and all officers of the said courts shall terminate on the same date."

Unlike the British Court for Japan, or even the United States Court for China, there was no formal final hearing in the British Supreme Court for China.

In honour of all those who served in or appeared before the British Supreme Court for China and Japan, it is appropriate to bring closure as it would have happened if the war had not intervened:

"Know all men, this court stands adjourned. God save the King."

CHAPTER 33

Summing Up

LADIES AND GENTLEMAN of the jury, you have now heard the evidence on the case of extraterritoriality as practiced in China, Japan and Korea by the British and Americans. What is the verdict of history?

Was it Gunboat Justice? Or, was it a necessary evil? Each one of us will have a different view.

Clearly, extraterritoriality is not a system that any country would willingly accept unless forced to by military or economic pressure.

Its original purpose was to allow foreigner to judge foreigner, and for the whole time extraterritoriality was practiced it served this purpose. For the majority of cases before all extraterritorial courts, this caused no problems when the parties were all nationals of the court concerned. Contractual disputes were resolved; tort claims were decided; divorces were granted and criminal were punished. The courts functioned as they would in their home countries.

Problems arose, however, when parties of different nationalities were involved, particularly when nationals of the host country had suffered at the hands of foreigners. Then, genuine problems arose. Chinese, Japanese and Koreans had to bring cases in foreign courts in foreign languages. For criminal cases, the prosecutors were also foreigners. They clearly lacked zeal in some cases and, in the case, of the British courts, English juries would not convict or only convict on lesser offences.

These shortcomings were recognized and after long struggles by both countries, ultimately, extraterritoriality was brought to an end, first in Japan and then in China, to much celebration. In Korea, there was nothing to celebrate, as extraterritoriality ended with Japan's annexation of the country.

What, however, was the result of extraterritoriality? Strangely, for the two main countries on which it was imposed, it produced completely different results. For Japan, extraterritoriality was an important impetus to legal, economic and political reforms that created a country that during World War II was able to occupy most of East Asia. While World War II ended in defeat, the structure of modern Japan as a rich democratic outward-looking country owes much to the reforms that were carried out in the late 19th century.

For China, extraterritoriality was an unmitigated disaster. It weakened the Manchu rule at the end of the Qing Dynasty, but did not bring it to an end. Indeed, towards the end, foreigners kept the Qing Dynasty alive because it suited their purposes. Extraterritoriality did eventually lead to the development of a modern legal system by the Nationalist Party. However, this was abolished in Mainland China when the Communists took over.

The legacy of extraterritoriality in Korea and Taiwan is more complex. Korea inherited a Japanese-based legal system at the end of the war. After decades of military dictatorship, this system has now contributed strongly to Korea's economic growth. The same can also be said of Taiwan, to which the Nationalist Party brought its modern legal system after the war.

Some will view extraterritoriality as having been a good thing, although in these days of general anti-Imperialism, their numbers will be small. Others, such as the Chinese Communists and the Chinese Nationalists consider it an evil system that oppressed their country. The Japanese view is more nuanced, no doubt because Japan suffered from yet also imposed extraterritoriality on others. For them, it was a necessary evil brought about by their undeveloped legal system. However, once they had developed their modern system, which remains in place to this day, had to be abolished.

For myself, I find it very hard to say. I have called this book Gunboat Justice because that is what extraterritoriality was: a system of justice imposed at the point of gunboat barrels.

Nevertheless, there were good things about the system – purely foreign cases were dealt with better than they would have been if tried in local Chinese or Japanese court. This led to many of the treaty ports, including Shanghai, Tianjin, Yokohama, and Kobe becoming and remaining to this day as major trading cities. There were bad things about the system. There were cases of injustice brought about by judges or juries favouring their own. But, no legal system is free from injustice.

The instability of the Chinese governments following the Republican Revolution in 1911 extended the life of extraterritoriality in China longer than it should have perhaps lasted. Extraterritoriality contributed, in no small part, to this instability. The fact that foreigners could rely on their own courts and authorities to protect them meant there was no strong pressure to ensure there was a stable government in China. A weak government suited them.

It is this era that now forms the cornerstone of how many Chinese, and particularly the Communist Party, see the world. Foreigners – to this day are seen as trying to split and weaken China. Mao threw all foreigners out in the 1950s for this reason. Even following Deng Xiaoping's reform and opening, China tightly guards it sovereignty. Almost all foreign investment must be through locally incorporated companies. Chinese courts do not enforce judgments of foreign courts. Anti-foreign and, in particular, anti-Japanese rhetoric is regularly spouted by senior leaders. China as it grows stronger shows no compunction about using gunboat diplomacy against its neighbours.

On Tiananmen Square, there are two slogans written on Tiananmen Gate on either side of the portrait of Chairman Mao. Most foreigners know one slogan reads "Long Live Chairman Mao." Most do not know that the other is "Long live the Unity of the People of the World." While 21st century Chinese leaders pay lip-service to the first slogan; it is the second slogan that forms the bedrock of Chinese thinking – only a strong unified government can control and protect China from foreign encroachments and explains why despite its many shortcomings, one party rule has survived so long in China.

No matter what your view of extraterritoriality, the one thing of which there can be no doubt is that it changed and continues to influence the course of history in East Asia.

—AND THERE IS NO FIRE-ENGINE!

Sapajou on Sino-Japanese relations in 1937. As valid today as it was then?

INDEX

Appeals threatened 103, 120, 130, 311

Decisions of, relied upon 257, 309

Jurisdiction 66-7, 104

Prize cases, WWI 273

Protests, formal

Chinese, by 137, 150-2, 217, 248-9, 264 (lack of), 403 (lack of), 429,

Japanese, by 103

British, by 162-4, 377, 413

Other powers, by 278-9

Provincial Courts (see Consular Courts, British)

Provisional Court (Shanghai) 334, 353-5, 361-5

Pu, Keng-lung 214

Purdy, Milton

Biography 294-5, 384

Judge 337-45, 338i, 356-8, 361

Lobingier, Charles, on 294

Qingdao – See Tsingtao

Raven, Frank 388-96, 388i, 403

Rees-Davies, William 263-4, 273

Reeks, Hugh 399-405, 429

Reid, Gilbert 275-9, 276i

Reinsch, Paul 275-8

Rennie, Richard

Biography 49-50, 49i, 144

Barrister 49-52, 55-7, 85

Chief Justice 131-2, 134-6, 140-1

Judge for Japan 104-5, 105i, 106i, 111i,

Republican Revolution (China) 10, 61, 260-66, 292, 454

Rights of Audience in non-national court 208, 316

Riots, anti-foreign

Canton 132-4, 330

Chungking 115

Foochow 114-7

Missionary, anti 3, 114-7

Shanghai 195-7, 197i, 333-4, 353

Yangtse Valley 147-8

Robertson, Russell 106

Rockhill, W.W. 217-8

Rodger, Hewitt Douglas (H.D.) 356-8, 361-2, 387

Roosevelt, Franklin 384, 395, 440, 450

Roosevelt, Theodore 194, 201, 204, 213, 219-20, 232-33, 294, 297

Ross, John 107-113

Ross, United States v (Ross Case) 107-113, 140, 289, 346, 445

Russo-Japanese War 193-5, 226, 236, 412

Satow, Ernest 27, 172, 177, 188, 199-200

Sausmarez, Havilland de 198-9, 199i, 263, 271-2, 275, 281-2, 298, 383

Secretary of State (US) 75, 110-2, 201-2, 213, 218, 219-20, 335, 365, 387, 418, 446-8

Secretary of State for Foreign Affairs (UK) 38, 60, 62, 103, 110-2, 151-2, 199, 242, 371, 378, 430, 446-8

Sedition 234- 43, 275-9, 321-3, 350

Sellett, Thomas 338i, 339-45, 363-4, 385

Seward, George 28, 44, 88

Seymour, Horace 447

www.ingramcontent.com/pod-product-compliance
Lightning Source LLC
Chambersburg PA
CBHW061545120626
46550CB00004B/1375